S0-DVC-737

CALIFORNIA
GPS
COMPANION

The GPS Companion is for the hundreds of days when you can't be in the wilderness or on the water.

The Companion makes any portable GPS a useful highway navigation tool. It includes the location of virtually every town in the state, no matter how small, plus landmarks like the Hearst Castle, the Half Dome summit, and major parks & beaches.

The Companion is compatible with every brand of GPS sold. It also includes handy reference information tailored for the State of California.

-Lists the coordinates for over 8100 cities and landmarks

-Includes all cities and towns indexed on normal State Highway maps plus THOUSANDS more.

-Based on US Government survey data

-Compact size to "go along" in car, boat or backpack

-Useful conversion charts and helpful hints

-After batteries the Companion is the best thing you can buy for your GPS.

CONTENTS

DATA FORMAT: DD-MM-SS

DATUM: NAD27

CAUTION: Airport data is not approved for aerial navigation.

California GPS Companion

Place Name	Latitude	Longitude	Type	Elev

A

Place Name	Latitude	Longitude	Type	Elev
Abbot, Mount	37 23 10N	118 47 00W	summit	13704
Abbott	39 01 14N	121 37 28W	city/town	43
Aberdeen	36 58 41N	118 15 09W	city/town	3906
Abilene	36 08 44N	119 03 10W	city/town	405
Abrams Lake Mobile	41 20 17N	122 21 15W	city/town	3710
Acampo	38 10 29N	121 16 39W	city/town	52
Acebedo	35 49 55N	120 12 03W	city/town	1580
Acolita	33 04 16N	115 11 02W	city/town	275
Acorn Lodge	37 31 25N	119 55 14W	locale	
Acrodectes Peak	36 51 39N	118 22 31W	summit	13183
Actis	34 57 31N	118 08 52W	city/town	2560
Acton	34 28 12N	118 11 45W	city/town	2720
Adams	38 51 23N	122 43 07W	city/town	2720
Adams Square	34 08 01N	118 14 25W	city/town	498
Adams Station	41 50 34N	123 59 29W	city/town	340
Adela	37 47 19N	120 51 44W	city/town	186
Adelaida	35 38 44N	120 52 21W	city/town	1400
Adelanto	34 34 58N	117 24 30W	city/town	2880
Adin	41 11 38N	120 56 39W	city/town	4205
Adin Airport	41 11 09N	120 57 07W	airport	4229

California GPS Companion

Place Name	Latitude	Longitude	Type	Elev
Admiral Standley S	39 38 48N	123 36 49W	park	
Adobe Art Center	37 41 51N	122 04 55W	building	
Adobe Corner	37 25 34N	122 15 55W	city/town	394
Adobe Fort -hist.	38 15 21N	122 35 01W	military	
Adobe Hills	37 59 48N	118 39 22W	locale	
Adorni Center	40 48 22N	124 09 35W	building	
Adorni Fishing Pr.	40 48 23N	124 09 37W	pier	
Advance	36 30 57N	118 54 06W	city/town	1600
Aeneas Beach	36 36 43N	121 53 47W	beach	
Aeolian Yacht Club	37 45 02N	122 14 02W	locale	
Aerial Acres	35 05 16N	117 47 28W	city/town	2430
Aerospace Museum	34 01 02N	118 16 59W	museum	
Aetna Springs	38 39 13N	122 28 54W	city/town	780
Afton (1)	39 25 12N	121 57 55W	city/town	75
Afton (2)	35 02 11N	116 22 44W	city/town	1408
Agassiz, Mount	37 06 42N	118 31 48W	summit	13891
Agate Beach (1)	41 08 40N	124 08 33W	beach	
Agate Beach (2)	37 53 51N	122 42 35W	beach	
Ager	41 51 59N	122 27 34W	city/town	2375
Aggie, Mount	37 32 46N	118 50 35W	summit	11561
Agnew	37 23 41N	121 57 29W	city/town	22
Agoura	34 08 35N	118 44 13W	city/town	899

California GPS Companion

Place Name	Latitude	Longitude	Type	Elev
Agoura Hills	34 08 11N	118 46 25W	city/town	1000
Agra	33 20 00N	117 29 57W	city/town	180
Agua Caliente	38 19 27N	122 29 13W	city/town	155
Agua Caliente Sprg	32 57 00N	116 17 36W	airport	1220
Agua Dulce	34 29 47N	118 19 29W	city/town	2520
Agua Dulce Airpark	34 30 14N	118 18 46W	airport	2660
Agua Fria	37 29 06N	120 01 09W	city/town	2000
Aguanga	33 26 34N	116 51 51W	city/town	1940
Ahlgren Cabin	41 21 17N	123 14 45W	building	5680
Ahmanson Theatre	34 03 29N	118 14 47W	building	
Ahwahnee	37 21 56N	119 43 31W	city/town	2321
Ahwahnee Hotel	37 44 47N	119 34 24W	building	
Aikens Arch	35 14 22N	115 44 52W	arch	
Ainsworth Corner	41 59 55N	121 33 31W	city/town	4067
Airport Dunes	33 56 49N	118 26 12W	locale	
Airport Marina	37 44 13N	122 12 43W	marina	
Akers	37 59 54N	121 16 57W	city/town	21
Al Tahoe	38 56 31N	119 58 57W	city/town	6260
Alabama Hill	38 21 18N	120 35 27W	city/town	3012
Alabama Hills	36 34 04N	118 05 20W	city/town	4550
Alabama House -his	38 23 48N	121 00 17W	building	237
Alameda (1)	35 14 16N	119 00 08W	city/town	332

California GPS Companion

Place Name	Latitude	Longitude	Type	Elev
Alameda (2)	37 45 55N	122 14 26W	city/town	30
Alameda Marina	37 46 38N	122 14 58W	marina	
Alameda Municipal	37 44 32N	122 13 51W	golf	
Alameda Naval Air	37 47 25N	122 19 31W	military	14
Alamere Falls	37 57 14N	122 46 57W	falls	
Alamitos	37 15 02N	121 51 58W	city/town	175
Alamitos Bay Beach	33 45 22N	118 07 50W	beach	
Alamitos Bay Yacht	33 44 45N	118 06 58W	locale	
Alamo	37 51 01N	122 01 52W	city/town	280
Alamo Oaks	37 50 22N	121 59 31W	city/town	520
Alamorio	32 58 45N	115 27 38W	city/town	-135
Alba	37 47 53N	121 02 19W	city/town	95
Albany	37 53 13N	122 17 48W	city/town	40
Alberhill	33 43 38N	117 23 56W	city/town	1240
Albinger Archaelog	34 16 51N	119 17 52W	museum	
Albion	39 13 25N	123 46 03W	city/town	178
Albrae	37 29 44N	121 59 18W	city/town	7
Alcatraz	37 49 37N	122 25 18W	building	
Alder Creek	38 38 05N	121 12 02W	city/town	150
Alder Springs (1)	37 03 58N	119 24 04W	city/town	4440
Alder Springs (2)	39 39 04N	122 43 28W	city/town	4440
Aldercroft Heights	37 09 39N	121 58 04W	city/town	1000

California GPS Companion

Place Name	Latitude	Longitude	Type	Elev
Alderglen Springs	38 50 07N	123 03 06W	city/town	450
Alderpoint	40 10 35N	123 36 38W	city/town	460
Alemandra	39 08 56N	121 41 13W	city/town	52
Alessandro	33 53 10N	117 16 10W	city/town	1530
Alford Place	40 13 06N	122 39 56W	city/town	1315
Algerine	37 54 40N	120 22 56W	city/town	1450
Algoma	41 15 24N	121 52 56W	city/town	3800
Algoso	35 21 35N	118 55 27W	city/town	430
Alhambra	34 05 43N	118 07 34W	city/town	500
Alice Arts Center	37 48 12N	122 15 53W	building	
Alice, Mount	37 07 24N	118 28 00W	summit	11630
Alicia	39 06 10N	121 34 50W	city/town	55
Alico	36 34 11N	117 57 44W	city/town	3672
Alisal -subdivis.	36 40 45N	121 37 00W	city/town	85
Aliso	33 43 37N	117 49 56W	city/town	91
Aliso Beach	33 30 36N	117 45 06W	beach	
Aliso Pier	33 30 31N	117 45 07W	pier	
Aliso Viejo	33 36 30N	117 44 40W	city/town	400
Alla	33 58 52N	118 25 44W	city/town	20
Allan Hancock Aud.	34 01 10N	118 17 02W	building	
Allan Hancock Coll	34 56 37N	120 25 15W	univ/coll	
Alleghany	39 28 11N	120 50 32W	city/town	4419

Place Name	Latitude	Longitude	Type	Elev
Allen	38 37 02N	120 06 35W	city/town	8100
Allen Ranch	35 25 28N	118 38 09W	locale	3740
Allendale	38 26 41N	121 56 31W	city/town	118
Allensworth	35 51 49N	119 23 17W	city/town	207
Alliance	40 53 19N	124 05 12W	city/town	30
Alliance Redwood	38 26 02N	122 58 19W	city/town	180
Allied Artists Stu	34 05 52N	118 17 01W	studio	
Alligator Head Arc	32 51 04N	117 16 21W	arch	
Alma College	37 10 56N	122 00 04W	univ/coll	
Almaden Country Cl	37 12 42N	121 52 04W	golf	
Almanor	40 13 03N	121 10 23W	city/town	4519
Almanor Country Cl	40 15 05N	121 08 21W	golf	4510
Almanor West	40 14 11N	121 12 12W	city/town	4700
Almansor Municipal	34 05 14N	118 06 40W	golf	
Almond	33 51 32N	117 59 02W	city/town	85
Almonte	37 53 24N	122 31 26W	city/town	10
Alondra Golf Cours	33 52 54N	118 20 26W	golf	
Alpaugh	35 53 16N	119 29 11W	city/town	210
Alpine (1)	32 50 06N	116 45 56W	city/town	1880
Alpine (2)	39 26 11N	123 34 56W	city/town	263
Alpine (3)	34 32 21N	118 06 20W	city/town	2850
Alpine Heights	32 49 05N	116 46 48W	city/town	1873

California GPS Companion

Place Name	Latitude	Longitude	Type	Elev
Alpine Meadows	39 10 43N	120 13 36W	city/town	6500
Alpine Meadows Ski	39 09 27N	120 14 17W	ski area	8637
Alpine Village	33 36 22N	116 28 08W	city/town	3970
Alray	34 19 42N	117 28 55W	city/town	3400
Alsace	33 58 43N	118 24 53W	city/town	15
Alta	39 12 24N	120 48 37W	city/town	3590
Alta Hill.	39 13 48N	121 04 32W	city/town	2640
Alta Loma	34 07 20N	117 35 50W	city/town	1390
Alta Mesa	37 23 56N	122 08 01W	city/town	100
Alta Schmidt House	39 44 39N	122 11 36W	museum	
Alta Sierra (1)	39 08 30N	121 03 10W	city/town	2300
Alta Sierra (2)	35 43 45N	118 32 55W	city/town	5678
Alta Sierra Estate	39 06 51N	121 03 15W	city/town	2260
Alta Sierra Ranche	39 06 16N	121 01 25W	city/town	1880
Alta Vineyards Mat	36 40 21N	119 41 08W	wine/vin	
Alta Vista	37 24 46N	118 32 30W	city/town	4585
Alta Vista Golf Cl	33 52 40N	117 51 05W	golf	
Alta Vista Park	39 13 39N	121 03 56W	city/town	2640
Altacanyada	34 13 20N	118 12 40W	city/town	1800
Altadena	34 11 23N	118 07 49W	city/town	1342
Altadena Golf Crs.	34 10 57N	118 07 03W	golf	
Altamont	37 44 38N	121 39 42W	city/town	740

California GPS Companion

Place Name	Latitude	Longitude	Type	Elev
Altamont Speedway	37 44 18N	121 33 40W	track	
Altaville	38 05 02N	120 33 39W	city/town	1540
Alten	38 22 53N	122 48 19W	city/town	100
Alto	37 54 16N	122 31 28W	city/town	27
Alton	40 32 51N	124 08 23W	city/town	60
Alturas	41 29 14N	120 32 29W	city/town	4366
Alturas Cal. Pines	41 24 44N	120 41 03W	airport	4398
Alturas Municipal	41 28 58N	120 33 55W	airport	4375
Alum Rock	37 21 58N	121 49 34W	city/town	149
Alum Rock	37 23 17N	121 47 16W	summit	1861
Alum Rock	37 23 43N	121 48 37W	pillar	
Alum Rock Park	37 23 52N	121 47 55W	park	
Alviso	37 25 34N	121 58 27W	city/town	4
Amador City	38 25 10N	120 49 23W	city/town	954
Amador County Muse	38 21 03N	120 46 22W	museum	
Amador Foothill Wi	38 31 48N	120 47 30W	wine/vin	
Amador-Livermore V	37 39 41N	121 52 26W	museum	
Amanico Ergina Vlg	37 46 57N	122 26 08W	city/town	130
Amarillo Beach	34 01 47N	118 42 19W	beach	
Ambassador Auditor	34 08 36N	118 09 20W	building	
Ambassador College	34 08 38N	118 09 28W	univ/coll	
Ambler	36 18 29N	119 16 53W	city/town	333

8

California GPS Companion

Place Name	Latitude	Longitude	Type	Elev
Amboy	34 33 28N	115 44 37W	city/town	639
Ambrose	41 30 07N	120 58 49W	city/town	4960
Amedee Army Air F.	40 15 58N	120 09 09W	military	4008
Amelia Earhart Pk.	37 47 09N	119 17 14W	summit	11982
American Canyon	38 10 30N	122 15 35W	city/town	60
American River Col	38 39 04N	121 20 53W	univ/coll	
American Victorian	39 15 44N	121 01 09W	museum	
Ames Research Cent	37 24 55N	122 03 45W	building	
Amos	33 07 05N	115 15 18W	city/town	260
Ampere	38 06 09N	121 14 32W	city/town	53
Amsterdam	37 25 49N	120 32 28W	city/town	215
Anacapa Island	34 00 16N	119 23 55W	island	
Anacapa Island Lt.	34 00 57N	119 21 32W	lighthous	
Anaheim	33 50 07N	117 54 49W	city/town	160
Anaheim Convention	33 48 05N	117 55 12W	building	
Anaheim Stadium	33 48 01N	117 52 55W	stadium	
Anchor Bay	38 48 10N	123 34 36W	city/town	120
Ancient Bristlecon	37 30 50N	118 10 52W	locale	
Anderson	40 26 54N	122 17 48W	city/town	430
Anderson Marsh Sta	38 55 32N	122 37 56W	park	
Anderson Valley H.	39 01 48N	123 23 05W	museum	
Andersonia	39 58 41N	123 48 22W	city/town	520

9

California GPS Companion

Place Name	Latitude	Longitude	Type	Elev
Andesite	41 31 57N	122 12 13W	city/town	4600
Andover	39 18 38N	120 14 46W	city/town	6400
Andrade Corner	34 38 55N	118 22 34W	city/town	3402
Andreas Falls	33 45 29N	116 37 00W	falls	
Andrew Molera Stat	36 17 00N	121 50 00W	park	
Angel Island	37 51 46N	122 25 51W	island	
Angel Island State	37 51 51N	122 25 51W	park	
Angeles Abbey Maus	33 53 48N	118 12 16W	building	
Angels Camp	38 04 06N	120 32 19W	city/town	1440
Angels Gate Light.	33 42 30N	118 15 03W	lighthous	
Angelus Oaks	34 08 45N	116 58 54W	city/town	5800
Angiola	35 59 21N	119 28 30W	city/town	200
Angle Falls	37 20 18N	119 34 11W	falls	
Angora Lookout	38 52 57N	120 03 13W	overlook	7290
Angus Hills Golf C	38 56 50N	121 02 27W	golf	
Angwin	38 34 33N	122 26 56W	city/town	1750
Angwin -Parrett	38 34 42N	122 26 06W	airport	1848
Anita	39 48 39N	121 58 38W	city/town	156
Anna Mills, Mount	36 28 30N	118 20 55W	summit	12064
Annandale Country	34 08 38N	118 10 23W	golf	
Annandale Golf Crs	34 08 45N	118 10 34W	golf	
Annapolis	38 43 19N	123 22 07W	city/town	780

California GPS Companion

Place Name	Latitude	Longitude	Type	Elev
Annette	35 39 03N	120 10 41W	city/town	2197
Ano Nuevo State R.	37 07 02N	122 19 33W	park	
Ansel	34 54 18N	118 09 12W	city/town	2510
Ansel Adams, Mount	37 41 52N	119 16 49W	summit	11760
Antelope	38 42 30N	121 19 44W	city/town	155
Antelope Acres	34 45 16N	118 17 19W	city/town	2424
Antelope Center	34 34 48N	117 58 06W	city/town	2645
Antelope Vly C C	34 36 22N	118 08 26W	golf	
Antelope Vly Ind.	34 39 01N	117 50 58W	museum	
Antes	36 18 31N	119 07 47W	city/town	403
Anthony Mill Ruins	36 00 25N	117 22 05W	locale	
Anthony Peak Look.	39 50 47N	122 57 48W	overlook	6954
Antioch	38 00 18N	121 48 17W	city/town	40
Antioch City Marin	38 01 11N	121 49 12W	marina	
Antlers	40 53 44N	122 22 12W	city/town	1080
Anton Stadium	39 09 02N	123 13 16W	stadium	
Antonio	34 50 07N	120 34 08W	city/town	240
Anza (1)	33 33 18N	116 40 22W	city/town	3918
Anza (2)	32 48 01N	115 29 51W	city/town	-47
Aperture Peak	37 07 06N	118 31 47W	summit	13265
Apex	38 43 37N	120 49 20W	city/town	1880
Apollo	35 20 30N	116 52 25W	city/town	3140

California GPS Companion

Place Name	Latitude	Longitude	Type	Elev
Apple Valley	34 30 03N	117 11 06W	city/town	2947
Apple Valley Arpt	34 34 44N	117 11 10W	airport	3059
Apple Valley Yacht	34 31 40N	117 13 32W	locale	
Applegate	39 00 03N	120 59 29W	city/town	2000
Aptos	36 58 38N	121 53 54W	city/town	100
Arastraville	37 59 53N	120 13 33W	city/town	3150
Araz Junction	32 44 50N	114 42 49W	city/town	200
Arbee	39 12 40N	121 59 41W	city/town	55
Arbios	36 46 36N	120 23 49W	city/town	167
Arboga	39 03 05N	121 33 17W	city/town	55
Arbolada	34 26 59N	119 15 26W	city/town	840
Arbor	37 57 42N	121 43 20W	city/town	96
Arbuckle	39 01 03N	122 03 24W	city/town	140
Arbuckle Golf Club	39 00 31N	122 08 19W	golf	
Arcade	38 28 33N	121 34 43W	city/town	29
Arcadia	34 08 23N	118 02 04W	city/town	485
Arcadia Golf Cours	34 06 05N	118 01 01W	golf	
Arcata	40 52 00N	124 04 54W	city/town	33
Arcata Airport	40 58 41N	124 06 31W	airport	218
Arch Beach	33 31 18N	117 45 50W	beach	
Arch of the Navarr	39 11 29N	123 45 51W	arch	
Arch Rock	33 54 16N	116 01 30W	locale	

California GPS Companion

Place Name	Latitude	Longitude	Type	Elev
Arch Rock	37 26 49N	119 04 22W	arch	
Arched Rock Beach	38 22 04N	123 04 18W	beach	
Archer	34 25 14N	115 21 53W	city/town	855
Arches, The	33 37 13N	117 55 21W	arch	40
Arcilla	33 47 00N	117 28 43W	city/town	960
Arden Town	38 34 27N	121 22 55W	city/town	57
Arena	37 22 15N	120 40 31W	city/town	141
Argonaut Winery	38 25 17N	120 54 02W	wine/vin	
Argos	34 43 33N	116 15 00W	city/town	2040
Arguello	34 34 42N	120 38 31W	city/town	120
Argus	35 44 50N	117 23 40W	city/town	1648
Arlanza	33 56 34N	117 27 53W	city/town	740
Arlight	34 34 40N	120 38 18W	city/town	200
Arlington	33 55 13N	117 26 44W	city/town	788
Arlington College	33 46 53N	118 06 31W	univ/coll	
Arlington Station	33 54 51N	117 26 25W	city/town	820
Arlynda Corners	40 35 42N	124 15 14W	city/town	20
Armand Hammer Mus.	34 03 33N	118 26 35W	museum	
Armistead	35 32 52N	117 55 36W	city/town	3063
Armona	36 18 57N	119 42 27W	city/town	236
Armstrong (1)	39 19 42N	120 14 07W	city/town	6160
Armstrong (2)	38 05 21N	121 16 25W	city/town	38

13

California GPS Companion

Place Name	Latitude	Longitude	Type	Elev
Armstrong Hill L.	38 32 33N	120 23 00W	overlook	5701
Armstrong Univ.	37 52 07N	122 16 06W	univ/coll	
Arnold (1)	38 15 20N	120 21 00W	city/town	3960
Arnold (2)	39 31 08N	123 23 33W	city/town	1226
Arnold Heights	33 53 37N	117 16 41W	city/town	1560
Aromas	36 53 19N	121 38 31W	city/town	130
Arrillaga Sports C	37 25 48N	122 09 38W	building	
Arrow Peak	36 55 42N	118 29 26W	summit	12958
Arrow Point	33 28 39N	118 32 18W	cape	
Arrowbear Lake	34 12 39N	117 04 57W	city/town	6087
Arrowhead -subdiv.	34 08 52N	117 17 11W	city/town	1232
Arrowhead Country	34 09 13N	117 16 29W	golf	
Arrowhead Highland	34 13 48N	117 15 43W	city/town	5200
Arrowhead Junction	34 56 34N	114 49 25W	city/town	1653
Arrowhead Spire	37 45 27N	119 35 15W	pillar	6210
Arrowhead Springs	34 11 12N	117 15 39W	city/town	1960
Arroyo De Los Frij	37 13 33N	122 24 30W	beach	
Arroyo Grande	35 07 07N	120 35 23W	city/town	80
Arroyo Seco Golf C	34 06 54N	118 10 08W	golf	
Arroyo Vista	38 43 24N	121 03 13W	city/town	980
Arroz	38 37 15N	121 58 12W	city/town	160
Artesia	33 51 57N	118 04 56W	city/town	51

California GPS Companion

Place Name	Latitude	Longitude	Type	Elev
Artois	39 37 11N	122 11 34W	city/town	165
Arvin	35 12 33N	118 49 39W	city/town	445
Asco	37 40 59N	121 52 18W	city/town	350
Ascot Speedway-his	34 04 04N	118 11 28W	track	
Ash Creek Butte	41 26 51N	122 02 52W	summit	8378
Ash Creek Falls	41 24 15N	122 08 07W	falls	
Ash Creek Junction	41 16 03N	122 04 36W	city/town	3437
Ash Creek State Wi	41 10 48N	121 04 26W	park	
Ash Creek Station	41 16 07N	121 56 37W	city/town	3700
Ash Hill	34 42 25N	116 03 15W	city/town	1940
Ashford Junction	35 54 35N	116 40 21W	city/town	-104
Ashford Mill	35 55 08N	116 41 02W	city/town	-98
Ashland	37 41 41N	122 06 46W	city/town	30
Ashrama	37 18 26N	121 28 07W	city/town	2140
Asilomar State Bch	36 37 27N	121 56 17W	park	
Asistencia de San	33 21 57N	117 04 27W	mission	
Aspen Springs	37 33 17N	118 42 44W	city/town	7125
Aspen Valley	37 49 39N	119 46 13W	city/town	6160
Aspendell	37 14 17N	118 35 51W	city/town	8400
Asti	38 45 47N	122 58 19W	city/town	267
Asuncion	35 30 54N	120 40 42W	city/town	820
Asylum	39 08 01N	123 11 58W	city/town	600

California GPS Companion

Place Name	Latitude	Longitude	Type	Elev
Atagam Beach	39 14 18N	120 02 42W	beach	
Atascadero	35 29 22N	120 40 11W	city/town	880
Atascadero State B	35 23 35N	120 51 52W	park	
Atchison Village	37 56 01N	122 22 14W	city/town	10
Athens	33 55 12N	118 16 49W	city/town	165
Atherton	37 27 41N	122 11 48W	city/town	60
Athlone	37 12 29N	120 21 25W	city/town	200
Atlanta	37 48 47N	121 07 11W	city/town	60
Atlas	38 25 45N	122 14 49W	city/town	1748
Atolia	35 18 53N	117 36 30W	city/town	3300
Atwater (1)	34 06 59N	118 15 20W	city/town	400
Atwater (2)	37 20 52N	120 36 29W	city/town	151
Atwood	33 51 56N	117 49 48W	city/town	249
Auberry	37 04 51N	119 29 04W	city/town	1960
Auburn	38 53 48N	121 04 33W	city/town	1359
Auburn Hills Mobil	38 55 34N	121 05 14W	city/town	1400
Auburn Lake Trails	38 54 52N	120 57 05W	city/town	1920
Auburn Mun. Airp.	38 57 09N	121 04 54W	airport	1520
Auckland	36 35 17N	119 06 21W	city/town	1280
Aukum	38 33 26N	120 43 32W	city/town	2140
Aurant	34 04 41N	118 09 48W	city/town	440
Aurora	37 39 36N	121 00 06W	city/town	85

California GPS Companion

Place Name	Latitude	Longitude	Type	Elev
Austin	37 14 33N	121 59 50W	city/town	430
Austin Creek State	38 34 01N	123 03 07W	park	
Avalon	33 20 34N	118 19 37W	city/town	30
Avalon -Catalina	33 24 17N	118 24 57W	airport	1602
Avalon Bay Seaplan	33 20 30N	118 18 58W	airport	0
Avalon Village	33 48 46N	118 15 47W	city/town	36
Avals Beach	38 13 54N	122 58 52W	beach	
Avena	37 50 35N	121 03 55W	city/town	77
Avenal	36 00 15N	120 07 41W	city/town	800
Avenales Observat.	35 11 22N	120 14 43W	overlook	2858
Avery	38 12 16N	120 22 08W	city/town	3387
Avery Place	40 10 55N	121 46 46W	city/town	1660
Avila Beach	35 10 48N	120 43 51W	city/town	20
Avila Place	41 02 35N	120 52 00W	city/town	4680
Avila State Beach	35 10 43N	120 43 57W	park	
Avinsino Corner	38 41 37N	120 40 32W	city/town	2475
Avocado	36 47 22N	119 24 11W	city/town	490
Avocado Heights	34 02 10N	117 59 25W	city/town	335
Avon	38 01 58N	122 04 27W	city/town	9
Azalea	41 16 42N	122 18 04W	city/town	3347
Azure Vista	32 43 10N	117 15 44W	city/town	140
Azusa	34 08 01N	117 54 24W	city/town	612

California GPS Companion

Place Name	Latitude	Longitude	Type	Elev
Azusa Greens Publ.	34 08 51N	117 55 11W	golf	
Azusa Pacific Coll	34 07 47N	117 53 16W	univ/coll	

𝔹

Place Name	Latitude	Longitude	Type	Elev
Babe Zaharias Golf	34 01 12N	117 56 00W	golf	
Backbone Ridge Lk.	40 53 23N	123 08 29W	overlook	4653
Baden	37 38 59N	122 25 59W	city/town	100
Badger	36 37 53N	119 00 44W	city/town	3030
Badger Pass Ski Ar	37 39 45N	119 39 48W	ski area	
Badlands	36 17 07N	120 46 36W	locale	
Badwater	36 13 47N	116 45 58W	city/town	-280
Bagdad	34 34 58N	115 52 29W	city/town	755
Bago, Mount	36 46 11N	118 26 18W	summit	11868
Bahia	38 05 48N	122 06 07W	city/town	6
Bailhache	38 36 13N	122 51 13W	city/town	100
Baird Park -subdiv	34 05 13N	118 10 49W	city/town	560
Bak	38 27 27N	122 40 13W	city/town	250
Baker (1)	35 15 54N	116 04 25W	city/town	923
Baker (2)	35 02 32N	117 40 00W	city/town	2500
Baker Airport	35 17 07N	116 04 57W	airport	922
Baker Beach	37 47 40N	122 28 56W	beach	
Baker Beach State	37 47 24N	122 29 04W	park	

California GPS Companion

Place Name	Latitude	Longitude	Type	Elev
Bakersfield	35 22 24N	119 01 04W	city/town	408
Bakersfield Colleg	35 24 32N	118 58 14W	univ/coll	684
Bakersfield C C	35 23 33N	118 56 23W	golf	
Bakersfield Mead.	35 26 00N	119 03 24W	airport	507
Bakersfield Munic.	35 19 29N	118 59 45W	airport	376
Bakersfield RioBr.	35 24 23N	118 51 10W	airport	830
Balance Rock	35 48 22N	118 39 04W	city/town	4120
Balboa	33 35 13N	117 54 00W	city/town	5
Balboa Beach	33 34 59N	117 54 02W	beach	
Balboa Island	33 35 40N	117 53 27W	city/town	6
Balboa Mun. Golf C	34 10 28N	118 29 46W	golf	
Balboa Pavilion	33 36 08N	117 53 53W	building	
Balboa Pier	33 35 57N	117 54 00W	pier	
Balboa Stadium	32 43 14N	117 09 03W	stadium	
Balch	35 02 34N	116 01 36W	city/town	1016
Balch Camp	36 54 11N	119 07 20W	city/town	1267
Balderson Station	38 56 05N	120 45 11W	city/town	3288
Baldinelli Viney.	38 31 23N	120 49 15W	wine/vin	
Baldwin Beach	38 56 37N	120 04 03W	beach	
Baldwin Park	34 05 07N	117 57 36W	city/town	374
Baldwin, Mount	37 31 57N	118 51 05W	summit	12690
Bale	38 33 15N	122 30 34W	city/town	279

California GPS Companion

Place Name	Latitude	Longitude	Type	Elev
Ballarat	36 02 52N	117 13 21W	city/town	1061
Ballard	34 38 09N	120 06 44W	city/town	660
Ballena	33 03 55N	116 44 45W	city/town	2480
Ballena Bay Marina	37 46 00N	122 17 05W	marina	
Ballico	37 27 16N	120 42 18W	city/town	150
Balloon Dome	37 27 51N	119 13 36W	summit	6881
Ballou	34 02 57N	117 36 22W	city/town	900
Baltimore Park	37 55 51N	122 31 53W	city/town	80
Baltimore Town	39 23 16N	120 32 21W	city/town	7300
Bancroft	37 56 02N	122 02 46W	city/town	80
Bancroft Point	32 44 13N	116 59 05W	city/town	780
Bancroft Ranch Hse	32 44 46N	117 00 02W	museum	
Bandini (1)	34 00 24N	118 10 01W	city/town	150
Bandini (2)	33 58 56N	118 07 02W	city/town	168
Banfield Place	40 05 12N	122 36 27W	city/town	1320
Bangle	33 49 28N	118 13 40W	city/town	25
Bangor	39 23 19N	121 24 15W	city/town	755
Bankhead Springs	32 38 59N	116 14 35W	city/town	3300
Banneker Homes	37 46 26N	122 25 28W	city/town	100
Banner	33 04 08N	116 32 43W	city/town	2755
Banner Crest	39 14 08N	121 01 05W	city/town	3020
Banner Peak	37 41 48N	119 11 39W	summit	12945

California GPS Companion

Place Name	Latitude	Longitude	Type	Elev
Banning	33 55 32N	116 52 32W	city/town	2400
Banning Municipal	33 55 23N	116 51 02W	airport	2219
Banning Residence	33 47 25N	118 15 29W	museum	
Bannings Beach	33 22 29N	118 21 10W	beach	
Bannister	35 15 56N	119 05 59W	city/town	342
Bannock	34 56 12N	114 51 47W	city/town	1730
Banta	37 45 16N	121 22 11W	city/town	21
Bar J Ranch	38 39 43N	121 00 35W	city/town	1200
Barbara Worth C C	32 48 07N	115 25 03W	golf	
Barber	39 42 53N	121 50 04W	city/town	186
Barber City	33 45 32N	118 01 24W	city/town	28
Barbie Hall of Fam	37 26 52N	122 09 35W	museum	
Barcroft, Mount	37 34 56N	118 14 52W	summit	13040
Bard	32 47 21N	114 33 19W	city/town	135
Bardi	37 45 53N	121 09 51W	city/town	49
Bardsdale	34 22 18N	118 55 55W	city/town	426
Barkerville	39 09 16N	122 33 41W	city/town	1450
Barlow	38 25 30N	122 51 27W	city/town	123
Barnard, Mount	36 37 43N	118 19 13W	summit	13990
Barnes Laboratory	37 25 45N	122 10 55W	building	
Barnhill Marina	37 47 17N	122 16 23W	marina	
Barnwell	35 17 35N	115 14 06W	city/town	4805

California GPS Companion

Place Name	Latitude	Longitude	Type	Elev
Baroda	34 41 12N	120 35 30W	city/town	10
Barona	32 56 09N	116 52 02W	city/town	1350
Barrett (1)	37 38 24N	120 17 05W	city/town	780
Barrett (2)	32 37 45N	116 27 35W	city/town	2640
Barrett Junction	32 36 41N	116 42 23W	city/town	900
Barro	38 31 34N	122 29 30W	city/town	230
Barstow (1)	34 53 55N	117 01 19W	city/town	2106
Barstow (2)	36 48 55N	119 58 08W	city/town	271
Barstow College	34 52 13N	117 01 23W	univ/coll	
Barsug	34 57 27N	120 34 19W	city/town	87
Bartle	41 15 28N	121 49 12W	city/town	3974
Bartlett	36 28 36N	118 01 48W	city/town	3640
Bartlett Springs	39 11 02N	122 42 12W	city/town	2126
Bartolo	34 00 23N	118 03 41W	city/town	200
Barton	38 27 17N	120 31 45W	city/town	3268
Basin	35 02 35N	116 17 39W	city/town	1217
Basin Mountain	37 17 50N	118 39 28W	summit	13240
Bass Lake	37 19 29N	119 33 55W	city/town	3425
Bass Lake Annex	37 16 17N	119 31 59W	city/town	3380
Bassett	34 02 59N	117 59 45W	city/town	285
Bassetts	39 37 11N	120 35 11W	city/town	5400
Bassi Falls	38 53 32N	120 19 48W	falls	

California GPS Companion

Place Name	Latitude	Longitude	Type	Elev
Batavia	38 24 23N	121 51 31W	city/town	60
Bateman Place	40 37 25N	121 44 15W	city/town	4240
Battery Point	41 44 48N	124 12 12W	cape	
Battery Point Is.	41 44 39N	124 12 07W	island	
Batto	38 17 01N	122 26 09W	city/town	82
Baumberg	37 37 15N	122 05 57W	city/town	10
Baxter	39 12 47N	120 46 48W	city/town	3900
Baxter, Mount	36 51 41N	118 21 54W	summit	13125
Bay Meadows Racetr	37 32 35N	122 17 46W	track	
Bay Park	32 46 54N	117 12 20W	city/town	60
Bay Shores	33 36 53N	117 54 36W	city/town	10
Bayles Place	40 08 58N	122 38 26W	city/town	1096
Bayley House	38 50 39N	121 00 50W	building	
Bayliss	39 34 58N	122 02 41W	city/town	109
Bayo Vista	38 02 13N	122 15 37W	city/town	40
Bayshore	37 42 23N	122 24 44W	city/town	25
Bayside	40 50 33N	124 03 45W	city/town	25
Bayside Golf Cours	40 50 51N	124 03 00W	golf	
Bayside Village	32 46 53N	117 12 09W	city/town	50
Bayside Vlg. -subd	37 46 59N	122 23 19W	city/town	10
Bayview	40 46 22N	124 10 58W	city/town	70
Bayview District	37 44 03N	122 23 25W	city/town	50

California GPS Companion

Place Name	Latitude	Longitude	Type	Elev
Baywood Golf & C C	40 50 33N	124 02 36W	golf	
Baywood Park	35 19 35N	120 50 03W	city/town	152
Baywood Park Beach	35 19 49N	120 50 35W	beach	
Beach State Park	37 37 57N	122 29 36W	park	
Beachcomer Marina	38 56 43N	119 58 36W	marina	
Beacon Station	35 07 57N	116 12 29W	city/town	1465
Beal Place	40 35 52N	121 44 55W	city/town	4520
Beale A F B	39 08 09N	121 26 11W	military	113
Beall Place	40 01 39N	123 49 43W	city/town	1720
Bealville	35 16 20N	118 37 31W	city/town	1820
Bean Hollow State	37 13 58N	122 24 50W	park	
Bear Canyon Falls	33 00 57N	114 40 11W	falls	
Bear Creek (1)	38 05 02N	121 14 30W	city/town	47
Bear Creek (2)	37 17 50N	120 24 59W	city/town	190
Bear Creek Falls	40 31 55N	121 56 45W	falls	
Bear Creek Spire	37 22 05N	118 46 00W	summit	13713
Bear River Pines	39 10 10N	120 58 01W	city/town	2520
Bear River Resort	38 32 51N	120 15 21W	ski area	5840
Bear Valley (1)	38 27 53N	120 02 20W	city/town	1120
Bear Valley (2)	37 34 08N	120 07 06W	city/town	2050
Bear Valley Ski Ar	38 29 32N	120 02 37W	ski area	
Beatrice (1)	38 38 36N	121 35 42W	city/town	20

California GPS Companion

Place Name	Latitude	Longitude	Type	Elev
Beatrice (2)	40 40 12N	124 12 05W	city/town	10
Beatty Junction	36 35 17N	116 56 32W	city/town	190
Beaumont	33 55 46N	116 58 35W	city/town	2620
BeauPre Golf Cours	40 57 38N	124 05 41W	golf	
Becker Racetrack	40 34 18N	123 33 11W	track	
Beckwourth	39 49 13N	120 22 40W	city/town	4900
Beckwourth Airport	39 49 05N	120 21 20W	airport	4894
Bee Rock	35 47 14N	120 56 17W	city/town	931
Beegum	40 20 42N	122 51 25W	city/town	1291
Beeks Place	33 49 13N	117 38 16W	city/town	2815
Behring Museum	37 47 59N	121 55 08W	museum	
Bel Air	34 05 00N	118 26 52W	city/town	750
Bel Air Country Cl	34 04 39N	118 26 47W	golf	
Belden	40 00 22N	121 14 53W	city/town	3400
Belfast	40 26 37N	120 27 02W	city/town	4128
Belfort	38 24 59N	119 15 58W	city/town	10200
Bell	33 58 39N	118 11 10W	city/town	135
Bell Gardens	33 57 55N	118 09 02W	city/town	122
Bell Mountain	34 37 27N	117 12 22W	city/town	3082
Bell Springs	39 57 07N	123 35 03W	city/town	3620
Bella Vista (1)	40 38 27N	122 13 53W	city/town	550
Bella Vista (2)	35 39 08N	118 19 18W	city/town	2720

California GPS Companion

Place Name	Latitude	Longitude	Type	Elev
Bella Vista Park	39 14 40N	121 02 59W	city/town	2840
Belle Haven	37 28 35N	122 09 30W	city/town	10
Belle Monte	37 31 09N	122 17 45W	city/town	400
Belleview (1)	38 00 47N	120 17 23W	city/town	2580
Belleview (2)	40 30 22N	124 07 11W	city/town	100
Bellevue	38 24 07N	122 42 45W	city/town	118
Bellflower	33 52 54N	118 06 58W	city/town	71
Bellflower Golf C.	33 53 41N	118 08 22W	golf	
Bellota	38 03 11N	121 00 46W	city/town	131
Belltown	34 00 42N	117 22 57W	city/town	830
Bellvale	37 18 43N	122 19 12W	city/town	240
Belmont	37 31 13N	122 16 29W	city/town	33
Belmont Country Cl	36 44 52N	119 38 23W	golf	
Belmont Pier	33 45 24N	118 08 51W	pier	
Belmont Shore	33 45 26N	118 08 10W	city/town	7
Belvedere (1)	37 52 22N	122 27 48W	city/town	300
Belvedere (2)	34 02 26N	118 10 06W	city/town	313
Belvedere Gardens	34 01 40N	118 09 43W	city/town	230
Belvedere Heights	33 59 01N	117 18 36W	city/town	1240
Ben Ali	38 37 19N	121 25 17W	city/town	50
Ben Hur	37 21 06N	119 57 24W	city/town	1750
Ben Lomond	37 05 21N	122 05 07W	city/town	360

California GPS Companion

Place Name	Latitude	Longitude	Type	Elev
Ben Weston Beach	33 21 43N	118 29 03W	beach	
Ben Weston Point	33 21 26N	118 29 17W	cape	
Bena	35 19 36N	118 44 20W	city/town	873
Benbow	40 04 07N	123 47 00W	city/town	400
Benbow Lake State	40 03 47N	123 47 37W	park	
Bend	40 15 19N	122 12 27W	city/town	340
Benicia	38 02 58N	122 09 27W	city/town	33
Benicia Capitol St	38 03 00N	122 09 29W	museum	
Benito	36 49 18N	120 26 07W	city/town	160
Benton	37 49 09N	118 28 32W	city/town	5377
Benton Crossing	37 41 57N	118 45 47W	city/town	6817
Benton Hot Springs	37 48 01N	118 31 41W	city/town	5626
Berenda	37 02 25N	120 09 09W	city/town	253
Berg	39 10 51N	121 37 35W	city/town	63
Berkeley	37 52 18N	122 16 18W	city/town	150
Berkeley Marina	37 52 05N	122 18 55W	marina	
Berkeley Pier	37 51 19N	122 20 16W	pier	
Berkeley Yacht Clb	37 51 54N	122 18 40W	locale	
Bermuda Dunes C C	33 44 32N	116 16 40W	golf	
Bern	35 41 21N	120 32 19W	city/town	840
Berry Creek	39 38 43N	121 24 08W	city/town	2050
Berry Creek Falls	37 10 11N	122 15 49W	falls	

California GPS Companion

Place Name	Latitude	Longitude	Type	Elev
Berry Glenn	41 19 03N	124 02 24W	city/town	41
Berryessa	37 23 11N	121 51 34W	city/town	144
Berryessa Highland	38 30 53N	122 11 12W	city/town	
Berryessa Marina	38 34 48N	122 14 52W	marina	
Bertram	33 22 42N	115 46 57W	city/town	-195
Bestville	41 18 03N	123 08 31W	city/town	2240
Beswick	41 58 01N	122 12 07W	city/town	2670
Bethany Bible Coll	37 04 31N	121 59 34W	univ/coll	
Bethany Park	37 04 33N	121 59 31W	city/town	840
Bethel Island	38 00 54N	121 38 22W	city/town	5
Bethune	34 04 47N	117 18 21W	city/town	1000
Betteravia	34 55 04N	120 30 50W	city/town	155
Betteravia Jct.	34 55 39N	120 31 58W	city/town	130
Betz Beach	33 29 34N	115 54 22W	beach	
Beulah Park	37 00 41N	122 01 21W	city/town	360
Beulah Picnic Grnd	32 50 56N	116 32 59W	city/town	
Beveridge	36 42 16N	117 54 51W	city/town	5590
Beverly Glen	34 06 28N	118 26 41W	city/town	1020
Beverly Hills	34 04 25N	118 23 58W	city/town	225
Bicentennial Mus.	39 15 48N	121 00 58W	museum	
Bicknell	34 49 00N	120 23 32W	city/town	760
Bidwell Canyon Mar	39 31 58N	121 27 18W	marina	

California GPS Companion

Place Name	Latitude	Longitude	Type	Elev
Bidwell Mansion	39 43 57N	121 50 32W	building	
Bidwell Municipal	39 46 06N	121 46 47W	golf	
Bieber	41 07 17N	121 08 35W	city/town	4127
Bieber -Southard	41 08 22N	121 07 25W	airport	4158
Big Bar (1)	40 44 28N	123 15 17W	city/town	1320
Big Bar (2)	38 18 43N	120 43 08W	city/town	620
Big Bar (3)	39 48 20N	121 26 13W	city/town	1420
Big Bear City	34 15 40N	116 50 39W	city/town	6757
Big Bear City Airp	34 15 49N	116 51 16W	airport	6748
Big Bear Lake	34 14 38N	116 54 38W	city/town	6754
Big Bear Solar Obs	34 15 30N	116 55 13W	observtry	
Big Bend (1)	41 01 15N	121 54 36W	city/town	1701
Big Bend (2)	39 18 20N	120 31 01W	city/town	5740
Big Bend (3)	39 41 54N	121 27 35W	city/town	2288
Big Bend (4)	38 14 11N	122 27 40W	city/town	20
Big Break Marina	38 00 46N	121 43 55W	marina	
Big Bunch	36 45 26N	119 32 14W	city/town	392
Big Creek	37 12 18N	119 14 42W	city/town	4920
Big Falls	34 05 09N	116 53 42W	falls	
Big Lagoon	41 09 38N	124 07 57W	city/town	40
Big Meadow	38 24 54N	120 06 51W	city/town	6560
Big Oak Flat	37 49 25N	120 15 26W	city/town	2840

29

California GPS Companion

Place Name	Latitude	Longitude	Type	Elev
Big Pine	37 09 54N	118 17 19W	city/town	3985
Big Pines	34 22 44N	117 41 21W	city/town	6862
Big Rock Beach	34 02 14N	118 36 52W	beach	
Big Rock Springs	34 26 07N	117 50 05W	city/town	3894
Big Sluice Box	39 00 29N	120 15 47W	locale	
Big Springs	41 35 44N	122 24 14W	city/town	2613
Big Sur	36 16 13N	121 48 23W	city/town	155
Big Trees	38 16 39N	120 18 34W	city/town	4682
Big Tujunga Dam	34 17 36N	118 11 15W	dam	2290
Bigelow	37 20 07N	118 18 48W	city/town	4040
Bigfoot Golf and C	40 57 14N	123 37 34W	golf	
Biggs	39 24 45N	121 42 42W	city/town	94
Bijou	38 56 48N	119 58 03W	city/town	6235
Bijou Golf Course	38 56 30N	119 57 53W	golf	
Bijou Park	38 56 58N	119 57 28W	city/town	6240
Bing Maloney Golf	38 30 03N	121 29 56W	golf	
Bingham	33 50 46N	118 03 30W	city/town	38
Binghamton	38 21 05N	121 49 18W	city/town	35
Binney Junction	39 09 27N	121 35 21W	city/town	83
Biola	36 48 08N	120 00 55W	city/town	251
Biola College	33 54 25N	118 00 54W	univ/coll	
Biola Junction	36 48 03N	119 52 04W	city/town	297

California GPS Companion

Place Name	Latitude	Longitude	Type	Elev
Birch Meadow Acres	39 09 17N	121 01 28W	city/town	2270
Birch Mountain	37 03 50N	118 25 05W	summit	13660
Birchville	39 19 40N	121 08 36W	city/town	1750
Birds Landing	38 07 58N	121 52 11W	city/town	58
Biscar State Wildl	40 33 20N	120 21 00W	park	
Bishop	37 21 49N	118 23 39W	city/town	4147
Bishop Airport	37 22 23N	118 21 48W	airport	4120
Biskra Palms	33 47 24N	116 15 08W	city/town	320
Bismarck	34 57 57N	116 51 31W	city/town	3060
Bissell	34 59 41N	118 00 05W	city/town	2700
Bitney Corner	39 13 55N	121 06 28W	city/town	2359
Bitterwater	36 22 49N	121 00 06W	city/town	1487
Bivalve	38 05 33N	122 49 34W	city/town	20
Bixby Knolls	33 50 08N	118 10 33W	city/town	82
Bixby Village Golf	33 46 15N	118 06 41W	golf	
Bixler	37 56 25N	121 37 16W	city/town	10
Black Butte	41 23 30N	122 21 36W	city/town	3920
Black Forest	40 15 33N	121 22 35W	city/town	4840
Black Giant	37 06 12N	118 38 50W	summit	13330
Black Kaweah	36 32 42N	118 30 56W	summit	13765
Black Lake Golf C.	35 02 52N	120 32 33W	golf	
Black Lands	38 03 27N	121 14 30W	city/town	44

31

California GPS Companion

Place Name	Latitude	Longitude	Type	Elev
Black Meadow Ldg.	34 21 07N	114 11 49W	city/town	470
Black Oak Golf Crs	38 58 05N	121 04 25W	golf	
Black Oaks	38 49 51N	122 49 53W	city/town	2000
Black Point	38 06 37N	122 30 16W	city/town	13
Black Point Beach	38 41 11N	123 25 53W	beach	
Black Winery	38 47 23N	122 59 25W	wine/vin	
Blackcap Mountain	37 04 20N	118 47 33W	summit	11559
Blackhawk C C	37 48 47N	121 55 08W	golf	
Blackrock	36 55 45N	118 13 57W	city/town	3845
Blacks Mountain	40 46 30N	121 11 20W	summit	7286
Blackslough Ldg.	37 59 40N	121 25 04W	city/town	7
Blacktop Peak	37 47 36N	119 11 47W	summit	12710
Blackwells Corner	35 36 54N	119 52 01W	city/town	644
Blairsden	39 46 52N	120 36 56W	city/town	4380
Blakes Landing	38 11 40N	122 55 06W	city/town	0
Blanchard	37 43 53N	120 19 28W	city/town	1040
Blanco (1)	36 40 43N	121 44 30W	city/town	20
Blanco (2)	36 02 10N	119 30 37W	city/town	207
Blanco Mountain	37 27 56N	118 09 42W	summit	11278
Blavo	39 34 18N	121 43 56W	city/town	138
Bleeker Laboratory	37 25 46N	122 10 55W	building	
Blind Beach	38 26 10N	123 07 15W	beach	

California GPS Companion

Place Name	Latitude	Longitude	Type	Elev
Blocksburg	40 16 34N	123 38 07W	city/town	1596
Bloody Mountain	37 33 38N	118 54 28W	summit	12544
Bloomfield	38 18 50N	122 51 00W	city/town	80
Bloomington	34 04 13N	117 23 42W	city/town	1090
Blue Canyon	39 15 26N	120 42 36W	city/town	4686
Blue Canyon Falls	36 55 53N	118 44 59W	falls	
Blue Canyon Peak	37 01 41N	118 42 29W	summit	11849
Blue Hills	37 17 17N	122 01 52W	city/town	318
Blue Jay	34 14 46N	117 12 32W	city/town	5200
Blue Lake	40 52 59N	123 58 58W	city/town	100
Blue Lake Museum	40 52 52N	123 59 20W	museum	
Blue Ridge Ski Lft	34 22 09N	117 41 31W	ski area	
Blue Tent	39 18 37N	120 58 21W	city/town	3136
Bluegum	39 35 01N	122 11 32W	city/town	145
Bluff Falls	40 24 49N	121 31 55W	falls	
Blunt	40 14 31N	122 17 24W	city/town	440
Bly	33 59 33N	117 29 38W	city/town	750
Blythe	33 36 37N	114 35 44W	city/town	267
Blythe Airport	33 37 08N	114 43 00W	airport	397
Boal	32 36 49N	117 05 18W	city/town	33
Boards Crossing	38 18 16N	120 13 59W	city/town	3880
Bob Hoaglin Place	40 05 40N	123 19 39W	city/town	2320

33

California GPS Companion

Place Name	Latitude	Longitude	Type	Elev
Boca	39 23 10N	120 05 35W	city/town	5540
Bodega	38 20 43N	122 58 22W	city/town	106
Bodega Bay	38 20 00N	123 02 49W	city/town	100
Bodega Dunes	38 20 09N	123 03 51W	locale	
Bodega Harbor	38 19 25N	123 02 48W	bay	
Bodega Island	38 19 12N	123 02 06W	locale	
Bodfish	35 35 17N	118 29 28W	city/town	2680
Bodie	38 12 44N	119 00 40W	city/town	8369
Bodie State Histor	38 12 56N	119 00 36W	park	
Bogue	39 05 53N	121 37 26W	city/town	53
Boiling Point	34 31 20N	118 15 41W	city/town	3160
Bolam	41 30 51N	122 14 53W	city/town	4417
Boles	41 32 21N	121 03 29W	city/town	4870
Bolinas	37 54 34N	122 41 07W	city/town	9
Bolinas Ridge	38 05 42N	122 47 05W	ridge	
Bollinger Place	39 50 37N	122 52 43W	city/town	5200
Bolsa Chica Beach	33 41 42N	118 02 48W	park	
Bolsa Knolls	36 44 02N	121 38 13W	city/town	140
Bolton Brown Mount	37 02 47N	118 26 25W	summit	13538
Bombay	38 41 13N	121 28 45W	city/town	35
Bombay Beach	33 21 01N	115 43 00W	beach	
Bombay Beach	33 21 03N	115 43 44W	city/town	-225

California GPS Companion

Place Name	Latitude	Longitude	Type	Elev
Bonanza Springs	38 51 52N	122 41 09W	city/town	2480
Bonds Corner	32 41 37N	115 20 11W	city/town	30
Bonetti	38 40 29N	120 27 13W	city/town	4640
Bonilla	38 16 41N	122 26 12W	city/town	65
Bonita (1)	32 39 28N	117 01 45W	city/town	118
Bonita (2)	36 57 09N	120 12 03W	city/town	206
Bonita Falls	34 13 49N	117 30 14W	falls	
Bonita Golf Course	32 39 23N	117 04 01W	golf	
Bonnefoy	38 21 38N	120 45 00W	city/town	1280
Bonnie Bell	33 56 57N	116 38 34W	city/town	1680
Bonnie View	39 22 57N	122 41 02W	city/town	3000
Bonny Doon	37 02 30N	122 08 58W	city/town	1250
Bonny Doon Beach	36 59 59N	122 10 50W	beach	
Bonsall	33 17 20N	117 13 29W	city/town	175
Boomer Beach	32 51 00N	117 16 24W	beach	
Boonville	39 00 33N	123 21 54W	city/town	400
Boonville Airport	39 00 45N	123 22 58W	airport	371
Bootjack	37 27 54N	119 53 08W	city/town	2242
Borden	36 55 48N	120 01 32W	city/town	270
Border Field State	32 32 34N	117 07 17W	park	
Boreal Ridge Ski A	39 19 54N	120 21 00W	ski area	7701
Bormister	41 21 19N	120 32 10W	city/town	4400

California GPS Companion

Place Name	Latitude	Longitude	Type	Elev
Boron	34 59 58N	117 38 56W	city/town	2460
Borosolvay	35 44 06N	117 24 03W	city/town	1680
Borrego	33 13 16N	116 20 00W	city/town	504
Borrego Badlands	33 14 54N	116 13 25W	locale	
Borrego Springs	33 15 21N	116 22 27W	city/town	590
Borrego Valley Air	33 15 35N	116 19 23W	airport	520
Boston Heights	34 03 35N	118 11 40W	city/town	400
Boston Ravine	39 12 29N	121 04 07W	city/town	2400
Bostonia	32 48 27N	116 56 08W	city/town	480
Botanical Gardens	34 07 55N	118 06 51W	park	
Boulder Bay	34 14 23N	116 56 44W	city/town	6760
Boulder Creek	37 07 34N	122 07 16W	city/town	493
Boulder Creek Golf	37 09 13N	122 09 30W	golf	
Boulder Oaks (1)	32 57 26N	116 55 29W	city/town	1474
Boulder Oaks (2)	32 43 54N	116 29 02W	city/town	3160
Boulder Park	32 39 32N	116 06 00W	city/town	2837
Boulevard	32 39 49N	116 16 22W	city/town	
Boundary Oak Golf	37 55 33N	122 00 07W	golf	
Bouquet Canyon Dam	34 34 39N	118 23 02W	dam	3011
Bouquet Junction	34 25 22N	118 32 23W	city/town	1175
Bourn Mansion	37 47 38N	122 25 55W	building	
Bowerbank	35 23 58N	119 24 27W	city/town	295

California GPS Companion

Place Name	Latitude	Longitude	Type	Elev
Bowerman Boat Lnch	40 53 27N	122 46 10W	locale	2362
Bowles	36 36 15N	119 45 00W	city/town	273
Bowling Ball Beach	38 52 15N	123 39 26W	beach	
Bowman	38 56 31N	121 02 47W	city/town	1620
Bowman Place	39 47 22N	123 33 42W	city/town	2320
Box Springs	33 56 48N	117 17 44W	city/town	1500
Boyers Landing	38 57 06N	121 50 17W	city/town	33
Boyes Hot Springs	38 18 50N	122 28 51W	city/town	160
Boyle Heights	34 02 02N	118 12 16W	city/town	330
Boys Republic	33 59 49N	117 43 25W	city/town	690
Brackney	37 04 08N	122 04 52W	city/town	300
Bracut	40 49 39N	124 04 56W	city/town	10
Bradbury	34 08 49N	117 58 12W	city/town	600
Bradbury Dam Obser	34 34 50N	119 58 40W	overlook	
Bradford Winery	38 17 44N	121 25 00W	wine/vin	
Bradley	35 51 48N	120 47 59W	city/town	541
Bradley Young Obs.	38 34 39N	122 25 41W	observtry	1900
Bradley, Mount (1)	36 43 43N	118 20 15W	summit	13289
Bradley, Mount (2)	41 13 18N	122 18 29W	summit	5556
Bradys	35 42 08N	117 52 04W	city/town	2500
Braemar Country Cl	34 08 34N	118 32 27W	golf	
Bragur	34 56 07N	120 32 44W	city/town	110

California GPS Companion

Place Name	Latitude	Longitude	Type	Elev
Brainard	40 48 44N	124 06 33W	city/town	3
Bramlet Place	40 15 38N	123 09 43W	city/town	2800
Brandon College	37 46 32N	122 25 05W	univ/coll	
Brandon Corner	38 35 09N	120 56 00W	city/town	777
Brandy City	39 32 16N	121 01 27W	city/town	3700
Brannan Island	38 08 48N	121 38 49W	island	
Brannon Island St.	38 06 55N	121 41 30W	park	
Branscomb	39 39 13N	123 37 28W	city/town	1570
Brant	35 17 30N	115 22 11W	city/town	3740
Brawley	32 58 43N	115 31 46W	city/town	-110
Brawley Municipal	32 59 35N	115 31 00W	airport	-129
Bray	41 38 39N	121 58 11W	city/town	4660
Brazil Beach	38 14 03N	122 57 20W	beach	
Brazos	38 12 30N	122 18 18W	city/town	6
Brea	33 55 00N	117 53 57W	city/town	360
Brea Chem	33 55 01N	117 52 06W	city/town	390
Brea Golf Club	33 54 43N	117 54 24W	golf	
Bredehoft Place	39 46 58N	122 56 18W	city/town	4700
Brela	38 34 31N	120 57 53W	city/town	960
Brents Junction	34 08 54N	118 41 49W	city/town	770
Brentwood (1)	34 03 07N	118 28 23W	city/town	360
Brentwood (2)	37 55 55N	121 41 41W	city/town	79

California GPS Companion

Place Name	Latitude	Longitude	Type	Elev
Brentwood C C	34 02 47N	118 29 02W	golf	
Brentwood Heights	34 03 49N	118 28 26W	city/town	440
Brentwood Park	38 02 42N	120 14 45W	city/town	3640
Brentwood Park-sub	34 03 18N	118 29 14W	city/town	425
Bretz Mill	37 02 15N	119 14 20W	city/town	3300
Brewer, Mount	36 42 31N	118 29 04W	summit	13570
Briarwood Canyon	38 40 30N	121 00 50W	city/town	1230
Briceburg	37 36 18N	119 57 57W	city/town	1200
Briceland	40 06 29N	123 53 56W	city/town	620
Brickyard Cove Mar	37 54 32N	122 23 25W	marina	
Bridalveil Fall	37 43 00N	119 38 45W	falls	
Bridgedale -subdiv	33 52 42N	118 19 40W	city/town	45
Bridgehaven	38 26 01N	123 05 59W	city/town	51
Bridgehead	38 00 18N	121 45 16W	city/town	40
Bridgeport (1)	38 15 21N	119 13 49W	city/town	6468
Bridgeport (2)	37 26 00N	120 00 12W	city/town	1500
Bridgeport (3)	39 17 30N	121 11 37W	city/town	567
Bridgeport -Bryant	38 15 44N	119 13 32W	airport	6468
Bridgeport Covered	39 17 33N	121 11 38W	bridge	
Bridgeville	40 28 10N	123 47 55W	city/town	646
Briggs Terrace	34 14 27N	118 13 33W	city/town	2400
Brighton	38 32 58N	121 24 58W	city/town	50

California GPS Companion

Place Name	Latitude	Longitude	Type	Elev
Brightside	37 35 57N	121 55 24W	city/town	205
Brisbane	37 40 51N	122 23 56W	city/town	100
Brito	36 59 33N	120 42 28W	city/town	108
Broadmoor	37 41 12N	122 28 54W	city/town	400
Broadview Farms	36 49 19N	120 30 21W	city/town	265
Broadway Jail -his	37 47 52N	122 24 18W	building	
Broadway Pier	32 42 55N	117 10 38W	pier	
Broadway Wharf	37 47 39N	122 16 36W	wharf	
Broadwell	34 52 26N	116 11 33W	city/town	1298
Brockman	40 57 50N	120 29 53W	city/town	5320
Brockman Cabin-his	40 02 08N	121 49 22W	building	1000
Brockmans Corner	37 22 34N	118 25 53W	city/town	4245
Brockway	39 13 36N	120 00 40W	city/town	6340
Brockway Golf Club	39 14 21N	120 01 57W	golf	
Brockway Vista	39 14 17N	120 00 51W	city/town	6400
Broderick	38 35 28N	121 30 58W	city/town	15
Broken Finger Peak	37 24 20N	118 43 00W	summit	13000
Bromela	35 01 04N	120 34 58W	city/town	52
Bronco	39 23 11N	120 01 18W	city/town	5340
Brookdale	37 06 23N	122 06 18W	city/town	440
Brookfield Village	37 44 07N	122 11 06W	city/town	18
Brookhurst	33 50 40N	117 57 28W	city/town	117

Place Name	Latitude	Longitude	Type	Elev
Brooklyn Heights	34 02 55N	118 12 40W	city/town	340
Brooklyn Hts. -sub	32 43 28N	117 07 46W	city/town	260
Brooks	38 44 30N	122 08 49W	city/town	350
Brooks Exh. Hall	37 46 44N	122 24 59W	building	
Brooks Island	37 53 47N	122 21 15W	island	159
Brooks Mill	41 16 46N	120 18 35W	city/town	5330
Brookshire	37 45 33N	122 01 38W	city/town	560
Brookside Golf Crs	34 10 11N	118 10 10W	golf	
Brooktrails	39 26 38N	123 23 03W	city/town	1640
Brooktrails Golf C	39 26 27N	123 23 05W	golf	
Brown	35 46 25N	117 50 57W	city/town	2392
Brown Place	40 01 31N	122 35 19W	city/town	1029
Browning	33 44 00N	117 48 05W	city/town	100
Browns Corner	38 40 40N	121 48 05W	city/town	75
Browns Flat	38 00 14N	120 23 03W	city/town	1960
Browns Island	38 02 20N	121 51 49W	island	
Browns Valley	39 14 32N	121 24 29W	city/town	268
Brownsville	39 28 24N	121 16 05W	city/town	2235
Brownsville Aero P	39 27 19N	121 17 28W	airport	2120
Bruceville	38 20 09N	121 24 58W	city/town	24
Bruhel Point	39 36 28N	123 47 07W	cape	
Brush Creek	39 41 26N	121 20 17W	city/town	3540

California GPS Companion

Place Name	Latitude	Longitude	Type	Elev
Bryants	38 43 08N	120 28 32W	city/town	4460
Bryman	34 40 29N	117 20 41W	city/town	2523
Bryn Mawr	34 02 54N	117 13 48W	city/town	1202
Bryson	35 48 24N	121 05 22W	city/town	978
Bryte	38 35 41N	121 32 26W	city/town	20
Buchanan	37 54 53N	120 11 15W	city/town	3100
Buchanan Field G.	37 58 47N	122 03 45W	golf	
Buchli	38 12 54N	122 19 54W	city/town	7
Buck Meadows	37 48 46N	120 03 48W	city/town	3006
Buckeye (1)	39 47 44N	121 18 11W	city/town	4960
Buckeye (2)	40 38 37N	122 23 47W	city/town	720
Buckeye (3)	38 55 26N	120 47 49W	city/town	2960
Buckhorn	34 24 03N	118 48 53W	city/town	600
Buckingham Park	39 00 56N	122 45 25W	city/town	1400
Bucks Lodge	39 52 32N	121 10 25W	city/town	5246
Bucksport	40 46 31N	124 11 28W	city/town	10
Bucktail	40 42 15N	122 50 56W	city/town	1738
Bucktown	38 23 27N	122 01 23W	city/town	283
Buellton	34 36 49N	120 11 30W	city/town	361
Buena	33 10 24N	117 12 28W	city/town	460
Buena Park	33 52 03N	117 59 50W	city/town	74
Buena Vista (1)	38 17 40N	120 54 44W	city/town	295

California GPS Companion

Place Name	Latitude	Longitude	Type	Elev
Buena Vista (2)	40 03 20N	121 51 59W	city/town	1760
Buena Vista (3)	38 17 23N	122 26 02W	city/town	105
Buena Vista (4)	37 42 40N	119 47 34W	city/town	5200
Buena Vista Wine C	38 17 58N	122 25 16W	wine/vin	
Buffalo Hill	38 54 31N	120 50 47W	city/town	2550
Buhach	37 20 11N	120 34 51W	city/town	155
Bull Creek	40 20 09N	124 01 31W	city/town	380
Bullard	38 36 33N	120 57 37W	city/town	1120
Bully Hill	40 47 52N	122 11 31W	city/town	1180
Bumblebee	38 13 35N	119 59 46W	city/town	6040
Bummerville	38 24 05N	120 30 17W	city/town	2949
Bunker	38 21 03N	121 45 26W	city/town	18
Bunker Hill (1)	34 04 53N	117 18 15W	city/town	1030
Bunker Hill (2)	38 25 36N	120 49 38W	city/town	940
Bunnell Cascade	37 44 43N	119 28 15W	falls	
Buntingville	40 17 09N	120 29 02W	city/town	4090
Burbank (1)	34 10 51N	118 18 29W	city/town	598
Burbank (2)	37 19 24N	121 55 50W	city/town	122
Burbank - Glendale	34 12 02N	118 21 30W	airport	775
Burbank Junction	34 11 07N	118 19 02W	city/town	600
Burbeck	39 25 48N	123 26 33W	city/town	680
Burdell	38 09 29N	122 33 51W	city/town	10

California GPS Companion

Place Name	Latitude	Longitude	Type	Elev
Burlingame	37 35 03N	122 21 54W	city/town	25
Burlingame C C	37 34 15N	122 21 45W	golf	
Burlington	40 18 31N	123 54 29W	city/town	180
Burness	36 45 54N	119 39 27W	city/town	346
Burney	40 52 57N	121 39 35W	city/town	3173
Burney Falls	41 00 39N	121 39 06W	falls	
Burnham	37 53 31N	121 08 52W	city/town	55
Burnham Pavilion	37 25 42N	122 09 48W	building	
Burnt Lava Flow Ge	41 29 16N	121 31 30W	locale	6186
Burnt Ranch	40 48 33N	123 28 23W	city/town	1473
Burnt Ranch Falls	40 49 35N	123 28 30W	falls	
Burr	36 14 43N	119 06 51W	city/town	350
Burrel	36 29 18N	119 59 03W	city/town	200
Burson	38 11 02N	120 53 22W	city/town	408
Burton Creek State	39 11 42N	120 08 30W	park	7175
Burton Mill	35 30 02N	118 24 22W	city/town	6720
Busch Gardens	34 07 46N	118 09 50W	park	
Bush	34 09 00N	115 42 08W	city/town	1205
Butano Falls	37 14 32N	122 19 01W	falls	
Butano Park	37 14 00N	122 19 34W	city/town	200
Butano State Park	37 13 22N	122 18 08W	park	
Butler	34 07 57N	117 57 52W	city/town	490

California GPS Companion

Place Name	Latitude	Longitude	Type	Elev
Butte City	39 27 53N	121 59 20W	city/town	87
Butte Creek C C	39 40 49N	121 46 18W	golf	
Butte Meadows	40 04 53N	121 33 00W	city/town	4351
Butte Street Jct.	34 01 05N	118 13 51W	city/town	220
Button Shell Beach	33 24 18N	118 22 05W	beach	
Buttonwillow	35 24 02N	119 28 07W	city/town	269
Buttonwillow Elk H	35 21 09N	119 28 43W	airport	326
Byron	37 52 02N	121 38 13W	city/town	26
Byron Airport	37 50 09N	121 38 13W	airport	65

ℂ

Place Name	Latitude	Longitude	Type	Elev
Caballero Country	34 09 37N	118 32 04W	golf	
Cabazon	33 55 03N	116 47 11W	city/town	1792
Cabin Cove	36 27 56N	118 39 11W	city/town	5960
Cable	35 10 09N	118 28 31W	city/town	3560
Cable Car Barn & M	37 47 41N	122 24 38W	museum	
Cabrillo Beach	33 42 34N	118 16 55W	beach	
Cabrillo Beach Yt.	33 43 29N	118 16 52W	locale	
Cabrillo College	36 59 20N	121 55 20W	univ/coll	
Cabrillo Fishing P	33 42 26N	118 16 27W	pier	
Cabrillo Harbor	33 25 13N	118 24 12W	bay	
Cabrillo Marina	33 43 17N	118 16 48W	marina	

California GPS Companion

Place Name	Latitude	Longitude	Type	Elev
Cabrillo Marine M.	33 42 34N	118 16 59W	museum	
Cabrillo National	32 40 15N	117 14 30W	park	
Cabrillo Pavillion	34 25 00N	119 40 04W	building	
Cabrillo, Point	36 37 18N	121 54 10W	cape	
Cachuma Village	34 35 10N	119 59 24W	city/town	620
Cactus	32 51 44N	114 53 46W	city/town	390
Cactus City	33 40 42N	115 57 47W	city/town	1668
Cactus Garden	33 07 50N	116 13 20W	garden	
Cadenasso	38 42 52N	122 07 41W	city/town	330
Cadiz	34 31 12N	115 30 43W	city/town	791
Cadiz Dunes	34 20 54N	115 22 38W	locale	
Cadwell	38 21 30N	122 46 36W	city/town	113
Cahoon Rock Look.	36 22 43N	118 41 16W	overlook	9278
Cahuilla	33 32 27N	116 44 35W	city/town	3629
Cahuilla Hills	33 41 19N	116 24 56W	city/town	920
Cain Rock	40 08 13N	123 35 30W	city/town	380
Cairns Corner	36 12 45N	119 08 05W	city/town	345
Cajon	34 17 56N	117 27 20W	city/town	3000
Cajon Heights -sub	32 47 28N	116 58 31W	city/town	480
Cajon Junction	34 18 42N	117 28 26W	city/town	3120
Cajon Speedway	32 49 20N	116 58 04W	track	
Cal Col Arts&Craft	37 50 09N	122 14 58W	univ/coll	

California GPS Companion

Place Name	Latitude	Longitude	Type	Elev
Cal Col of Medicin	34 03 48N	118 12 39W	univ/coll	
Cal St U Domingue	33 51 51N	118 15 15W	univ/coll	
Cal St U Fresno	36 48 45N	119 44 44W	univ/coll	
Cal St U Hayward	37 56 42N	121 58 34W	univ/coll	
Cal St. Fullerton	33 52 49N	117 53 05W	univ/coll	
Cal St. Hayward	37 39 29N	122 03 17W	univ/coll	
Cal St. Long Beach	33 46 35N	118 06 48W	univ/coll	
Cal St. Los Angel.	34 04 01N	118 10 00W	univ/coll	
Cal St. San Bern.	34 10 58N	117 19 31W	univ/coll	
Cal-Ida	39 31 34N	121 00 53W	city/town	3575
Cal. Concordia Col	37 46 21N	122 10 53W	univ/coll	
Cal. Hist. Soc. SF	37 47 36N	122 25 42W	museum	
Calabasas	34 09 28N	118 38 15W	city/town	928
Calabasas Golf	34 08 32N	118 39 18W	golf	
Calabasas Highland	34 07 51N	118 38 40W	city/town	1400
Calada	35 34 47N	115 22 14W	city/town	2750
Calaveras Big Tree	38 16 19N	120 17 12W	park	
Calaveras Point	37 28 01N	122 03 00W	cape	
Calaveritas	38 09 29N	120 36 32W	city/town	1120
Calavo Gardens	32 45 46N	116 57 37W	city/town	800
Calawee Cove Beach	38 59 57N	120 05 50W	beach	
Calders Corner	35 23 01N	119 15 01W	city/town	328

California GPS Companion

Place Name	Latitude	Longitude	Type	Elev
Caldor	38 36 22N	120 25 54W	city/town	4440
Caldwell Pines	38 50 44N	122 48 25W	city/town	3200
Calexico	32 40 44N	115 29 53W	city/town	2
Calexico Internat.	32 40 10N	115 30 47W	airport	0
Calexico Lodge	32 39 58N	116 16 48W	city/town	3880
Calflax	36 20 33N	120 06 07W	city/town	272
Calgro	36 29 23N	119 17 05W	city/town	340
Calico (1)	35 37 58N	119 12 20W	city/town	397
Calico (2)	34 56 56N	116 51 51W	city/town	2280
Caliente	35 17 28N	118 37 37W	city/town	1298
California Baptist	33 55 48N	117 25 29W	univ/coll	
California Bighorn	36 51 37N	118 19 52W	park	
California City	35 07 33N	117 59 06W	city/town	2360
California City Mu	35 09 06N	118 00 50W	airport	2437
California Country	34 02 24N	118 00 46W	golf	
California Crafts	37 48 21N	122 25 16W	museum	
California Falls	37 54 58N	119 26 21W	falls	
California Golf Cl	37 38 48N	122 26 13W	golf	
California Heights	33 49 36N	118 10 33W	city/town	78
California Hot Spr	35 52 49N	118 40 22W	city/town	3074
California Memor.	37 52 17N	122 15 01W	stadium	
California Valley	35 19 12N	120 00 21W	city/town	1970

California GPS Companion

Place Name	Latitude	Longitude	Type	Elev
California Western	32 43 03N	117 15 32W	univ/coll	
Calimesa	34 00 14N	117 03 40W	city/town	2400
Calipatria	33 07 32N	115 30 48W	city/town	184
Calipatria Municip	33 07 47N	115 31 18W	airport	-180
Calistoga	38 34 44N	122 34 43W	city/town	362
Calla	37 46 33N	121 10 55W	city/town	44
Callahan	41 18 35N	122 48 01W	city/town	3123
Callender	35 03 11N	120 35 43W	city/town	93
Callender Dunes	35 04 00N	120 37 15W	locale	
Calneva	40 09 10N	120 00 28W	city/town	4005
Calpack	37 17 49N	120 21 04W	city/town	214
Calpella	39 14 01N	123 12 10W	city/town	673
Calpine	39 39 59N	120 26 19W	city/town	4958
Caltech Peak	36 41 20N	118 23 20W	summit	13832
Calvada Springs	35 58 06N	115 53 39W	city/town	2590
Calville	40 56 11N	124 05 57W	city/town	15
Calvin Laboratory	37 52 16N	122 15 11W	building	
Calwa	36 42 38N	119 45 27W	city/town	290
Calzona	34 07 44N	114 24 37W	city/town	465
Camanche Village	38 16 12N	120 58 20W	city/town	270
Camarillo	34 12 59N	119 02 12W	city/town	
Camarillo Airport	34 12 49N	119 05 39W	airport	75

California GPS Companion

Place Name	Latitude	Longitude	Type	Elev
Cambria	35 33 51N	121 04 47W	city/town	65
Cambria Pines	35 34 03N	121 05 35W	city/town	200
Cambrian Golf Club	37 15 10N	121 56 04W	golf	
Cambrian Park	37 15 25N	121 55 47W	city/town	230
Cambridge Oaks	38 40 01N	121 00 09W	city/town	1160
Camden	36 25 52N	119 47 49W	city/town	234
Camelot Golf Cours	35 01 48N	118 11 33W	golf	2787
Cameo	36 45 53N	119 42 08W	city/town	330
Cameron (1)	39 16 21N	123 33 12W	city/town	1400
Cameron (2)	35 05 48N	118 17 48W	city/town	3800
Cameron Airpark	38 41 02N	120 59 13W	airport	1286
Cameron Airpark Es	38 40 52N	120 59 15W	city/town	1240
Cameron Corners	32 37 44N	116 28 13W	city/town	2620
Cameron Creek Colo	36 19 02N	119 12 14W	city/town	362
Cameron Park	38 40 08N	120 59 10W	city/town	1200
Cameron Park C C	38 40 02N	120 59 00W	golf	
Camiaca Peak	38 03 36N	119 19 23W	summit	11739
Camino	38 44 18N	120 40 26W	city/town	3160
Camino Falls	37 25 14N	119 25 04W	falls	
Camp Bartlett	34 25 41N	119 06 26W	city/town	1160
Camp Connell	38 18 34N	120 16 38W	city/town	4840
Camp Dix -historic	34 57 48N	119 26 41W	locale	2859

California GPS Companion

Place Name	Latitude	Longitude	Type	Elev
Camp Drum -hist.	33 47 06N	118 15 24W	military	
Camp Dunlap Naval	33 15 15N	115 28 09W	military	
Camp Earnest	38 00 47N	120 13 30W	city/town	3440
Camp Eighteen	39 37 37N	121 10 09W	city/town	3950
Camp Evers	37 02 34N	122 01 26W	city/town	527
Camp Klamath	41 32 26N	124 02 55W	city/town	20
Camp Meeker	38 25 31N	122 57 30W	city/town	400
Camp Nelson	36 08 34N	118 36 30W	city/town	4770
Camp Owens	35 46 07N	118 25 48W	city/town	2720
Camp Pardee	38 14 53N	120 50 36W	city/town	680
Camp Pendola	38 12 53N	120 08 53W	city/town	4780
Camp Richardson	38 56 04N	120 02 21W	city/town	6240
Camp Richardson XC	38 55 45N	120 02 15W	ski area	
Camp Rose	38 36 55N	122 49 48W	city/town	200
Camp Sierra	37 11 26N	119 15 32W	city/town	4520
Camp Spaulding	39 19 09N	120 38 13W	city/town	5180
Camp Thayer	38 29 28N	123 03 45W	city/town	50
Campana	38 53 03N	120 31 10W	city/town	4780
Campbell (1)	41 14 24N	120 16 46W	city/town	5260
Campbell (2)	37 17 14N	121 56 56W	city/town	196
Campbell Hot Sprg.	39 34 30N	120 20 49W	city/town	5000
Campbellville	40 01 33N	121 43 19W	city/town	3925

California GPS Companion

Place Name	Latitude	Longitude	Type	Elev
Camphora	36 27 11N	121 22 12W	city/town	168
Campito Mountain	37 29 57N	118 12 01W	summit	11543
Campo	32 36 23N	116 28 05W	city/town	2600
Campo Seco (1)	37 56 20N	120 24 54W	city/town	1475
Campo Seco (2)	38 13 38N	120 51 08W	city/town	560
Camptonville	39 27 07N	121 02 51W	city/town	2800
Camron-Stanford H.	37 48 05N	122 15 40W	museum	
Camulos	34 24 24N	118 45 21W	city/town	740
Cana	39 50 25N	121 59 35W	city/town	167
Canada College	37 26 53N	122 15 50W	univ/coll	
Canby	41 26 38N	120 52 09W	city/town	4312
Canby Cross	41 49 08N	121 32 33W	city/town	4063
Candlestick Park	37 42 48N	122 23 07W	park	
Candlewood C C	33 55 49N	118 02 03W	golf	
Canebrake	35 43 42N	118 08 15W	city/town	3020
Cannery Row	36 36 48N	121 53 48W	city/town	20
Cannon	38 18 16N	121 56 46W	city/town	90
Cannonball Beach	41 07 54N	124 09 40W	beach	
Canoga Park	34 12 04N	118 35 50W	city/town	795
Cantil	35 18 32N	117 58 03W	city/town	2025
Cantrall Mill	41 19 09N	120 19 35W	city/town	6030
Cantua Creek	36 30 05N	120 18 55W	city/town	295

California GPS Companion

Place Name	Latitude	Longitude	Type	Elev
Canyon	37 49 54N	122 11 12W	city/town	622
Canyon Acres	33 33 11N	117 46 18W	city/town	120
Canyon City	32 35 42N	116 31 37W	city/town	2250
Canyon Creek Falls	40 56 04N	123 01 10W	falls	
Canyon Crest Golf	33 57 04N	117 20 16W	golf	
Canyon Crest Hts.	33 58 50N	117 19 41W	city/town	1060
Canyon Lake	33 41 06N	117 16 20W	city/town	1440
Canyon Lakes Golf	37 45 47N	121 56 35W	golf	
Canyon Oaks Golf C	39 45 41N	121 46 43W	golf	
Canyondam	40 10 19N	121 04 18W	city/town	4620
Capay (1)	38 42 28N	122 02 49W	city/town	204
Capay (2)	39 47 48N	122 05 00W	city/town	187
Capay Dam	38 42 48N	122 05 00W	dam	209
Cape Horn (1)	38 29 27N	119 57 57W	city/town	8000
Cape Horn (2)	39 08 08N	123 38 03W	city/town	1057
Cape Horn (3)	39 07 45N	120 55 25W	city/town	2660
Cape Mendocino Lt.	40 26 25N	124 24 21W	lighthous	
Cape San Martin	35 53 20N	121 27 43W	cape	
Capetown	40 27 59N	124 21 58W	city/town	60
Capistrano Beach	33 27 45N	117 40 15W	city/town	160
Capital Hill	35 37 40N	120 40 47W	city/town	640
Capitan	34 27 48N	120 02 32W	city/town	40

California GPS Companion

Place Name	Latitude	Longitude	Type	Elev
Capitola	36 58 31N	121 57 08W	city/town	50
Capitola Beach	36 58 18N	121 57 02W	beach	
Capitola State Bch	36 58 19N	121 56 54W	park	
Captain Roberts Bo	39 28 15N	120 07 58W	locale	5930
Caravan Mobile Hom	39 07 37N	123 09 31W	city/town	660
Carbon Beach	34 02 20N	118 39 28W	beach	
Carbon Canyon Dam	33 54 49N	117 50 18W	dam	475
Carbona	37 41 46N	121 24 40W	city/town	130
Carbondale	38 24 32N	121 00 21W	city/town	215
Card Place	39 48 29N	123 24 13W	city/town	820
Cardiff State Bch.	33 00 36N	117 16 42W	park	
Cardiff-by-the-Sea	33 01 18N	117 16 49W	city/town	100
Cardinal Mountain	36 59 58N	118 24 50W	summit	13397
Caribou	40 04 50N	121 09 24W	city/town	3280
Carillon, Mount	36 35 33N	118 16 38W	summit	13552
Carlotta	40 32 15N	124 03 34W	city/town	124
Carlsbad	33 09 29N	117 20 59W	city/town	50
Carlsbad McClellan	33 07 41N	117 16 49W	airport	328
Carlton	33 54 07N	117 50 11W	city/town	391
Carlton Hills	32 51 10N	116 59 38W	city/town	420
Carlton Oaks Golf	32 50 31N	117 00 33W	golf	
Carmel Beach (1)	38 22 24N	123 04 35W	beach	

California GPS Companion

Place Name	Latitude	Longitude	Type	Elev
Carmel Beach (2)	36 33 01N	121 55 41W	beach	
Carmel River State	36 31 56N	121 55 33W	park	
Carmel Valley	36 28 47N	121 43 53W	city/town	400
Carmel Valley Airp	36 28 54N	121 43 48W	airport	450
Carmel-By-The-Sea	36 33 19N	121 55 20W	city/town	200
Carmelita Gardens	34 08 47N	118 09 34W	park	
Carmen City	38 02 51N	120 41 23W	city/town	1244
Carmenita	33 53 29N	118 02 43W	city/town	75
Carmet	38 22 28N	123 04 31W	city/town	80
Carmichael	38 37 02N	121 19 38W	city/town	123
Carnadero	36 58 35N	121 32 32W	city/town	170
Carnegie Lib.-his.	38 45 13N	121 17 04W	building	
Carnegie Pub. Libr	39 55 45N	122 10 48W	building	
Carnelian Bay	39 13 37N	120 04 51W	city/town	6238
Carnelian Heights	39 12 35N	120 06 02W	city/town	6860
Carpenter	37 36 48N	122 02 36W	city/town	35
Carpenter Place	39 44 05N	122 55 43W	city/town	3400
Carpenteria Botan.	37 03 15N	119 25 36W	garden	3800
Carpinteria	34 23 56N	119 31 03W	city/town	14
Carpinteria State	34 23 31N	119 31 13W	park	
Carquinez Bridge	38 03 41N	122 13 27W	bridge	
Carquinez Heights	38 04 35N	122 14 20W	city/town	120

California GPS Companion

Place Name	Latitude	Longitude	Type	Elev
Carquinez Strait L	38 04 19N	122 14 06W	lighthous	
Carr	34 55 52N	120 30 39W	city/town	152
Carrizo Badlands	32 50 34N	116 04 44W	locale	
Carrizo Falls	33 01 15N	114 41 17W	falls	
Carrolton	37 47 55N	121 04 09W	city/town	82
Carrville	41 03 54N	122 42 11W	city/town	2420
Carson	33 49 53N	118 16 52W	city/town	37
Carson Falls	38 29 21N	119 40 54W	falls	
Carson Hill	38 01 42N	120 30 20W	city/town	1441
Carson Mansion	40 48 19N	124 09 29W	building	
Cartago	36 19 15N	118 01 32W	city/town	3620
Cartoon Art Museum	37 46 46N	122 23 31W	museum	
Caruthers	36 32 34N	119 49 56W	city/town	244
Carvin Creek Homes	39 37 43N	120 34 37W	city/town	5700
Casa Adobe Rafael	34 09 57N	118 15 47W	building	
Casa Blanca	33 55 59N	117 24 06W	city/town	880
Casa Ciele	37 45 24N	122 25 43W	building	
Casa d l Cerritos	35 18 07N	118 28 01W	building	
Casa de Adobe	34 05 56N	118 12 16W	building	
Casa de Oro	32 44 56N	116 58 48W	city/town	460
Casa Del Adobe	34 35 13N	118 06 38W	building	
Casa Diablo Hot Sp	37 38 47N	118 54 54W	locale	7290

California GPS Companion

Place Name	Latitude	Longitude	Type	Elev
Casa Joaquin Murie	37 52 06N	122 15 05W	building	
Casa Juvan	34 30 56N	118 10 09W	building	
Casa Loma (1)	39 12 02N	120 46 32W	city/town	4020
Casa Loma (2)	33 49 37N	117 01 52W	city/town	1520
Cascade	39 42 00N	121 10 38W	city/town	4063
Cascade Falls	38 12 14N	119 33 25W	falls	
Cascade Shores	39 15 54N	120 54 36W	city/town	3280
Cascadel Woods	37 13 50N	119 27 15W	city/town	3660
Casey Corner	39 11 50N	121 10 37W	city/town	1423
Casitas Springs	34 22 17N	119 18 20W	city/town	285
Casmalia	34 50 17N	120 31 49W	city/town	294
Caspar	39 21 49N	123 48 53W	city/town	160
Cassel	40 55 09N	121 32 48W	city/town	3199
Castaic	34 29 20N	118 37 19W	city/town	1232
Castaic Junction	34 26 27N	118 36 20W	city/town	1016
Castaic Lake Dam	34 31 10N	118 36 22W	dam	1240
Castaic Lake State	34 32 05N	118 36 39W	park	
Castella	41 08 19N	122 19 00W	city/town	1950
Castellammare	34 02 33N	118 33 37W	city/town	300
Castle A F B	37 22 49N	120 34 05W	military	188
Castle Crag	41 09 46N	122 17 27W	city/town	2150
Castle Crags State	41 10 16N	122 21 02W	park	

California GPS Companion

Place Name	Latitude	Longitude	Type	Elev
Castle Gardens	37 21 24N	120 34 47W	city/town	165
Castle Park	32 36 37N	117 04 00W	city/town	120
Castle Rock Beach	34 02 26N	118 33 45W	beach	
Castle Rock Falls	37 13 35N	122 06 17W	falls	
Castle Rock Nat'l.	41 45 43N	124 14 54W	park	
Castle Rock Spring	38 46 13N	122 42 56W	city/town	2320
Castle Rock State	37 13 54N	122 06 57W	park	
Castlewood Country	37 38 02N	121 53 38W	golf	
Castro City	37 24 09N	122 06 09W	city/town	55
Castro Valley	37 41 39N	122 05 07W	city/town	180
Castroville	36 45 57N	121 45 25W	city/town	23
Caswell	34 43 20N	118 47 51W	city/town	2960
Catalina Air-Sea	33 44 57N	118 16 29W	airport	5
Catalina Harbor	33 25 50N	118 30 21W	bay	
Catfish Beach	40 18 41N	121 10 32W	beach	
Cathedral City	33 46 47N	116 27 52W	city/town	400
Cathedral Spires	37 42 49N	119 37 54W	pillar	6907
Catheys Valley	37 25 57N	120 05 49W	city/town	1321
Catillo De San Joa	37 48 38N	122 28 33W	military	
Catlett	38 50 43N	121 32 15W	city/town	33
Cave City	38 12 09N	120 30 27W	city/town	1614
Cave Country	38 04 31N	120 23 52W	locale	

California GPS Companion

Place Name	Latitude	Longitude	Type	Elev
Cave Rock	40 37 45N	121 41 02W	pillar	
Cavin	34 23 43N	118 50 55W	city/town	540
Cawelo	35 29 58N	119 09 53W	city/town	425
Cayley	37 43 49N	121 35 58W	city/town	500
Cayton	41 03 43N	121 37 58W	city/town	3070
Cayucos	35 26 34N	120 53 28W	city/town	60
Cayucos Beach	35 26 55N	120 54 17W	beach	
Cayucos State Bch.	35 26 56N	120 54 15W	park	
Cazadero	38 32 00N	123 05 03W	city/town	117
CBS Studios	34 08 41N	118 23 24W	studio	
Cecile	36 42 03N	119 43 00W	city/town	304
Cecilville	41 08 28N	123 08 20W	city/town	2360
Cedar Creek Falls	32 59 22N	116 43 46W	falls	
Cedar Crest (1)	39 11 52N	121 00 21W	city/town	2940
Cedar Crest (2)	37 14 42N	119 12 01W	city/town	7068
Cedar Glen	34 15 14N	117 09 50W	city/town	5400
Cedar Grove (1)	36 47 27N	118 40 10W	city/town	4600
Cedar Grove (2)	38 45 10N	120 37 56W	city/town	3480
Cedar Mill	39 56 39N	120 55 20W	city/town	3420
Cedar Mountain Win	37 39 56N	121 42 10W	wine/vin	
Cedar Pass Ski Ar.	41 33 22N	120 15 36W	ski area	
Cedar Ridge (1)	39 11 56N	121 01 12W	city/town	2890

California GPS Companion

Place Name	Latitude	Longitude	Type	Elev
Cedar Ridge (2)	38 03 57N	120 16 33W	city/town	3760
Cedar Rock Lodge	38 01 18N	120 14 45W	city/town	3604
Cedar Slope	36 08 43N	118 34 39W	city/town	5800
Cedar Spring Dam	34 18 18N	117 18 48W	dam	3363
Cedar Springs	34 21 02N	117 53 03W	city/town	6840
Cedar Stock	40 50 47N	122 49 43W	city/town	2428
Cedarbrook	36 42 25N	119 00 26W	city/town	4200
Cedarpines Park	34 15 00N	117 19 30W	city/town	4800
Cedarville	41 31 45N	120 10 20W	city/town	4630
Cedarville Airport	41 33 09N	120 09 58W	airport	4623
Cedric Wright Mt.	36 54 13N	118 23 20W	summit	12372
Cella	36 41 30N	119 27 14W	city/town	365
Ceneda	35 21 16N	117 53 47W	city/town	1946
Centennial Peak	36 37 40N	118 29 25W	summit	13228
Center Mountain	38 08 41N	119 29 17W	summit	11273
Center Peak	36 43 20N	118 21 40W	summit	12760
Centerville (1)	36 44 02N	119 29 49W	city/town	393
Centerville (2)	39 47 16N	121 39 15W	city/town	640
Centerville (3)	40 31 06N	122 29 03W	city/town	860
Centerville Beach	40 34 25N	124 20 56W	locale	
Centerville Dist.	37 33 15N	121 59 53W	city/town	56
Central	38 23 34N	121 34 19W	city/town	1

California GPS Companion

Place Name	Latitude	Longitude	Type	Elev
Central Camp	37 20 58N	119 28 58W	city/town	5380
Central Costa Coll	37 58 14N	122 20 10W	univ/coll	
Centralia	38 19 13N	121 14 37W	city/town	65
Century City	34 03 20N	118 25 01W	city/town	300
Ceres	37 35 42N	120 57 24W	city/town	90
Cerritos	33 51 30N	118 03 50W	city/town	51
Cerritos College	33 53 12N	118 05 45W	univ/coll	
Cerritos Iron-Wood	33 52 51N	118 06 19W	golf	
Cerro	37 59 30N	122 31 49W	city/town	80
Cerro Coso Junior	35 34 03N	117 40 02W	univ/coll	
Cerro Gordo Peak	36 32 16N	117 47 08W	summit	9184
Cerro Villa Height	33 49 36N	117 48 12W	city/town	500
Chabot College	37 38 28N	122 06 17W	univ/coll	
Chabot Observatory	37 47 14N	122 10 37W	observtry	
Chabot Terrace	38 08 50N	122 14 42W	city/town	140
Chabot-Las Positas	37 42 37N	121 48 03W	univ/coll	
Chadbourne	38 14 38N	122 04 58W	city/town	36
Chaffee	35 04 00N	118 10 13W	city/town	2820
Chaffey Union J C	34 08 51N	117 34 24W	univ/coll	
Chagoopa Falls	36 28 17N	118 24 19W	falls	
Chalfant Valley	37 31 46N	118 21 45W	city/town	4258
Chalk Bank Landing	41 54 44N	121 38 30W	city/town	4080

California GPS Companion

Place Name	Latitude	Longitude	Type	Elev
Challenge	39 29 15N	121 13 21W	city/town	2557
Chamberlands Est.	39 04 10N	120 09 05W	city/town	6440
Chambers Lodge	39 04 24N	120 08 25W	city/town	6240
Chambless	34 33 41N	115 32 38W	city/town	717
Champagne	34 02 04N	117 33 45W	city/town	850
Champagne Fountain	37 16 33N	122 00 27W	city/town	318
Chanchelulla Peak	40 28 24N	122 59 24W	summit	6399
Chaney Ranch	36 39 21N	120 34 41W	city/town	406
Channel Islands N.	34 00 15N	119 23 47W	park	
Channel Marina	37 55 21N	122 22 13W	marina	
Chapman (1)	37 55 08N	122 30 57W	city/town	420
Chapman (2)	34 08 54N	118 04 57W	city/town	700
Chapman College	33 47 33N	117 51 03W	univ/coll	
Chapmantown	39 43 14N	121 48 56W	city/town	205
Chappo	33 17 35N	117 21 40W	city/town	57
Charles Spinetta V	38 32 34N	120 46 59W	wine/vin	
Charter Oak	34 06 11N	117 50 42W	city/town	740
Charter Oak Mobile	34 06 01N	117 49 37W	city/town	820
Charybdis	37 05 16N	118 40 04W	summit	13091
Chase	35 11 02N	115 30 09W	city/town	3805
Chateau Shasta Mob	41 18 03N	122 18 57W	city/town	3450
Chatsworth	34 15 26N	118 36 01W	city/town	950

California GPS Companion

Place Name	Latitude	Longitude	Type	Elev
Chatsworth Lake Ma	34 14 27N	118 38 10W	city/town	950
Chaw'se Reg Indian	38 25 30N	120 38 30W	museum	
Cheeseville	41 31 16N	122 53 55W	city/town	2788
Chemehuevi Valley	34 31 39N	114 25 51W	airport	619
Chemeketa Park	37 09 45N	121 58 47W	city/town	1000
Chemurgic	37 27 51N	120 55 04W	city/town	75
Cherokee (1)	39 38 47N	121 32 14W	city/town	1325
Cherokee (2)	37 58 54N	120 14 48W	city/town	2800
Cherokee (3)	38 09 31N	121 14 32W	city/town	65
Cherokee (4)	39 22 13N	121 02 31W	city/town	2575
Cherokee Strip	35 28 02N	119 15 35W	city/town	330
Cherry Creek Acres	39 06 15N	121 04 54W	city/town	1720
Cherry Valley	33 58 21N	116 58 35W	city/town	2820
Chester	40 18 23N	121 13 51W	city/town	4528
Chester -Rogers F	40 17 14N	121 14 19W	airport	4525
Chevy Chase Golf C	34 10 19N	118 12 04W	golf	
Chianti	38 44 14N	122 56 28W	city/town	240
Chico	39 43 43N	121 50 11W	city/town	195
Chico -Ranchaero	39 43 14N	121 52 03W	airport	173
Chico Municipal	39 47 43N	121 51 30W	airport	238
Chico Museum	39 43 47N	121 50 28W	museum	
Chico State Colleg	39 43 42N	121 50 51W	univ/coll	

California GPS Companion

Place Name	Latitude	Longitude	Type	Elev
Chicory Wharf	38 16 10N	121 38 20W	wharf	5
Chilcoot	39 47 52N	120 08 19W	city/town	5020
Childrens Multicul	37 46 42N	122 25 43W	museum	
Childrens Museum	37 19 42N	121 53 24W	museum	
Childrens Pool Bch	32 50 52N	117 16 39W	beach	
Childs Meadows	40 21 37N	121 29 27W	city/town	4920
Chilnualna Fall	37 33 50N	119 36 59W	falls	
China Beach	37 47 24N	122 29 15W	beach	
China Cove Beach	33 35 53N	117 52 43W	beach	
China Gardens	41 02 16N	123 08 07W	garden	4000
China Lake	35 39 03N	117 39 39W	city/town	2262
China Lake Golf Cl	35 39 42N	117 38 26W	golf	
Chinatown (1)	37 48 00N	122 16 09W	city/town	36
Chinatown (2)	37 47 48N	122 24 27W	city/town	125
Chinese Camp	37 52 16N	120 25 56W	city/town	1261
Chinese Peak Ski A	37 13 38N	119 09 20W	ski area	8705
Chino	34 00 44N	117 41 17W	city/town	750
Chino Airport	33 58 30N	117 38 12W	airport	650
Chino Hills	33 53 37N	117 43 35W	city/town	1200
Chinowths Corner	36 19 37N	119 20 05W	city/town	313
Chinquapin Falls	37 40 01N	119 45 21W	falls	
Chipps	38 03 05N	121 54 50W	city/town	7

California GPS Companion

Place Name	Latitude	Longitude	Type	Elev
Chipps Island	38 03 19N	121 54 39W	island	
Chiquita	38 38 06N	122 52 24W	city/town	154
Chiriaco Summit	33 39 39N	115 43 14W	city/town	1710
Chiriaco Summit	33 39 55N	115 42 37W	airport	1713
Chittenden	36 54 12N	121 36 26W	city/town	130
Chloride City	36 42 24N	116 52 53W	city/town	4760
Chocolate Peak	37 08 40N	118 32 56W	summit	11658
Cholame	35 43 26N	120 17 44W	city/town	1157
Chololo Falls	36 03 35N	118 38 39W	falls	
Chorro	35 19 36N	120 40 36W	city/town	640
Chowchilla	37 07 23N	120 15 33W	city/town	240
Chowchilla Airport	37 06 44N	120 14 48W	airport	242
Chrisman	34 17 52N	119 18 04W	city/town	60
Christensen	41 16 51N	120 34 03W	city/town	4400
Christi Beach	34 01 36N	119 52 30W	beach	
Christie	38 00 11N	122 12 20W	city/town	270
Chrome	39 43 45N	122 32 54W	city/town	932
Chualar	36 34 14N	121 31 03W	city/town	105
Chubbuck	34 21 54N	115 17 07W	city/town	1010
Chula Vista	32 38 24N	117 05 00W	city/town	70
Chula Vista Munic.	32 39 41N	117 01 59W	golf	
Churn Creek Golf C	40 30 26N	122 19 08W	golf	

California GPS Companion

Place Name	Latitude	Longitude	Type	Elev
Cidar Pass Ski Cou	41 33 18N	120 15 49W	ski area	6100
Cienega	34 01 16N	118 19 39W	city/town	120
Cima	35 14 16N	115 29 54W	city/town	4175
Cimarron	36 17 55N	119 48 46W	city/town	216
Cinco	35 15 48N	118 02 07W	city/town	2150
Cincotta	36 45 41N	119 45 13W	city/town	310
Cinder Flats State	40 56 55N	121 30 34W	park	
Cinnabar Springs	41 57 54N	122 52 24W	city/town	3430
Cirque Peak	36 28 37N	118 14 10W	summit	12900
Cisco	39 18 06N	120 32 45W	city/town	5923
Cisco Grove	39 18 36N	120 32 20W	city/town	5660
Citro	36 23 34N	119 01 25W	city/town	500
Citrona	38 38 01N	121 58 13W	city/town	163
Citrus	38 36 24N	121 15 56W	city/town	110
Citrus Heights	38 42 26N	121 16 48W	city/town	150
Citrus Junior Coll	34 08 06N	117 53 00W	univ/coll	
City College (1)	33 47 25N	118 10 25W	univ/coll	
City College (2)	33 58 12N	117 22 54W	univ/coll	
City College of SF	37 43 33N	122 27 04W	univ/coll	
City Terrace	34 03 00N	118 10 55W	city/town	620
Civic Center Audit	37 46 41N	122 24 58W	building	
Clair	33 48 24N	117 59 01W	city/town	70

California GPS Companion

Place Name	Latitude	Longitude	Type	Elev
Clairemont	32 47 50N	117 11 30W	city/town	240
Clam Beach	40 59 41N	124 06 39W	city/town	19
Clam Beach (1)	40 59 47N	124 06 54W	beach	
Clam Beach (2)	38 30 56N	123 15 11W	beach	
Claraville	35 26 32N	118 19 43W	city/town	6300
Clare Mill	39 24 59N	123 25 37W	city/town	
Claremont	34 05 48N	117 43 08W	city/town	1169
Claremont Country	37 50 15N	122 14 31W	golf	
Claremont Golf Crs	34 06 47N	117 42 56W	golf	
Claremont Mens Col	34 06 04N	117 42 27W	univ/coll	
Clarence King, Mt.	36 50 13N	118 26 45W	summit	12905
Claribel	37 42 52N	120 49 28W	city/town	187
Clark Field -hist.	35 15 08N	120 39 38W	airport	130
Clark, Mount	37 41 47N	119 25 39W	summit	11522
Clarke Memorial M.	40 48 13N	124 10 00W	museum	
Clarksburg	38 25 14N	121 31 34W	city/town	14
Clarksburg Marina	38 25 07N	121 31 29W	marina	
Clarksville	38 39 18N	121 03 05W	city/town	673
Clarsona	38 22 26N	120 58 57W	city/town	2711
Claus	37 41 12N	120 55 08W	city/town	117
Claussenius	38 50 48N	120 36 46W	city/town	4240
Clay	38 20 10N	121 09 30W	city/town	102

California GPS Companion

Place Name	Latitude	Longitude	Type	Elev
Claypipers Theatre	38 26 28N	120 51 14W	building	
Clayton (1)	38 54 29N	121 18 40W	city/town	135
Clayton (2)	37 56 28N	121 56 05W	city/town	394
Clayton Historical	37 56 29N	121 56 01W	museum	
Clear Creek (1)	41 42 34N	123 26 57W	city/town	970
Clear Creek (2)	40 17 53N	121 02 51W	city/town	4940
Clear Creek Jct.	40 17 39N	121 03 58W	city/town	4910
Clear Lake State P	39 00 34N	122 48 38W	park	
Clearing House	37 39 54N	119 51 59W	city/town	1550
Clearlake	38 57 30N	122 37 31W	city/town	1400
Clearlake Highland	38 57 20N	122 38 30W	city/town	1340
Clearlake Oaks	39 01 35N	122 40 15W	city/town	1360
Clearlake Park	38 58 00N	122 39 00W	city/town	1360
Clearwater	33 53 47N	118 09 33W	city/town	72
Clement Junction	34 00 51N	118 14 16W	city/town	215
Clements	38 11 27N	121 05 14W	city/town	131
Cleone	39 29 24N	123 47 04W	city/town	67
Cliff Haven	33 37 57N	117 54 53W	city/town	99
Cliff House	37 46 42N	122 30 46W	building	
Clifton	33 49 39N	118 22 44W	city/town	163
Clima	38 14 58N	122 04 14W	city/town	30
Clint	36 25 53N	119 46 21W	city/town	240

California GPS Companion

Place Name	Latitude	Longitude	Type	Elev
Clinton	38 22 34N	120 40 02W	city/town	2000
Clio	39 44 36N	120 34 45W	city/town	4420
Clipper Gap	38 58 10N	121 00 59W	city/town	1670
Clipper Mills	39 31 58N	121 09 23W	city/town	3550
Clockspring Viney.	38 32 32N	120 47 55W	wine/vin	
Clotho	36 43 17N	119 36 32W	city/town	347
Cloudripper	37 08 33N	118 31 46W	summit	13525
Clover Creek Falls	40 39 22N	122 01 00W	falls	
Clover Flat	32 39 43N	116 24 49W	city/town	3000
Cloverdale (1)	40 28 25N	122 28 29W	city/town	892
Cloverdale (2)	38 48 20N	123 00 58W	city/town	316
Cloverdale Municip	38 46 27N	122 59 31W	airport	272
Clovis	36 49 31N	119 42 07W	city/town	361
Clyde (1)	32 55 00N	114 57 55W	city/town	385
Clyde (2)	38 01 32N	122 01 42W	city/town	35
Clyde Spires	37 08 24N	118 38 51W	summit	12955
Coachella	33 40 49N	116 10 23W	city/town	-71
Coal Oil Point	34 24 26N	119 52 38W	cape	33
Coalinga	36 08 23N	120 21 33W	city/town	667
Coalinga Harris R.	36 14 52N	120 14 15W	airport	470
Coalinga Municipal	36 09 37N	120 21 37W	airport	714
Coarsegold	37 15 44N	119 42 00W	city/town	2206

California GPS Companion

Place Name	Latitude	Longitude	Type	Elev
Coast Royale Beach	33 30 19N	117 44 51W	beach	
Cobb	38 49 20N	122 43 19W	city/town	2600
Coburn	36 17 19N	121 09 06W	city/town	263
Cochrane	37 43 52N	121 21 31W	city/town	48
Cockatoo Grove	32 38 35N	116 58 59W	city/town	540
Cocklebur Beach	37 52 01N	120 52 09W	beach	
Codfish Falls	38 59 50N	120 57 13W	falls	
Codora	39 27 32N	122 01 16W	city/town	85
Coffee	41 06 11N	122 46 37W	city/town	3000
Coffee Creek	41 05 21N	122 42 28W	city/town	2500
Cogswell College	37 47 28N	122 24 18W	univ/coll	
Cogswell Polytech.	37 44 56N	122 24 50W	univ/coll	
Cohasset	39 55 32N	121 43 48W	city/town	2820
Col of Alameda	37 46 52N	122 16 41W	univ/coll	
Col of Notre Dame	37 31 01N	122 17 02W	univ/coll	
Col of St Albert	37 50 51N	122 14 52W	univ/coll	
Col of the Dessert	33 43 56N	116 23 12W	univ/coll	
Col of the Redwood	40 41 54N	124 11 50W	univ/coll	
Col of the Sequoia	36 19 25N	119 18 49W	univ/coll	
Col of the Siskiyo	41 24 44N	122 23 17W	univ/coll	3580
Cold Fork	40 10 19N	122 40 20W	city/town	1360
Cold Springs (1)	38 09 45N	120 03 08W	city/town	5640

California GPS Companion

Place Name	Latitude	Longitude	Type	Elev
Cold Springs (2)	38 44 31N	120 52 09W	city/town	1202
Cold Springs Golf	38 44 46N	120 52 53W	golf	
Cole	42 00 08N	122 38 21W	city/town	2880
Coleman	39 10 39N	120 58 29W	city/town	2525
Coleman Beach	38 21 55N	123 04 12W	beach	
Coleville	38 33 59N	119 30 22W	city/town	5171
Colfax	39 06 03N	120 57 08W	city/town	2440
Colfax Spring	37 49 15N	120 01 36W	city/town	3133
Colima	33 56 41N	118 00 46W	city/town	200
Coliseum Gardens	37 45 26N	122 11 48W	park	
College City	39 00 21N	122 00 30W	city/town	70
College Heights	34 06 24N	117 41 18W	city/town	1290
College Park	37 20 32N	121 53 55W	city/town	70
College Terrace	37 25 18N	122 09 01W	city/town	46
Collegeville	37 54 18N	121 08 47W	city/town	59
Collierville	38 12 53N	121 16 04W	city/town	57
Collins	38 09 57N	122 15 05W	city/town	40
Collinsville	38 04 37N	121 50 56W	city/town	3
Colma	37 40 37N	122 27 31W	city/town	100
Coloma	38 48 00N	120 53 21W	city/town	784
Coloma Road State	38 42 40N	120 56 31W	park	
Coloma Winery	38 47 39N	120 53 23W	wine/vin	

California GPS Companion

Place Name	Latitude	Longitude	Type	Elev
Colonia Manzanilla	33 45 38N	117 56 00W	city/town	76
Colosseum Mountain	36 54 29N	118 22 16W	summit	12473
Colton	34 04 26N	117 18 46W	city/town	1000
Columbia	38 02 11N	120 24 01W	city/town	2143
Columbia Airport	38 01 49N	120 24 52W	airport	2118
Columbia College	38 01 48N	120 23 06W	univ/coll	2333
Columbia Historic	38 01 58N	120 23 51W	park	
Columbia Picture S	34 05 46N	118 19 13W	studio	
Columbian Gardens	37 43 48N	122 11 17W	park	
Columbine Peak	37 05 18N	118 32 56W	summit	12652
Columbus Tower	37 47 47N	122 24 13W	building	
Colusa	39 12 52N	122 00 30W	city/town	61
Colusa Carnegie Lb	39 12 50N	122 00 29W	building	
Colusa County Airp	39 10 44N	121 59 36W	airport	47
Colusa Golf & C C	39 11 36N	122 00 01W	golf	
Colusa Junction	39 08 52N	121 39 33W	city/town	55
Cometa	37 51 24N	120 56 42W	city/town	135
Commerce	34 00 02N	118 09 32W	city/town	146
Community Center	34 16 09N	118 44 12W	city/town	905
Como	33 41 56N	117 47 34W	city/town	70
Comptche	39 15 54N	123 35 24W	city/town	640
Compton	33 53 45N	118 13 09W	city/town	66

California GPS Companion

Place Name	Latitude	Longitude	Type	Elev
Compton Airport	33 53 24N	118 14 37W	airport	97
Compton College	33 52 39N	118 12 33W	univ/coll	
Compton Par Three	33 53 40N	118 11 03W	golf	
Comstock Acres	39 09 33N	120 08 55W	city/town	6340
Conant	41 06 46N	122 19 28W	city/town	1960
Conaway	38 40 38N	121 40 19W	city/town	33
Concannon Winery	37 40 01N	121 44 20W	wine/vin	
Concepcion	34 27 13N	120 27 14W	city/town	115
Concord	37 58 41N	122 01 48W	city/town	80
Concord -Buchanan	37 59 22N	122 03 25W	airport	23
Concord Municipal	38 00 50N	122 01 06W	golf	
Concord Pavilion	37 57 33N	121 56 13W	building	
Condor Obs. Site 1	34 31 16N	118 53 40W	locale	2811
Condor Obs. Site 2	34 48 42N	119 08 49W	locale	8810
Condor Observation	34 48 47N	119 08 40W	tower	8831
Conejo	36 31 06N	119 43 05W	city/town	263
Confederate Corner	36 38 41N	121 39 48W	city/town	47
Confidence	38 02 51N	120 12 01W	city/town	4080
Coniston	38 24 54N	121 33 33W	city/town	0
Conklin Sawmill-hi	41 21 04N	120 56 00W	building	
Conner	35 10 48N	119 06 54W	city/town	293
Conness, Mount	37 58 02N	119 19 09W	summit	12590

California GPS Companion

Place Name	Latitude	Longitude	Type	Elev
Conrad Viano Winer	38 00 16N	122 06 00W	wine/vin	
Contra Costa Golf	37 58 17N	122 04 51W	golf	
Cooks Beach	38 47 23N	123 33 36W	beach	
Cooks Valley	40 00 05N	123 47 06W	city/town	480
Cooley Landing	37 28 36N	122 07 14W	city/town	10
Coolidge Springs	33 23 39N	116 02 58W	city/town	-180
Cooper (1)	36 42 52N	121 42 58W	city/town	20
Cooper (2)	39 13 11N	123 00 11W	city/town	2000
Cooperstown	37 44 36N	120 32 37W	city/town	280
Copco	41 59 00N	122 21 37W	city/town	2575
Copeland	39 57 20N	122 03 45W	city/town	205
Copic	41 51 55N	121 20 27W	city/town	4035
Copper City (1)	39 43 23N	122 48 30W	city/town	5820
Copper City (2)	35 21 03N	117 11 05W	city/town	3833
Copperopolis	37 58 52N	120 38 27W	city/town	990
Coppervale	40 20 48N	120 54 14W	city/town	5200
Coppervale Ski Tow	40 20 43N	120 54 10W	ski area	5821
Copple Place	40 00 31N	122 37 43W	city/town	1440
Coquette Falls	41 26 50N	122 12 49W	falls	
Coram	40 42 37N	122 26 25W	city/town	640
Corcoran	36 05 53N	119 33 34W	city/town	207
Corcoran Airport	36 06 08N	119 35 41W	airport	197

California GPS Companion

Place Name	Latitude	Longitude	Type	Elev
Corcoran, Mount	36 32 20N	118 14 57W	summit	13760
Cordelia	38 12 38N	122 08 05W	city/town	20
Cordelia Junction	38 13 01N	122 08 19W	city/town	18
Cordero Junction	38 17 16N	121 57 12W	city/town	80
Cordova	38 30 37N	121 28 27W	city/town	20
Cordova Golf Cours	38 32 12N	121 20 48W	golf	
Corlieu Falls	37 24 58N	119 37 25W	falls	
Cornell (1)	41 47 58N	121 19 06W	city/town	4115
Cornell (2)	34 06 52N	118 46 37W	city/town	800
Corning	39 55 40N	122 10 41W	city/town	272
Corning Municipal	39 56 37N	122 10 16W	airport	292
Cornwall	38 01 14N	121 52 40W	city/town	40
Coromar	34 26 03N	119 52 00W	city/town	40
Corona	33 52 31N	117 33 56W	city/town	678
Corona del Mar	33 35 53N	117 52 20W	city/town	80
Corona Del Mar St.	33 35 37N	117 52 27W	park	
Corona Municipal	33 53 51N	117 36 08W	airport	533
Coronado	32 41 09N	117 10 56W	city/town	20
Coronado City Bch.	32 41 05N	117 11 13W	beach	
Coronado C C	32 41 36N	117 11 20W	golf	
Coronado Heights	32 36 03N	117 07 37W	city/town	11
Coronado Shores B.	32 40 35N	117 10 25W	beach	

California GPS Companion

Place Name	Latitude	Longitude	Type	Elev
Coronado Yacht Clb	32 40 54N	117 10 25W	locale	
Corporal	36 55 47N	121 32 49W	city/town	160
Corral Beach	34 01 59N	118 43 56W	beach	
Corral State Beach	34 01 59N	118 44 00W	park	
Corralitos	36 59 19N	121 48 19W	city/town	270
Corte Madera	37 55 32N	122 31 35W	city/town	27
Cortena	39 13 09N	122 11 06W	city/town	77
Cortez	37 28 31N	120 44 19W	city/town	140
Cory	39 46 06N	122 08 55W	city/town	230
Coso	35 58 42N	117 55 43W	city/town	3340
Coso Junction	36 02 42N	117 56 47W	city/town	3368
Coso Peak	36 12 10N	117 42 47W	summit	8160
Costa Mesa	33 38 28N	117 55 04W	city/town	101
Cosumne	38 29 33N	121 10 26W	city/town	110
Cosy Dell	34 16 44N	117 27 10W	city/town	2800
Cota	33 50 22N	118 12 24W	city/town	35
Cotati	38 19 37N	122 42 22W	city/town	110
Cotners Corner	34 28 17N	117 10 15W	city/town	2986
Cottage Corners	36 52 10N	121 23 58W	city/town	259
Cottage Gardens	34 06 22N	117 16 05W	city/town	1048
Cottage Grove	41 36 10N	123 30 16W	city/town	840
Cottage Springs	38 21 22N	120 12 39W	city/town	5820

California GPS Companion

Place Name	Latitude	Longitude	Type	Elev
Cotton Center	36 03 58N	119 08 31W	city/town	372
Cottonwood (1)	38 39 30N	121 58 12W	city/town	161
Cottonwood (2)	40 23 09N	122 16 47W	city/town	420
Cottonwood Botanic	39 32 54N	120 18 52W	trail	5600
Cougar	41 35 00N	122 11 03W	city/town	4872
Coulterville	37 42 38N	120 11 49W	city/town	1683
Counsman	38 44 58N	121 29 29W	city/town	35
Country Club Park	34 03 01N	118 19 13W	city/town	180
Country Mobile Est	34 28 59N	117 49 48W	city/town	3440
Courtland	38 19 52N	121 34 03W	city/town	10
Covelo	39 47 35N	123 14 49W	city/town	1398
Covelo -Round Vly	39 47 24N	123 15 59W	airport	1434
Covina	34 05 24N	117 53 22W	city/town	546
Cow Creek	38 14 26N	119 59 28W	city/town	6040
Cowan Heights	33 46 40N	117 46 23W	city/town	113
Cowell	37 57 10N	121 59 18W	city/town	280
Cowell Beach	36 57 40N	122 01 26W	beach	
Cox	33 50 20N	114 46 19W	city/town	810
Cox Stadium	37 43 29N	122 28 38W	stadium	
Coyote	37 13 00N	121 44 22W	city/town	255
Coyote Point	37 35 31N	122 19 09W	cape	
Coyote Point Yacht	37 35 16N	122 18 53W	bay	

California GPS Companion

Place Name	Latitude	Longitude	Type	Elev
Coyote Valley Rnch	39 13 55N	123 09 59W	city/town	760
Coyote Wells	32 44 19N	115 58 00W	city/town	290
Coyoteville	38 33 05N	120 41 20W	city/town	2160
Cozzens Corner	38 42 04N	122 57 03W	city/town	194
Crabtree	36 50 37N	119 05 20W	city/town	4000
Crabtree Place	40 09 13N	123 21 01W	city/town	2580
Crafton	34 03 47N	117 07 15W	city/town	1752
Cragmont -subdiv.	37 53 43N	122 15 50W	city/town	750
Craig	39 20 15N	121 33 47W	city/town	90
Cranmore	38 59 17N	121 48 20W	city/town	36
Crannell	41 00 43N	124 05 01W	city/town	200
Crater	37 12 58N	117 41 11W	city/town	5300
Crater Crest	38 07 21N	119 20 10W	summit	11394
Crater Mountain	36 55 19N	118 25 19W	summit	12874
Crater Peak	40 41 53N	121 37 13W	summit	8677
Creed	38 14 36N	121 51 15W	city/town	36
Creegan	37 17 31N	120 27 43W	city/town	170
Crescent -subdiv.	34 05 27N	118 22 24W	city/town	240
Crescent Beach	41 43 50N	124 09 15W	beach	
Crescent City	41 45 22N	124 12 02W	city/town	44
Crescent City J Mc	41 46 48N	124 14 11W	airport	57
Crescent City Lt.	41 44 39N	124 12 06W	lighthous	

78

California GPS Companion

Place Name	Latitude	Longitude	Type	Elev
Crescent Mills	40 05 48N	120 54 35W	city/town	3520
Crescent Ridge Vlg	38 39 12N	121 04 40W	city/town	700
Cressey	37 25 11N	120 39 59W	city/town	165
Crest	40 43 29N	120 22 09W	city/town	5443
Crest Park	34 14 02N	117 11 44W	city/town	5640
Cresta	39 50 37N	121 24 12W	city/town	1560
Cresta Dam	39 52 34N	121 22 21W	dam	1693
Crestline	34 14 31N	117 17 05W	city/town	4720
Crestmore	34 02 40N	117 23 43W	city/town	980
Creston (1)	35 31 08N	120 31 22W	city/town	1115
Creston (2)	38 12 33N	122 12 11W	city/town	310
Crestview	37 45 09N	118 59 00W	city/town	7518
Crocker Nuclear La	38 32 12N	121 45 05W	building	
Crocker Place	39 33 25N	123 03 14W	city/town	2600
Crocker, Mount	37 28 58N	118 49 26W	summit	12457
Crockett	38 03 09N	122 12 43W	city/town	118
Crockett Historic.	38 03 20N	122 13 13W	museum	
Crockett Marina	38 03 25N	122 13 35W	marina	
Croft	38 34 54N	120 26 01W	city/town	4520
Crolona Heights	38 03 17N	122 13 03W	city/town	140
Cromberg	39 51 37N	120 41 26W	city/town	4280
Crome	35 26 30N	119 11 57W	city/town	342

California GPS Companion

Place Name	Latitude	Longitude	Type	Elev
Cromir	36 48 16N	120 25 15W	city/town	161
Cronese Valley	35 06 00N	116 16 21W	city/town	1099
Crooks Peak	36 34 28N	118 17 25W	summit	14180
Cross Mountain	36 44 11N	118 30 08W	summit	12185
Cross Roads	34 12 52N	114 12 54W	city/town	395
Crossley Reflector	37 20 18N	121 38 34W	locale	
Crow Canyon C C	37 47 21N	121 57 28W	golf	
Crowley	39 24 33N	123 25 28W	city/town	1350
Crown	38 16 00N	122 39 21W	city/town	31
Crown Jewel	34 04 38N	117 12 33W	city/town	1227
Crown Point	38 06 39N	119 27 24W	summit	11346
Crown Point Shores	32 47 07N	117 13 52W	beach	
Crown Rock	36 57 16N	118 52 13W	pillar	9342
Crown Village	38 41 43N	121 05 03W	city/town	740
Crows Landing	37 23 38N	121 04 14W	city/town	111
Crucero	35 02 50N	116 09 53W	city/town	1014
Crystal Cove	33 34 31N	117 50 26W	city/town	40
Crystal Lake	39 19 22N	120 34 09W	city/town	5753
Crystal Pier	32 47 45N	117 15 27W	pier	
Crystal Spring	34 14 00N	118 06 00W	city/town	5086
Crystal Spring Dam	37 31 43N	122 21 40W	dam	284
Crystal Springs G.	37 33 27N	122 22 48W	golf	

California GPS Companion

Place Name	Latitude	Longitude	Type	Elev
Crystalaire C C	34 28 24N	117 50 48W	golf	
Cubbler Place	39 45 10N	123 08 55W	city/town	1600
Cucamonga Winery H	34 06 26N	117 36 34W	park	
Cudahy	33 57 38N	118 11 04W	city/town	121
Cuesta-by-the-Sea	35 19 06N	120 50 45W	city/town	20
Culver City	34 01 16N	118 23 44W	city/town	94
Culver Garden -sub	33 59 34N	118 25 39W	city/town	30
Culver Junction	34 01 42N	118 23 22W	city/town	108
Cummings	39 50 00N	123 37 51W	city/town	1320
Cunard	38 48 50N	121 41 05W	city/town	20
Cunningham	38 21 45N	122 46 36W	city/town	100
Cupertino	37 19 23N	122 01 52W	city/town	236
Curlew	32 56 00N	115 24 17W	city/town	-93
Currier Gymnasium	34 03 44N	117 09 44W	building	
Curry Village	37 44 13N	119 34 18W	city/town	4000
Curtain Falls	39 39 47N	121 18 11W	falls	1200
Curtis	41 12 02N	121 45 56W	city/town	4500
Curtner	37 28 11N	121 55 21W	city/town	30
Cushenbury	34 21 14N	116 51 27W	city/town	4280
Cushing	35 25 34N	120 36 11W	city/town	930
Cutler	36 31 24N	119 17 09W	city/town	358
Cutten	40 46 12N	124 08 30W	city/town	200

California GPS Companion

Place Name	Latitude	Longitude	Type	Elev
Cuttings Wharf	38 13 36N	122 18 28W	city/town	5
Cuyama	34 56 07N	119 36 51W	city/town	2261
Cuyamaca State Pk.	32 56 09N	116 33 42W	park	
Cygnus	38 09 10N	122 05 17W	city/town	5
Cypave	33 55 10N	118 19 38W	city/town	55
Cypress	33 49 01N	118 02 11W	city/town	36
Cypress Grove (1)	38 09 57N	122 53 58W	city/town	5
Cypress Grove (2)	33 59 28N	118 25 13W	city/town	27
Cypress Hill	39 13 43N	121 03 30W	city/town	2660
Cypress Hills Golf	37 40 58N	122 26 52W	golf	
Cypress Junior Col	33 49 42N	118 01 28W	univ/coll	
Cypress Park -sub.	34 05 32N	118 13 25W	city/town	360
Cypress Point Golf	36 34 45N	121 57 46W	golf	

𝔻

Place Name	Latitude	Longitude	Type	Elev
D Flourney	41 14 24N	120 31 53W	city/town	4400
D L Bliss State Pk	38 58 56N	120 05 42W	park	
Dade, Mount	37 22 54N	118 46 42W	summit	13400
Dagget -Barstow D.	34 51 13N	116 47 12W	airport	1927
Daggett	34 51 48N	116 53 14W	city/town	2003
Dagon	38 20 41N	120 57 37W	city/town	258
D'Agostini Winery	38 32 00N	120 46 01W	wine/vin	

California GPS Companion

Place Name	Latitude	Longitude	Type	Elev
Daguerra Dam	39 12 32N	121 26 33W	dam	130
Dairy Valley	33 51 30N	118 03 50W	city/town	45
Dairyland	37 01 06N	120 18 34W	city/town	181
Dairyville	40 07 48N	122 07 12W	city/town	247
Daisie	38 18 53N	121 38 34W	city/town	24
Dales	40 18 50N	122 04 14W	city/town	604
Dallidet Adobe	35 16 51N	120 39 19W	building	
Dalton	41 56 11N	121 25 06W	city/town	4037
Daly City	37 42 21N	122 27 39W	city/town	300
Dan Ryan Place	41 08 59N	120 48 58W	city/town	4920
Dana	41 06 42N	121 33 49W	city/town	3336
Dana Point	33 27 38N	117 42 51W	cape	
Dana Point	33 28 01N	117 41 50W	city/town	160
Dana Point Harbor	33 27 35N	117 41 41W	harbor	
Dana, Mount	37 53 59N	119 13 13W	summit	13053
Danburg Beach	38 00 54N	119 08 05W	beach	
Danby	34 38 08N	115 20 50W	city/town	1352
Danielson	38 14 18N	122 06 14W	city/town	34
Dantes View	36 13 16N	116 43 29W	summit	5475
Dantoni	39 09 54N	121 30 55W	city/town	85
Dantuma Place	40 17 37N	121 47 56W	city/town	3060
Danville	37 49 18N	121 59 56W	city/town	368

California GPS Companion

Place Name	Latitude	Longitude	Type	Elev
Daphnedale Park	41 30 33N	120 32 38W	city/town	4460
Dardanelle	38 20 28N	119 49 58W	city/town	5765
Dark Day Boat Ramp	39 25 54N	121 06 19W	locale	1900
Darlington	38 43 45N	120 24 02W	city/town	4200
Darlingtonia	41 50 11N	123 56 31W	city/town	480
Darrah	37 31 05N	119 50 03W	city/town	3150
Darwin	36 16 05N	117 35 27W	city/town	4746
Darwin Falls	36 19 15N	117 31 25W	falls	
Darwin, Mount	37 10 01N	118 40 14W	summit	13830
Date City	32 47 35N	115 18 33W	city/town	5
Daulton	37 07 09N	119 58 52W	city/town	400
Davenport	37 00 42N	122 11 27W	city/town	65
Davenport Landing	37 01 28N	122 12 53W	city/town	65
David Marks Tennis	34 01 23N	118 17 23W	stadium	
Davie Stadium	37 48 59N	122 13 45W	stadium	
Davies Symphony Ha	37 46 40N	122 25 09W	building	
Davis	38 32 42N	121 44 22W	city/town	50
Davis -University	38 31 53N	121 47 11W	airport	68
Davis -Yolo County	38 34 44N	121 51 23W	airport	98
Davis Creek	41 44 00N	120 22 15W	city/town	4835
Davis Golf Course	38 35 09N	121 46 22W	golf	
Davis Point	38 03 09N	122 15 33W	cape	

California GPS Companion

Place Name	Latitude	Longitude	Type	Elev
Dawes	38 56 57N	123 05 02W	city/town	500
Dawson Place	39 55 26N	122 42 23W	city/town	5480
Day	41 12 42N	121 22 24W	city/town	3655
Dayton	39 38 55N	121 52 16W	city/town	140
Dayton Avenue	34 05 02N	118 13 18W	city/town	340
De Anza College	37 19 18N	122 02 40W	univ/coll	
De Anza Desert C C	33 17 18N	116 23 11W	golf	
De Bell Municipal	34 12 18N	118 18 09W	golf	
De Luz	33 26 13N	117 19 25W	city/town	360
Deacon Lee Place	41 28 51N	122 55 41W	city/town	3920
Deadhorse Falls	40 17 37N	121 42 07W	falls	
Deadwood (1)	39 44 33N	121 31 25W	city/town	1710
Deadwood (2)	40 43 10N	122 43 57W	city/town	2800
Deadwood (3)	38 00 15N	120 06 26W	city/town	4780
Dean	36 31 15N	121 27 40W	city/town	120
Dean Place	39 13 24N	121 46 48W	city/town	660
Dearborn Park	37 15 32N	122 19 01W	city/town	400
Death Valley Jct.	36 18 08N	116 24 46W	city/town	2040
Death Valley Nat'l	37 00 01N	117 07 31W	park	
Death Valley Natrl	36 17 06N	116 45 52W	bridge	
Death Vly Airport	36 27 49N	116 52 53W	airport	-211
Death Vly Stovepip	36 36 14N	117 09 33W	airport	25

California GPS Companion

Place Name	Latitude	Longitude	Type	Elev
Deaver Vineyards	38 32 28N	120 47 41W	wine/vin	
DeCamp	39 26 25N	123 21 18W	city/town	1340
Declez	34 03 55N	117 29 01W	city/town	1030
Declezville	34 02 40N	117 28 50W	city/town	940
Dedrick	40 51 46N	123 02 08W	city/town	2505
Deep Springs	37 22 18N	117 59 03W	city/town	5220
Deer Creek	40 15 36N	121 23 31W	city/town	4780
Deer Creek Colony	35 58 42N	118 59 57W	city/town	539
Deer Creek Falls	40 12 09N	121 30 44W	falls	
Deer Creek Park	39 15 30N	120 56 46W	city/town	3580
Deer Crossing	36 41 24N	119 02 52W	city/town	3140
Deer Lake Highland	34 17 02N	118 35 45W	city/town	1440
Deer Park Ski Area	39 11 12N	120 11 53W	ski area	6600
Deer Vally Golf L.	40 05 13N	120 54 46W	golf	
Deer View	38 50 36N	120 40 00W	city/town	3340
Deerhorn Mountain	36 42 48N	118 24 32W	summit	13265
Deetz	41 21 29N	122 22 56W	city/town	3795
DeHaven	39 39 37N	123 47 02W	city/town	40
Dehesa	32 46 53N	116 51 08W	city/town	503
Del Amo	33 50 47N	118 12 34W	city/town	38
Del Dios	33 04 22N	117 07 06W	city/town	350
Del Loma	40 46 43N	123 19 52W	city/town	1180

California GPS Companion

Place Name	Latitude	Longitude	Type	Elev
Del Mar	32 57 34N	117 15 52W	city/town	120
Del Mar Heights	32 56 54N	117 15 36W	city/town	350
Del Mar Race Track	32 58 35N	117 15 42W	track	
Del Monte	36 36 03N	121 52 05W	city/town	20
Del Monte Beach	36 36 15N	121 52 15W	beach	
Del Monte Golf Crs	36 35 10N	121 52 14W	golf	
Del Monte Heights	36 36 42N	121 49 52W	city/town	160
Del Norte Golf Crs	41 50 04N	124 05 51W	golf	
Del Paso	38 39 10N	121 28 20W	city/town	30
Del Paso C C	38 37 14N	121 23 10W	golf	
Del Paso Heights	38 38 10N	121 25 09W	city/town	50
Del Ray (1)	33 59 07N	118 25 28W	city/town	16
Del Rey (2)	36 39 33N	119 35 34W	city/town	340
Del Rey Oaks	36 35 36N	121 50 02W	city/town	100
Del Rio Country Cl	33 00 34N	115 31 15W	golf	
Del Rio Golf and C	37 44 36N	121 00 13W	golf	
Del Rio Woods	38 37 23N	122 50 18W	city/town	140
Del Rosa	34 08 56N	117 14 33W	city/town	1320
Del Sur	34 41 23N	118 17 16W	city/town	2422
Del Valle	34 25 10N	118 39 20W	city/town	920
Del Valle State Re	37 35 47N	121 42 47W	park	
Delano	35 46 08N	119 14 46W	city/town	316

Place Name	Latitude	Longitude	Type	Elev
Delano Municipal	35 44 44N	119 14 11W	airport	314
Delevan	39 21 15N	122 11 24W	city/town	86
Delft Colony	36 30 43N	119 26 42W	city/town	311
Delhi	37 25 56N	120 46 39W	city/town	117
Delleker	39 48 32N	120 29 49W	city/town	4840
Delmonico Place	39 58 32N	123 19 02W	city/town	2400
Delphos	39 11 25N	122 10 08W	city/town	77
Delta (1)	33 55 11N	118 19 15W	city/town	65
Delta (2)	40 56 40N	122 25 25W	city/town	1137
Delta View Golf C.	38 00 33N	121 54 35W	golf	
DeLuz	33 21 32N	117 16 12W	city/town	580
Demuth	41 20 16N	121 15 54W	city/town	4250
Denair	37 31 35N	120 47 45W	city/town	124
Denis	34 37 34N	118 07 27W	city/town	2577
Denny	40 56 39N	123 23 08W	city/town	1520
Denverton	38 13 29N	121 53 47W	city/town	7
Derby Acres	35 14 50N	119 35 40W	city/town	1366
Derner	41 17 57N	120 33 34W	city/town	4400
Des Moines	33 55 55N	117 58 01W	city/town	279
DeSabla	39 52 26N	121 36 06W	city/town	2780
Descanso	32 51 10N	116 36 54W	city/town	3396
Descanso Gardens	34 12 06N	118 12 41W	park	

California GPS Companion

Place Name	Latitude	Longitude	Type	Elev
Descanso Junction	32 50 28N	116 36 43W	city/town	3380
Desert Aire Golf C	34 36 02N	118 03 35W	golf	
Desert Beach	33 30 46N	115 55 35W	city/town	-220
Desert Camp	33 32 01N	115 58 57W	city/town	-200
Desert Center	33 42 45N	115 24 05W	city/town	906
Desert Center Airp	33 44 55N	115 19 22W	airport	559
Desert Heights	34 12 04N	116 08 27W	city/town	2230
Desert Hot Springs	33 57 40N	116 30 03W	city/town	1100
Desert Lake	35 00 09N	117 41 53W	city/town	2400
Desert Lodge	33 12 38N	116 19 35W	city/town	540
Desert Shores	33 24 15N	116 02 20W	city/town	-200
Desert View	33 48 05N	116 38 24W	city/town	8720
Desert View Highl.	34 35 27N	118 09 06W	city/town	2700
Devil Canyon	34 11 52N	117 19 54W	city/town	1840
Devils Cauldron	36 31 05N	121 57 15W	locale	
Devils Crags	37 02 12N	118 37 06W	summit	12400
Devils Elbow	39 20 45N	122 25 40W	city/town	1000
Devils Garden Vist	38 37 58N	120 10 19W	locale	7600
Devils Hole	34 17 50N	117 07 01W	locale	
Devils Kitchen	40 03 49N	121 41 20W	locale	
Devils Postpile N.	37 36 54N	119 05 08W	park	
Devils Rock Garden	40 39 09N	121 33 32W	locale	

California GPS Companion

Place Name	Latitude	Longitude	Type	Elev
Devils Slide	37 34 28N	122 31 09W	locale	
Devils Slide Beach	37 33 55N	122 30 48W	beach	
Devils Speedway	36 19 22N	116 52 42W	locale	
Devon	34 50 31N	120 31 06W	city/town	294
Devonshire Golf Co	34 15 35N	118 36 58W	golf	
Devore	34 12 59N	117 24 02W	city/town	2022
Devore Heights	34 14 14N	117 24 53W	city/town	2492
Dew Drop	39 05 14N	121 05 08W	city/town	1434
Dewitt	38 04 04N	122 32 19W	city/town	40
DeYoung Museum	37 46 17N	122 28 05W	museum	
Di Giorgio	35 15 10N	118 51 02W	city/town	480
Diablo	37 50 06N	121 57 25W	city/town	560
Diablo Country Clb	37 50 08N	121 57 29W	golf	
Diablo Hills Golf	37 54 51N	122 02 45W	golf	
Diablo Valley Coll	37 58 09N	122 04 14W	univ/coll	
Diablo, Mount	37 52 54N	121 54 46W	summit	3849
Diamond	38 01 18N	121 53 32W	city/town	40
Diamond Bar	34 01 43N	117 48 34W	city/town	720
Diamond Bar Golf C	34 00 30N	117 49 14W	golf	
Diamond Heights V.	37 44 45N	122 26 26W	city/town	625
Diamond Oaks Mun.	38 46 13N	121 17 09W	golf	
Diamond Peak	36 49 35N	118 23 26W	summit	13126

California GPS Companion

Place Name	Latitude	Longitude	Type	Elev
Diamond Springs	38 41 41N	120 48 50W	city/town	1778
Dibble Place	41 11 22N	120 53 45W	city/town	4400
Dickson Art Center	34 04 32N	118 26 25W	building	
Digger Bay Marina	40 43 34N	122 23 30W	marina	1080
Dillard	38 24 05N	121 15 21W	city/town	80
Dillon Beach	38 15 03N	122 57 51W	city/town	80
Dinkey Creek	37 05 10N	119 09 24W	city/town	5840
Dinsmore	40 29 30N	123 36 21W	city/town	2401
Dinsmore Airport	40 29 34N	123 35 59W	airport	2375
Dinsmores	40 43 12N	123 44 16W	city/town	4460
Dinuba	36 32 36N	119 23 10W	city/town	330
Dirigo	41 08 58N	122 18 34W	city/town	2000
Disappointment Pk.	37 04 04N	118 28 01W	summit	13917
Discovery Bay	37 54 31N	121 35 57W	city/town	10
Discovery Bay C C	37 53 45N	121 35 38W	golf	
Discovery Pinnacle	36 33 27N	118 17 25W	summit	13750
Disney Studios	34 09 24N	118 19 25W	studio	
Disney, Mount	39 17 41N	120 20 23W	summit	7953
Disneyland	33 48 37N	117 55 05W	locale	
Ditch Camp Five	38 45 55N	120 32 50W	city/town	
Dixie	40 56 39N	121 10 15W	city/town	4526
Dixieland	32 47 27N	115 46 10W	city/town	-40

California GPS Companion

Place Name	Latitude	Longitude	Type	Elev
Dixon	38 26 44N	121 49 20W	city/town	60
Dobbins	39 22 18N	121 12 18W	city/town	720
Doble	34 17 55N	116 49 15W	city/town	6821
Dodge Place	39 54 14N	121 40 42W	city/town	1860
Dodge Ridge Ski Ar	38 11 11N	119 56 57W	ski area	7410
Dodgeland	39 32 41N	121 54 24W	city/town	100
Dodger Stadium	34 04 25N	118 14 23W	stadium	
Doelger City -sub.	37 45 27N	122 29 26W	city/town	275
Dog Town	38 10 13N	119 11 47W	city/town	7087
Doghouse Junction	32 36 01N	116 50 25W	city/town	3305
Dogtown (1)	39 35 19N	122 42 42W	city/town	4906
Dogtown (2)	38 12 50N	121 05 15W	city/town	150
Dogtown (3)	37 42 08N	120 07 37W	city/town	2575
Doheny State Beach	33 27 44N	117 40 48W	park	
Dolanco Junction	33 50 42N	118 17 57W	city/town	40
Dollar Point	39 11 17N	120 05 56W	city/town	6480
Dolley	33 51 56N	118 05 25W	city/town	57
Dolomite	36 33 11N	117 56 40W	city/town	3673
Dolores	33 49 59N	118 13 32W	city/town	31
Dominguez	33 50 05N	118 13 04W	city/town	30
Dominguez Golf Crs	33 50 54N	118 16 38W	golf	
Dominguez Junction	33 51 48N	118 13 01W	city/town	52

California GPS Companion

Place Name	Latitude	Longitude	Type	Elev
Dominican College	37 58 49N	122 30 48W	univ/coll	
Donner	39 18 59N	120 19 52W	city/town	7020
Donner Laboratory	37 52 28N	122 15 20W	building	
Donner Lake Vlg.	39 19 31N	120 17 05W	city/town	5950
Donner Memorial St	39 19 12N	120 14 31W	park	
Donner Pines Tract	39 19 45N	120 14 41W	city/town	5980
Donner Summit Ski	39 19 25N	120 19 44W	ski area	7200
Donner Woods	39 19 05N	120 17 22W	city/town	5940
Donohue Peak	37 46 31N	119 13 50W	summit	12023
Dora Belle	37 06 46N	119 19 12W	city/town	5800
Doran Beach	38 18 49N	123 02 19W	beach	
Dorr Place	38 37 14N	123 05 26W	city/town	660
Dorrington	38 18 05N	120 16 34W	city/town	4800
Dorris	41 58 03N	121 55 01W	city/town	4240
Dorris -Butte Vly	41 53 13N	121 58 32W	airport	4239
Dos Cabezas	32 44 45N	116 08 22W	city/town	1720
Dos Palmas Corners	33 55 29N	116 30 04W	city/town	825
Dos Palos	36 59 10N	120 37 32W	city/town	116
Dos Palos Y	37 02 56N	120 38 04W	city/town	110
Dos Rios	39 43 01N	123 21 08W	city/town	926
Douds Landing	38 12 46N	120 19 28W	city/town	3500
Dougherty (1)	38 09 45N	121 14 32W	city/town	64

93

California GPS Companion

Place Name	Latitude	Longitude	Type	Elev
Dougherty (2)	37 42 40N	121 54 31W	city/town	350
Dougherty Peak	36 55 14N	118 32 45W	summit	12244
Douglas City	40 39 08N	122 56 37W	city/town	1651
Douglas Flat	38 06 52N	120 27 14W	city/town	1965
Douglas Junction	33 51 21N	118 09 50W	city/town	50
Douglas Park	41 47 15N	124 03 42W	city/town	140
Dow	35 30 15N	119 10 18W	city/town	425
Downey	33 56 24N	118 07 54W	city/town	119
Downey Art Museum	33 57 11N	118 08 11W	museum	
Downey Road	33 58 08N	118 06 19W	city/town	150
Downieville	39 33 34N	120 49 33W	city/town	2899
Downtown Shoreline	33 45 37N	118 11 05W	locale	
Doyle	40 01 41N	120 06 10W	city/town	4267
Doyle State Wildl.	40 03 55N	120 02 45W	park	
Doyles Corner	40 52 39N	121 33 33W	city/town	3203
Dozier	38 17 08N	121 48 56W	city/town	18
Drake	34 28 14N	120 18 10W	city/town	80
Drake Stadium	34 04 18N	118 26 51W	stadium	
Drakes Bay	38 00 43N	122 55 05W	bay	
Drakes Beach	38 01 39N	122 57 38W	beach	
Drakes Head	38 02 21N	122 54 51W	cape	
Drakesbad	40 26 40N	121 24 12W	city/town	5700

California GPS Companion

Place Name	Latitude	Longitude	Type	Elev
Drawbridge	37 27 59N	121 58 26W	city/town	5
Dresser	37 35 33N	121 57 17W	city/town	120
Driftwood Beach	38 11 48N	122 57 54W	beach	
Driftwood Marina	38 01 05N	121 44 55W	marina	
Dry Lagoon State P	41 11 24N	124 07 14W	park	
Dryden Park Munic.	37 36 50N	121 00 08W	golf	
Drytown	38 26 28N	120 51 12W	city/town	640
Duarte	34 08 22N	117 58 35W	city/town	510
Dubakella Mountain	40 23 03N	123 08 42W	summit	5881
Dublin	37 42 08N	121 56 05W	city/town	380
Dubois, Mount	37 47 01N	118 20 29W	summit	13559
Ducor	35 53 30N	119 02 47W	city/town	545
Dudmore	33 51 24N	118 21 00W	city/town	85
Dufour	38 45 43N	121 50 31W	city/town	66
Dugan	38 36 16N	120 57 28W	city/town	1104
Dulah	34 18 45N	119 21 32W	city/town	20
Dulzura	32 38 39N	116 46 50W	city/town	1045
Dumbarton Bridge	37 30 01N	122 07 31W	bridge	
Dumbarton Point	37 30 01N	122 06 00W	cape	
Dumont	35 41 35N	116 10 30W	city/town	1080
Duncan Springs	38 57 08N	123 07 25W	city/town	760
Duncans Mills	38 27 14N	123 03 14W	city/town	29

California GPS Companion

Place Name	Latitude	Longitude	Type	Elev
Dunderberg Mill	38 06 14N	119 14 58W	city/town	8600
Dunderberg Peak	38 03 53N	119 16 22W	summit	12374
Dunes	32 46 59N	114 47 47W	city/town	320
Dunes Beach	37 29 02N	122 27 06W	beach	
Dunlap	36 44 18N	119 07 12W	city/town	1914
Dunlap Acres	34 01 52N	117 06 24W	city/town	2119
Dunlap Place	39 51 14N	123 25 51W	city/town	890
Dunmovin	36 05 19N	117 57 37W	city/town	3502
Dunn	35 02 42N	116 26 13W	city/town	1600
Dunneville	36 56 26N	121 24 34W	city/town	187
Dunnigan	38 53 07N	121 58 07W	city/town	68
Dunsmuir	41 12 30N	122 16 15W	city/town	2289
Dunsmuir Municipal	41 15 47N	122 16 19W	airport	3258
Durham	39 38 47N	121 47 56W	city/town	158
Durmid	33 25 51N	115 49 56W	city/town	-190
Dustin Acres	35 13 10N	119 23 23W	city/town	380
Dutch Flat	39 12 22N	120 50 12W	city/town	3144
Dutton	38 04 34N	121 52 56W	city/town	6
Dwight D Eisenhow.	34 01 22N	117 55 45W	golf	
Dyer	33 42 36N	117 51 13W	city/town	52

California GPS Companion

Place Name	Latitude	Longitude	Type	Elev

𝔼

Place Name	Latitude	Longitude	Type	Elev
Eagle Falls	38 57 07N	120 06 37W	falls	
Eagle Mountain	33 51 27N	115 29 11W	city/town	1280
Eagle Rock	34 08 20N	118 12 47W	city/town	566
Eagle Scout Peak	36 32 44N	118 33 38W	summit	12040
Eagle Tree	38 12 05N	121 30 44W	city/town	3
Eagles Nest	33 17 17N	116 35 36W	city/town	4500
Eagles Nest Golf C	41 50 08N	122 50 25W	golf	
Eagles Peak Ski Ar	39 58 25N	120 07 10W	ski area	
Eagleville (1)	41 18 59N	120 06 53W	city/town	4640
Eagleville (2)	39 34 46N	121 05 43W	city/town	3747
Eagleville Airport	41 18 27N	120 02 31W	airport	4497
Earlimart	35 53 03N	119 16 17W	city/town	283
Earp	34 09 53N	114 18 01W	city/town	388
East Arboga	39 03 25N	121 33 02W	city/town	55
East Beach	34 25 00N	119 39 47W	beach	
East Biggs	39 24 55N	121 39 10W	city/town	117
East Blythe	33 36 38N	114 34 23W	city/town	268
East Colton Hts	34 02 54N	117 17 50W	city/town	995
East Farmersville	36 18 06N	119 11 38W	city/town	360
East Garrison	36 39 11N	121 43 53W	city/town	160

California GPS Companion

Place Name	Latitude	Longitude	Type	Elev
East Gridley	39 21 48N	121 39 39W	city/town	95
East Highlands	34 06 35N	117 10 11W	city/town	1330
East Irvine	33 40 33N	117 45 32W	city/town	195
East Los Angeles	34 01 26N	118 10 16W	city/town	261
East Nicolaus	38 54 37N	121 32 38W	city/town	40
East Orosi	36 32 53N	119 15 35W	city/town	390
East Palo Alto	37 28 08N	122 08 24W	city/town	15
East Pasadena	34 08 46N	118 05 36W	city/town	700
East Petaluma	38 14 24N	122 37 59W	city/town	15
East Pleasanton	37 40 25N	121 49 44W	city/town	382
East Quincy	39 56 03N	120 53 49W	city/town	3500
East Richmond	37 56 37N	122 18 51W	city/town	290
East San Diego	32 44 58N	117 06 33W	city/town	360
East San Gabriel	34 05 30N	118 05 25W	city/town	365
East Side	38 08 07N	121 14 32W	city/town	63
East Vidette	36 44 36N	118 23 58W	summit	13350
East Whittier	33 57 48N	118 01 02W	city/town	310
East Windsor	38 32 39N	122 48 03W	city/town	110
Easter Cross	32 50 23N	117 14 37W	city/town	800
Easter Hill Vlg.	37 55 25N	122 20 36W	city/town	40
Eastman Place	40 30 41N	121 43 53W	city/town	4050
Eastmont (1)	37 46 09N	122 10 16W	city/town	90

California GPS Companion

Place Name	Latitude	Longitude	Type	Elev
Eastmont (2)	34 01 25N	118 09 15W	city/town	210
Easton	36 39 01N	119 47 23W	city/town	273
Eastport	37 50 23N	122 10 46W	city/town	760
Eaton Canyon Park	34 09 57N	118 04 43W	golf	
Eberly	37 34 21N	121 59 32W	city/town	45
Echo	35 18 03N	116 48 15W	city/town	3200
Echo Island Beacon	38 06 52N	122 03 48W	locale	
Echo Lake	38 50 02N	120 02 26W	city/town	7440
Echo Ridge Estates	39 14 50N	121 03 00W	city/town	2700
Echo Ridge Trails	39 14 50N	121 03 20W	city/town	2480
Eckley	38 03 14N	122 12 06W	city/town	20
Eden	33 52 41N	117 03 15W	city/town	1430
Eden Gardens	32 59 14N	117 15 26W	city/town	180
Eden Hot Springs	33 53 44N	117 03 16W	city/town	1700
Edendale	38 29 06N	123 00 06W	city/town	80
Edendale -subdiv.	34 05 24N	118 15 30W	city/town	480
Edenvale	37 15 54N	121 49 01W	city/town	182
Eder	39 17 59N	120 17 29W	city/town	6720
Edgar	32 47 20N	115 43 57W	city/town	-35
Edgemar	37 39 14N	122 29 23W	city/town	125
Edgemont	33 55 13N	117 16 40W	city/town	1537
Edgewood	41 27 30N	122 25 50W	city/town	2953

California GPS Companion

Place Name	Latitude	Longitude	Type	Elev
Edison	35 20 51N	118 52 15W	city/town	564
Edison Building	34 03 02N	118 15 10W	building	
Edmiston	36 46 44N	119 32 22W	city/town	403
Edmundson Acres	35 13 44N	118 49 20W	city/town	480
Edna	35 12 14N	120 36 43W	city/town	241
Edom	33 48 25N	116 23 25W	city/town	215
Edwards	34 55 34N	117 56 03W	city/town	2400
Edwards A F B	34 54 17N	117 53 01W	military	2302
Edwards Track Stad	37 52 08N	122 15 50W	stadium	
Edwin	38 22 43N	120 59 12W	city/town	280
Eel Point	32 54 02N	118 32 40W	cape	
Egan	33 43 56N	117 00 40W	city/town	1517
Ehrman Mansion	39 03 12N	120 06 46W	building	
Eighteen-Inch Tele	33 21 12N	116 51 38W	observtry	
Eighteenmile House	37 07 40N	119 52 10W	building	
Eightmile House	38 03 28N	121 15 28W	building	
Eileen	41 57 47N	123 06 15W	city/town	4040
Eisen, Mount	36 29 54N	118 33 59W	summit	12160
El Bonita	38 30 44N	122 58 58W	city/town	50
El Cajon	32 47 41N	116 57 42W	city/town	435
El Camino	40 02 28N	122 10 10W	city/town	257
El Camino College	33 53 06N	118 19 35W	univ/coll	

California GPS Companion

Place Name	Latitude	Longitude	Type	Elev
El Camino C C	33 11 05N	117 19 21W	golf	
El Campo	37 53 51N	122 27 51W	city/town	10
El Capitan	37 44 03N	119 38 12W	summit	7569
El Capitan Beach	34 27 35N	120 01 35W	beach	
El Capitan Dam	32 53 02N	116 48 30W	dam	750
El Cariso Golf Crs	34 18 45N	118 24 45W	golf	
El Casco	33 58 52N	117 07 03W	city/town	1840
El Centro	32 47 31N	115 33 44W	city/town	-40
El Cerrito (1)	33 50 26N	117 31 19W	city/town	861
El Cerrito (2)	37 54 57N	122 18 38W	city/town	66
El Dorado	38 40 58N	120 50 48W	city/town	1602
El Dorado Beach	38 56 42N	119 58 30W	beach	
El Dorado Golf Crs	33 42 42N	116 20 17W	golf	
El Dorado Hills	38 39 35N	121 04 06W	golf	
El Dorado Marina	38 43 07N	121 06 02W	marina	
El Dorado Park	33 48 11N	118 05 34W	golf	
El Granada	37 30 10N	122 28 06W	city/town	50
El Granada Beach	37 30 01N	122 28 11W	beach	
El Macero	38 32 49N	121 41 35W	city/town	32
El Macero Golf &CC	38 32 35N	121 41 01W	golf	
El Matador State B	34 02 17N	118 52 55W	park	
El Merrie Dell	34 17 43N	118 22 40W	city/town	1430

California GPS Companion

Place Name	Latitude	Longitude	Type	Elev
El Mirador	36 10 40N	119 01 03W	city/town	480
El Mirage	34 36 08N	117 37 49W	city/town	2913
El Modena	33 47 16N	117 48 31W	city/town	276
El Monte	34 04 07N	118 01 36W	city/town	283
El Monte Airport	34 05 09N	118 02 05W	airport	296
El Nido (1)	33 51 56N	118 21 38W	city/town	96
El Nido (2)	37 08 06N	120 29 28W	city/town	139
El Nido (3)	34 02 37N	118 44 18W	city/town	750
El Niguel Country	33 30 47N	117 43 03W	golf	
El Pescador State	34 02 20N	118 53 27W	park	
El Pinal	37 58 50N	121 16 52W	city/town	20
El Portal	37 40 29N	119 46 59W	city/town	1919
El Rancho Mobile H	33 53 15N	118 11 27W	city/town	61
El Rancho Verde CC	34 08 59N	117 22 29W	golf	
El Rio	34 13 56N	119 10 18W	city/town	79
El Rio Villa	38 32 05N	121 56 35W	city/town	123
El Rita	35 13 03N	118 33 20W	city/town	2700
El Rivino Country	34 02 05N	117 22 58W	golf	
El Roble	39 05 23N	123 10 47W	city/town	560
El Segundo	33 55 09N	118 24 56W	city/town	100
El Segundo Golf Co	33 54 37N	118 23 35W	golf	
El Sereno	34 04 52N	118 10 37W	city/town	450

California GPS Companion

Place Name	Latitude	Longitude	Type	Elev
El Sobrante	37 58 38N	122 17 39W	city/town	160
El Sueno	34 26 37N	119 46 13W	city/town	220
El Toro	33 37 33N	117 41 34W	city/town	440
El Verano	38 17 52N	122 29 26W	city/town	107
Elayon	34 21 52N	118 31 21W	city/town	1400
Elba	36 13 52N	119 18 44W	city/town	306
Elders Corner	38 57 24N	121 06 00W	city/town	1354
Elderwood	36 28 18N	119 07 17W	city/town	490
Eldridge	38 20 56N	122 30 35W	city/town	190
Eldton	37 43 34N	122 26 54W	city/town	300
Electra	38 19 56N	120 40 13W	city/town	760
Electra Peak	37 42 18N	119 15 34W	summit	12442
Elftman	33 50 25N	118 13 20W	city/town	27
Elk (1)	39 07 49N	123 43 00W	city/town	140
Elk (2)	36 45 01N	119 29 31W	city/town	41
Elk Creek	39 36 19N	122 32 17W	city/town	750
Elk Grove	38 24 32N	121 22 14W	city/town	51
Elk Grove -Sunset	38 23 37N	121 19 55W	airport	54
Elk River	40 44 11N	124 10 23W	city/town	55
Elkhorn	36 49 28N	121 44 22W	city/town	8
Elkhorn Country Cl	38 03 06N	121 19 34W	golf	
Elkhorn Yacht Club	36 48 49N	121 47 09W	locale	

103

California GPS Companion

Place Name	Latitude	Longitude	Type	Elev
Ella Falls	36 43 55N	118 58 39W	falls	
Ellicott	36 55 18N	121 50 09W	city/town	157
Ellicott Bridge	38 57 38N	120 28 55W	bridge	3520
Elliott Corner	37 27 46N	119 46 25W	city/town	2961
Ellis	33 46 19N	117 13 06W	city/town	1415
Ellis Place	36 31 16N	119 01 05W	city/town	880
Ellwood	34 25 54N	119 53 13W	city/town	100
Ellwood Pier	34 25 50N	119 55 25W	pier	
Elm View	36 32 51N	119 47 25W	city/town	255
Elmar Beach	37 28 28N	122 26 49W	beach	
Elmco	35 59 33N	119 02 31W	city/town	463
Elmhurst -subdiv.	37 45 07N	122 10 15W	city/town	35
Elmira	38 20 54N	121 54 32W	city/town	70
Elmo	35 40 46N	119 19 46W	city/town	297
Elmore Desert Rnch	33 06 13N	115 47 59W	city/town	-190
Elora	35 08 17N	115 31 41W	city/town	3405
Elsa	36 15 03N	121 08 16W	city/town	287
Elsey	39 36 27N	121 35 36W	city/town	650
Elvas	38 35 00N	121 26 51W	city/town	25
Elverta	38 42 50N	121 27 42W	city/town	50
Elvira	32 50 15N	117 13 57W	city/town	100
Embarcadero	38 14 24N	122 26 55W	city/town	10

California GPS Companion

Place Name	Latitude	Longitude	Type	Elev
Embarcadero Center	37 47 41N	122 23 50W	building	
Embarcadero Marina	32 42 17N	117 09 45W	park	
Embarcadero Plaza	37 47 46N	122 23 44W	park	
Emerald Bay (1)	38 57 36N	120 05 49W	city/town	6240
Emerald Bay (2)	33 33 09N	117 48 30W	city/town	40
Emerald Bay Overl.	38 57 16N	120 06 33W	overlook	
Emerald Bay State	38 57 16N	120 05 35W	park	
Emerald Hills Golf	37 27 13N	122 15 47W	golf	
Emerald Peak	37 09 58N	118 45 43W	summit	12546
Emerson Lake Golf	40 21 47N	120 38 39W	golf	
Emerson, Mount	37 14 32N	118 39 09W	summit	13118
Emeryville	37 49 53N	122 17 03W	city/town	15
Emeryville Marina	37 50 24N	122 18 43W	marina	
Emigrant Gap	39 17 49N	120 40 18W	city/town	5140
Emigrant Gap -Blue	39 16 29N	120 42 33W	airport	5284
Emigrant Trail Mus	39 19 25N	120 13 50W	museum	
Emma Wood State B.	34 17 07N	119 19 29W	park	
Emmaton	38 04 49N	121 43 52W	city/town	3
Empire	37 38 18N	120 54 04W	city/town	115
Empire Landing	33 25 37N	118 26 01W	beach	
Empire Mine State	39 12 24N	121 02 42W	park	
Empire Mountain	36 28 02N	118 34 31W	summit	11509

California GPS Companion

Place Name	Latitude	Longitude	Type	Elev
Encanto	32 42 43N	117 02 58W	city/town	240
Enchanted Hills	38 22 59N	122 25 30W	city/town	1080
Encinal	39 12 56N	121 39 38W	city/town	66
Encinal Beach	34 02 20N	118 53 21W	beach	
Encinal Yacht Club	37 46 57N	122 15 43W	locale	
Encinitas	33 02 13N	117 17 28W	city/town	91
Encino	34 09 33N	118 30 01W	city/town	780
Encino Municipal	34 10 14N	118 29 14W	golf	
Engineer Springs	32 37 41N	116 45 51W	city/town	1300
Englewood	40 23 48N	123 56 16W	city/town	392
English Town	37 10 46N	121 50 17W	city/town	1360
Ennis	34 00 34N	117 25 43W	city/town	920
Ensley	38 48 27N	121 40 18W	city/town	20
Enson	36 33 33N	119 22 27W	city/town	345
Enterprise (1)	38 32 25N	120 50 46W	city/town	860
Enterprise (2)	40 33 50N	122 20 30W	city/town	530
Enterprise (3)	39 21 48N	122 56 58W	city/town	2803
Epworth	34 18 54N	118 53 28W	city/town	869
Equestrian Village	38 43 24N	121 04 25W	city/town	640
Erickson	41 39 01N	122 06 48W	city/town	5016
Ericsson, Mount	36 41 50N	118 24 46W	summit	13608
Escalle	37 56 36N	122 32 38W	city/town	350

California GPS Companion

Place Name	Latitude	Longitude	Type	Elev
Escalon	37 47 51N	120 59 44W	city/town	117
Escondido	33 07 09N	117 05 08W	city/town	684
Escondido Beach	34 01 29N	118 46 03W	beach	
Escondido Junction	33 10 54N	117 22 04W	city/town	40
Escondido Village	37 25 35N	122 09 15W	city/town	50
Esparto	38 41 32N	122 00 58W	city/town	191
Esperanza	33 52 32N	117 45 21W	city/town	360
Esquon	39 36 21N	121 45 57W	city/town	139
Essex (1)	40 54 22N	124 02 03W	city/town	80
Essex (2)	34 44 01N	115 14 39W	city/town	1745
Estelle	33 10 35N	115 30 28W	city/town	174
Estero Bay	35 25 46N	120 55 45W	bay	
Estrella	35 42 20N	120 36 33W	city/town	770
Estrellita	40 51 34N	122 47 23W	city/town	2395
Etheda Springs	36 41 39N	119 00 23W	city/town	4220
Etiwanda	34 07 34N	117 31 22W	city/town	1359
Etna	41 27 25N	122 53 37W	city/town	2929
Ettawa Springs	38 51 04N	122 41 42W	city/town	1960
Ettersburg	40 08 19N	123 59 46W	city/town	679
Eucalyptus Hills	32 52 47N	116 56 45W	city/town	700
Eugene	37 53 35N	120 50 45W	city/town	177
Eureka	40 48 08N	124 09 45W	city/town	44

California GPS Companion

Place Name	Latitude	Longitude	Type	Elev
Eureka -Kneeland	40 43 09N	123 55 39W	airport	2737
Eureka -Murray	40 48 15N	124 06 53W	airport	7
Eureka Boat Launch	40 48 29N	124 09 12W	locale	
Eureka Mun Auditor	40 47 48N	124 09 51W	building	
Eureka Mun. Golf	40 45 18N	124 10 03W	golf	
Eureka Mun. Airprt	40 46 51N	124 12 44W	airport	20
Evans Place	41 03 36N	120 13 43W	city/town	6060
Evelyn	36 08 48N	116 18 55W	city/town	1875
Everglade	38 58 57N	121 45 59W	city/town	25
Evergreen	37 18 35N	121 46 57W	city/town	240
Evergreen Estates	39 14 37N	121 02 39W	city/town	2870
Excelsior Mountain	38 01 28N	119 18 15W	summit	12446
Exchequer Dam	37 35 11N	120 16 06W	dam	707
Exeter	36 17 46N	119 08 28W	city/town	386
Exeter-Thunderhawk	36 14 34N	119 08 58W	airport	340
Exploratorium	37 48 14N	122 26 52W	building	
Exposition Park	34 00 54N	118 17 08W	park	

F

Facht Place	40 14 33N	121 57 44W	city/town	920
Faery Falls	41 15 41N	122 20 03W	falls	
Fagan	39 20 10N	121 40 57W	city/town	90

California GPS Companion

Place Name	Latitude	Longitude	Type	Elev
Fair Oaks (1)	39 22 43N	123 20 25W	city/town	1440
Fair Oaks (2)	37 57 19N	121 15 27W	city/town	22
Fair Oaks (3)	38 38 41N	121 16 16W	city/town	172
Fair Play	38 35 37N	120 39 34W	city/town	2320
Fairbanks	38 51 57N	120 40 09W	city/town	3680
Fairfax	37 59 14N	122 35 16W	city/town	120
Fairfield	38 14 58N	122 02 20W	city/town	20
Fairhaven	40 47 07N	124 12 06W	city/town	10
Fairmead	37 04 35N	120 11 31W	city/town	252
Fairmont	34 44 05N	118 25 26W	city/town	2784
Fairmont Park Golf	34 00 04N	117 22 38W	golf	
Fairoaks	35 07 04N	120 36 05W	city/town	85
Fairport	41 59 07N	120 19 15W	city/town	4730
Fairview (1)	35 55 33N	118 29 38W	city/town	3519
Fairview (2)	34 18 55N	118 54 50W	city/town	842
Fairview (3)	40 49 00N	122 45 56W	city/town	2362
Fairville	38 10 41N	122 26 40W	city/town	5
Fales Hot Springs	38 21 04N	119 23 57W	city/town	7330
Fall River Mills	41 00 17N	121 26 14W	city/town	3291
Fall River Mills	41 01 07N	121 25 59W	airport	3323
Fallbrook	33 22 35N	117 15 01W	city/town	685
Fallbrook Commun.	33 21 15N	117 15 03W	airport	708

California GPS Companion

Place Name	Latitude	Longitude	Type	Elev
Fallbrook Country	33 20 30N	117 11 27W	golf	
Fallbrook Junction	33 13 24N	117 23 36W	city/town	50
Fallen Leaf	38 52 59N	120 04 18W	city/town	6440
Fallen Leaf Marina	38 52 48N	120 03 53W	marina	
Falling Springs	34 18 06N	117 50 18W	city/town	3920
Fallon	38 16 29N	122 54 17W	city/town	80
False Klamath	41 35 31N	124 05 39W	city/town	140
Famoso	35 35 53N	119 12 26W	city/town	422
Famoso Poso-Kern	35 35 47N	119 07 39W	airport	635
Fandango Pass Mas.	41 49 45N	120 15 40W	site	
Fane	36 22 12N	119 08 01W	city/town	403
Fannette Island	38 57 15N	120 05 58W	island	
Farallon Islands	37 44 00N	123 02 00W	island	
Faria	34 19 05N	119 23 12W	city/town	10
Farley	39 36 53N	123 21 58W	city/town	1067
Farmersville	36 17 52N	119 12 21W	city/town	360
Farmington	37 55 48N	120 59 57W	city/town	110
Farquhar, Mount	36 43 43N	118 29 53W	summit	12893
Farr	33 07 49N	117 19 43W	city/town	60
Farwell	37 35 54N	121 56 39W	city/town	161
Favinger Place	40 02 41N	121 58 35W	city/town	500
Fawnskin	34 16 05N	116 56 30W	city/town	5756

California GPS Companion

Place Name	Latitude	Longitude	Type	Elev
Fayette	36 12 07N	119 03 50W	city/town	405
Feather Falls	39 35 36N	121 15 19W	city/town	2980
Feather Falls	39 38 35N	121 16 24W	falls	
Feather Peak	37 19 33N	118 46 37W	summit	13240
Feather River Coll	39 57 10N	120 58 19W	univ/coll	3560
Feather River Inn	39 47 13N	120 38 06W	golf	
Feather River Inn	39 47 26N	120 37 43W	city/town	4480
Feather River Park	39 46 42N	120 37 43W	city/town	4340
Felix	38 01 42N	120 42 53W	city/town	1120
Fellows	35 10 43N	119 32 25W	city/town	1350
Fellows Marina	33 45 51N	118 14 38W	marina	
Felton	37 03 05N	122 04 20W	city/town	286
Femmons	37 56 18N	120 01 17W	city/town	4102
Fenestra Winery	37 38 31N	121 47 42W	wine/vin	
Fenner	34 48 57N	115 10 42W	city/town	2105
Fergus	37 19 10N	120 32 14W	city/town	155
Fern	40 41 18N	121 55 50W	city/town	2720
Fern Ann Falls	34 17 05N	118 36 56W	city/town	1450
Fern Falls	39 42 50N	120 39 55W	falls	
Fern Valley	33 45 31N	116 41 50W	city/town	5700
Fernald Point	34 25 08N	119 37 09W	cape	
Fernbridge	40 36 59N	124 12 00W	city/town	40

California GPS Companion

Place Name	Latitude	Longitude	Type	Elev
Fernbrook	32 58 05N	116 54 39W	city/town	1218
Ferndale	40 34 35N	124 15 46W	city/town	50
Ferndale Museum	40 34 42N	124 15 44W	museum	
Fernside -subdiv.	37 45 55N	122 13 40W	city/town	7
Fernwood (1)	34 04 46N	118 36 06W	city/town	1000
Fernwood (2)	40 52 09N	123 50 58W	city/town	2720
Ferrum	33 27 31N	115 51 36W	city/town	-195
Ferry Building	37 47 44N	122 23 33W	building	
Fetters Hot Sprgs	38 19 12N	122 29 06W	city/town	137
Fickle Hill	40 51 50N	124 02 30W	city/town	1120
Fiddlers Green	39 43 44N	122 42 51W	city/town	2160
Fiddletown	38 30 14N	120 45 16W	city/town	1687
Fieldbrook	40 57 57N	124 02 04W	city/town	186
Fields Landing	40 43 29N	124 12 50W	city/town	30
Fiftytwo-Inch Tel.	33 21 26N	116 51 32W	observtry	
Fig Garden Golf Co	36 51 03N	119 50 14W	golf	
Fig Orchard	35 18 31N	118 34 54W	city/town	1560
Figarden	36 49 22N	119 51 41W	city/town	310
Fillmore	34 23 57N	118 55 02W	city/town	469
Fin Dome	36 48 47N	118 24 45W	summit	11693
Fine Gold	37 11 27N	119 37 04W	city/town	1400
Finger Peak	37 01 48N	118 43 46W	summit	12404

California GPS Companion

Place Name	Latitude	Longitude	Type	Elev
Finger Peaks	38 05 13N	119 24 17W	summit	11390
Finley	39 00 16N	122 52 28W	city/town	1340
Finley Place	40 17 36N	121 47 31W	city/town	3150
Finnegan Falls	37 39 30N	121 13 45W	falls	
Firebaugh	36 51 32N	120 27 18W	city/town	151
Firebaugh Airport	36 51 35N	120 27 52W	airport	157
Firebrick	38 20 04N	120 55 27W	city/town	380
Firehouse Number 1	39 15 48N	121 01 00W	museum	
Firestone Park	33 57 47N	118 13 54W	city/town	135
First Falls	37 07 35N	118 26 39W	falls	
Fish Camp	37 28 43N	119 38 22W	city/town	4980
Fish Rock	38 48 18N	123 35 03W	city/town	200
Fish Rock Beach	38 48 12N	123 34 51W	beach	
Fish Springs	37 04 30N	118 15 10W	city/town	3965
Fishel	34 18 45N	115 14 29W	city/town	885
Fisher (1)	40 56 30N	124 07 02W	city/town	100
Fisher (2)	41 02 11N	122 23 32W	city/town	1680
Fisher Place	38 14 07N	120 26 59W	city/town	2680
Fishermans Wh-Mont	36 36 17N	121 53 29W	wharf	
Fishermans Wh-SF	37 48 37N	122 25 01W	wharf	
Fiske, Mount	37 08 10N	118 40 00W	summit	13524
Five Brooks	38 00 04N	122 45 24W	city/town	180

Place Name	Latitude	Longitude	Type	Elev
Five Corners	37 49 37N	121 08 35W	city/town	50
Five Mile Terrace	38 44 18N	120 42 43W	city/town	2920
Five Points (1)	35 03 05N	118 30 42W	city/town	6720
Five Points (2)	36 25 46N	120 06 07W	city/town	221
Five Points (3)	38 17 27N	121 38 36W	city/town	0
Five Points (4)	39 52 16N	120 34 17W	city/town	6810
Five Points (5)	32 44 35N	117 11 02W	city/town	100
Five Points (6)	34 03 44N	118 01 06W	city/town	288
Flamingo Heights	34 14 26N	116 26 17W	city/town	3463
Flat Rock Point	33 47 49N	118 24 26W	cape	
Flatiron Butte	38 11 45N	119 29 32W	summit	11381
Fleener Place	41 50 52N	121 35 22W	city/town	4263
Fleetridge	32 43 40N	117 14 50W	city/town	220
Fleishhacker Zoo	37 43 58N	122 29 57W	park	
Fleta	35 00 12N	118 09 26W	city/town	2640
Fletcher Hills	32 49 21N	116 58 40W	golf	
Fletcher Peak	37 47 31N	119 20 04W	summit	11408
Fletcher Place	41 44 15N	120 30 49W	city/town	4766
Flinn Springs	32 51 18N	116 51 06W	city/town	800
Flonellis	38 34 10N	120 57 49W	city/town	940
Florence	33 58 28N	118 14 50W	city/town	149
Florence Peak	36 24 23N	118 33 00W	summit	12432

California GPS Companion

Place Name	Latitude	Longitude	Type	Elev
Florence, Mount	37 44 24N	119 18 55W	summit	12561
Florin	38 29 46N	121 24 28W	city/town	34
Floriston	39 23 41N	120 01 13W	city/town	5400
Flosden Acres	38 08 11N	122 15 04W	city/town	10
Flourney (1)	41 14 06N	120 17 50W	city/town	5060
Flournoy (2)	39 55 14N	122 26 06W	city/town	564
Floyd	36 44 06N	119 59 31W	city/town	244
Fluhr	37 21 46N	120 34 36W	city/town	170
Flumeville	38 55 46N	123 42 31W	city/town	174
Flynn	34 58 43N	115 43 53W	city/town	1837
Foerster Peak	37 41 24N	119 17 23W	summit	12058
Folger Peak	38 29 45N	119 48 52W	summit	9680
Folsom	38 40 41N	121 10 30W	city/town	218
Folsom Junction	38 40 06N	121 10 52W	city/town	180
Folsom Lake State	38 43 54N	121 07 55W	park	
Folsom Marina Boat	38 43 04N	121 06 00W	marina	
Folsom State Pris.	38 41 43N	121 09 41W	building	
Fondo	33 06 41N	115 37 25W	city/town	-206
Fontana	34 05 32N	117 26 03W	city/town	1232
Fontenay Villa	37 04 52N	121 58 23W	city/town	1040
Foothill College	37 21 42N	122 07 37W	univ/coll	
Foothill Farms	38 40 35N	121 20 07W	city/town	131

California GPS Companion

Place Name	Latitude	Longitude	Type	Elev
Foppiano	38 01 19N	121 14 25W	city/town	37
Forbestown	39 31 02N	121 15 58W	city/town	2760
Ford Center	37 25 43N	122 09 48W	building	
Ford City	35 09 16N	119 27 19W	city/town	875
Ford House Museum	39 18 17N	123 47 56W	museum	
Ford Park Golf Crs	33 57 21N	118 09 15W	golf	
Fore Bay Golf Club	37 05 49N	121 01 34W	golf	
Forebay	39 14 12N	120 44 08W	city/town	4419
Forest	39 29 29N	120 51 07W	city/town	4760
Forest Falls	34 05 18N	116 55 10W	city/town	5600
Forest Glen	40 22 24N	123 19 27W	city/town	2300
Forest Hill -sub.	37 44 51N	122 27 45W	city/town	600
Forest Hills	38 30 29N	122 55 24W	city/town	60
Forest Knolls (1)	38 00 55N	122 41 15W	city/town	256
Forest Knolls (2)	39 14 18N	121 00 15W	city/town	3160
Forest Lake	38 49 05N	122 43 00W	city/town	2600
Forest Park (1)	37 08 02N	122 08 15W	city/town	620
Forest Park (2)	34 26 50N	118 25 40W	city/town	1680
Forest Ranch	39 52 56N	121 40 18W	city/town	2357
Forest Springs	37 08 20N	122 08 52W	city/town	800
Foresta	37 41 54N	119 45 15W	city/town	4350
Foresta Falls	37 41 34N	119 45 32W	falls	

California GPS Companion

Place Name	Latitude	Longitude	Type	Elev
Foresthill	39 01 13N	120 49 01W	city/town	3225
Forestville	38 28 25N	122 53 21W	city/town	160
Fornis	38 53 33N	120 51 37W	city/town	2380
Fort Bidwell	41 51 38N	120 09 01W	city/town	4555
Fort Bidwell Airp.	41 52 34N	120 08 48W	airport	4602
Fort Bragg	39 26 45N	123 48 15W	city/town	100
Fort Crook Museum	41 00 10N	121 26 45W	museum	
Fort Dick	41 52 05N	124 08 52W	city/town	47
Fort Funston -hist	37 42 45N	122 29 57W	military	
Fort Goff	41 51 44N	123 15 20W	city/town	1320
Fort Grizzly Site	38 31 26N	120 28 42W	locale	
Fort Humboldt St.	40 46 39N	124 11 12W	park	
Fort Irwin	35 15 46N	116 41 02W	city/town	2580
Fort Jones (1)	41 36 28N	122 50 21W	city/town	2747
Fort Jones (2)	38 15 27N	120 25 07W	city/town	3040
Fort Jones Histor.	41 35 47N	122 50 24W	locale	2735
Fort Jones Museum	41 36 25N	122 50 30W	museum	
Fort Jones-Scott V	41 33 29N	122 51 19W	airport	2728
Fort MacArthur Mil	33 42 43N	118 17 43W	museum	
Fort Mason Histor.	37 48 20N	122 25 40W	park	
Fort McDowell	37 51 46N	122 25 18W	city/town	33
Fort Monroe -hist.	37 42 37N	119 41 39W	locale	5630

California GPS Companion

Place Name	Latitude	Longitude	Type	Elev
Fort Ord Golf Crs	36 37 49N	121 49 11W	golf	
Fort Ord Village	36 37 25N	121 50 01W	city/town	120
Fort Piute	35 06 54N	114 59 04W	city/town	2835
Fort Point Nat'l	37 48 38N	122 28 32W	park	
Fort Romie	36 24 01N	121 20 43W	city/town	185
Fort Rosecrans	32 41 03N	117 14 43W	city/town	57
Fort Ross	38 30 51N	123 14 33W	city/town	113
Fort Ross State H.	38 30 59N	123 14 24W	park	
Fort Seward	40 13 23N	123 38 32W	city/town	322
Fort Tejon State H	34 52 22N	118 53 57W	park	
Fort Washington CC	36 53 08N	119 45 32W	golf	
Fort Winfield Scot	37 48 06N	122 28 21W	city/town	225
Fortman Marina	37 46 48N	122 15 18W	marina	
Fortuna	40 35 54N	124 09 22W	city/town	61
Fortuna -Rohnerv.	40 33 14N	124 07 57W	airport	392
Fossil Falls	35 58 12N	117 54 29W	falls	
Foster (1)	41 15 14N	122 57 28W	city/town	6800
Foster (2)	32 54 30N	116 55 31W	city/town	452
Foster City	37 33 31N	122 16 12W	city/town	3
Fountain Place	38 51 04N	119 55 59W	city/town	7820
Fountain Springs	35 53 28N	118 54 53W	city/town	800
Fountain Valley	33 42 33N	117 57 10W	city/town	28

California GPS Companion

Place Name	Latitude	Longitude	Type	Elev
Four Acres	39 00 31N	120 47 15W	city/town	1200
Four Corners (1)	32 58 40N	116 46 35W	city/town	1921
Four Corners (2)	37 57 23N	122 02 18W	city/town	45
Four Corners (3)	40 56 18N	121 36 20W	city/town	3185
Four Corners (4)	38 16 33N	122 27 35W	city/town	52
Four Gables	37 18 22N	118 41 40W	summit	12720
Four Pines	39 36 36N	123 00 42W	city/town	4360
Four Points	34 32 33N	118 01 45W	city/town	2750
Fourth Crossing	38 07 53N	120 38 01W	city/town	937
Fouts Springs	39 21 12N	122 39 50W	city/town	1720
Fowler	36 37 50N	119 40 39W	city/town	305
Fowler Museum	34 04 22N	118 26 32W	museum	
Fowler Place	40 12 08N	122 33 34W	city/town	775
Fox Hills Country	33 59 15N	118 23 06W	golf	
Frances	33 42 43N	117 45 49W	city/town	190
Francis Beach	37 28 10N	122 26 42W	beach	
Franciscan Village	38 42 25N	121 04 50W	city/town	720
Franklin	38 22 45N	121 27 12W	city/town	18
Franklin Canyon	38 00 22N	122 13 04W	golf	
Franklin Field	38 18 17N	121 25 46W	airport	21
Fraser Point	34 03 36N	119 55 45W	cape	
Frazier Corners	40 38 15N	122 14 08W	city/town	535

California GPS Companion

Place Name	Latitude	Longitude	Type	Elev
Frazier Falls	39 42 25N	120 38 29W	falls	
Frazier Gardens	40 02 52N	123 26 40W	garden	
Frazier Park	34 49 22N	118 56 38W	city/town	4767
Fraziers Landing	39 00 18N	121 49 05W	city/town	40
Freda	34 06 08N	114 54 35W	city/town	885
Fredalba	34 12 06N	117 07 53W	city/town	5520
Frederick Douglass	37 46 47N	122 25 35W	city/town	90
Frederickburg	38 49 44N	119 47 09W	city/town	5070
Fredericks	38 22 25N	122 47 37W	city/town	115
Fredericksburg	38 49 43N	119 47 10W	city/town	5100
Freedom	36 56 07N	121 46 19W	city/town	120
Freeman	35 36 06N	117 54 07W	city/town	3186
Freeport	38 27 43N	121 30 02W	city/town	14
Freestone	38 22 21N	122 54 52W	city/town	120
Fremont (1)	37 32 54N	121 59 15W	city/town	53
Fremont (2)	35 11 30N	117 34 33W	city/town	2817
Fremont (3)	38 40 36N	121 38 02W	city/town	20
Fremont Ford State	37 18 07N	120 55 27W	park	
Fremont Peak State	36 45 39N	121 30 05W	park	
Fremont Raceways	37 29 52N	121 57 56W	track	12
Fremont Stadium	37 33 27N	121 58 33W	stadium	
Fremont Weir State	38 45 49N	121 39 16W	park	

California GPS Companion

Place Name	Latitude	Longitude	Type	Elev
French Camp	37 53 03N	121 16 12W	city/town	23
French Corral	39 18 22N	121 09 37W	city/town	522
French Gulch	40 42 03N	122 38 14W	city/town	1355
French Hill	41 49 30N	123 58 17W	city/town	1850
French Meadows Boa	39 06 47N	120 25 35W	locale	5150
Frenchtown (1)	38 38 29N	120 54 37W	city/town	1180
Frenchtown (2)	39 23 17N	121 15 14W	city/town	1450
Fresh Pond	38 45 37N	120 31 44W	city/town	3600
Freshwater	40 45 42N	124 03 38W	city/town	100
Freshwater Corners	40 47 08N	124 05 03W	city/town	9
Fresno	36 44 52N	119 46 17W	city/town	296
Fresno - Chandler	36 43 56N	119 49 11W	airport	278
Fresno -Sierra Sky	36 50 24N	119 52 13W	airport	321
Fresno Air Termin.	36 46 34N	119 43 05W	airport	333
Fresno Airways	36 46 40N	119 42 17W	golf	
Fresno City Colleg	36 46 03N	119 47 49W	univ/coll	
Fresno Crossing	37 14 14N	119 46 27W	city/town	1102
Fresno Natural His	36 46 07N	119 43 50W	museum	
Friant	36 59 16N	119 42 39W	city/town	340
Friend Place	40 29 09N	123 21 45W	city/town	3260
Friendly Hills	33 57 13N	118 00 10W	city/town	318
Friendly Hills C C	33 57 44N	117 59 27W	golf	

California GPS Companion

Place Name	Latitude			Longitude			Type	Elev
Friendship Village	37	46	42N	122	25	46W	city/town	110
Frink	33	21	45N	115	38	50W	city/town	-170
Frost	34	30	39N	117	16	36W	city/town	2760
Frost Amphitheatre	37	25	51N	122	09	54W	building	
Fruitdale	32	36	06N	117	05	30W	city/town	10
Fruitland	40	17	45N	123	49	27W	city/town	1000
Fruitridge Manor	38	31	30N	121	26	28W	city/town	29
Fruitvale	35	23	00N	119	04	56W	city/town	393
Fruto	39	35	24N	122	26	56W	city/town	620
Fuchs	38	20	51N	120	27	18W	city/town	2600
Fudenna Stadium	37	33	12N	121	59	25W	stadium	
Fuller	32	51	37N	115	24	19W	city/town	-72
Fuller Acres	35	18	00N	118	54	39W	city/town	415
Fuller Park -sub.	33	52	07N	117	58	38W	city/town	93
Fullerton	33	52	13N	117	55	28W	city/town	155
Fullerton Dam	33	53	48N	117	53	05W	dam	290
Fullerton Golf Clb	33	54	15N	117	55	29W	golf	
Fullerton Junior C	33	52	32N	117	54	24W	univ/coll	
Fullerton Municip.	33	52	19N	117	58	47W	airport	96
Fulton	38	29	47N	122	46	08W	city/town	132
Fulton Wells	33	56	34N	118	04	54W	city/town	125
Funeral Peak	36	06	11N	116	37	22W	summit	6384

California GPS Companion

G

Place Name	Latitude	Longitude	Type	Elev
Gabb, Mount	37 22 36N	118 48 06W	summit	13111
Gabilan Acres	36 45 19N	121 37 06W	city/town	200
Gage	33 58 31N	118 07 33W	city/town	150
Gale	34 51 22N	116 50 29W	city/town	1990
Galivan	33 34 10N	117 40 23W	city/town	280
Gallagher Beach	33 22 14N	118 20 52W	beach	
Gallatin Beach	40 33 31N	120 46 08W	beach	
Gallaway	38 52 09N	123 39 08W	city/town	88
Gallinas	38 01 13N	122 31 27W	city/town	40
Gallinas Beach	38 00 56N	122 30 14W	beach	
Galt	38 15 17N	121 17 56W	city/town	47
Ganns	38 24 16N	120 09 29W	city/town	6760
Garberville	40 06 01N	123 47 38W	city/town	533
Garberville Airprt	40 05 09N	123 48 49W	airport	546
Garden Air Golf	33 59 32N	117 02 49W	golf	
Garden Farms	35 25 05N	120 36 19W	city/town	952
Garden Grove	33 46 26N	117 56 26W	city/town	87
Garden Grove Muni.	33 45 09N	117 54 39W	golf	
Garden Park -sub.	34 05 26N	117 16 07W	city/town	1040
Garden Valley	38 51 15N	120 51 30W	city/town	1941

California GPS Companion

Place Name	Latitude	Longitude	Type	Elev
Gardena	33 53 18N	118 18 29W	city/town	53
Gardenland	38 36 40N	121 28 26W	city/town	21
Gardiner, Mount	36 48 21N	118 27 32W	summit	12907
Garey	34 53 19N	120 18 50W	city/town	379
Garlic Falls	36 51 43N	118 57 08W	falls	
Garlock	35 24 09N	117 47 21W	city/town	2160
Garnet	33 54 07N	116 32 41W	city/town	714
Garnsey	34 10 07N	118 24 04W	city/town	655
Garrapata State Pk	36 27 38N	121 54 47W	park	
Garvanza	34 06 59N	118 10 46W	city/town	610
Gas Point	40 24 56N	122 32 00W	city/town	607
Gasquet	41 50 44N	123 58 06W	city/town	356
Gasquet -Ward Fld.	41 50 44N	123 59 04W	airport	356
Gaston	39 23 39N	120 44 26W	city/town	5060
Gate Place	39 55 45N	120 34 36W	city/town	5800
Gateley	38 00 26N	122 18 32W	city/town	60
Gateway	39 19 34N	120 12 09W	city/town	5950
Gato	34 27 27N	120 22 36W	city/town	60
Gavilan Junior Col	36 58 22N	121 34 01W	univ/coll	
Gaviota	34 28 18N	120 12 50W	city/town	98
Gaviota Beach	34 28 15N	120 13 25W	beach	
Gaviota Beach Stat	34 28 20N	120 13 38W	park	

124

California GPS Companion

Place Name	Latitude	Longitude	Type	Elev
Gayley, Mount	37 06 11N	118 29 58W	summit	13510
Gazelle	41 31 15N	122 31 09W	city/town	2755
Gelatt	39 19 16N	120 17 25W	city/town	5950
Gemco	34 12 33N	118 26 12W	city/town	755
Gemini	37 17 49N	118 48 56W	summit	12866
Gendarme Peak	37 07 37N	118 31 50W	summit	13241
Gene Autry Western	34 08 56N	118 16 51W	museum	
Genesee	40 02 35N	120 45 10W	city/town	3680
Genevra	39 04 12N	122 05 26W	city/town	95
Genevra, Mount	36 41 03N	118 25 56W	summit	13055
George A F B	34 35 02N	117 23 03W	military	2875
Georgetown	38 54 25N	120 50 15W	city/town	2649
Georgetown Airport	38 55 15N	120 51 52W	airport	2588
Gepford	36 23 54N	119 48 30W	city/town	235
Gerber	40 03 23N	122 08 57W	city/town	241
Gerstle Cove	38 33 50N	123 19 34W	bay	
Geyserville	38 42 28N	122 54 05W	city/town	206
Giant	37 59 26N	122 21 22W	city/town	20
Gibbs, Mount	37 52 37N	119 12 42W	summit	12764
Gibson	41 00 43N	122 24 28W	city/town	1400
Gibson House Mus.	38 39 45N	121 46 22W	museum	
Gibsonville	39 44 25N	120 54 28W	city/town	5440

California GPS Companion

Place Name	Latitude	Longitude	Type	Elev
Giffen Cantua Rnch	36 28 29N	120 23 29W	city/town	440
Gilbert, Mount	37 08 14N	118 35 48W	summit	13103
Gilberts (1)	38 38 13N	120 29 30W	city/town	4200
Gilberts (2)	39 00 42N	120 28 16W	city/town	5640
Gilcrest Peak	38 00 39N	119 13 46W	summit	11575
Gillete	36 10 26N	119 02 07W	city/town	445
Gilliam Place	40 08 14N	122 35 13W	city/town	1060
Gillis (1)	37 56 03N	121 22 55W	city/town	0
Gillis (2)	41 57 30N	122 05 45W	city/town	4270
Gilman Hot Springs	33 50 09N	116 59 17W	city/town	1520
Gilroy	37 00 21N	121 34 02W	city/town	200
Gilroy Country Clb	37 00 49N	121 37 07W	golf	
Ginzton Laboratory	37 25 44N	122 10 27W	building	
Giraud Peak	37 04 39N	118 34 16W	summit	12585
Girvan	40 30 46N	122 22 44W	city/town	460
Glacier Point	37 43 51N	119 34 22W	cliff	7214
Glamis	32 59 51N	115 04 16W	city/town	335
Glasgow	34 59 01N	115 52 08W	city/town	1418
Gleason Beach	38 23 23N	123 05 04W	beach	
Glen Arbor	37 04 28N	122 04 52W	city/town	340
Glen Avon	34 00 42N	117 29 02W	city/town	750
Glen Avon Golf Crs	34 00 18N	117 28 36W	golf	

California GPS Companion

Place Name	Latitude	Longitude	Type	Elev
Glen Ellen	38 21 51N	122 31 23W	city/town	230
Glen Frazer	37 59 54N	122 09 42W	city/town	300
Glen Ivy Hot Sprgs	33 45 24N	117 29 36W	locale	
Glen Martin	34 08 45N	116 59 05W	city/town	5620
Glen Oaks	32 50 18N	116 48 11W	city/town	1320
Glen Oaks Golf Crs	34 06 58N	117 51 56W	golf	
Glen Valley	33 51 43N	117 19 31W	city/town	1640
Glenblair	39 27 28N	123 43 27W	city/town	120
Glenbrook (1)	38 51 06N	122 45 27W	city/town	2300
Glenbrook (2)	39 14 32N	121 02 04W	city/town	2700
Glenbrook Resort	38 51 04N	122 45 22W	locale	
Glenburn	41 03 41N	121 29 21W	city/town	3314
Glencoe	38 21 15N	120 35 02W	city/town	2721
Glencove	38 04 07N	122 12 21W	city/town	20
Glendale (1)	40 54 00N	124 00 57W	city/town	90
Glendale (2)	34 08 33N	118 15 15W	city/town	510
Glendale Civic Aud	34 09 59N	118 13 51W	building	
Glendale College	34 10 03N	118 13 38W	univ/coll	
Glendale Junction	34 04 31N	118 13 27W	city/town	320
Glendora	34 08 10N	117 51 52W	city/town	776
Glendora C C	34 07 46N	117 49 11W	golf	
Gleneagles Int'l	37 42 56N	122 25 00W	golf	

California GPS Companion

Place Name	Latitude	Longitude	Type	Elev
Glenhaven	39 01 35N	122 43 55W	city/town	1360
Glenn	39 31 19N	122 00 46W	city/town	95
Glenn County Golf	39 35 01N	122 13 14W	golf	
Glennville	35 43 44N	118 42 10W	city/town	3188
Glenridge -subdiv.	37 44 21N	122 26 09W	city/town	480
Glenridge Park	39 02 40N	120 07 24W	city/town	6320
Glenview (1)	32 49 56N	116 54 18W	city/town	597
Glenview (2)	38 54 00N	122 45 29W	city/town	2440
Glenview (3)	34 07 28N	118 36 02W	city/town	1200
Glenwood	37 06 30N	121 59 08W	city/town	891
Globe	36 06 04N	118 49 38W	city/town	820
Globe Mill	40 53 04N	123 01 22W	city/town	
Glorietta (1)	36 50 16N	119 42 31W	city/town	362
Glorietta (2)	37 51 44N	122 10 01W	city/town	600
Glorietta Bay Mar.	32 40 53N	117 10 25W	marina	
Gloster	34 57 22N	118 08 52W	city/town	2560
Goat Mountain	36 52 12N	118 34 24W	summit	12207
Goat Rock	38 34 54N	123 07 13W	city/town	874
Goat Rock Beach	38 26 48N	123 07 31W	beach	
Goddard, Mount	37 06 12N	118 43 07W	summit	13568
Goethe, Mount	37 12 23N	118 42 07W	summit	13264
Goffs	34 55 09N	115 03 43W	city/town	2587

California GPS Companion

Place Name	Latitude	Longitude	Type	Elev
Goggins	39 02 27N	120 30 25W	city/town	4520
Gold Bluffs Beach	41 23 48N	124 04 02W	beach	
Gold Flat	39 14 46N	121 01 24W	city/town	2640
Gold Hill (1)	38 45 40N	120 53 01W	city/town	1605
Gold Hill (2)	38 54 06N	121 10 50W	city/town	347
Gold Hill Vineyard	38 47 17N	120 53 34W	wine/vin	
Gold Hills C C	40 38 12N	122 20 40W	golf	
Gold Mine Hill	37 44 31N	122 26 13W	city/town	625
Gold Mine Ski Area	34 13 35N	116 51 49W	ski area	
Gold Ridge	38 45 12N	120 34 02W	city/town	4040
Gold Run	39 10 51N	120 51 17W	city/town	3222
Gold Trail Park	38 45 10N	120 50 56W	city/town	1720
Golden Chain Mobil	38 56 17N	121 05 30W	city/town	1420
Golden Circle Vly	33 09 27N	117 07 22W	golf	
Golden Gate Bridge	37 49 11N	122 28 40W	bridge	
Golden Gate Nat'l	37 51 00N	122 31 00W	park	
Golden Gate Park	37 46 07N	122 30 15W	golf	
Golden Gate Park	37 46 09N	122 28 45W	park	
Golden Gate Park C	37 46 22N	122 27 33W	consrvtry	
Golden Gate Park S	37 46 05N	122 29 30W	stadium	
Golden Gate Yacht	37 48 28N	122 26 28W	locale	
Golden Hills Golf	35 08 56N	118 29 35W	golf	

129

California GPS Companion

Place Name	Latitude	Longitude	Type	Elev
Golden St Model RR	37 55 03N	122 23 00W	museum	
Golden West Colleg	33 44 02N	118 00 10W	univ/coll	
Goldleaf	36 43 20N	119 43 01W	city/town	306
Goldstone	35 17 50N	116 54 47W	city/town	3243
Goldtree	35 19 19N	120 40 53W	city/town	440
Goldwyn Studios	34 05 21N	118 20 47W	studio	
Goler Heights	35 25 37N	117 44 42W	city/town	2570
Goleta	34 26 09N	119 49 36W	city/town	20
Goleta Beach State	34 25 02N	119 49 43W	park	
Goleta Point	34 24 16N	119 50 35W	cape	
Gomez	41 02 10N	121 30 55W	city/town	3340
Gonzales	36 30 24N	121 26 36W	city/town	131
Goodale	36 22 41N	119 02 36W	city/town	470
Goodale Mountain	36 58 20N	118 23 15W	summit	12790
Goode, Mount	37 07 20N	118 34 02W	summit	13092
Goodmans Corner	38 12 18N	120 59 10W	city/town	176
Goodmill	36 46 51N	119 01 21W	city/town	3700
Goodyear Blimp Bas	33 51 23N	118 16 38W	airport	21
Goodyears Bar	39 32 24N	120 53 00W	city/town	2680
Goosenest	41 43 14N	122 13 19W	summit	8280
Gorda	35 55 57N	121 28 04W	city/town	158
Gordola	36 58 31N	122 08 00W	city/town	80

California GPS Companion

Place Name	Latitude	Longitude	Type	Elev
Gordon	36 53 46N	119 43 44W	city/town	392
Gorman	34 47 46N	118 51 06W	city/town	3811
Gosford	35 18 40N	119 05 26W	city/town	361
Goshen	36 21 04N	119 25 09W	city/town	282
Gottsville	41 52 03N	122 44 24W	city/town	1870
Gould, Mount	36 46 47N	118 22 38W	summit	13005
Government Camp	40 41 30N	122 23 21W	city/town	9050
Governors Village	38 41 20N	121 04 49W	city/town	760
Grabtown	37 25 20N	122 20 34W	city/town	1640
Grace Cathedral	37 47 30N	122 24 43W	mission	
Grace Hudson Mus.	39 08 53N	123 12 17W	museum	
Graeagle	39 45 59N	120 37 03W	city/town	4000
Graeagle Meadows	39 45 45N	120 36 08W	golf	
Graham Place	40 25 36N	123 24 25W	city/town	1840
Graino	39 02 09N	121 57 40W	city/town	41
Granada Hills	34 15 53N	118 31 20W	city/town	1032
Grand Island	39 03 58N	121 52 02W	city/town	44
Grand Sentinel	36 47 01N	118 35 00W	pillar	8504
Grand Terrace	34 02 02N	117 18 46W	city/town	1040
Grandview	34 53 24N	117 06 21W	city/town	2230
Grangeville	36 20 37N	119 42 28W	city/town	246
Granite Bay Golf	38 44 58N	121 12 06W	golf	

California GPS Companion

Place Name	Latitude	Longitude	Type	Elev
Granite Hills Vin.	38 45 54N	120 45 42W	wine/vin	
Granite Springs	37 42 04N	120 17 41W	city/town	1400
Graniteville	39 26 27N	120 44 19W	city/town	4960
Granlibakken Ski A	39 09 18N	120 09 19W	ski area	
Grant (1)	36 15 20N	117 59 35W	city/town	3730
Grant (2)	38 35 25N	122 50 48W	city/town	110
Grant Grove Vlg.	36 44 24N	118 57 42W	city/town	6600
Grant Lake Overlk.	37 48 47N	119 06 14W	overlook	7720
Grantville	32 47 15N	117 05 47W	city/town	170
Grape	34 05 53N	117 27 48W	city/town	1230
Grape Festival Bld	38 08 19N	121 15 49W	building	
Grapeland	34 07 30N	117 33 42W	city/town	1370
Grapevine	34 56 30N	118 55 45W	city/town	1758
Grapit	39 40 52N	122 11 35W	city/town	220
Grass Flat	39 40 33N	120 56 03W	city/town	4840
Grass Lake	41 38 06N	122 11 25W	city/town	5065
Grass Valley	39 13 09N	121 03 36W	city/town	2411
Grass Vly -Nevada	39 13 26N	121 00 08W	airport	3151
Graton	38 26 11N	122 52 07W	city/town	120
Graumans Chinese T	34 06 08N	118 20 24W	building	
Gravenstein	38 24 17N	122 48 24W	city/town	70
Gravesboro	36 46 23N	119 24 38W	city/town	480

132

California GPS Companion

Place Name	Latitude	Longitude	Type	Elev
Graveyard Peak	37 26 59N	118 59 16W	summit	11520
Gray Falls	40 51 15N	123 28 54W	falls	
Gray Peak	37 40 27N	119 25 06W	summit	11574
Gray Whale Cove St	37 33 56N	122 30 48W	park	
Grays Flat	40 01 04N	121 03 45W	city/town	2780
Grayson	37 33 50N	121 10 42W	city/town	55
Great West Arch	37 42 02N	123 00 45W	arch	
Greekstore	39 04 37N	120 33 27W	city/town	5680
Green	38 20 45N	121 38 19W	city/town	25
Green Brae	37 56 55N	122 31 25W	city/town	28
Green Hills C C	37 36 19N	122 24 41W	golf	
Green Springs Rnch	38 42 06N	121 02 01W	city/town	1050
Green Springs Vly.	38 42 35N	121 02 50W	city/town	1080
Green Tree C C	34 30 09N	117 18 48W	golf	
Green Valley	34 37 18N	118 24 47W	city/town	2928
Green Valley Acres	38 42 45N	121 04 15W	city/town	680
Green Valley Golf	38 15 26N	122 10 04W	golf	
Green Valley Lake	34 14 27N	117 04 35W	city/town	6920
Green Valley Recr.	34 14 12N	117 04 27W	locale	
Greenacres	35 23 00N	119 06 32W	city/town	379
Greendale	38 22 25N	121 35 06W	city/town	2
Greenfield (1)	36 19 15N	121 14 34W	city/town	280

California GPS Companion

Place Name	Latitude	Longitude	Type	Elev
Greenfiled (2)	35 16 08N	119 00 07W	city/town	346
Greensport	34 04 03N	117 06 12W	city/town	2122
Greenstone Winery	38 18 38N	120 58 00W	wine/vin	
Greenview	41 33 03N	122 54 16W	city/town	2812
Greenville (1)	40 08 23N	120 57 00W	city/town	3580
Greenville (2)	39 26 12N	121 10 35W	city/town	2200
Greenwater	36 10 46N	116 36 56W	city/town	4300
Greenwich Village	34 10 53N	118 51 49W	city/town	780
Greenwood (1)	39 41 46N	122 11 36W	city/town	228
Greenwood (2)	38 53 48N	120 54 42W	city/town	1615
Greenwood Creek St	39 07 39N	123 43 00W	park	
Gregg	36 52 54N	119 56 09W	city/town	295
Gregorys Monument	36 42 05N	118 23 41W	summit	13907
Grenada	41 38 50N	122 31 08W	city/town	2590
Grey Butte	38 03 07N	119 20 49W	summit	11365
Greystone Mansion	34 05 31N	118 24 02W	building	
Grider Island	37 33 25N	121 08 01W	locale	
Gridley	39 21 50N	121 41 33W	city/town	91
Gridley Colony	39 21 03N	121 39 40W	city/town	93
Griffin Place	39 58 10N	122 47 07W	city/town	4760
Griffith Observato	34 07 07N	118 17 58W	observtry	
Grimes	39 04 28N	121 53 34W	city/town	47

California GPS Companion

Place Name	Latitude	Longitude	Type	Elev
Griminger	38 43 11N	120 24 33W	city/town	4920
Grizzlie Place	41 54 04N	120 38 22W	city/town	5210
Grizzly Bay	38 07 05N	122 01 20W	bay	
Grizzly Flat	38 38 11N	120 31 35W	city/town	3880
Grizzly Island	38 09 05N	121 58 18W	island	
Grossmont	32 46 42N	116 59 15W	city/town	800
Grossmont College	32 48 59N	117 00 19W	univ/coll	
Grotto Hills	35 09 38N	115 12 52W	locale	4893
Grove	39 26 13N	123 39 30W	city/town	100
Groveland	37 50 18N	120 13 54W	city/town	2846
Groveland Pine Mt.	37 51 41N	120 10 42W	airport	2930
Grover Beach	35 07 18N	120 37 13W	city/town	60
Grover Hot Springs	38 42 02N	119 50 12W	park	
Guadalcanal Vlg.	38 07 07N	122 17 34W	city/town	8
Guadalupe	34 58 18N	120 34 15W	city/town	85
Guadalupe College	37 12 33N	121 58 24W	univ/coll	
Guadalupe Dunes	35 00 20N	120 37 24W	locale	
Gualala	38 45 57N	123 31 37W	city/town	67
Gualala -Ocean Rdg	38 48 04N	123 31 49W	airport	940
Guasti	34 03 54N	117 35 08W	city/town	965
Guatay	32 50 56N	116 33 23W	city/town	4000
Guerneville	38 30 07N	122 59 42W	city/town	56

California GPS Companion

Place Name	Latitude	Longitude	Type	Elev
Guernewood	38 29 34N	123 00 50W	city/town	80
Guernewood Park	38 29 49N	123 00 41W	city/town	60
Guernsey	36 12 47N	119 38 24W	city/town	218
Guernsey Mill	35 50 03N	118 36 56W	city/town	5520
Guild	38 08 43N	121 14 33W	city/town	60
Guinda	38 49 45N	122 11 34W	city/town	355
Gulf	35 10 46N	119 09 33W	city/town	290
Gum	34 55 12N	120 31 14W	city/town	150
Gustine	37 15 28N	120 59 52W	city/town	96
Gustine Airport	37 15 45N	120 57 47W	airport	75
Guyot, Mount	36 30 32N	118 21 43W	summit	12300
Gypsite	35 19 52N	117 55 49W	city/town	1960

Ⴌ

Place Name	Latitude	Longitude	Type	Elev
Hacienda	38 30 41N	122 55 36W	city/town	100
Hacienda del Flora	32 37 02N	116 29 58W	city/town	2620
Hacienda Golf Club	33 57 36N	117 56 45W	golf	
Hacienda Heights	33 59 35N	117 58 04W	city/town	460
Hacienda Mobile Hm	37 39 59N	121 50 47W	city/town	400
Hackamore	41 33 07N	121 07 21W	city/town	4714
Hacketsville	40 29 15N	124 10 13W	city/town	240
Hackmans Falls	39 33 33N	120 37 29W	falls	

California GPS Companion

Place Name	Latitude	Longitude	Type	Elev
Haeckel, Mount	37 09 01N	118 39 38W	summit	13435
Haggin Museum	37 57 39N	121 18 43W	museum	
Haggin Oaks Golf	38 38 00N	121 24 08W	golf	
Hagginwood	38 37 39N	121 25 53W	city/town	40
Haight	38 05 34N	121 14 31W	city/town	50
Haight-Ashbury	37 46 12N	122 26 45W	city/town	270
Haines	34 19 29N	119 06 07W	city/town	215
Haiwee	36 08 48N	117 58 30W	city/town	3970
Halcon	33 49 38N	118 01 39W	city/town	47
Halcyon	35 06 12N	120 35 41W	city/town	60
Hale Place	38 30 30N	123 02 08W	city/town	220
Hale Telescope	33 21 23N	116 51 50W	observtry	5571
Hale, Mount	36 35 14N	118 18 50W	summit	13491
Hales Grove	39 49 04N	123 46 52W	city/town	1140
Half Dome	37 44 46N	119 31 55W	summit	8842
Half Moon Bay	37 27 49N	122 25 39W	city/town	69
Half Moon Bay	37 29 00N	122 28 15W	bay	
Half Moon Bay Arpt	37 30 49N	122 30 03W	airport	67
Halfmoon Beach	40 40 48N	120 47 20W	beach	
Halfway House	35 35 23N	118 57 34W	city/town	1096
Hall Station	37 35 12N	122 03 51W	city/town	15
Hallelujah Jct.	39 46 32N	120 02 18W	city/town	4980

California GPS Companion

Place Name	Latitude	Longitude	Type	Elev
Halloran Springs	35 22 21N	115 53 23W	city/town	3000
Halls Corner	36 20 33N	119 48 20W	city/town	226
Halls Flat	40 45 22N	121 15 29W	city/town	5710
Halvern	37 37 31N	122 03 05W	city/town	15
Hamblin	36 19 47N	119 36 32W	city/town	248
Hambone	41 20 06N	121 41 48W	city/town	4410
Hamburg	41 46 59N	123 03 33W	city/town	1592
Hamburg Farms	36 52 46N	120 45 46W	city/town	223
Hamilton Beach	33 21 14N	118 19 43W	beach	
Hamilton Branch	40 16 30N	121 05 25W	city/town	4620
Hamilton City	39 44 34N	122 00 45W	city/town	150
Hamlet	38 12 28N	122 55 28W	city/town	40
Hammer Place	40 07 11N	122 42 58W	city/town	1560
Hammil	37 40 43N	118 24 10W	city/town	4586
Hammond (1)	36 27 56N	118 51 37W	city/town	1170
Hammond (2)	36 45 35N	119 47 10W	city/town	296
Hammonton	39 11 35N	121 25 11W	city/town	128
Hams	38 22 27N	120 27 40W	city/town	2960
Hancock Park -sub.	34 04 04N	118 19 54W	city/town	220
Hanford	36 19 39N	119 38 41W	city/town	247
Hanford Municipal	36 19 06N	119 37 43W	airport	242
Hanna Mountain	38 11 20N	119 29 06W	summit	11486

California GPS Companion

Place Name	Latitude	Longitude	Type	Elev
Hannchen	41 50 25N	121 24 12W	city/town	4040
Hansen	33 49 02N	118 00 35W	city/town	58
Hansen Dam Golf	34 15 36N	118 23 31W	golf	
Hansen Laboratory	37 25 42N	122 10 24W	building	
Happy Camp	41 47 36N	123 22 42W	city/town	1087
Happy Camp Airport	41 47 26N	123 23 20W	airport	1209
Happy Valley (1)	38 40 55N	120 33 44W	city/town	3720
Happy Valley (2)	34 05 01N	118 11 58W	city/town	600
Haraszthy Falls	38 17 34N	122 25 04W	falls	
Harbin Mountain	38 47 31N	122 38 43W	summit	12585
Harbin Springs	38 47 16N	122 39 16W	city/town	1560
Harbin Springs Ann	38 47 32N	122 39 37W	city/town	1700
Harbison Canyon	32 49 13N	116 49 45W	city/town	840
Harbor Beach	33 12 18N	117 23 36W	beach	
Harbor City	33 47 24N	118 17 49W	city/town	48
Harbor Hills	33 46 49N	118 18 50W	city/town	200
Harbor Park Golf	33 47 10N	118 17 19W	golf	
Harbor Side	32 36 36N	117 04 50W	city/town	50
Harden Flat	37 48 40N	119 56 47W	city/town	3479
Harden Gardens	37 54 01N	119 39 47W	garden	
Harder Stadium	34 25 13N	119 51 12W	stadium	
Harding Golf Crs	34 08 23N	118 16 56W	golf	

California GPS Companion

Place Name	Latitude	Longitude	Type	Elev
Harding Park Mun.	37 43 21N	122 29 15W	golf	
Hardwick	36 24 05N	119 43 04W	city/town	245
Hardy	39 42 45N	123 48 07W	city/town	30
Hardy Place	39 48 04N	122 56 59W	city/town	4560
Harlem	36 23 57N	121 15 09W	city/town	200
Harlem Springs	34 07 17N	117 13 31W	city/town	1411
Harlow Place	41 08 43N	121 40 33W	city/town	4320
Harmon Gymnasium	37 52 10N	122 15 40W	building	
Harmony	35 30 31N	121 01 18W	city/town	175
Harmony Acres	34 08 37N	116 06 31W	city/town	2360
Harmony Grove	33 05 46N	117 08 04W	city/town	560
Harold	34 32 42N	118 06 31W	city/town	2830
Harp	37 34 50N	120 59 02W	city/town	80
Harper	41 12 54N	120 55 50W	city/town	4250
Harpertown	35 17 41N	118 55 21W	city/town	395
Harrington	38 57 32N	122 00 59W	city/town	135
Harris	40 05 03N	123 39 27W	city/town	2260
Harris Point	34 04 34N	120 22 02W	cape	
Harrisburg	36 21 50N	117 06 38W	city/town	5040
Harrison Park	33 01 34N	116 34 06W	city/town	4520
Harry A Merlo St.	41 11 00N	124 06 25W	park	
Harry Floyd Terrac	38 07 45N	122 14 13W	city/town	140

California GPS Companion

Place Name	Latitude	Longitude	Type	Elev
Hart	35 17 20N	115 06 09W	city/town	4495
Hartland	36 39 16N	118 57 24W	city/town	4400
Hartley	38 25 02N	121 56 45W	city/town	116
Harts Place	35 30 03N	117 56 52W	city/town	3086
Harvard	34 57 04N	116 39 50W	city/town	1822
Harvey Monroe Hall	37 57 37N	119 17 51W	locale	11033
Harvey West Stad.	36 59 00N	122 02 06W	stadium	
Haskell Creek Home	39 38 05N	120 33 06W	city/town	5800
Hatch	37 29 23N	120 57 16W	city/town	70
Hatchet Creek Fall	40 52 31N	121 56 26W	falls	
Hatfield	41 59 53N	121 31 06W	city/town	4047
Hathaway Pines	38 11 31N	120 21 52W	city/town	3320
Hathaway Place	35 10 01N	120 17 54W	city/town	980
Havasu Lake	34 28 56N	114 24 47W	city/town	500
Havasu Palms	34 23 56N	114 16 47W	city/town	480
Haven	40 00 34N	121 13 45W	city/town	2320
Haven Place	40 10 57N	122 40 29W	city/town	1310
Havilah	35 31 04N	118 31 04W	city/town	3140
Hawaiian Gardens	33 49 53N	118 04 19W	city/town	29
Hawes	38 05 39N	121 14 46W	city/town	48
Hawkins Bar	40 52 13N	123 31 18W	city/town	760
Hawkinsville	41 45 39N	122 37 15W	city/town	2486

California GPS Companion

Place Name	Latitude	Longitude	Type	Elev
Hawley	39 48 39N	120 21 14W	city/town	4880
Hawthorne	33 54 59N	118 21 06W	city/town	69
Hawthorne Municip.	33 55 22N	118 20 06W	airport	63
Hayden	35 02 41N	115 36 37W	city/town	2493
Hayden Hill	40 59 44N	120 53 10W	city/town	5740
Hayes	34 04 27N	118 01 19W	city/town	292
Hayes Truck Museum	38 40 35N	121 43 43W	museum	
Hayfield	33 42 17N	115 38 01W	city/town	1403
Hayfork	40 33 16N	123 10 55W	city/town	2327
Hayfork Airport	40 32 49N	123 10 54W	airport	2321
Hays Place	39 40 38N	122 54 36W	city/town	3140
Haystack	38 13 24N	122 36 32W	city/town	40
Hayward (1)	37 38 34N	120 22 13W	city/town	650
Hayward (2)	37 40 08N	122 04 47W	city/town	111
Hayward Air Term.	37 39 33N	122 07 20W	airport	47
Hayward Golf Crs	37 37 26N	122 02 46W	golf	
Hayward Park	37 33 16N	122 18 44W	city/town	15
Hazelton	35 02 32N	119 23 01W	city/town	775
Headley Peak	37 41 19N	118 17 08W	summit	12676
Healdsburg	38 36 38N	122 52 05W	city/town	106
Healdsburg Municip	38 39 12N	122 53 57W	airport	278
Hearst	39 29 30N	123 12 49W	city/town	1320

California GPS Companion

Place Name	Latitude	Longitude	Type	Elev
Hearst Anthropolog	37 52 11N	122 15 15W	museum	
Hearst Castle	35 41 07N	121 10 00W	building	
Hearst Gymnasium	37 52 11N	122 15 21W	building	
Hearst Ranch	35 39 25N	121 11 14W	locale	
Hearst San Simeon	35 41 06N	121 10 10W	park	
Heart Bar Campgrnd	34 09 31N	116 47 09W	city/town	
Heart Bar State Pk	34 08 41N	116 45 54W	park	
Hearts Desire	38 07 58N	122 53 32W	beach	
Heartwell Golf Crs	33 49 52N	118 06 10W	golf	
Heath Place	39 49 27N	123 22 48W	city/town	2080
Heather Glen	39 01 06N	120 58 51W	city/town	2060
Heavenly Vly Ski A	38 56 16N	119 54 28W	ski area	10000
Heavenly Vly Ski L	38 56 05N	119 56 25W	ski area	
Heber	32 43 51N	115 31 44W	city/town	-15
Hector	34 48 14N	116 27 06W	city/town	1878
Heeser Addition	39 24 55N	123 46 11W	city/town	310
Helena	40 46 25N	123 07 38W	city/town	1404
Helendale	34 44 38N	117 19 25W	city/town	2430
Helendale Sun Hill	34 45 28N	117 29 48W	airport	2984
Hellhole Palms	33 14 12N	116 26 22W	city/town	1760
Hellman Tennis Sta	37 52 12N	122 15 50W	stadium	
Hells Half Acre	39 28 50N	120 50 39W	locale	

California GPS Companion

Place Name	Latitude	Longitude	Type	Elev
Helltown	39 48 42N	121 39 31W	city/town	800
Helm	36 31 54N	120 05 50W	city/town	185
Helm Corner	36 05 53N	119 38 34W	city/town	188
Hemet	33 44 51N	116 58 16W	city/town	1596
Hemet -Ryan Airprt	33 44 02N	117 01 21W	airport	1512
Henderson	37 28 46N	122 09 52W	city/town	10
Henderson Village	38 06 03N	121 18 16W	city/town	29
Hendrys Beach	34 24 03N	119 44 18W	beach	
Hendy Grove	39 04 37N	123 27 45W	city/town	196
Hendy Woods State	39 04 16N	123 27 55W	park	
Henley	41 54 08N	122 33 44W	city/town	2200
Henleyville	39 57 43N	122 19 32W	city/town	435
Henry	35 29 23N	120 38 49W	city/town	846
Henry, Mount	37 11 00N	118 49 35W	summit	12196
Henshaw	34 00 08N	117 27 45W	city/town	770
Heppe Bridge	41 41 56N	121 32 32W	arch	
Herald	38 17 45N	121 14 36W	city/town	71
Hercraff Place	40 12 30N	122 32 41W	city/town	753
Hercules	38 01 02N	122 17 15W	city/town	60
Hercules Wharf	38 01 22N	122 17 29W	wharf	
Herlong	40 08 37N	120 08 01W	city/town	4092
Herlong Airport	40 08 19N	120 10 43W	airport	4055

California GPS Companion

Place Name	Latitude	Longitude	Type	Elev
Herlong Junction	40 07 29N	120 14 44W	city/town	4005
Hermosa Beach	33 51 44N	118 23 55W	city/town	15
Hermosa Beach Pav.	33 51 55N	118 23 36W	locale	
Hermosillo -sub.	33 52 45N	118 17 42W	city/town	32
Herndon	36 50 12N	119 54 59W	city/town	295
Herpoco	38 00 42N	122 16 12W	city/town	60
Herrin Labs	37 25 48N	122 10 15W	building	
Hershey	38 55 32N	121 59 44W	city/town	115
Hesperia	34 25 35N	117 18 00W	city/town	3191
Hesperia Airport	34 22 38N	117 18 57W	airport	3390
Hess Mill	38 06 09N	120 14 12W	city/town	3320
Hessel	38 20 54N	122 46 34W	city/town	130
Hetch Hetchy Jct.	37 48 04N	120 29 12W	city/town	950
Hewes Park	33 46 50N	117 48 55W	city/town	240
Hewitt	34 11 59N	118 23 21W	city/town	740
Hi Vista	34 44 06N	117 46 35W	city/town	3050
Hibbards Wharf	37 46 43N	122 15 04W	wharf	
Hickman	37 37 25N	120 45 10W	city/town	171
Hickok Ranch	38 43 02N	121 02 44W	city/town	1000
Hickson	34 15 26N	118 28 00W	city/town	910
Hicksville	38 19 38N	121 19 20W	city/town	40
Hidden Falls	33 38 11N	116 30 33W	falls	

California GPS Companion

Place Name	Latitude	Longitude	Type	Elev
Hidden Hills	34 09 37N	118 39 05W	city/town	1100
Hidden Palms	33 49 13N	116 18 02W	city/town	400
Hidden Palms State	33 37 24N	116 24 10W	park	
Hidden River	34 10 42N	116 18 26W	city/town	2786
Hidden Springs	34 19 06N	118 07 49W	city/town	3120
Hidden Valley (1)	38 45 51N	121 09 44W	city/town	430
Hidden Valley (2)	38 42 25N	121 05 27W	city/town	500
Higby	36 17 06N	119 17 13W	city/town	325
Higgins Corner	39 02 34N	121 05 38W	city/town	1416
High Sierra Park	38 04 55N	120 08 47W	city/town	4700
Highcroft	38 30 07N	122 56 33W	city/town	100
Highgrove	34 00 57N	117 19 57W	city/town	949
Highland	34 07 42N	117 12 28W	city/town	1315
Highland Art Cent.	40 43 58N	122 56 20W	building	
Highland College	34 08 00N	118 10 27W	univ/coll	
Highland Park (1)	39 11 05N	121 01 36W	city/town	2740
Highland Park (2)	38 33 28N	121 29 15W	city/town	15
Highland Park (3)	34 06 43N	118 11 53W	city/town	600
Highland Park -sub	37 47 52N	122 13 35W	city/town	200
Highland Sprgs -1	33 58 10N	116 56 29W	city/town	3000
Highland Sprgs -2	38 56 14N	122 54 21W	city/town	1500
Highland Village	38 42 24N	121 04 15W	city/town	740

California GPS Companion

Place Name	Latitude	Longitude	Type	Elev
Hights Corner	35 26 36N	119 12 05W	city/town	340
Highway City	36 48 39N	119 53 02W	city/town	295
Highway Highlands	34 14 04N	118 15 31W	city/town	1675
Hilarita	37 53 03N	122 28 15W	city/town	16
Hildreth	37 06 32N	119 37 55W	city/town	1220
Hilgard, Mount	37 21 39N	118 49 31W	summit	13361
Hillcrest (1)	32 44 52N	117 09 24W	city/town	300
Hillcrest (2)	40 51 50N	121 54 27W	city/town	3125
Hillcrest C C	34 03 00N	118 24 18W	golf	
Hillgrove	34 01 00N	117 58 45W	city/town	329
Hillmaid	36 24 50N	119 08 02W	city/town	436
Hills Ferry	37 20 56N	120 58 43W	city/town	70
Hills Flat	39 13 27N	121 03 08W	city/town	2460
Hillsborough	37 34 27N	122 22 42W	city/town	500
Hillsborough Park	37 33 18N	122 21 28W	city/town	350
Hillsdale (1)	37 32 11N	122 18 16W	city/town	50
Hillsdale (2)	32 46 45N	116 55 38W	city/town	784
Hilmar	37 24 31N	120 50 57W	city/town	89
Hilt	41 59 42N	122 37 20W	city/town	2901
Hilton	38 30 17N	122 56 21W	city/town	70
Hilton, Mount	40 57 24N	123 03 08W	summit	8964
Hinda	33 57 10N	117 03 26W	city/town	2170

California GPS Companion

Place Name	Latitude	Longitude	Type	Elev
Hinkley	34 56 05N	117 11 54W	city/town	2162
Hinsdale	39 00 55N	121 46 40W	city/town	30
Hinton	39 22 31N	120 04 22W	city/town	5500
Hiouchi	41 47 34N	124 04 15W	city/town	163
Hirschdale	39 22 07N	120 04 30W	city/town	5500
Hitchcock, Mount	36 33 16N	118 18 39W	summit	13184
Hite Cove	37 38 27N	119 50 53W	city/town	1600
Hobart	34 00 44N	118 12 14W	city/town	190
Hobart Mills	39 24 02N	120 10 58W	city/town	5880
Hobergs	38 50 37N	122 43 24W	city/town	3026
Hoboken	40 52 59N	123 26 01W	city/town	1120
Hodge	34 48 56N	117 11 33W	city/town	2273
Hoffman Point	36 41 32N	119 11 50W	city/town	1525
Hoffman, Mount	41 36 39N	121 33 12W	summit	7913
Hogue, Mount	37 43 57N	118 18 11W	summit	12751
Holcomb Village	33 21 03N	116 44 12W	city/town	3280
Holiday Harbor Res	40 48 09N	122 18 33W	city/town	1150
Holiday Hill Ski L	34 21 53N	117 40 42W	ski area	
Hollis	35 40 03N	119 11 25W	city/town	416
Hollister	36 51 09N	121 24 02W	city/town	290
Hollister -Frazier	36 57 11N	121 27 55W	airport	151
Hollister Municip	36 53 24N	121 24 25W	airport	233

California GPS Companion

Place Name	Latitude	Longitude	Type	Elev
Hollydale (1)	38 30 19N	122 55 08W	city/town	440
Hollydale (2)	33 54 53N	118 09 39W	city/town	80
Hollywood	34 05 54N	118 19 33W	city/town	320
Hollywood Beach	34 09 51N	119 13 46W	beach	
Hollywood Beach	34 10 02N	119 13 47W	city/town	10
Hollywood by the S	34 09 38N	119 13 30W	city/town	10
Hollywood Riviera	33 48 51N	118 22 56W	city/town	140
Holmes	40 25 07N	123 56 22W	city/town	145
Holt	37 56 04N	121 25 34W	city/town	8
Holtville	32 48 40N	115 22 46W	city/town	-11
Holtville Airport	32 50 25N	115 16 02W	airport	59
Holy City	37 09 25N	121 58 40W	city/town	1240
Holy Names College	37 48 09N	122 11 10W	univ/coll	
Holy Redeemer Coll	37 45 32N	122 09 19W	univ/coll	
Home Gardens	33 52 41N	117 31 12W	city/town	680
Home Junction	34 02 09N	118 26 02W	city/town	158
Homeland	33 44 35N	117 06 30W	city/town	1608
Homelands	32 44 30N	116 58 18W	city/town	600
Homer	34 55 12N	114 56 10W	city/town	2135
Homestead	41 54 49N	121 25 19W	city/town	4036
Homewood	39 05 13N	120 09 33W	city/town	6238
Homewood Seaplane	39 05 11N	120 09 36W	airport	6229

California GPS Companion

Place Name	Latitude	Longitude	Type	Elev
Homewood Ski Area	39 04 48N	120 09 59W	ski area	7360
Honby	34 25 16N	118 29 29W	city/town	1300
Honcut	39 19 45N	121 31 58W	city/town	106
Honda	34 36 56N	120 37 57W	city/town	100
Honey Lake State W	40 17 55N	120 22 31W	park	4010
Honeydew	40 14 40N	124 07 18W	city/town	360
Honker Bay	38 03 55N	121 55 41W	bay	
Hood	38 22 06N	121 30 59W	city/town	7
Hood Junction	38 21 49N	121 30 31W	city/town	10
Hooker	40 18 03N	122 19 33W	city/town	527
Hookston	37 56 29N	122 03 06W	city/town	65
Hookton	40 40 24N	124 13 02W	city/town	10
Hoopa	41 03 02N	123 40 23W	city/town	1720
Hoopa Airport	41 02 34N	123 40 06W	airport	356
Hooper	41 16 05N	122 09 38W	city/town	3720
Hooper Beach	36 58 13N	121 57 15W	beach	
Hooper, Mount	37 17 33N	118 53 37W	summit	12349
Hooperville	41 40 44N	122 50 52W	city/town	3017
Hoover Pavilion	37 26 29N	122 10 03W	building	
Hope Ranch	34 25 19N	119 46 12W	city/town	140
Hopeton	37 29 30N	120 31 48W	city/town	180
Hopkins, Mount	37 27 50N	118 48 43W	summit	12302

California GPS Companion

Place Name	Latitude	Longitude	Type	Elev
Hopland	38 58 23N	123 06 55W	city/town	486
Hoppaw	41 31 28N	124 01 44W	city/town	30
Hornbrook	41 54 37N	122 33 17W	city/town	2154
Hornitos	37 30 08N	120 14 14W	city/town	821
Horse Creek	41 49 27N	122 59 45W	city/town	1705
Horse Lake	40 40 27N	120 24 11W	city/town	5094
Horstville	39 01 41N	121 23 26W	city/town	110
Hoskin	41 42 32N	123 21 44W	city/town	2260
Hot Springs (1)	41 08 47N	121 02 15W	city/town	4180
Hot Springs (2)	40 01 08N	121 01 58W	city/town	2840
Hotlum	41 28 27N	122 18 48W	city/town	4140
Hough Springs	39 09 45N	122 36 40W	city/town	1550
Houghton Place	39 48 18N	122 40 38W	city/town	3840
House-on-the-Hill	37 32 37N	122 20 13W	building	
Houze Place	34 46 07N	117 37 30W	city/town	2947
Hovley	33 00 09N	115 31 15W	city/town	-138
Howard	41 18 47N	122 16 33W	city/town	4143
Howard Landing	38 13 44N	121 36 00W	city/town	5
Howard Springs	38 51 30N	122 40 25W	city/town	2140
Howell Mountain	38 34 53N	122 27 00W	city/town	1675
Howell Place	34 28 09N	119 07 08W	city/town	2720
Howland Flat	39 42 54N	120 53 08W	city/town	5640

California GPS Companion

Place Name	Latitude	Longitude	Type	Elev
Huasna	35 07 22N	120 23 33W	city/town	790
Hub	36 24 08N	119 48 29W	city/town	233
Hubert Place	35 10 08N	120 15 59W	city/town	1220
Hudner	36 54 00N	121 27 01W	city/town	203
Hughes Mill	39 05 28N	120 46 43W	city/town	3500
Hughes Place	39 43 40N	121 24 04W	city/town	2525
Hughes Stadium	38 32 26N	121 29 06W	stadium	
Hughson	37 35 49N	120 51 54W	city/town	123
Hulburd Grove	32 51 43N	116 37 20W	city/town	3440
Hull Mountain	39 31 19N	122 56 07W	summit	6873
Humboldt Bay Marit	40 48 22N	124 09 20W	museum	
Humboldt Redwoods	40 19 21N	123 59 34W	park	
Humboldt State U.	40 52 38N	124 04 33W	univ/coll	
Hume	36 47 06N	118 54 46W	city/town	5400
Hume Station	36 47 40N	118 54 15W	city/town	5280
Humpherys College	38 00 41N	121 18 56W	univ/coll	
Humphreys	34 24 37N	118 26 23W	city/town	1490
Humphreys, Mount	37 16 14N	118 40 22W	summit	13986
Hunewill Peak	38 09 33N	119 26 34W	summit	11713
Hungry Valley St.	34 45 01N	118 51 30W	park	
Hunter Place	40 10 46N	124 00 51W	city/town	880
Hunter-Liggett	36 00 37N	121 14 15W	city/town	1060

California GPS Companion

Place Name	Latitude	Longitude	Type	Elev
Hunters Point	37 43 28N	122 22 06W	cape	
Huntington Beach	33 39 37N	117 59 54W	city/town	28
Huntington Beach	33 40 22N	118 00 21W	golf	
Huntington Falls	37 46 07N	122 28 23W	falls	
Huntington Harbour	33 43 16N	118 03 48W	city/town	25
Huntington Lake	37 13 54N	119 14 06W	city/town	7040
Huntington Park	33 58 54N	118 13 27W	city/town	170
Huntington Sea Clf	33 40 34N	118 00 53W	golf	
Huntington, Mount	37 28 11N	118 46 36W	summit	12405
Huntley	37 45 31N	120 56 46W	city/town	130
Hurd Peak	37 08 29N	118 33 55W	summit	12219
Hurlbut	38 24 46N	122 50 15W	city/town	180
Hurleton	39 29 51N	121 23 11W	city/town	1596
Huron	36 12 10N	120 06 07W	city/town	368
Hutt	34 54 28N	117 04 28W	city/town	2150
Hutton, Mount	37 07 33N	118 47 53W	summit	11998
Huxley, Mount	37 08 13N	118 40 55W	summit	13117
Hyampom	40 37 03N	123 27 05W	city/town	1285
Hyampom Airport	40 37 39N	123 28 14W	airport	1250
Hyde Park	33 58 50N	118 19 47W	city/town	160
Hyde Street Pier	37 48 33N	122 25 10W	pier	
Hydesville	40 32 52N	124 05 46W	city/town	380

California GPS Companion

Place Name	Latitude	Longitude	Type	Elev
Hydril	36 00 46N	120 05 51W	city/town	1040
Hyperion	33 55 34N	118 25 55W	city/town	40
Ibis	34 56 24N	114 47 30W	city/town	1449
Iceland	39 22 32N	120 01 30W	city/town	5400
Ickes, Mount	36 55 59N	118 26 25W	summit	12968
Idlewild (1)	41 53 55N	123 46 15W	city/town	1240
Idlewild (2)	39 06 32N	120 09 30W	city/town	6240
Idlewild (3)	35 48 39N	118 40 16W	city/town	3720
Idlewild Inn -hist	37 10 07N	121 59 39W	building	
Idria	36 25 01N	120 40 24W	city/town	2440
Idyllwild	33 44 24N	116 43 05W	city/town	5400
Igerna	41 24 06N	122 22 42W	city/town	3701
Ignacio	38 04 13N	122 32 15W	city/town	24
Igo	40 30 20N	122 32 26W	city/town	1095
Illilouette Fall	37 42 50N	119 33 39W	falls	
Ilmon	35 18 45N	118 41 35W	city/town	1006
Imhoff	36 12 52N	119 19 48W	city/town	292
Immaculate Heart C	34 06 26N	118 18 32W	univ/coll	
Imola	38 16 43N	122 16 46W	city/town	10
Imperial	32 50 51N	115 34 07W	city/town	60

Place Name	Latitude	Longitude	Type	Elev
Imperial Beach	32 35 02N	117 06 44W	city/town	20
Imperial County A.	32 50 03N	115 34 43W	airport	-56
Imperial Dam	32 53 00N	114 28 01W	dam	181
Imperial Valley C.	32 47 22N	115 33 51W	univ/coll	
Inca	33 48 03N	114 45 56W	city/town	724
Inceville	34 02 18N	118 33 16W	city/town	19
Incline	37 39 38N	119 51 06W	city/town	1550
Independence (1)	38 20 57N	120 30 45W	city/town	2622
Independence (2)	36 48 10N	118 11 57W	city/town	3936
Independence Airp.	36 48 49N	118 12 18W	airport	3900
Independence Peak	36 45 39N	118 19 53W	summit	11744
Indian Beach (1)	38 08 13N	122 53 43W	beach	
Indian Beach (2)	39 01 23N	122 43 24W	beach	
Indian Creek C C	38 48 11N	121 11 17W	golf	
Indian Falls	40 03 25N	120 57 46W	city/town	3280
Indian Falls	40 03 42N	120 57 38W	falls	3200
Indian Gulch	37 26 22N	120 11 45W	city/town	960
Indian Head Beach	36 39 55N	121 49 13W	locale	
Indian Hills Golf	33 59 07N	117 27 22W	golf	
Indian Peak	37 41 31N	118 18 44W	summit	11297
Indian Rock	36 52 07N	118 20 20W	summit	12205
Indian Springs (1)	37 03 02N	119 43 53W	city/town	520

California GPS Companion

Place Name	Latitude	Longitude	Type	Elev
Indian Springs (2)	34 19 56N	118 19 58W	city/town	1940
Indian Springs (3)	32 43 13N	116 52 48W	city/town	880
Indian Springs (4)	39 44 01N	123 22 22W	city/town	880
Indian Village	36 26 57N	116 52 24W	city/town	210
Indian Wells (1)	35 39 55N	117 52 20W	city/town	2755
Indian Wells (2)	33 43 07N	116 18 27W	city/town	100
Indian Wells Golf	33 43 15N	116 19 33W	golf	
Indianola (1)	40 48 46N	124 04 55W	city/town	40
Indianola (2)	40 41 11N	124 13 56W	city/town	40
Indio	33 43 14N	116 12 53W	city/town	-14
Indio Hills	33 49 52N	116 13 50W	city/town	12
Industry	34 01 11N	117 57 28W	city/town	329
Ingle	36 43 17N	120 15 20W	city/town	163
Inglenook	39 31 47N	123 45 28W	city/town	90
Ingleside	37 43 23N	122 27 07W	city/town	300
Inglewood	33 57 42N	118 21 08W	city/town	110
Inglewood C C	33 57 30N	118 20 17W	golf	
Ingomar	37 10 49N	120 58 02W	city/town	90
Ingot	40 43 40N	122 04 41W	city/town	1074
Ingram	38 53 25N	123 10 15W	city/town	808
Inperial Gables	33 07 39N	114 55 42W	city/town	1280
Inskip	39 59 24N	121 32 24W	city/town	4816

Place Name	Latitude	Longitude	Type	Elev
Institute of Molec	37 25 27N	122 08 27W	building	
International Aren	32 45 18N	117 12 42W	arena	
International C C	32 39 53N	115 30 39W	golf	
International Race	33 39 43N	117 44 44W	track	
Inverness	38 06 04N	122 51 21W	city/town	80
Inverness Park	38 03 50N	122 49 18W	city/town	100
Inwood	40 31 27N	121 57 22W	city/town	2046
Inyokern	35 38 49N	117 48 42W	city/town	2433
Inyokern Airport	35 39 31N	117 49 46W	airport	2455
Ione	38 21 10N	120 55 54W	city/town	298
Iowa City	39 17 30N	121 28 35W	city/town	180
Iowa Hill	39 06 31N	120 51 30W	city/town	2840
Iremel	34 55 24N	120 31 32W	city/town	139
Iris	33 11 43N	115 24 13W	city/town	77
Irish Town	39 48 45N	121 37 29W	city/town	2200
Irma	34 25 46N	119 45 09W	city/town	220
Irmulco	39 25 20N	123 30 59W	city/town	407
Iron Mountain	40 40 15N	122 31 23W	city/town	2700
Ironsides	33 48 40N	118 18 19W	city/town	65
Ironsides Museum	40 52 06N	123 31 08W	museum	
Irrigosa	36 53 28N	119 59 11W	city/town	275
Irvine	33 40 10N	117 49 20W	city/town	70

California GPS Companion

Place Name	Latitude	Longitude	Type	Elev
Irvine Coast C C	33 36 07N	117 52 50W	golf	
Irvine, Mount	36 33 17N	118 15 49W	summit	13770
Irvings Crest	32 58 47N	116 54 41W	city/town	1380
Irvington District	37 31 22N	121 58 14W	city/town	40
Irwin	37 23 49N	120 50 56W	city/town	95
Irwindale	34 06 25N	117 56 04W	city/town	467
Irwindale Raceway	34 07 33N	117 56 15W	track	
Isabella Main Dam	35 38 46N	118 28 53W	dam	2635
Isabella Marina #2	35 39 06N	118 29 00W	marina	
Ishi Pishi Falls	41 22 55N	123 29 55W	falls	
Isla Vista	34 24 48N	119 51 36W	city/town	35
Isla Vista Theater	34 24 41N	119 51 14W	building	
Island Beach	36 48 17N	121 47 13W	beach	
Island Mountain	40 01 35N	123 29 21W	city/town	520
Island Yacht Club	37 46 33N	122 14 52W	locale	
Isleton	38 09 43N	121 36 38W	city/town	5
Isosceles Peak	37 05 34N	118 32 41W	summit	12321
Italian Gardens	33 24 40N	118 22 56W	garden	
Italian Swiss Clny	36 55 52N	120 06 20W	city/town	246
Ivanhoe	36 23 14N	119 13 01W	city/town	362
Ivanpah	35 20 26N	115 18 35W	city/town	3508
Iverson Indian Rch	38 56 08N	123 40 57W	city/town	180

California GPS Companion

Place Name	Latitude	Longitude	Type	Elev
Ivesta	36 43 19N	119 38 08W	city/town	341
Ivory	36 34 07N	119 25 21W	city/town	335
Izaak Walton, Mt.	37 28 12N	118 53 17W	summit	12099

𝕁

Place Name	Latitude	Longitude	Type	Elev
J Paul Getty Mus.	34 02 42N	118 33 51W	museum	
Jacinto	39 34 52N	122 00 20W	city/town	105
Jack London Square	37 47 39N	122 16 29W	park	
Jackon London Mar.	37 47 37N	122 16 29W	marina	
Jacksnipe	38 11 34N	122 04 01W	city/town	8
Jackson	38 20 56N	120 46 23W	city/town	1240
Jackson -Westover	38 22 36N	120 47 38W	airport	1690
Jackson Falls	34 27 56N	119 03 14W	falls	2400
Jackson State For.	39 23 33N	123 38 52W	park	
Jackson Valley Vin	38 17 36N	120 56 50W	wine/vin	
Jacobs Corner	38 40 18N	121 53 36W	city/town	123
Jacumba	32 37 03N	116 11 20W	city/town	2829
Jacumba Airport	32 37 00N	116 09 53W	airport	2820
Jalama	34 29 53N	120 29 37W	city/town	120
Jamacha	32 44 30N	116 54 38W	city/town	367
Jamacha Junction	32 44 23N	116 56 33W	city/town	344
James	39 39 12N	121 32 55W	city/town	920

California GPS Companion

Place Name	Latitude	Longitude	Type	Elev
Jamesan	36 43 12N	120 12 32W	city/town	175
Jamesburg	36 22 11N	121 35 21W	city/town	1720
Jamestown	37 57 12N	120 25 18W	city/town	1406
Jamul	32 43 01N	116 52 31W	city/town	993
Janes Place	40 47 22N	123 42 56W	city/town	3000
Janesville	40 17 48N	120 31 23W	city/town	4236
Japanese Tea Gardn	37 46 11N	122 28 07W	park	
Jarvis Landing	37 31 46N	122 03 45W	city/town	10
Jasmin	35 44 34N	119 08 38W	city/town	450
Jastro	35 22 36N	119 04 17W	city/town	395
Java	34 53 15N	114 43 35W	city/town	1066
Jawbone Falls	38 00 30N	119 58 15W	falls	
Jayhawk	38 43 53N	120 57 55W	city/town	1160
Jefferson	34 01 06N	118 16 16W	city/town	200
Jefferson Park	34 01 38N	118 19 00W	city/town	145
Jellico	40 50 42N	121 17 30W	city/town	5133
Jenks Place	39 42 31N	122 50 50W	city/town	5297
Jenner	38 26 59N	123 06 52W	city/town	80
Jenny Lind	38 05 42N	120 52 08W	city/town	243
Jepson, Mount	37 05 19N	118 29 42W	summit	13390
Jerome	41 43 54N	121 59 57W	city/town	4470
Jerseydale	37 33 49N	119 51 23W	city/town	3750

California GPS Companion

Place Name	Latitude	Longitude	Type	Elev
Jesmond Dene	33 10 49N	117 06 30W	city/town	900
Jesus Maria	38 17 08N	120 38 47W	city/town	1040
Jet	37 25 58N	121 05 56W	city/town	113
Jetty Beach	36 48 35N	121 47 20W	beach	
Jewell	38 02 12N	122 44 41W	city/town	100
Jewish Community M	37 47 35N	122 23 30W	museum	
Jim Leggett Place	39 51 46N	123 25 10W	city/town	1400
Jimgrey	34 58 37N	117 28 00W	city/town	2420
Jims Camp	41 49 59N	122 35 05W	city/town	100
Jimtown	38 40 00N	122 49 07W	city/town	174
Jodar Vineyard and	38 46 11N	120 46 01W	wine/vin	
Joe Devel Peak	36 30 53N	118 17 45W	summit	13325
Joes Landing	38 46 48N	121 36 09W	city/town	20
Joesphine	39 05 39N	121 48 00W	city/town	38
Jofegan	33 18 54N	117 19 53W	city/town	100
Johannesburg	35 22 22N	117 38 02W	city/town	3536
John Little State	36 07 08N	121 37 47W	park	
John Muir Hst Site	37 59 29N	122 07 56W	locale	
John Muir Rock	37 13 05N	118 49 22W	pillar	8290
John Rains House	34 06 40N	117 36 36W	locale	
Johnny Carson Tele	34 01 23N	118 17 04W	building	
Johnson Creek Fall	41 27 34N	122 55 09W	falls	

California GPS Companion

Place Name	Latitude	Longitude	Type	Elev
Johnson Park	40 55 04N	121 37 34W	city/town	3180
Johnson Peak	36 25 11N	118 19 55W	summit	11371
Johnson, Mount	37 07 44N	118 35 06W	summit	12868
Johnsondale	35 58 29N	118 32 24W	city/town	3535
Johnsons	41 21 02N	123 52 15W	city/town	160
Johnsons Landing	33 28 07N	118 31 52W	beach	
Johnston Corner	36 55 43N	121 42 15W	city/town	70
Johnstons Corner	34 49 49N	117 10 46W	city/town	2318
Johnstonville	40 23 04N	120 35 11W	city/town	4139
Johnstown	32 50 17N	116 53 45W	city/town	600
Johnsville	39 45 39N	120 41 40W	city/town	5160
Jolon	35 58 15N	121 10 30W	city/town	960
Jonata Park	34 39 04N	120 11 00W	city/town	515
Jones Corner	36 03 57N	119 06 22W	city/town	398
Jones Place	38 50 59N	120 22 10W	city/town	4280
Jones Valley Mar.	40 44 40N	122 12 28W	marina	1070
Jonesville	40 06 45N	121 27 58W	city/town	5045
Jordan Park -sub.	37 47 05N	122 27 20W	city/town	215
Jordan peak Look.	36 10 53N	118 35 51W	overlook	9115
Jordan, Mount	36 41 00N	118 26 55W	summit	13344
Joshua	35 16 16N	115 26 55W	city/town	3984
Joshua Tree	34 08 05N	116 18 44W	city/town	2728

California GPS Companion

Place Name	Latitude	Longitude	Type	Elev
Joshua Tree Nat'l	33 55 00N	115 55 00W	park	
Joshua Tree-Hi Des	34 09 18N	116 15 08W	airport	2464
Jovista	35 47 51N	119 10 55W	city/town	405
Juan	35 21 59N	115 05 14W	city/town	4195
Juarez Old Adobe	38 17 18N	122 16 24W	locale	
Jug Handle State R	39 22 28N	123 48 15W	park	
Julian	33 04 43N	116 36 04W	city/town	4220
Julius Caesar, Mt.	37 21 24N	118 46 51W	summit	13196
Juncal Dam	34 29 32N	119 30 25W	dam	2224
Junction Camp	34 43 54N	119 58 45W	city/town	3440
Junction City	40 44 00N	123 03 09W	city/town	1475
Junction House (1)	39 19 00N	120 48 36W	city/town	4328
Junction House (2)	39 44 26N	121 17 27W	city/town	3520
Junction Peak	36 41 31N	118 21 53W	summit	13888
Junction Ranch	36 04 26N	117 30 43W	city/town	5724
June Lake	37 46 47N	119 04 28W	city/town	7640
June Lake Junction	37 48 45N	119 03 12W	city/town	7684
June Mtn Ski Area	37 45 05N	119 04 18W	ski area	10115
June Mtn Ski Lodge	37 45 57N	119 05 17W	ski area	7520
Junior Museum	37 45 52N	122 26 14W	museum	
Juniper	41 28 48N	120 34 18W	city/town	4350
Juniper Hills	34 26 39N	117 56 04W	city/town	4284

California GPS Companion

Place Name	Latitude	Longitude	Type	Elev
Juniper Serra Mus.	32 45 33N	117 11 35W	museum	
Juniper Springs	33 45 58N	117 05 00W	city/town	2120
Junipero Serra Bld	34 03 12N	118 14 45W	building	
Jupiter	38 07 21N	120 16 54W	city/town	2800
Jurupa Hills C C	33 58 34N	117 26 24W	golf	

𝕂

Place Name	Latitude	Longitude	Type	Elev
K Flourney	41 13 24N	120 31 49W	city/town	4410
Kadota	37 17 42N	120 24 40W	city/town	190
Kaiser	34 05 38N	117 29 17W	city/town	1170
Kalina	41 59 43N	121 25 09W	city/town	4045
Kanawyers	36 47 43N	118 35 02W	city/town	5035
Kandra	41 49 34N	121 23 56W	city/town	4046
Kane Spring	33 06 33N	115 50 07W	city/town	-166
Karlo	40 33 02N	120 18 52W	city/town	4434
Karly Vineyards	38 32 09N	120 49 33W	wine/vin	
Karnak	38 47 06N	121 39 16W	city/town	17
Kathryn	33 42 15N	117 45 09W	city/town	230
Kauffman	41 14 02N	120 27 59W	city/town	4430
Kaweah	36 28 11N	118 55 03W	city/town	960
Kaweah Queen	36 33 18N	118 30 31W	summit	13382
Kaweah, Mount	36 31 35N	118 28 39W	summit	13802

California GPS Companion

Place Name	Latitude	Longitude	Type	Elev
Kayandee	35 20 51N	118 59 39W	city/town	395
Kearsarge	36 48 25N	118 06 59W	city/town	3763
Kearsarge Peak	36 47 21N	118 20 47W	summit	12598
Kecks Corner	35 40 15N	120 04 51W	city/town	845
Keddie	40 00 54N	120 57 36W	city/town	3200
Keeler	36 29 14N	117 52 23W	city/town	3609
Keenbrook	34 14 58N	117 27 24W	city/town	2440
Keene	35 13 25N	118 33 41W	city/town	2600
Kegg	41 41 22N	121 59 09W	city/town	4420
Kehoe Beach	38 09 18N	122 56 52W	beach	
Keith	34 23 39N	118 57 33W	city/town	460
Keith, Mount	36 42 01N	118 20 33W	summit	13977
Kekawaka	40 05 44N	123 31 05W	city/town	440
Kelham Beach	37 59 33N	122 48 54W	beach	100
Keller Place	39 42 56N	122 54 24W	city/town	4240
Kellers Beach	37 55 15N	122 23 08W	beach	
Kelley House Mus.	39 18 19N	123 47 53W	museum	
Kellogg	38 37 56N	122 40 22W	city/town	520
Kellogg Road Beach	41 52 10N	124 12 41W	beach	
Kelly Ridge Golf	39 32 00N	121 28 23W	golf	
Kelsey	38 47 56N	120 49 11W	city/town	1925
Kelseyville	38 58 41N	122 50 18W	city/town	1386

165

California GPS Companion

Place Name	Latitude	Longitude	Type	Elev
Kelso	35 00 45N	115 39 10W	city/town	2125
Kennedy Meadow	38 18 42N	119 44 41W	city/town	6402
Kennedy Mountain	36 52 44N	118 40 03W	summit	11433
Kenneth Hahn State	34 00 31N	118 21 52W	park	
Kenny	39 55 19N	123 53 51W	city/town	1600
Kensington	37 54 38N	122 16 45W	city/town	600
Kentfield	37 57 08N	122 33 22W	city/town	80
Kenton Mill	34 38 23N	116 21 16W	city/town	1960
Kentwood-In-The-Pi	33 04 18N	116 34 29W	city/town	4280
Kenwood	38 24 50N	122 32 42W	city/town	415
Kenwood Estates	39 09 16N	121 04 03W	city/town	2200
Kenworthy Vineyard	38 31 05N	120 49 00W	wine/vin	
Keough Hot Springs	37 15 17N	118 22 34W	city/town	4200
Kephart	41 35 21N	121 18 47W	city/town	4321
Kerckhoff Dam	37 07 42N	119 31 28W	dam	971
Kerens	34 57 59N	115 48 21W	city/town	1621
Kerman	36 43 25N	120 03 32W	city/town	216
Kern City	35 21 14N	119 04 21W	city/town	384
Kern City Golf Crs	35 20 51N	119 04 05W	golf	
Kern Lake	35 08 24N	119 04 26W	city/town	281
Kern Peak	36 18 28N	118 17 12W	summit	11510
Kern River State P	35 26 12N	118 53 31W	park	

California GPS Companion .

Place Name	Latitude	Longitude	Type	Elev
Kernell	35 45 25N	119 20 35W	city/town	250
Kernville	35 45 17N	118 25 28W	city/town	2706
Kernville-Kern Vly	35 43 41N	118 25 11W	airport	2614
Kester	34 10 27N	118 25 24W	city/town	680
Keswick	40 37 21N	122 27 53W	city/town	780
Kett	40 36 26N	122 27 46W	city/town	730
Kettenpom	40 09 27N	123 27 35W	city/town	3468
Kettle Dome	36 56 53N	118 47 06W	pillar	9446
Kettle Rock	40 08 27N	120 43 29W	summit	7820
Kettleman	38 06 58N	121 14 32W	city/town	57
Kettleman City	36 00 30N	119 57 39W	city/town	234
Kettleman Station	35 59 56N	119 57 46W	city/town	290
Kevet	34 21 44N	119 02 22W	city/town	305
Keyes	37 33 24N	120 54 52W	city/town	93
Keyesville	35 37 33N	118 30 36W	city/town	2880
Keys View	33 55 38N	116 11 09W	summit	5185
Keystone (1)	37 50 07N	120 30 24W	city/town	1055
Keystone (2)	33 49 31N	118 16 46W	city/town	35
Kezar Pavilion	37 46 03N	122 27 09W	building	
Kezar Stadium	37 46 00N	122 27 19W	stadium	
Kibesillah	39 35 25N	123 46 36W	city/town	122
Kickapoo Waterfall	41 07 26N	122 48 55W	falls	

California GPS Companion

Place Name	Latitude	Longitude	Type	Elev
Kid Mountain	37 06 03N	118 25 49W	summit	11896
Kid Peak	36 52 41N	118 33 03W	summit	11458
Kiesel	38 39 47N	121 36 56W	city/town	20
Kilaga Springs	38 58 16N	121 14 49W	city/town	580
Kilkare Woods	37 37 42N	121 54 40W	city/town	840
Kilowatt	35 23 56N	119 26 47W	city/town	276
Kimball	34 15 24N	119 11 18W	city/town	130
Kincaid	34 07 43N	117 56 05W	city/town	570
King City	36 12 46N	121 07 30W	city/town	330
King City -Mesa DR	36 13 40N	121 07 18W	airport	370
King Farms	38 43 36N	121 41 25W	city/town	35
King Harbor Marina	33 50 50N	118 23 45W	marina	
King Salmon	40 44 22N	124 13 03W	city/town	13
Kings Beach	39 14 16N	120 01 32W	city/town	6280
Kings Beach State	39 14 11N	120 01 37W	park	6240
Kings Canyon Nat'l	36 57 00N	118 36 00W	park	
Kings Canyon Overl	36 43 11N	118 53 46W	overlook	
Kings Cavern Geol.	36 55 17N	118 59 20W	locale	6140
Kings County C C	36 25 20N	119 40 18W	golf	
Kings Creek Falls	40 27 34N	121 26 19W	falls	
Kingsburg	36 30 50N	119 33 11W	city/town	297
Kingsville	38 40 36N	120 52 29W	city/town	1522

California GPS Companion

Place Name	Latitude	Longitude	Type	Elev
Kingswood Estates	39 15 19N	120 03 45W	city/town	6980
Kingvale	39 19 16N	120 25 40W	city/town	6118
Kinner Falls	41 00 17N	121 53 01W	falls	
Kinyon	41 16 17N	121 53 35W	city/town	
Kirby Beach	37 49 36N	122 29 20W	beach	
Kirkville	38 54 32N	121 47 30W	city/town	35
Kirkwood (1)	39 51 19N	122 09 39W	city/town	220
Kirkwood (2)	38 42 10N	120 04 18W	city/town	7682
Kirkwood Ski Area	38 40 42N	120 02 31W	ski area	9000
Kiska	40 04 06N	122 09 34W	city/town	240
Kismet	37 02 50N	120 05 33W	city/town	275
Kister	39 49 20N	121 21 44W	city/town	4840
Kit Carson	38 40 15N	120 06 45W	city/town	7280
Kit Carson Resort	38 40 02N	120 06 29W	locale	7320
Kiva Beach	38 56 26N	120 03 00W	city/town	6240
Kiva Beach	38 56 27N	120 02 55W	beach	
Klamath	41 31 36N	124 02 14W	city/town	28
Klamath Glen	41 30 46N	123 59 34W	city/town	80
Klamath Glen -McB.	41 30 43N	123 59 44W	airport	42
Klamath River	41 51 41N	122 49 28W	city/town	1750
Klau	35 37 31N	120 53 26W	city/town	1080
Klinefelter	34 54 02N	114 45 58W	city/town	1233

California GPS Companion

Place Name	Latitude	Longitude	Type	Elev
Klondike	34 40 06N	116 00 08W	city/town	1660
Knapp Estate	41 43 50N	123 58 30W	locale	400
Kneeland	40 45 41N	123 59 37W	city/town	
Knights Ferry	37 49 11N	120 40 16W	city/town	200
Knights Foundry-hi	38 23 37N	120 47 56W	locale	
Knights Landing	38 47 59N	121 43 02W	city/town	33
Knights Landing Br	38 48 02N	121 43 01W	bridge	
Knightsen	37 58 08N	121 40 01W	city/town	25
Knob	40 23 20N	122 59 13W	city/town	3100
Knollwood Golf Crs	34 17 20N	118 29 56W	golf	
Knotts Berry Farm	33 50 33N	117 59 51W	locale	
Knowland State Arb	37 45 15N	122 07 57W	arboretum	
Knowles	37 13 12N	119 52 23W	city/town	980
Knowles Corner	38 21 09N	122 48 51W	city/town	156
Knowles Junction	37 12 10N	119 54 29W	city/town	892
Knoxville	38 49 40N	122 20 22W	city/town	1320
Koip Peak	37 48 49N	119 12 04W	summit	12979
Komandorski Vlg.	37 42 58N	121 54 28W	city/town	360
Korbel (1)	40 52 14N	123 57 26W	city/town	150
Korbel (2)	38 30 28N	122 57 48W	city/town	61
Korblex	40 54 13N	124 04 13W	city/town	40
Koreatown -subdiv.	34 03 28N	118 18 00W	city/town	190

California GPS Companion

Place Name	Latitude	Longitude	Type	Elev
Koshland Mansion	37 47 21N	122 27 17W	building	
Kramer	34 59 40N	117 35 06W	city/town	2492
Kramer Arch	34 57 04N	116 50 31W	arch	
Kramer Hills	34 55 15N	117 28 04W	city/town	2728
Kramer Junction	34 59 33N	117 32 27W	city/town	2473
Kramm	39 33 11N	121 35 01W	city/town	410
Kratka Ridge Ski A	34 21 04N	117 53 50W	ski area	6800
Kres	39 11 55N	121 00 36W	city/town	2849
Kresge Auditorium	37 25 25N	122 10 02W	building	
Krug	38 31 05N	122 28 50W	city/town	230
Kruse Rhododendron	38 35 38N	123 19 52W	park	
Kuna Peak	37 48 46N	119 12 24W	summit	13002
Kyburz	38 46 29N	120 17 45W	city/town	4047

𝕃

L A City College	34 05 12N	118 17 35W	univ/coll	
L A College Aircr.	33 56 52N	118 23 41W	univ/coll	
L A Harbor College	33 47 03N	118 16 52W	univ/coll	
L A Pacific Colleg	34 06 10N	118 10 54W	univ/coll	
L A Southwest Col.	33 55 47N	118 18 22W	univ/coll	
L A Valley J C	34 10 31N	118 25 16W	univ/coll	
La Barr Meadows	39 10 29N	121 02 39W	city/town	2479

California GPS Companion

Place Name	Latitude	Longitude	Type	Elev
La Canada C C	34 12 53N	118 11 13W	golf	
La Canada Flintrid	34 11 57N	118 11 13W	city/town	1193
La Casa De Rancho	33 50 22N	118 11 41W	building	
La Casita d Arroyo	34 08 29N	118 09 57W	building	
La Costa Beach	34 02 16N	118 38 29W	beach	
La Costa C C	33 05 30N	117 15 48W	golf	
La Crescenta	34 13 27N	118 14 21W	city/town	1720
La Cresta	32 48 40N	116 51 45W	city/town	1640
La Cresta Village	38 39 44N	121 04 55W	city/town	900
La Delta	34 38 32N	117 20 37W	city/town	2600
La Fetra	34 08 20N	117 52 50W	city/town	700
La Fresa	33 52 22N	118 20 06W	city/town	62
La Grange	37 39 49N	120 27 45W	city/town	258
La Grange Dam	37 40 20N	120 26 39W	dam	297
La Habra	33 55 55N	117 56 43W	city/town	298
La Habra Heights	33 57 39N	117 56 59W	city/town	700
La Honda	37 19 09N	122 16 23W	city/town	440
La Honda Park	38 07 14N	120 29 43W	city/town	1823
La Jolla (1)	32 50 50N	117 16 24W	city/town	100
La Jolla (2)	33 51 27N	117 52 32W	city/town	200
La Jolla Amago	33 16 58N	116 51 45W	city/town	2760
La Jolla Bay	32 51 13N	117 15 48W	bay	

California GPS Companion

Place Name	Latitude	Longitude	Type	Elev
La Jolla Beach	34 04 58N	119 02 04W	beach	
La Jolla C C	32 50 16N	117 16 03W	golf	
La Jolla Cont. Art	32 50 40N	117 16 37W	museum	
La Jolla Hermosa	32 49 05N	117 16 10W	city/town	100
La Jolla Ranch	36 43 42N	120 36 07W	city/town	342
La Jolla Shores B.	32 51 41N	117 15 16W	beach	
La Mesa	32 46 04N	117 01 20W	city/town	507
La Mirada	33 55 02N	118 00 40W	city/town	181
La Mirada County	33 54 45N	117 59 50W	golf	
La Paco	34 10 07N	118 21 27W	city/town	602
La Palma	33 50 47N	118 02 45W	city/town	44
La Paloma	33 46 51N	117 48 13W	city/town	270
La Panza	35 21 40N	120 12 52W	city/town	1880
La Patera	34 26 15N	119 50 28W	city/town	34
La Piedra State B.	34 02 19N	118 53 10W	park	
La Playa	32 42 33N	117 14 10W	beach	
La Playa	32 42 44N	117 14 40W	city/town	60
La Porte	39 40 56N	120 58 59W	city/town	4959
La Presa	32 42 29N	116 59 47W	city/town	351
La Puente	34 01 12N	117 56 55W	city/town	360
La Quinta (1)	34 19 40N	118 38 23W	city/town	1950
La Quinta (2)	33 39 48N	116 18 33W	city/town	120

California GPS Companion

Place Name	Latitude	Longitude	Type	Elev
La Rinconada C C	37 15 23N	121 58 32W	golf	
La Salle	34 38 52N	120 31 31W	city/town	47
La Selva Beach	36 56 12N	121 51 49W	city/town	76
La Sierra	33 55 15N	117 29 44W	city/town	740
La Sierra College	33 54 38N	117 29 57W	univ/coll	
La Sierra Heights	33 56 39N	117 29 08W	city/town	800
La Verne	34 06 03N	117 46 01W	city/town	1060
La Verne -Brackett	34 05 29N	117 46 54W	airport	1011
La Verne College	34 06 02N	117 46 20W	univ/coll	1046
La Vina	36 52 50N	120 06 34W	city/town	231
Lacjac	36 36 42N	119 28 59W	city/town	347
Lackey Place	35 37 56N	118 38 45W	city/town	3800
Lafayette	37 53 09N	122 07 01W	city/town	302
Lagol	34 16 10N	118 56 59W	city/town	390
Laguna	33 58 36N	118 08 20W	city/town	145
Laguna Beach	33 32 32N	117 46 56W	city/town	70
Laguna Beach C C	33 30 45N	117 44 51W	golf	
Laguna Heights	37 47 01N	122 25 34W	city/town	175
Laguna Hills	33 36 45N	117 42 43W	city/town	360
Laguna Junction	32 48 34N	116 30 42W	city/town	4085
Laguna Niguel	33 31 21N	117 42 24W	city/town	420
Laguna Point Beach	39 29 26N	123 47 45W	beach	

174

California GPS Companion

Place Name	Latitude	Longitude	Type	Elev
Laguna Seca Race T	36 35 00N	121 44 54W	track	1554
Laguna West	38 25 30N	121 28 20W	city/town	33
Lagunitas	38 00 41N	122 42 04W	city/town	240
Lagunitas C C	37 57 41N	122 34 09W	golf	
Laird Landing	41 52 23N	121 43 23W	city/town	4088
Lairds Corner	36 03 05N	119 13 52W	city/town	317
Lairds Landing	38 09 34N	122 54 41W	city/town	0
Lairport	33 55 20N	118 22 40W	city/town	95
Lake Almanor C C	40 16 11N	121 07 30W	golf	
Lake Alpine	38 28 43N	120 00 10W	city/town	7400
Lake Arrowhead	34 14 54N	117 11 18W	city/town	5191
Lake Chabot Muni.	37 44 21N	122 07 16W	golf	
Lake City (1)	39 21 31N	120 56 26W	city/town	3390
Lake City (2)	41 38 34N	120 12 57W	city/town	4559
Lake Elsinore	33 40 05N	117 19 35W	city/town	1306
Lake Forest (1)	39 11 04N	120 06 49W	city/town	6264
Lake Forest (2)	33 38 49N	117 41 18W	city/town	480
Lake Hills Estates	38 43 55N	121 05 04W	city/town	520
Lake Hughes	34 40 37N	118 26 40W	city/town	3240
Lake Isabella	35 37 05N	118 28 20W	city/town	2460
Lake Lindero C C	34 09 25N	118 47 22W	golf	
Lake Los Angeles	34 36 45N	117 49 38W	city/town	2655

California GPS Companion

Place Name	Latitude	Longitude	Type	Elev
Lake Mary	37 36 00N	119 00 01W	city/town	0
Lake Merced C C	37 41 52N	122 28 30W	golf	
Lake of the Pines	39 02 23N	121 03 20W	city/town	1520
Lake of the Woods	34 49 03N	118 59 44W	city/town	5133
Lake Oroville St.	39 33 49N	121 27 19W	park	
Lake Redding Golf	40 35 55N	122 23 50W	golf	
Lake San Marcos	33 07 34N	117 12 27W	city/town	520
Lake Shastina Golf	41 30 48N	122 22 11W	golf	
Lake Tahoe -South	38 53 37N	119 59 43W	airport	6264
Lake Tahoe Com Col	38 55 33N	119 58 15W	univ/coll	
Lake Tahoe Golf C.	38 52 14N	120 00 37W	golf	
Lake Tamarisk	33 44 20N	115 23 20W	city/town	720
Lake Valley	38 55 48N	120 00 13W	city/town	6240
Lake View Terrace	34 16 35N	118 21 37W	city/town	1160
Lake Wildwood	39 13 59N	121 11 58W	city/town	1500
Lakehead	40 54 19N	122 22 41W	city/town	1200
Lakeland Village	33 38 19N	117 20 35W	city/town	1300
Lakeport	39 02 35N	122 54 53W	city/town	1343
Lakeport -Lampson	38 59 24N	122 53 58W	airport	1378
Lakeridge Oaks	38 42 43N	121 06 30W	city/town	520
Lakeshore (1)	37 15 11N	119 10 26W	city/town	7000
Lakeshore (2)	40 52 48N	122 23 15W	city/town	1120

California GPS Companion

Place Name	Latitude	Longitude	Type	Elev
Lakeshore (3)	38 48 55N	121 06 42W	city/town	680
Lakeside	32 51 26N	116 55 17W	city/town	400
Lakeside Farms	32 52 01N	116 56 21W	city/town	390
Lakeside Golf Club	34 08 43N	118 20 48W	golf	
Lakeside Golf Crs	32 51 48N	116 56 07W	golf	
Lakeside Marina	38 57 31N	119 57 02W	marina	
Lakeside Park	34 13 41N	118 38 45W	city/town	1000
Lakeview (1)	35 05 41N	119 06 31W	city/town	374
Lakeview (2)	39 19 42N	120 15 45W	city/town	6000
Lakeview (3)	33 50 19N	117 07 02W	city/town	1450
Lakeview (4)	32 50 34N	116 54 12W	city/town	560
Lakeview (5)	34 33 27N	118 08 33W	city/town	2910
Lakeview Hot Sprgs	33 50 18N	117 08 41W	city/town	1426
Lakeview Junction	41 28 34N	120 32 12W	city/town	4363
Lakeview Resort	40 48 52N	122 17 27W	city/town	1150
Lakeville	38 11 57N	122 32 46W	city/town	9
Lakewood	33 51 13N	118 07 59W	city/town	50
Lakewood Golf Crs	33 50 15N	118 08 52W	golf	
Lakin	41 22 42N	121 33 40W	city/town	4130
Lamanda Park	34 08 53N	118 05 35W	city/town	740
Lamarck, Mount	37 11 42N	118 40 13W	summit	13417
Lamoine	40 58 41N	122 25 47W	city/town	1238

California GPS Companion

Place Name	Latitude	Longitude	Type	Elev
Lamont	35 15 35N	118 54 48W	city/town	400
Lanare	36 25 50N	119 55 48W	city/town	205
Lancaster	34 41 53N	118 08 09W	city/town	2355
Lancaster Museum	34 41 53N	118 08 11W	museum	
Lancaster-Genl Fox	34 44 27N	118 13 08W	airport	2347
Landco	35 22 46N	119 03 37W	city/town	395
Lander Crossing	39 04 09N	120 58 39W	city/town	2280
Landers	34 15 58N	116 23 32W	city/town	3083
Lane	38 00 10N	121 14 57W	city/town	34
Lane Redwood Flat	39 53 48N	123 45 04W	city/town	670
Lanfair	35 07 33N	115 10 58W	city/town	4050
Lang	34 25 54N	118 22 36W	city/town	1680
Langille Peak	37 06 03N	118 37 02W	summit	11991
Langley, Mount	36 31 24N	118 14 17W	summit	14026
LaPurisima Mission	34 40 45N	120 25 21W	park	
Larabee	40 24 22N	123 55 41W	city/town	160
Largo	39 01 18N	123 07 44W	city/town	522
Largo Vista	34 25 37N	117 45 55W	city/town	4760
Larkmead	38 33 32N	122 31 19W	city/town	300
Larkspur	37 56 03N	122 32 03W	city/town	43
Larson	37 55 46N	121 12 38W	city/town	35
Las Cantilles	34 30 27N	118 27 04W	city/town	1750

California GPS Companion

Place Name	Latitude	Longitude	Type	Elev
Las Casetas	34 12 30N	118 09 55W	city/town	0
Las Cruces	34 30 29N	120 13 41W	city/town	320
Las Flores (1)	33 17 09N	117 27 05W	city/town	80
Las Flores (2)	34 02 14N	118 38 06W	city/town	18
Las Flores (3)	40 04 19N	122 09 42W	city/town	250
Las Flores Ranch	34 02 13N	118 37 41W	beach	
Las Gallinas	38 01 14N	122 32 15W	city/town	9
Las Juntas	37 55 55N	122 03 12W	city/town	80
Las Lomas (1)	36 51 55N	121 44 02W	city/town	41
Las Lomas (2)	38 40 38N	123 08 03W	city/town	1920
Las Lomas (3)	34 08 37N	117 56 45W	city/town	590
Las Palmas	36 45 27N	119 41 58W	city/town	331
Las Posadas State	38 33 32N	122 24 28W	park	
Las Positas Golf C	37 41 55N	121 49 22W	golf	
Las Tunas Beach	34 02 22N	118 35 34W	beach	
Las Tunas State B.	34 02 21N	118 35 47W	park	
Lasco	40 25 21N	120 58 18W	city/town	5520
Lassen College	40 25 53N	120 37 53W	univ/coll	
Lassen Peak	40 29 16N	121 30 14W	summit	10457
Lassen Speedway	40 35 01N	122 19 48W	track	
Lassen Volcanic N.	40 28 52N	121 22 56W	park	
Last Chance	39 06 41N	120 37 25W	city/town	4600

California GPS Companion

Place Name	Latitude	Longitude	Type	Elev
Last Chance Mount	37 16 49N	117 41 55W	summit	8456
Lathrop	37 49 22N	121 16 32W	city/town	22
Laton	36 26 00N	119 41 09W	city/town	255
Latrobe	38 33 35N	120 58 58W	city/town	780
Laughlin	39 16 47N	123 14 00W	city/town	863
Laurel (1)	37 07 00N	121 57 55W	city/town	900
Laurel (2)	37 31 55N	122 18 24W	city/town	75
Laurel Beach	39 07 19N	122 51 06W	beach	
Laurel Mountain	37 34 50N	118 53 30W	summit	11812
Lauro Dam	34 27 14N	119 43 33W	dam	549
Lava Beds National	41 45 12N	121 30 20W	park	
Lavic	34 43 40N	116 18 45W	city/town	2173
Lawndale (1)	38 25 17N	122 34 09W	city/town	431
Lawndale (2)	33 53 14N	118 21 06W	city/town	55
Lawrence	37 22 12N	121 59 41W	city/town	60
Lawrence Berkeley	37 52 39N	122 14 59W	locale	
Laws	37 24 03N	118 20 41W	city/town	4113
Lawson Peak	36 33 40N	118 30 50W	summit	13140
Laytonville	39 41 18N	123 28 54W	city/town	1650
Le Conte Falls	37 55 24N	119 27 05W	falls	
Le Conte, Mount	36 32 27N	118 15 04W	summit	13960
Le Grand	37 13 43N	120 14 50W	city/town	253

California GPS Companion

Place Name	Latitude	Longitude	Type	Elev
Leadfield	36 50 48N	117 03 30W	city/town	4040
Leaf	41 38 32N	122 00 03W	city/town	4681
Leavitt	40 23 46N	120 31 30W	city/town	4108
Leavitt Falls	38 19 10N	119 33 43W	falls	
Leavitt Peak	38 17 11N	119 39 00W	summit	11569
Lebec	34 50 30N	118 51 50W	city/town	3570
Leduc Acres	39 11 33N	121 01 02W	city/town	2700
Lee Vining	37 57 27N	119 07 15W	city/town	6781
Lee Vining Airport	37 57 29N	119 06 23W	airport	6802
Lee Vining Peak	37 58 20N	119 11 53W	summit	11691
Leesdale	34 11 48N	119 05 56W	city/town	
Leesville	39 11 22N	122 25 21W	city/town	1430
Leffingwell	33 56 00N	117 59 32W	city/town	240
Leggett	39 51 57N	123 42 47W	city/town	952
Lehamite Falls	37 45 45N	119 34 40W	falls	
Leimert Park -sub.	34 00 25N	118 19 50W	city/town	120
Leisure Town	38 21 58N	121 56 37W	city/town	97
Leisure World Golf	33 36 47N	117 43 42W	golf	
LeMoine House	38 26 26N	120 51 10W	building	
Lemon Grove	32 44 33N	117 01 50W	city/town	440
Lemon Heights	33 45 32N	117 46 52W	city/town	500
Lemona	33 58 49N	117 19 30W	city/town	1100

California GPS Companion

Place Name	Latitude	Longitude	Type	Elev
Lemoncove	36 22 58N	119 01 25W	city/town	518
Lemoore	36 18 03N	119 46 55W	city/town	225
Lemoore Naval Air	36 19 58N	119 57 07W	military	234
Lennox	33 56 17N	118 21 06W	city/town	71
Lento	34 28 22N	120 09 34W	city/town	85
Lenwood	34 52 36N	117 06 11W	city/town	2260
Leo Carrillo State	34 02 39N	118 56 18W	park	
Leon	34 33 29N	117 18 20W	city/town	2683
Leona Valley	34 37 06N	118 17 14W	city/town	3133
Leonard	41 08 05N	121 01 47W	city/town	4180
Leonardi	38 52 55N	120 32 07W	city/town	4660
Lerdo	35 29 25N	119 09 06W	city/town	412
Lerona	37 07 46N	119 25 49W	city/town	2800
Lester Beach	39 00 02N	120 06 00W	beach	
Leucadia	33 04 05N	117 18 09W	city/town	54
Levis	36 37 25N	120 24 19W	city/town	208
Lew Galbraith Golf	37 43 08N	122 11 43W	golf	
Lewis, Mount	37 50 30N	119 11 23W	summit	12296
Lewiston	40 42 27N	122 48 23W	city/town	1826
Lexington Dam	37 12 05N	121 59 17W	dam	660
Liberty	38 17 04N	122 42 03W	city/town	70
Lick	37 17 14N	121 50 41W	city/town	160

California GPS Companion

Place Name	Latitude	Longitude	Type	Elev
Lick Mountain	41 59 09N	123 08 20W	summit	4423
Lido Isle	33 36 14N	117 54 59W	city/town	10
Lido Peninsula	33 36 45N	117 55 29W	cape	11
Likely	41 13 50N	120 30 11W	city/town	4447
Lilac	33 17 16N	117 04 59W	city/town	730
Limantour Beach	38 01 42N	122 53 51W	beach	
Limon	34 19 14N	119 06 25W	city/town	211
Limoneira	34 19 49N	119 07 29W	city/town	280
Lincoln	38 53 30N	121 17 31W	city/town	164
Lincoln Acres	32 40 04N	117 04 19W	city/town	100
Lincoln Beach	36 57 38N	121 59 37W	beach	
Lincoln Crest	34 35 13N	118 18 14W	city/town	3619
Lincoln Heights	34 04 14N	118 12 15W	city/town	400
Lincoln Municipal	38 54 32N	121 21 04W	airport	119
Lincoln Park Muni.	37 47 00N	122 29 40W	golf	
Lincoln Village -1	38 00 19N	121 19 38W	city/town	10
Lincoln Village -2	33 49 40N	118 13 19W	city/town	27
Linda	39 07 40N	121 32 59W	city/town	65
Linda Falls	38 33 21N	122 26 28W	falls	
Linda Rose	33 31 45N	117 10 28W	city/town	1040
Linda Vista (1)	32 47 00N	117 10 14W	city/town	350
Linda Vista (2)	34 10 17N	118 10 34W	city/town	1000

California GPS Companion

Place Name	Latitude	Longitude	Type	Elev
Lindale Greens C C	38 28 46N	121 25 01W	golf	
Lindcove	36 21 28N	119 03 49W	city/town	460
Linden	38 01 17N	121 04 58W	city/town	87
Lindsay	36 12 11N	119 05 14W	city/town	383
Lindsay Museum	37 55 25N	122 04 26W	museum	
Lingard	37 14 25N	120 23 47W	city/town	187
Linne	35 34 21N	120 34 05W	city/town	1070
Linnie	35 49 59N	117 51 58W	city/town	2580
Lion Slide Falls	40 52 21N	121 53 31W	falls	
Lion Wash Falls	40 52 18N	121 53 05W	falls	
Lippincott Mount	36 31 16N	118 33 43W	summit	12260
Lira	39 08 43N	121 52 00W	city/town	40
Liskey	41 50 56N	121 24 32W	city/town	4035
Lisko	36 05 49N	119 02 11W	city/town	430
List	36 16 34N	119 07 37W	city/town	377
Litchfield	40 22 58N	120 23 10W	city/town	4068
Little Corona Del	33 35 25N	117 52 07W	beach	
Little Golden Gate	40 27 40N	123 50 25W	bridge	
Little Italy -sub.	37 48 03N	122 24 35W	city/town	75
Little Lake	35 56 12N	117 54 21W	city/town	3140
Little Morongo Hts	34 05 44N	116 31 09W	city/town	2840
Little Nellie Fall	37 43 13N	119 47 00W	falls	

California GPS Companion

Place Name	Latitude	Longitude	Type	Elev
Little Norway	38 49 29N	120 02 08W	city/town	7208
Little Osaka	37 47 09N	122 25 44W	city/town	150
Little Penny	38 55 22N	123 27 24W	city/town	900
Little River	39 16 15N	123 47 14W	city/town	80
Little River Airp.	39 15 43N	123 45 13W	airport	572
Little River Golf	39 16 20N	123 46 40W	golf	
Little River State	41 00 59N	124 06 31W	beach	
Little Shasta	41 42 43N	122 23 25W	city/town	2705
Little Tokyo -sub.	34 02 52N	118 14 25W	city/town	265
Little Valley	40 53 40N	121 10 35W	city/town	4183
Littlerock	34 31 16N	117 58 58W	city/town	2830
Live Oak (1)	39 16 33N	121 39 32W	city/town	75
Live Oak (2)	38 29 03N	121 04 23W	city/town	185
Live Oak Acres	34 24 25N	119 18 27W	city/town	420
Live Oak Springs	32 41 26N	116 20 01W	city/town	3880
Livermore	37 40 55N	121 46 01W	city/town	486
Livermore Municip.	37 41 36N	121 49 13W	airport	397
Livermore N A S	37 41 07N	121 42 23W	military	
Livermore Valley C	37 38 44N	121 46 31W	wine/vin	
Livermore Valley S	37 40 06N	121 45 31W	stadium	
Livermore Yacht Cl	37 48 42N	121 33 29W	locale	
Livingston	37 23 13N	120 43 21W	city/town	133

California GPS Companion

Place Name	Latitude	Longitude	Type	Elev
Llanada	36 36 33N	120 54 56W	city/town	1420
Llano	38 24 43N	122 47 36W	city/town	78
Llano Race Track	34 29 35N	117 46 38W	track	
Llewellyn Falls	38 27 38N	119 36 15W	falls	
Lobitos	37 22 59N	122 23 57W	city/town	165
Locans	36 43 25N	119 39 44W	city/town	329
Loch Lomond	38 51 48N	122 43 06W	city/town	2800
Locke	38 15 02N	121 30 30W	city/town	5
Lockeford	38 09 49N	121 08 56W	city/town	104
Lockhart	35 00 53N	117 19 48W	city/town	2060
Lockwood	35 56 12N	121 04 50W	city/town	980
Lodi	38 07 49N	121 16 17W	city/town	51
Lodi -Kingdon Aprk	38 05 29N	121 21 33W	airport	15
Lodi Airpark -Prec	38 05 02N	121 18 58W	airport	25
Lodi Airport	38 12 08N	121 16 09W	airport	58
Lodi Junction	38 07 42N	121 14 32W	city/town	62
Lodoga	39 18 07N	122 29 17W	city/town	1250
Logan (1)	41 45 37N	122 26 18W	city/town	2749
Logan (2)	36 54 25N	121 37 50W	city/town	230
Logan Heights -sub	32 41 57N	117 07 43W	city/town	70
Logandale	39 26 14N	122 11 27W	city/town	102
Loganville	39 34 05N	120 39 58W	city/town	3909

California GPS Companion

Place Name	Latitude	Longitude	Type	Elev
Loghry State Park	37 14 56N	122 06 40W	park	
Lois	36 01 07N	119 01 36W	city/town	479
Lokern	35 24 00N	119 32 42W	city/town	275
Lokoya	38 22 24N	122 25 36W	city/town	1700
Loleta	40 38 28N	124 13 27W	city/town	20
Loma	36 15 28N	119 17 11W	city/town	319
Loma Linda	34 02 54N	117 15 37W	city/town	1160
Loma Linda Univ.	34 03 09N	117 15 48W	univ/coll	
Loma Mar	37 16 16N	122 18 27W	city/town	320
Loma Portal	32 44 38N	117 13 05W	city/town	40
Loma Rica	39 18 43N	121 25 00W	city/town	401
Lombard	38 11 27N	122 15 18W	city/town	57
Lombardi	38 26 46N	120 03 55W	city/town	6920
Lomita	33 47 32N	118 18 51W	city/town	90
Lomita Park	37 37 00N	122 24 12W	city/town	25
Lomita Railroad M.	33 47 55N	118 19 02W	museum	
Lomo (1)	39 13 15N	121 38 26W	city/town	66
Lomo (2)	40 02 19N	121 36 54W	city/town	3797
Lompico	37 06 20N	122 03 06W	city/town	800
Lompoc	34 38 21N	120 27 25W	city/town	104
Lompoc Airport	34 39 56N	120 28 00W	airport	87
London	36 28 34N	119 26 32W	city/town	295

California GPS Companion

Place Name	Latitude	Longitude	Type	Elev
Lone Hill Manor M.	34 05 50N	117 49 51W	city/town	790
Lone Pine	36 36 22N	118 03 43W	city/town	3733
Lone Pine Airport	36 35 17N	118 03 07W	airport	3680
Lone Pine Peak	36 33 42N	118 13 27W	summit	12944
Lone Star (1)	39 42 34N	122 48 29W	city/town	5300
Lone Star (2)	36 42 02N	119 40 49W	city/town	317
Lone Star Junction	40 37 58N	123 52 34W	city/town	2157
Lone Tree Golf Crs	37 58 14N	121 48 23W	golf	
Lone Tree Point	38 02 13N	122 16 23W	cape	
Lone Wolf Colony	34 28 14N	117 09 18W	city/town	2993
Long Barn	38 05 35N	120 08 00W	city/town	4963
Long Beach	33 46 01N	118 11 18W	city/town	29
Long Beach Airport	33 49 03N	118 09 05W	airport	57
Long Beach Arena	33 45 50N	118 11 15W	arena	
Long Beach City C.	33 50 07N	118 08 08W	univ/coll	43
Long Beach Conv. C	33 45 53N	118 11 18W	building	
Long Beach Marina	33 45 10N	118 06 37W	marina	
Long Beach Museum	33 45 48N	118 09 50W	museum	
Long Beach Yacht C	33 45 11N	118 06 46W	locale	
Long Bell State Ga	41 27 07N	121 21 59W	park	
Long Mountain	37 40 07N	119 17 42W	summit	11502
Longvale	39 33 19N	123 25 43W	city/town	1180

California GPS Companion

Place Name	Latitude	Longitude	Type	Elev
Longview	34 29 37N	117 53 45W	city/town	3228
Longville	40 08 52N	121 14 37W	city/town	4361
Lonoak	36 16 39N	120 56 31W	city/town	880
Lonoke	37 01 33N	121 34 37W	city/town	205
Lonsmith	35 20 25N	118 55 21W	city/town	420
Lookout	41 12 29N	121 09 15W	city/town	4160
Lookout Junction	41 15 31N	121 14 01W	city/town	4240
Loomis	38 49 17N	121 11 31W	city/town	399
Loomis Corners	40 35 18N	122 18 17W	city/town	550
Loon Point	34 24 46N	119 34 31W	cape	
Loope	38 39 55N	119 41 42W	city/town	6160
Lopez Dam	35 11 22N	120 29 18W	dam	520
Lopez Point	36 01 14N	121 33 59W	cape	
Loraine	35 18 17N	118 26 09W	city/town	2665
Loren Miller Homes	37 46 22N	122 26 11W	city/town	200
Lorenzo Beach	33 28 25N	118 33 56W	beach	
Lorenzo Station	37 41 33N	122 07 44W	city/town	34
Loretta Falls	41 59 36N	123 32 05W	falls	
Lort	36 20 34N	119 09 12W	city/town	388
Los Alamitos	33 48 11N	118 04 18W	city/town	22
Los Alamitos Army	33 47 24N	118 03 07W	military	35
Los Alamitos Jct.	33 48 21N	117 59 54W	city/town	65

California GPS Companion

Place Name	Latitude	Longitude	Type	Elev
Los Alamitos Racet	33 48 27N	118 02 36W	track	
Los Alamos	34 44 40N	120 16 38W	city/town	575
Los Altos (1)	37 23 07N	122 06 47W	city/town	165
Los Altos (2)	33 47 38N	118 07 28W	city/town	14
Los Altos C C	37 21 02N	122 05 45W	golf	
Los Altos Hills	37 22 47N	122 08 11W	city/town	240
Los Amigos Golf C.	33 56 10N	118 09 36W	golf	
Los Angelas -Whit.	34 15 35N	118 24 48W	airport	1002
Los Angeles C C	34 04 10N	118 25 20W	golf	
Los Angeles Childr	34 03 16N	118 14 23W	museum	
Los Angeles Civic	34 03 25N	118 14 43W	building	
Los Angeles Colis.	34 00 50N	118 17 12W	stadium	
Los Angeles Conven	34 02 36N	118 16 08W	building	
Los Angeles Int'l	33 56 33N	118 24 29W	airport	126
Los Angeles Marit.	33 44 20N	118 16 40W	museum	
Los Angeles Swim S	34 00 44N	118 17 18W	stadium	
Los Angeles Tennis	34 04 12N	118 26 50W	building	
Los Angeles Zoo	34 08 51N	118 17 21W	park	
Los Angeles, City	34 03 08N	118 14 34W	city/town	330
Los Banos	37 03 30N	120 50 56W	city/town	120
Los Banos -Seaplan	37 03 29N	121 07 33W	airport	544
Los Banos Municip.	37 03 46N	120 52 09W	airport	119

California GPS Companion

Place Name	Latitude	Longitude	Type	Elev
Los Berros	35 04 44N	120 32 30W	city/town	216
Los Coyotes C C	33 53 23N	117 58 43W	golf	
Los Encinos State	34 09 38N	118 29 55W	park	
Los Gatos	37 13 36N	121 58 25W	city/town	390
Los Guilicos	38 25 36N	122 34 50W	city/town	460
Los Medanos	38 00 44N	121 51 01W	city/town	39
Los Medanos Colleg	38 00 19N	121 51 38W	univ/coll	
Los Molinos	40 01 17N	122 05 57W	city/town	220
Los Nietos	33 58 06N	118 04 11W	city/town	154
Los Nietos Jct.	33 57 41N	118 04 10W	city/town	150
Los Olivos	34 40 04N	120 06 50W	city/town	825
Los Osos	35 18 40N	120 49 53W	city/town	126
Los Padres Dam	36 23 09N	121 40 02W	dam	1040
Los Posas C C	34 15 02N	119 04 15W	golf	
Los Robles Greens	34 10 31N	118 52 40W	golf	
Los Serranos	33 58 22N	117 42 26W	city/town	620
Los Serranos C C	33 58 10N	117 42 00W	golf	
Los Terrentos	32 50 05N	116 37 16W	city/town	3299
Los Trancos Woods	37 20 58N	122 11 54W	city/town	1000
Los Tules	33 17 00N	116 37 13W	city/town	3400
Los Verdes Golf C.	33 45 15N	118 23 59W	golf	
Lost Arrow	37 45 23N	119 35 35W	pillar	6410

California GPS Companion

Place Name	Latitude	Longitude	Type	Elev
Lost City	38 05 12N	120 44 55W	city/town	1060
Lost Hills	35 36 59N	119 41 36W	city/town	300
Lost Hills Airport	35 37 24N	119 41 10W	airport	274
Lost Palms Trail	33 43 14N	115 46 40W	locale	
Lotus	38 48 06N	120 54 27W	city/town	720
Lovdal	38 36 01N	121 33 05W	city/town	35
Lovelock	39 53 29N	121 34 36W	city/town	3140
Lovers Point	36 37 36N	121 54 52W	cape	
Loves Falls	39 34 51N	120 36 22W	falls	
Lowell	38 10 27N	122 15 08W	city/town	45
Lower Deer Creek F	40 10 06N	121 34 51W	falls	3020
Lower Forni	38 48 11N	120 13 41W	city/town	6920
Lower Lake	38 54 38N	122 36 33W	city/town	1372
Lower Rainbow Fall	37 35 40N	119 05 17W	falls	
Lower Town	38 22 03N	119 07 08W	city/town	7640
Lower Yosemite Fls	37 45 05N	119 35 44W	falls	
Lowes Corner	36 05 40N	119 13 52W	city/town	313
Lowrey	40 00 50N	122 33 08W	city/town	825
Loyalton	39 40 35N	120 14 24W	city/town	4936
Loyola Corners	37 21 08N	122 05 06W	city/town	235
Loyola Univ. (1)	34 02 57N	118 16 13W	univ/coll	
Loyola Univ. (2)	33 58 15N	118 24 57W	univ/coll	

California GPS Companion

Place Name	Latitude	Longitude	Type	Elev
Lucca	36 14 43N	119 05 20W	city/town	360
Lucerne (1)	39 05 25N	122 47 43W	city/town	1332
Lucerne (2)	36 22 51N	119 39 48W	city/town	256
Lucerne Valley	34 26 38N	116 58 01W	city/town	2946
Lucia	36 01 15N	121 32 58W	city/town	400
Luckie Place	40 34 25N	123 12 25W	city/town	2788
Ludlow	34 43 16N	116 09 33W	city/town	1775
Lugo	34 22 02N	117 20 29W	city/town	3430
Lumer	36 02 15N	118 59 25W	city/town	499
Lumpkin	39 36 36N	121 12 28W	city/town	3585
Lund	38 19 50N	121 38 34W	city/town	25
Lundy	38 01 39N	119 14 26W	city/town	7840
Luther Burbank Gar	38 26 09N	122 42 40W	park	
Luzon	38 00 52N	122 15 01W	city/town	80
Lyell, Mount	37 44 22N	119 16 14W	summit	13114
Lyman Springs	40 18 34N	121 46 00W	city/town	3440
Lynwood	33 55 49N	118 12 38W	city/town	86
Lynwood Gardens	33 54 37N	118 11 28W	city/town	76
Lynwood Hills	32 38 43N	117 03 03W	city/town	260
Lyonsville	40 18 34N	121 44 13W	city/town	3780
Lyoth	37 42 57N	121 22 50W	city/town	77
Lytle Creek	34 15 33N	117 29 57W	city/town	3400

Place Name	Latitude	Longitude	Type	Elev
Lytton	38 39 34N	122 52 14W	city/town	185

M

Place Name	Latitude	Longitude	Type	Elev
Mabie	39 47 37N	120 31 13W	city/town	4820
Macabee Beach	36 36 57N	121 53 54W	beach	
Macdoel	41 49 37N	122 00 15W	city/town	4264
Mace Meadows Golf	38 27 13N	120 32 00W	golf	
Mackenson	38 06 58N	121 40 49W	city/town	9
MacKerricher State	39 29 36N	123 47 33W	park	
Maclure, Mount	37 44 37N	119 16 47W	summit	12880
Macomber Palms	33 47 55N	116 15 16W	city/town	460
Madeline	41 03 04N	120 28 28W	city/town	5314
Madera	36 57 41N	120 03 35W	city/town	275
Madera Country Clb	37 01 46N	120 04 08W	golf	
Madera Municipal	36 59 08N	120 06 43W	airport	253
Madison	38 40 46N	121 58 02W	city/town	151
Madrone	37 09 02N	121 40 14W	city/town	370
Madrone Soda Sprgs	37 09 57N	121 30 44W	city/town	1520
Magalia	39 48 44N	121 34 38W	city/town	2400
Magnolia	36 01 22N	118 59 39W	city/town	507
Magnolia Avenue	33 57 26N	117 25 03W	city/town	780
Magnolia Park	34 10 04N	118 20 47W	city/town	590

California GPS Companion

Place Name	Latitude	Longitude	Type	Elev
Magra	39 08 57N	120 53 44W	city/town	2880
Magunden	35 21 54N	118 56 02W	city/town	425
Mahogany Peak	40 32 48N	120 44 07W	summit	7194
Mahou Riviera	34 00 48N	118 48 20W	city/town	235
Maidenhair Falls	33 14 12N	116 26 19W	falls	
Main Beach	33 32 30N	117 47 02W	beach	
Maine Prairie	38 18 29N	121 45 28W	city/town	11
Majors	36 58 57N	122 08 32W	city/town	108
Malaga	36 41 01N	119 43 58W	city/town	297
Malakoff Digging S	39 22 26N	120 54 49W	park	4280
Malby Crossing	38 36 48N	121 04 12W	city/town	460
Malcolm X Square	37 46 52N	122 25 43W	city/town	110
Malibu	34 00 18N	118 48 33W	city/town	112
Malibu Beach	34 01 55N	118 41 15W	beach	
Malibu Beach	34 01 58N	118 41 15W	city/town	13
Malibu Bluff State	34 01 57N	118 42 19W	park	
Malibu Bowl	34 03 40N	118 44 22W	city/town	1250
Malibu Creek State	34 06 12N	118 43 59W	park	
Malibu Hills	34 02 51N	118 44 36W	city/town	1000
Malibu Junction	34 08 36N	118 45 22W	city/town	854
Malibu Lagoon Mus.	34 02 04N	118 40 43W	museum	
Malibu Lagoon St.	34 02 00N	118 40 42W	park	

California GPS Companion

Place Name	Latitude	Longitude	Type	Elev
Malibu Mar Vista	34 03 42N	118 45 51W	city/town	1825
Malibu Pier	34 02 10N	118 40 30W	pier	
Malibu Point	34 01 52N	118 40 53W	cape	
Malibu Vista	34 02 52N	118 46 24W	city/town	1000
Malibu West	34 02 14N	118 50 29W	city/town	50
Mallethead Rock	41 28 47N	122 37 22W	pillar	5286
Mallory, Mount	36 32 54N	118 15 44W	summit	13850
Maltby	38 00 54N	122 04 09W	city/town	5
Maltha	35 25 17N	118 59 47W	city/town	450
Mammoth	41 43 50N	121 21 14W	city/town	4201
Mammoth Lakes	37 38 55N	118 58 16W	city/town	7920
Mammoth Lakes Airp	37 37 26N	118 50 19W	airport	7128
Mammoth Mountain	37 37 51N	119 01 54W	summit	11053
Mammoth Mountain S	37 39 02N	119 02 11W	ski area	
Mammoth Peak	37 51 19N	119 15 45W	summit	12117
Mammoth Rock	37 36 54N	118 59 26W	pillar	9110
Mammoth Visitor Ce	37 38 52N	118 57 29W	building	
Manchester	38 58 13N	123 41 13W	city/town	110
Mandalay Beach	34 11 46N	119 14 47W	beach	
Manhattan Beach	33 53 05N	118 24 36W	city/town	100
Manhattan Beach	37 25 51N	122 26 20W	beach	
Manhattan Beach St	33 53 15N	118 24 50W	park	

California GPS Companion

Place Name	Latitude	Longitude	Type	Elev
Manila	40 51 07N	124 09 40W	city/town	12
Manix	34 58 55N	116 35 36W	city/town	1763
Mankas Corner	38 17 11N	122 06 21W	city/town	120
Manlove	38 33 15N	121 22 16W	city/town	45
Mann Laboratory	38 32 30N	121 45 16W	building	
Manolith	35 07 14N	118 22 19W	city/town	3920
Manor	37 59 27N	122 35 23W	city/town	160
Manresa State Bch.	36 55 27N	121 51 20W	park	
Manteca	37 47 51N	121 12 54W	city/town	38
Manteca Junction	37 51 49N	121 13 40W	city/town	25
Manton	40 26 07N	121 52 08W	city/town	1997
Manuel Mill	38 15 40N	120 21 36W	city/town	3760
Manzana	38 26 42N	122 52 15W	city/town	120
Manzanar	36 44 24N	118 04 47W	city/town	3720
Manzanita (1)	32 40 08N	116 17 20W	city/town	3508
Manzanita (2)	37 52 54N	122 30 59W	city/town	8
Manzanita Acres	38 44 17N	121 02 58W	city/town	820
Manzanita Lake	40 32 08N	121 33 35W	city/town	5880
Maple Creek	40 45 45N	123 52 05W	city/town	412
Maple Falls	41 38 41N	123 10 45W	falls	
Maple Grove	40 28 09N	123 49 57W	city/town	520
Mar Vista	34 00 17N	118 25 48W	city/town	69

California GPS Companion

Place Name	Latitude	Longitude	Type	Elev
Mar Vista Gardens	33 59 35N	118 24 38W	park	
Marble Falls	36 33 22N	118 47 28W	falls	
Marble Mountain	38 38 58N	121 01 58W	city/town	1130
Marble Place	39 27 30N	123 34 17W	city/town	1600
Marcel	35 11 25N	118 30 59W	city/town	3240
March Air Force B.	33 52 50N	117 15 34W	military	1533
March Field	33 54 00N	117 15 15W	city/town	1528
Marchant	38 49 23N	121 40 44W	city/town	20
Marconi	38 08 38N	122 52 38W	city/town	80
Marcus Garvey Sq.	37 46 53N	122 26 02W	city/town	120
Mare Island	38 05 44N	122 16 17W	island	
Maredith Mill	39 38 23N	120 52 52W	city/town	5260
Margarita Peak	33 26 39N	117 23 22W	summit	3189
Marian Place	40 18 36N	121 49 13W	city/town	2580
Maricopa	35 03 32N	119 24 00W	city/town	854
Mariemont	38 42 53N	120 56 20W	city/town	1160
Marigold	34 04 40N	117 14 26W	city/town	1103
Marin City	37 52 07N	122 30 29W	city/town	200
Marin County Civic	37 59 50N	122 31 42W	building	
Marin Headlands St	37 49 31N	122 30 23W	park	
Marin Junior Col.	37 57 21N	122 32 50W	univ/coll	
Marina	36 41 04N	121 48 04W	city/town	60

California GPS Companion

Place Name	Latitude	Longitude	Type	Elev
Marina District	37 48 11N	122 26 11W	city/town	20
Marina Golf Course	37 41 52N	122 11 11W	golf	
Marina Pacifica	33 45 37N	118 06 55W	marina	
Marina State Park	36 41 29N	121 48 28W	park	
Marina Village	38 42 55N	121 05 18W	city/town	700
Marine Street Bch.	32 50 13N	117 16 50W	beach	
Marine World	37 31 53N	122 15 50W	park	
Marinwood	38 02 18N	122 32 12W	city/town	30
Marion Peak	36 57 24N	118 31 19W	summit	12719
Mariposa	37 29 06N	119 57 55W	city/town	1950
Maritime Museum	32 43 10N	117 10 23W	museum	
Mark Edson Dam	38 54 14N	120 36 11W	dam	4242
Mark West Springs	38 32 57N	122 43 09W	city/town	439
Marklee Village	38 41 23N	119 47 50W	city/town	5840
Markleeville	38 41 42N	119 46 45W	city/town	5501
Markleeville -Alp.	38 44 09N	119 45 58W	airport	5867
Marks Place	39 42 12N	123 09 24W	city/town	1700
Marlboro	33 48 45N	117 51 29W	city/town	180
Marne	34 00 20N	117 54 20W	city/town	404
Mars	35 25 30N	116 53 20W	city/town	3280
Marsh Creek Spring	37 53 34N	121 51 10W	city/town	600
Marsh Mill	39 26 40N	120 42 09W	city/town	5840

California GPS Companion

Place Name	Latitude	Longitude	Type	Elev
Marshall	38 09 38N	122 53 35W	city/town	10
Marshall Beach	38 09 45N	122 54 49W	beach	
Marshall Canyon	34 08 53N	117 44 53W	golf	
Marshall Gold Disc	38 48 02N	120 53 28W	museum	
Marshall Junction	37 00 50N	119 34 05W	city/town	1225
Martell	38 22 01N	120 47 42W	city/town	1490
Martin Luther King	37 46 50N	122 26 02W	city/town	120
Martinez (1)	38 01 10N	122 07 59W	city/town	23
Martinez (2)	38 01 24N	120 22 43W	city/town	2160
Martinez (3)	33 33 46N	116 09 08W	city/town	-135
Martinez Historic.	38 01 10N	122 08 03W	museum	
Martinez Place	35 17 17N	120 09 54W	city/town	1940
Martinez Yacht Har	38 01 38N	122 08 10W	locale	
Martins	34 33 58N	118 39 32W	city/town	2700
Martins Beach	37 22 30N	122 24 25W	city/town	40
Martinus Corner	35 56 24N	121 07 05W	city/town	939
Mary Aaron Memor.	39 08 34N	121 35 19W	building	
Mary Austin, Mount	36 48 57N	118 21 43W	summit	13048
Mary Ellen Place	40 07 12N	122 37 52W	city/town	1580
Marymount College	33 44 41N	118 23 50W	univ/coll	
Marysville	39 08 45N	121 35 25W	city/town	63
Marysville Munic.	39 02 12N	121 33 50W	golf	

California GPS Companion

Place Name	Latitude	Longitude	Type	Elev
Marysville Yuba C.	39 05 51N	121 34 11W	airport	62
Mascorini Place	36 21 22N	121 31 22W	city/town	2380
Massack	39 55 34N	120 50 12W	city/town	3640
Massacre Natural B	40 29 43N	123 06 04W	arch	
Matchin	36 19 31N	119 07 45W	city/town	407
Mateo Coast State	37 28 40N	122 26 54W	beach	
Mather	37 52 56N	119 51 17W	city/town	4522
Mather A F B	38 33 19N	121 17 49W	military	96
Mather Field	38 34 00N	121 17 45W	city/town	90
Matheson	40 39 47N	122 27 36W	city/town	600
Mathews Mill	37 07 24N	119 22 19W	city/town	3100
Mathias Botanical	34 03 55N	118 26 55W	park	
Matilija	34 26 27N	119 15 36W	city/town	755
Matilija Dam	34 29 05N	119 18 31W	dam	1125
Matilija Springs	34 29 00N	119 18 16W	city/town	959
Mattei	36 42 01N	119 41 27W	city/town	311
Matterhorn Peak	38 05 34N	119 22 49W	summit	12264
Mattole Beach	40 17 21N	124 21 22W	beach	
Mattos	37 32 46N	122 00 59W	city/town	38
Maxson	34 04 34N	118 00 25W	city/town	313
Maxwell	39 16 35N	122 11 25W	city/town	91
May	33 53 42N	117 29 24W	city/town	695

California GPS Companion

Place Name	Latitude	Longitude	Type	Elev
Mayaro	39 49 27N	121 25 16W	city/town	1960
Mayfair	35 20 11N	118 54 48W	city/town	432
Mayfield -subdiv.	37 25 35N	122 08 28W	city/town	29
Mayhew	38 33 55N	121 20 59W	city/town	56
Maywood	33 59 12N	118 11 04W	city/town	155
McAdie, Mount	36 33 02N	118 16 33W	summit	13796
McArthur (1)	41 19 54N	120 32 11W	city/town	4370
McArthur (2)	41 03 01N	121 23 53W	city/town	3311
McAvoy	38 02 19N	121 57 33W	city/town	16
McAvoy Boat Harbor	38 02 28N	121 57 23W	locale	
McCampbell	33 58 17N	118 06 45W	city/town	145
McCann	40 19 25N	123 50 06W	city/town	200
McCann Stadium	38 53 26N	121 04 18W	stadium	
McCartney Place	40 10 27N	122 33 38W	city/town	825
McClellan A F B	38 40 03N	121 24 01W	military	75
McClellan Place	40 29 14N	123 25 08W	city/town	1760
McCloud	41 15 21N	122 08 18W	city/town	3254
McCloud Golf Club	41 14 21N	122 08 07W	golf	
McClure Place (1)	40 16 03N	121 49 27W	city/town	1640
McClure Place (2)	39 47 34N	123 02 03W	city/town	2060
McClures Beach	38 11 15N	122 57 51W	beach	
McColl	40 43 38N	122 19 43W	city/town	1000

California GPS Companion

Place Name	Latitude	Longitude	Type	Elev
McConnel	38 21 45N	121 20 45W	city/town	49
McConnel Place	38 47 49N	120 26 49W	city/town	4600
McConnell State Pk	37 24 55N	120 42 36W	park	
McCulloh	38 57 16N	120 31 30W	city/town	4840
McDonald	38 11 18N	122 54 30W	city/town	120
McDonald Peak	40 56 27N	120 24 41W	summit	7931
McDonalds Swim St.	34 01 27N	118 17 16W	stadium	
McDonnell Douglas	33 44 50N	118 02 04W	airport	65
McDuffie, Mount	37 04 26N	118 38 34W	summit	13271
McFarland	35 40 41N	119 13 42W	city/town	350
McGarva	41 17 17N	120 33 37W	city/town	4400
McGee, Mount	37 08 20N	118 44 14W	summit	12969
McGill	38 11 55N	122 26 08W	city/town	9
McGrath State Bch.	34 13 35N	119 15 41W	park	
McGuire Boat Ramp	39 07 16N	120 25 31W	locale	5300
McHenry	37 42 27N	121 00 11W	city/town	98
McKay (1)	35 47 01N	120 43 27W	city/town	610
McKay (2)	38 14 49N	120 18 26W	city/town	4120
McKenzie Place	40 17 41N	121 54 03W	city/town	1680
McKinleyville	40 56 48N	124 05 58W	city/town	140
McKittrick	35 18 20N	119 37 18W	city/town	1051
McManus	38 47 57N	120 31 59W	city/town	4280

California GPS Companion

Place Name	Latitude	Longitude	Type	Elev
McNear	38 13 43N	122 36 47W	city/town	10
McNears Beach	37 59 36N	122 27 08W	city/town	20
McNeil	34 10 17N	118 20 52W	city/town	595
McPherson	33 47 16N	117 49 34W	city/town	253
McRae Opera House	38 45 08N	121 17 04W	building	
Meadow Brook	38 51 34N	120 49 59W	city/town	2280
Meadow Country Clb	37 58 24N	122 37 04W	golf	
Meadow Lake Park	39 19 40N	120 12 30W	city/town	5920
Meadow Lakes	37 04 49N	119 25 47W	city/town	4440
Meadow Valley	39 55 47N	121 03 35W	city/town	3782
Meadow Vista	39 00 04N	121 01 15W	city/town	1720
Meadowbrook Golf C	37 57 04N	122 05 52W	golf	
Meadowbrook Woods	34 14 04N	117 12 05W	city/town	5600
Meadowlark C C	33 43 06N	118 01 52W	golf	
Meadowlark Golf C.	34 40 36N	118 14 16W	golf	
Meadowood Estates	39 45 07N	122 10 45W	city/town	251
Meadowsweet	37 55 23N	122 30 30W	city/town	10
Meares	41 37 15N	121 11 52W	city/town	4420
Mecca	33 34 18N	116 04 35W	city/town	-180
Medicine Mount (1)	41 33 50N	121 36 39W	summit	7580
Medicine Mount (2)	41 29 43N	123 19 01W	summit	6832
Meeks Bay	39 02 04N	120 07 23W	city/town	6239

California GPS Companion

Place Name	Latitude	Longitude	Type	Elev
Meiners Oaks	34 26 49N	119 16 42W	city/town	750
Meinert	37 56 39N	122 01 35W	city/town	70
Meins Landing	38 08 23N	121 54 22W	city/town	8
Meiss	38 38 18N	120 20 07W	city/town	5480
Melbourne	39 17 00N	123 38 59W	city/town	174
Melita	38 27 24N	122 38 09W	city/town	310
Mello	39 12 24N	121 33 44W	city/town	70
Meloland	32 48 11N	115 26 48W	city/town	-55
Melones	38 00 45N	120 29 51W	city/town	780
Melrose -subdiv.	37 46 12N	122 12 15W	city/town	40
Melsons Corner	38 36 37N	120 42 13W	city/town	2060
Melvin	36 48 31N	119 42 00W	city/town	358
Memorial Auditor.	38 34 44N	121 29 03W	building	
Memorial Lighthous	41 03 29N	124 08 30W	lighthous	
Memorial Stadium	39 09 37N	121 35 04W	stadium	
Mendel, Mount	37 10 30N	118 40 49W	summit	13691
Mendenhall Springs	37 35 18N	121 38 48W	city/town	1800
Mendocino	39 18 28N	123 47 54W	city/town	120
Mendocino Art Cent	39 18 25N	123 48 08W	building	
Mendocino Coast Bt	39 24 43N	123 48 45W	garden	
Mendocino College	39 11 12N	123 13 04W	univ/coll	
Mendocino County M	39 24 47N	123 20 42W	museum	

205

California GPS Companion

Place Name	Latitude	Longitude	Type	Elev
Mendocino Headland	39 18 31N	123 48 27W	park	
Mendota	36 45 13N	120 22 50W	city/town	170
Mendota Airport	36 45 28N	120 22 16W	airport	162
Menifee	33 43 42N	117 08 44W	city/town	1479
Menlo Baths	41 15 57N	120 04 58W	city/town	4561
Menlo Country Club	37 26 50N	122 14 05W	golf	
Menlo Park	37 27 14N	122 10 52W	city/town	60
Menlo School & Col	37 27 25N	122 11 26W	univ/coll	
Menning Golf Cours	40 31 31N	122 22 30W	golf	
Mentone	34 04 12N	117 08 01W	city/town	1660
Merazo	38 13 03N	122 22 19W	city/town	14
Merced	37 18 08N	120 28 55W	city/town	171
Merced Falls	37 31 23N	120 19 53W	city/town	350
Merced Golf Club	37 22 51N	120 27 00W	golf	
Merced Municipal	37 17 04N	120 30 49W	airport	153
Mercey Hot Springs	36 42 15N	120 51 33W	city/town	1160
Mercuryville	38 46 34N	122 49 15W	city/town	2703
Meridian (1)	35 06 27N	118 54 48W	city/town	428
Meridian (2)	37 19 23N	121 58 07W	city/town	132
Meridian (3)	39 08 36N	121 54 48W	city/town	47
Merlin	39 53 18N	121 21 57W	city/town	1760
Merriam Peak	37 18 34N	118 45 51W	summit	13103

California GPS Companion

Place Name	Latitude	Longitude	Type	Elev
Merril Natural Br.	41 43 41N	121 32 53W	arch	
Merrills Landing	39 52 42N	122 02 19W	city/town	178
Merrimac	39 45 58N	121 18 23W	city/town	3960
Merritt	38 36 51N	121 45 34W	city/town	52
Merryman	36 19 33N	119 06 16W	city/town	437
Mesa Camp	37 30 28N	118 34 21W	city/town	5710
Mesa Grande	33 10 49N	116 46 06W	city/town	3230
Mesa Verde C C	33 40 50N	117 56 13W	golf	
Mesaville	33 41 39N	114 38 57W	city/town	415
Mesquite	33 01 17N	115 06 27W	city/town	295
Mesquite Oasis	32 55 11N	116 13 04W	city/town	680
Metropolitan J C	34 02 06N	118 15 55W	univ/coll	
Mettah	41 18 37N	123 52 15W	city/town	160
Mettler	35 03 50N	118 58 09W	city/town	539
Metz	36 21 18N	121 12 38W	city/town	235
Mevers	38 51 22N	120 00 43W	city/town	6360
Mexican Colony	35 28 08N	119 16 04W	city/town	327
Mexican Museum	37 48 25N	122 25 47W	museum	
Meyers	37 45 31N	121 00 06W	city/town	102
Meyers Place (1)	40 16 01N	121 55 10W	city/town	2100
Meyers Place (2)	39 37 09N	122 41 28W	city/town	2800
MGM Studios	34 00 54N	118 24 07W	studio	

California GPS Companion

Place Name	Latitude	Longitude	Type	Elev
Mi-Wuk Village	38 03 57N	120 11 02W	city/town	4687
Micaflores	33 48 15N	117 54 25W	city/town	138
Michigan Bluff	39 02 35N	120 44 25W	city/town	3520
Midas	39 13 00N	120 45 24W	city/town	4140
Midco	34 56 11N	120 27 42W	city/town	195
Middle Falls	41 14 38N	122 00 31W	falls	
Middle Palisade	37 04 12N	118 28 09W	summit	14012
Middleman Falls	34 14 56N	117 25 09W	falls	
Middleton	38 12 24N	122 15 43W	city/town	50
Middletown	38 45 09N	122 36 50W	city/town	1105
Midland	33 51 40N	114 48 05W	city/town	968
Midoil	35 09 30N	119 31 18W	city/town	1337
Midpines	37 32 40N	119 55 10W	city/town	2575
Midvalley	36 17 53N	119 23 14W	city/town	292
Midway (1)	40 30 08N	121 57 55W	city/town	2160
Midway (2)	37 42 53N	121 33 25W	city/town	352
Midway (3)	35 01 58N	116 28 14W	city/town	1686
Midway City	33 44 41N	117 59 18W	city/town	40
Midway Mountain	36 38 38N	118 29 00W	summit	13666
Mikon	38 35 15N	121 32 14W	city/town	17
Mildred Falls	33 00 51N	116 42 50W	falls	
Mile High	34 24 46N	117 46 23W	city/town	5200

California GPS Companion

Place Name	Latitude	Longitude	Type	Elev
Mile Rock Lighth.	37 47 33N	122 30 34W	lighthous	
Miles	35 11 08N	120 42 08W	city/town	40
Milestone Mountain	36 38 08N	118 29 03W	summit	13641
Miley	36 37 20N	119 32 46W	city/town	340
Milford	40 10 17N	120 22 17W	city/town	4220
Mill City	37 37 22N	118 59 29W	city/town	8645
Mill Creek	40 19 35N	121 31 18W	city/town	4720
Mill Valley	37 54 22N	122 32 38W	city/town	80
Millbrae	37 35 55N	122 23 10W	city/town	50
Millbrae Meadows	37 36 08N	122 24 58W	city/town	250
Miller	36 57 26N	121 32 37W	city/town	155
Miller Farms	33 34 27N	114 37 10W	city/town	258
Miller Place	40 27 57N	123 25 42W	city/town	2240
Millers Landing	38 57 24N	121 50 19W	city/town	33
Millers Ranch	36 15 07N	121 25 44W	city/town	620
Millersville	35 18 14N	118 27 25W	city/town	2519
Millerton	38 06 33N	122 50 40W	city/town	32
Millerton Lake St.	37 01 13N	119 40 01W	park	
Milligan	34 16 36N	115 10 10W	city/town	735
Milligan District	38 20 53N	120 41 59W	city/town	1580
Mills	38 24 48N	122 50 32W	city/town	182
Mills College	37 46 47N	122 10 51W	univ/coll	

California GPS Companion

Place Name	Latitude	Longitude	Type	Elev
Mills Orchard	39 44 16N	122 03 19W	city/town	175
Mills Orchards	39 16 39N	122 16 26W	city/town	149
Mills, Mount	37 23 36N	118 47 19W	summit	13468
Millspaugh	36 02 46N	117 27 36W	city/town	6156
Millux	35 10 49N	119 11 52W	city/town	291
Millville	40 32 58N	122 10 27W	city/town	511
Milo	36 13 13N	118 48 59W	city/town	1800
Milpitas	37 25 42N	121 54 20W	city/town	19
Milton	38 01 55N	120 51 04W	city/town	382
Mina	39 57 54N	123 21 26W	city/town	1879
Minaret Falls	37 38 27N	119 05 38W	falls	
Minarets	37 39 43N	119 10 38W	summit	12255
Mineral	40 20 52N	121 35 38W	city/town	4907
Mineral King	36 27 03N	118 35 38W	city/town	7830
Mineral Slide	39 47 07N	121 37 08W	city/town	1000
Minkler	36 43 26N	119 27 26W	city/town	395
Minnelusa	34 15 59N	116 53 30W	city/town	6280
Minneola	34 50 46N	116 46 34W	city/town	1910
Minnesota	40 39 44N	122 29 16W	city/town	1600
Minnesota Flat	39 26 58N	120 49 48W	city/town	4360
Mint Canyon	34 25 45N	118 26 29W	city/town	1540
Minter Village	35 30 13N	119 10 55W	city/town	418

California GPS Companion

Place Name	Latitude	Longitude	Type	Elev
Minturn	37 08 23N	120 16 24W	city/town	237
Mira Loma	33 59 33N	117 30 56W	city/town	700
Mira Mesa	32 54 56N	117 08 35W	city/town	440
Mira Monte	34 26 01N	119 17 03W	city/town	650
Mira Vista C C	37 55 58N	122 18 03W	golf	
Mirabel Heights	38 29 26N	122 53 22W	city/town	120
Mirabel Park	38 29 36N	122 53 41W	city/town	80
Miracle Hot Spring	35 34 33N	118 32 01W	city/town	2366
Miracosta College	33 11 24N	117 18 05W	univ/coll	
Mirador	36 10 01N	119 02 06W	city/town	445
Miraleste	33 45 08N	118 19 31W	city/town	770
Miramar (1)	32 53 37N	117 07 03W	city/town	510
Miramar (2)	37 29 35N	122 27 20W	city/town	40
Miramar Beach	37 29 36N	122 27 33W	beach	
Miramar Naval Air	32 52 08N	117 06 28W	military	
Miramonte	36 41 33N	119 03 05W	city/town	3095
Miranda	40 14 05N	123 49 21W	city/town	331
Misery Hill	41 24 20N	122 11 49W	summit	13760
Miss. LaPurisima	34 40 17N	120 25 19W	mission	
Miss. San Antonio	36 00 55N	121 14 57W	mission	
Miss. San Buenav.	34 16 54N	119 17 50W	mission	
Miss. San Carlos	36 32 33N	121 55 07W	mission	

California GPS Companion

Place Name	Latitude	Longitude	Type	Elev
Miss. San Fernando	34 16 26N	118 27 38W	mission	
Miss. San Francis.	38 17 44N	122 26 44W	mission	
Miss. San Gabriel	34 05 50N	118 06 25W	mission	
Miss. San Jose d	37 31 58N	121 55 05W	mission	
Miss. San Luis Ob.	35 16 51N	120 39 47W	mission	
Miss. San Luis Re.	33 13 59N	117 19 09W	mission	
Miss. Santa Clara	37 21 00N	121 56 35W	mission	88
Miss. Santa Ines	34 35 41N	120 08 08W	mission	
Miss. Soledad	36 24 17N	121 21 18W	mission	
Mission (1)	34 31 10N	118 14 24W	city/town	3330
Mission (2)	34 26 17N	119 44 23W	city/town	200
Mission Bay Yacht	32 46 40N	117 14 53W	locale	
Mission Beach	32 46 57N	117 15 05W	city/town	10
Mission District	37 45 36N	122 25 05W	city/town	50
Mission Dolores	37 45 51N	122 25 33W	mission	
Mission Highlands	38 19 11N	122 27 24W	city/town	960
Mission Hills (1)	34 15 26N	118 27 58W	city/town	910
Mission Hills (2)	32 45 10N	117 11 10W	city/town	260
Mission Hills Golf	34 14 50N	118 28 36W	golf	
Mission Junction	34 03 45N	118 13 36W	city/town	300
Mission San Jose D	37 31 59N	121 55 09W	city/town	309
Mission San Jose P	37 31 40N	121 55 21W	park	

California GPS Companion

Place Name	Latitude	Longitude	Type	Elev
Mission Springs	37 03 59N	122 01 53W	city/town	340
Mission Viejo	33 36 00N	117 40 16W	city/town	400
Mission Viejo Golf	33 34 48N	117 39 48W	golf	
Missouri Triangle	35 26 20N	119 41 21W	city/town	559
Mist Falls	36 48 49N	118 32 52W	falls	
Mitchell Caverns S	34 56 27N	115 30 49W	park	
Mitchell Corner	36 19 36N	119 12 19W	city/town	365
Mitchell Place	39 57 33N	122 43 01W	city/town	5440
Mitchells Corner	35 13 25N	118 50 29W	city/town	461
Miwok Beach	38 21 38N	123 04 04W	beach	
Moccasin (1)	37 48 39N	120 17 56W	city/town	950
Moccasin (2)	40 04 37N	120 56 07W	city/town	3560
Mock	36 32 37N	117 55 57W	city/town	3630
Mococo	38 01 32N	122 06 54W	city/town	20
Modesto	37 38 21N	120 59 45W	city/town	87
Modesto City-Count	37 37 32N	120 57 15W	airport	97
Modesto Junior Col	37 39 09N	121 00 31W	univ/coll	
Modjeska	33 42 33N	117 37 31W	city/town	1320
Moffett Fld Naval	37 24 54N	122 02 53W	airport	34
Mohawk	39 46 44N	120 38 04W	city/town	4360
Mojave	35 03 09N	118 10 23W	city/town	2757
Mojave Airport	35 03 29N	118 09 03W	airport	2787

Place Name	Latitude	Longitude	Type	Elev
Mojave Base	35 19 50N	116 53 59W	city/town	3060
Mojave Heights	34 34 07N	117 19 29W	city/town	2740
Mokelumne Beach	38 12 24N	121 04 42W	beach	
Mokelumne City	38 15 11N	121 26 17W	city/town	21
Mokelumne Hill	38 18 02N	120 42 19W	city/town	1474
Mokelumne Peak	38 32 17N	120 05 37W	summit	9334
Mole Pier	32 42 43N	117 10 39W	pier	
Molena	38 07 33N	121 52 32W	city/town	37
Molino (1)	34 07 32N	117 11 41W	city/town	1354
Molino (2)	38 25 33N	122 50 49W	city/town	165
Molus	36 28 05N	121 23 35W	city/town	165
Monaco	33 52 23N	118 21 30W	city/town	95
Monada	38 02 13N	121 16 38W	city/town	28
Monastery Beach	36 31 25N	121 55 34W	beach	
Moneta -subdivis.	33 52 48N	118 19 00W	city/town	43
Monkeyface Falls	34 05 55N	116 57 20W	falls	
Monmouth	36 33 58N	119 44 21W	city/town	275
Mono Basin Nat'l	37 57 01N	119 03 30W	park	
Mono City	38 02 27N	119 08 37W	city/town	6769
Mono Hot Springs	37 19 36N	119 01 00W	city/town	6780
Mono Mills	37 53 15N	118 57 30W	city/town	7358
Mono Rock	37 26 20N	118 47 36W	summit	11555

Place Name	Latitude	Longitude	Type	Elev
Mono Vista	37 59 52N	120 16 08W	city/town	3000
Monola	37 08 37N	118 14 34W	city/town	3905
Monolith	35 07 12N	118 22 24W	city/town	3965
Monroe	38 27 10N	122 45 01W	city/town	120
Monrovia	34 08 53N	117 59 53W	city/town	560
Mons	33 55 14N	116 44 47W	city/town	1560
Monsanto	38 01 34N	122 03 16W	city/town	10
Monson	36 29 32N	119 20 08W	city/town	322
Monstad Pier	33 50 20N	118 23 27W	pier	
Monta Vista	37 19 22N	122 03 25W	city/town	320
Montague	41 43 42N	122 31 36W	city/town	2538
Montague -Siskiyou	41 46 53N	122 28 05W	airport	2648
Montague -Yreka R.	41 43 49N	122 32 44W	airport	2527
Montalvin Manor	37 59 44N	122 19 54W	city/town	35
Montalvo	34 15 14N	119 12 10W	city/town	109
Montana De Oro St.	35 15 50N	120 51 44W	park	
Montara	37 32 32N	122 30 54W	city/town	113
Montara Beach	37 32 49N	122 30 50W	beach	64
Montara State Bch.	37 32 56N	122 30 48W	park	
Montclair	34 04 39N	117 41 20W	city/town	1060
Monte Nido	34 04 51N	118 41 10W	city/town	590
Monte Rio	38 27 56N	123 00 28W	city/town	200

California GPS Companion

Place Name	Latitude	Longitude	Type	Elev
Monte Rosa	38 30 14N	123 01 34W	city/town	120
Monte Sereno	37 14 11N	121 59 29W	city/town	503
Monte Toyon	36 59 47N	121 53 42W	city/town	260
Monte Vista	39 11 12N	120 49 54W	city/town	3320
Montebello	34 00 34N	118 06 16W	city/town	200
Montebello Munic.	34 01 49N	118 08 01W	golf	
Montecito	34 26 12N	119 37 52W	city/town	50
Montecito C C	34 25 33N	119 39 18W	golf	
Monterey	36 36 01N	121 53 37W	city/town	60
Monterey Bay	36 48 00N	121 54 00W	bay	
Monterey Bay Aquar	36 37 06N	121 54 01W	aquarium	
Monterey Harbor	36 36 42N	121 53 40W	harbor	
Monterey Marina	36 36 13N	121 53 23W	marina	
Monterey Park	34 03 45N	118 07 19W	city/town	381
Monterey Park Golf	34 03 30N	118 09 40W	golf	
Monterey Peninsula	36 35 13N	121 50 34W	airport	254
Monterey Peninsula	36 35 26N	121 53 00W	univ/coll	
Monterey State Bch	36 36 05N	121 52 59W	park	
Montesano	38 29 14N	123 00 58W	city/town	160
Montevina Winery	38 30 57N	120 47 45W	wine/vin	
Montezuma (1)	38 05 26N	121 52 18W	city/town	5
Montezuma (2)	37 54 17N	120 27 09W	city/town	1275

California GPS Companion

Place Name	Latitude	Longitude	Type	Elev
Montgomery	39 14 01N	123 23 19W	city/town	800
Montgomery City	37 49 43N	118 25 48W	city/town	6420
Montgomery Creek	40 50 30N	121 55 21W	city/town	2140
Montgomery Creek F	40 50 17N	121 55 38W	falls	
Montgomery Peak	37 50 19N	118 21 20W	summit	13441
Montgomery Place	40 05 12N	122 34 30W	city/town	872
Montgomery Village	38 26 40N	122 41 15W	city/town	200
Montpelier	37 32 42N	120 42 18W	city/town	213
Montrose	34 12 23N	118 13 24W	city/town	1260
Moody	33 50 17N	118 02 42W	city/town	42
Moondunes Beach	39 14 15N	120 02 30W	beach	
Mooney Flat	39 12 56N	121 16 24W	city/town	760
Moonlight St. Bch.	33 02 53N	117 17 46W	park	
Moonridge	34 14 07N	116 51 17W	city/town	7280
Moonstone	41 01 49N	124 06 30W	city/town	120
Moonstone Bch (1)	33 23 20N	118 22 01W	beach	
Moonstone Bch (2)	41 01 49N	124 06 40W	beach	77
Moonstone Bch (3)	35 34 30N	121 06 46W	beach	
Moore	35 23 22N	115 15 49W	city/town	3282
Moores Flat	39 25 09N	120 50 59W	city/town	4120
Moorpark	34 17 08N	118 52 52W	city/town	513
Moorpark College	34 18 00N	118 49 56W	univ/coll	

California GPS Companion

Place Name	Latitude	Longitude	Type	Elev
Moorpark Home Acre	34 15 56N	118 54 51W	city/town	440
Moraga	37 50 06N	122 07 43W	city/town	490
Moraga Country Clb	37 50 10N	122 08 10W	golf	
Moraga Town	37 50 36N	122 07 20W	city/town	490
Moran	40 54 06N	120 29 21W	city/town	5286
Moreland Mill	35 30 26N	118 21 15W	city/town	7740
Morena	32 46 51N	117 12 25W	city/town	15
Morena Dam	32 41 10N	116 32 47W	dam	3052
Morena Village	32 40 46N	116 30 15W	city/town	3200
Moreno (1)	32 52 24N	116 55 27W	city/town	420
Moreno (2)	33 55 03N	117 09 25W	city/town	1597
Moreno Valley	33 56 15N	117 13 47W	city/town	16
Morettis Junction	33 11 58N	116 42 34W	city/town	2760
Morgan Hill	37 07 50N	121 39 12W	city/town	350
Morgan Springs	40 21 44N	121 30 36W	city/town	4850
Morgans Landing	38 19 42N	121 34 29W	city/town	21
Mormon	37 57 01N	121 15 53W	city/town	
Mormon Bar	37 27 44N	119 56 49W	city/town	1800
Mormon Island Dam	38 41 56N	121 07 03W	dam	481
Morningside Park	33 57 35N	118 19 32W	city/town	215
Moro Rock	36 32 39N	118 45 51W	summit	6725
Morongo Valley	34 02 49N	116 34 48W	city/town	2538

218

California GPS Companion

Place Name	Latitude	Longitude	Type	Elev
Morris Dailey Aud.	37 20 07N	121 52 56W	building	
Morrison	38 42 35N	120 19 24W	city/town	5280
Morrison Planetar.	37 46 12N	122 27 52W	building	
Morrison, Mount	37 33 42N	118 51 32W	summit	12268
Morristown	39 39 09N	120 54 13W	city/town	5220
Morro Bay	35 20 16N	120 51 01W	bay	
Morro Bay	35 21 57N	120 50 56W	city/town	100
Morro Bay Nat. His	35 20 49N	120 50 36W	museum	
Morro Bay State Pk	35 21 14N	120 49 54W	park	
Morro Rock	35 22 10N	120 52 00W	summit	578
Morro Strand State	35 25 40N	120 52 55W	park	
Morse	36 50 16N	121 29 32W	city/town	207
Mortero Palms	32 43 09N	116 09 03W	city/town	2000
Mortmar	33 31 18N	115 56 06W	city/town	-200
Morton	33 54 50N	118 10 59W	city/town	82
Moscone Conv Cent.	37 47 01N	122 23 58W	building	
Moss (1)	32 59 52N	115 24 25W	city/town	-100
Moss (2)	36 47 55N	121 47 06W	city/town	3
Moss Beach	36 36 36N	121 56 50W	beach	
Moss Beach	37 31 39N	122 30 44W	city/town	100
Moss Landing	36 48 16N	121 47 09W	city/town	10
Moss Landing Mar.	36 48 01N	121 47 17W	marina	

California GPS Companion

Place Name	Latitude	Longitude	Type	Elev
Moss Landing State	36 48 49N	121 47 22W	park	
Mossbrae Falls	41 14 30N	122 15 57W	falls	
Mossdale	37 47 05N	121 18 27W	city/town	10
Motion	40 40 28N	122 27 34W	city/town	594
Motor City	38 44 02N	120 44 22W	city/town	
Mott	41 15 36N	122 16 28W	city/town	3154
Mount Baldy	34 14 10N	117 39 33W	city/town	4200
Mount Baldy Vis. C	34 14 15N	117 39 16W	locale	4800
Mount Bullion	37 30 10N	120 02 33W	city/town	2176
Mount Diablo State	37 51 46N	121 55 48W	park	
Mount Eden	37 38 10N	122 05 56W	city/town	40
Mount Eden Station	37 38 09N	122 06 47W	city/town	
Mount Hannah Lodge	38 53 16N	122 43 46W	city/town	2590
Mount Hebron	41 47 14N	122 00 11W	city/town	4256
Mount Hermon	37 03 04N	122 03 27W	city/town	400
Mount High E. Area	34 22 09N	117 40 44W	ski area	7565
Mount High E. Lift	34 21 51N	117 40 44W	ski area	8140
Mount High W. Area	34 21 17N	117 44 23W	ski area	7320
Mount High W. Lift	34 22 19N	117 41 37W	ski area	7898
Mount Hope House	39 31 01N	121 13 00W	city/town	2950
Mount Hough State	40 01 15N	120 54 15W	park	
Mount Jackson	38 30 48N	122 54 14W	city/town	80

California GPS Companion

Place Name	Latitude	Longitude	Type	Elev
Mount Laguna	32 52 20N	116 25 03W	city/town	5960
Mount Pleasant	39 36 45N	120 58 39W	city/town	4537
Mount Reba Ski Ar.	38 29 44N	120 02 53W	ski area	8495
Mount Shasta	41 18 36N	122 18 34W	city/town	3554
Mount Shasta Ski P	41 19 20N	122 12 07W	ski area	5520
Mount Signal	32 40 42N	115 38 18W	city/town	-17
Mount Tamalpais St	37 54 14N	122 35 42W	park	
Mount Tom Lookout	37 22 33N	119 10 43W	overlook	9026
Mount Vernon	39 10 25N	121 45 08W	city/town	99
Mount Washington	34 05 57N	118 13 10W	city/town	700
Mount Waterman Ski	34 20 46N	117 55 58W	ski area	7800
Mount Whitney Golf	36 34 43N	118 03 40W	golf	3691
Mount Wilson	34 13 35N	118 03 55W	city/town	5680
Mount Wilson Obser	34 13 33N	118 03 23W	observtry	
Mountain Center	33 42 15N	116 43 30W	city/town	4520
Mountain Gate	40 42 59N	122 19 50W	city/town	886
Mountain Home (1)	36 14 05N	118 41 42W	city/town	6020
Mountain Home (2)	37 07 16N	121 47 41W	city/town	960
Mountain Home Vil.	34 06 02N	116 59 54W	city/town	3720
Mountain Meadows	34 04 56N	117 46 50W	golf	
Mountain Mesa	35 38 22N	118 24 17W	city/town	2663
Mountain Pass	35 28 13N	115 32 39W	city/town	4730

221

California GPS Companion

Place Name	Latitude	Longitude	Type	Elev
Mountain Ranch	38 13 42N	120 32 23W	city/town	2117
Mountain Top Jct.	34 23 25N	117 34 31W	city/town	4780
Mountain View (1)	34 30 23N	117 21 28W	city/town	3059
Mountain View (2)	37 23 10N	122 04 58W	city/town	97
Mountain View C C	33 52 35N	117 36 31W	golf	
Mountclef Village	34 14 04N	118 52 40W	city/town	773
Mowry Landing	37 30 22N	122 01 04W	city/town	5
Mudd College	34 06 21N	117 42 34W	univ/coll	
Mugginsville	41 34 25N	122 57 02W	city/town	2934
Muir (1)	37 59 26N	122 07 45W	city/town	110
Muir (2)	39 23 54N	123 20 38W	city/town	1380
Muir Beach	37 51 35N	122 34 33W	beach	
Muir Woods Nat'l	37 53 46N	122 34 45W	park	
Muir, Mount	36 33 50N	118 17 28W	summit	14012
Mulford	37 42 34N	122 10 43W	city/town	20
Mulford Gardens	37 42 17N	122 10 43W	city/town	15
Mulkey Place	41 51 54N	120 38 16W	city/town	5040
Mundo	33 16 25N	115 34 06W	city/town	-195
Munger Peak	36 52 27N	118 34 45W	summit	12076
Municipal Golf Crs	33 53 40N	118 08 22W	golf	
Munyon	33 02 26N	115 24 51W	city/town	-110
Muriel Peak	37 12 58N	118 41 30W	summit	12942

California GPS Companion

Place Name	Latitude	Longitude	Type	Elev
Murietta Farm	36 39 06N	120 27 30W	city/town	255
Muriettas Well Win	37 39 35N	121 44 01W	wine/vin	
Muroc Naval Air St	35 03 43N	118 09 19W	military	
Murphy Place	40 17 36N	123 13 13W	city/town	3300
Murphy Windmill	37 45 54N	122 30 27W	building	
Murphys	38 08 15N	120 27 31W	city/town	2171
Murray	36 05 39N	120 00 09W	city/town	256
Murray Park	37 56 40N	122 33 09W	city/town	73
Murrieta	33 33 14N	117 12 47W	city/town	1093
Murrieta Hot Sprgs	33 33 38N	117 09 26W	city/town	1160
Murrietta -Bear Cr	33 33 56N	117 14 23W	airport	1120
Murrietta-French V	33 34 34N	117 07 41W	airport	1347
Muscatel	36 47 34N	119 51 30W	city/town	296
Muscle Shoals	34 21 23N	119 26 30W	city/town	20
Muscoy	34 09 15N	117 20 36W	city/town	1385
Musee Mecanique	37 46 43N	122 30 46W	museum	
Museum of Am Herr.	37 26 44N	122 09 56W	museum	
Museum of Am Treas	32 41 00N	117 05 41W	museum	
Museum of Flying	34 01 03N	118 27 03W	museum	
Museum of Ophthalm	37 48 24N	122 25 09W	museum	
M. of Russian Cult	37 47 07N	122 26 25W	museum	
Museum of Science	34 00 58N	118 17 05W	museum	

California GPS Companion

Place Name	Latitude	Longitude	Type	Elev
Museum of Toleranc	34 03 13N	118 24 02W	museum	
Myers Flat	40 15 59N	123 52 09W	city/town	204
Myford	33 43 43N	117 46 50W	city/town	123
Myoma	33 45 05N	116 16 39W	city/town	71
Myricks Corner	35 30 59N	119 17 24W	city/town	347
Mystic	39 26 15N	120 01 08W	city/town	5140

N

Place Name	Latitude	Longitude	Type	Elev
Nacimiento	35 48 33N	120 44 26W	city/town	620
Nacomis Indian R.	38 59 10N	123 03 25W	city/town	760
Nadeau	33 57 56N	118 14 32W	city/town	138
Nanceville	36 04 10N	119 04 20W	city/town	417
Napa	38 17 50N	122 17 04W	city/town	17
Napa -Seaplane	38 35 29N	122 15 33W	airport	440
Napa College	38 16 24N	122 16 25W	univ/coll	
Napa County Airprt	38 12 47N	122 16 50W	airport	33
Napa Junction	38 11 15N	122 14 59W	city/town	74
Napa Soda Springs	38 23 27N	122 16 42W	city/town	760
Napa Valley C C	38 19 04N	122 14 24W	golf	
Naples (1)	33 45 16N	118 07 22W	city/town	5
Naples (2)	34 26 27N	119 57 29W	city/town	90
Naples Beach	37 29 19N	122 27 17W	beach	

California GPS Companion

Place Name	Latitude	Longitude	Type	Elev
Naranjo	36 24 17N	119 03 42W	city/town	465
Narlon	34 48 38N	120 35 52W	city/town	141
Narod	34 03 29N	117 41 01W	city/town	950
Nashmead	39 49 21N	123 24 49W	city/town	820
Nashua	36 44 29N	121 45 53W	city/town	16
Nashville	38 34 44N	120 50 39W	city/town	840
National City	32 40 41N	117 05 54W	city/town	100
National City Mun.	32 39 52N	117 05 03W	golf	
National Maritime	37 48 23N	122 25 22W	museum	
Natividad	36 43 58N	121 35 44W	city/town	161
Natoma	38 39 18N	121 10 49W	city/town	162
Natural Arch (1)	34 02 22N	118 34 32W	arch	
Natural Arch (2)	34 52 55N	116 05 59W	arch	
Natural Bridge (1)	36 21 33N	118 22 26W	arch	
Natural Bridge (2)	38 03 17N	120 28 34W	arch	
Natural History M.	34 01 01N	118 17 17W	museum	
Naud Junction	34 03 38N	118 14 07W	city/town	290
Navarro	39 09 07N	123 32 27W	city/town	272
Navelencia	36 41 00N	119 23 05W	city/town	419
Naylor Place	34 36 16N	118 39 52W	city/town	1635
NBC-TV Studios	34 09 11N	118 19 55W	studio	
Neafus Peak	40 08 26N	123 31 59W	summit	3980

California GPS Companion

Place Name	Latitude	Longitude	Type	Elev
Neal	37 24 49N	122 08 34W	city/town	45
Nealeys Corner	34 11 14N	117 26 18W	city/town	2044
Nebelhorn	38 48 41N	120 02 00W	city/town	7390
Nebo	34 52 48N	116 57 24W	city/town	2040
Need	38 18 08N	121 19 25W	city/town	40
Needham Mountain	36 27 15N	118 32 11W	summit	12467
Needle Rock Vis. C	39 56 35N	123 57 48W	center	
Needles	34 50 53N	114 36 48W	city/town	488
Needles Airport	34 45 58N	114 37 23W	airport	983
Needles Lookout	36 06 34N	118 29 01W	overlook	8254
Neff	33 48 34N	117 55 55W	city/town	123
Nelson	39 33 08N	121 45 52W	city/town	121
Nelson Mill	39 25 53N	120 59 52W	city/town	3200
Nelsons Crossing	39 39 50N	121 12 53W	city/town	3100
Neponset	36 43 43N	121 47 00W	city/town	20
Neroly	37 59 22N	121 44 58W	city/town	75
Nervo	38 41 16N	122 52 45W	city/town	220
Nestor	32 34 33N	117 05 00W	city/town	30
Neufeld	35 37 10N	119 19 54W	city/town	322
Nevada	34 03 56N	117 13 02W	city/town	1990
Nevada City	39 15 42N	121 00 54W	city/town	2525
Nevada County Golf	39 13 56N	121 02 48W	golf	

California GPS Companion

Place Name	Latitude	Longitude	Type	Elev
Nevada Fall	37 43 31N	119 31 58W	falls	
Nevin	34 00 51N	118 14 43W	city/town	212
New Almaden	37 10 34N	121 49 11W	city/town	440
New Auberry	37 05 36N	119 29 46W	city/town	2080
New Bridge Marina	38 01 07N	121 45 07W	marina	
New Brighton State	36 58 43N	121 56 05W	park	
New Chicago	38 26 14N	120 50 07W	city/town	940
New Chinatown	34 03 45N	118 14 17W	city/town	310
New Cuyama	34 56 49N	119 41 04W	city/town	2150
New Cuyama Airport	34 56 14N	119 41 18W	airport	2203
New Dunn	35 02 58N	116 25 31W	city/town	1560
New Hope	38 13 35N	121 25 22W	city/town	10
New Hope Landing	38 13 41N	121 29 23W	city/town	0
New Monterey	36 36 53N	121 54 04W	city/town	140
New Pine Creek	41 59 34N	120 17 46W	city/town	4850
Newark	37 31 47N	122 02 21W	city/town	16
Newark Pavilion	37 32 00N	122 01 53W	building	
Newberry Springs	34 49 38N	116 41 15W	city/town	1840
Newburg	40 36 00N	124 07 25W	city/town	158
Newbury Park	34 11 03N	118 54 35W	city/town	620
Newcastle	38 52 27N	121 07 56W	city/town	920
Newcomb Pier	34 00 30N	118 29 49W	pier	

California GPS Companion

Place Name	Latitude	Longitude	Type	Elev
Newcomb, Mount	36 32 23N	118 17 36W	summit	13410
Newell	41 53 18N	121 22 16W	city/town	4045
Newhall	34 23 05N	118 31 48W	city/town	1272
Newlove	37 59 38N	121 45 42W	city/town	70
Newman	37 18 50N	121 01 11W	city/town	91
Newman Springs	39 11 47N	122 42 53W	city/town	2120
Newport	39 34 39N	123 46 25W	city/town	120
Newport Bay	33 36 30N	117 54 30W	bay	
Newport Beach	33 35 26N	117 55 05W	beach	
Newport Beach	33 37 08N	117 55 41W	city/town	5
Newport Heights	33 37 09N	117 55 21W	city/town	85
Newport Pier	33 36 24N	117 55 46W	pier	
Newsom Springs	35 07 21N	120 32 39W	city/town	400
Newton Observatory	38 34 20N	122 25 58W	observtry	
Newton Park -sub.	34 05 27N	118 10 42W	city/town	580
Newtown (1)	38 10 08N	121 40 45W	city/town	10
Newtown (2)	38 42 16N	120 40 41W	city/town	2440
Newtown (3)	40 39 26N	122 23 43W	city/town	780
Newtown (4)	39 15 10N	121 06 08W	city/town	
Newville	39 47 28N	122 31 38W	city/town	630
Nicasio	38 03 42N	122 41 51W	city/town	200
Nice	39 07 24N	122 50 50W	city/town	1380

228

California GPS Companion

Place Name	Latitude	Longitude	Type	Elev
Nicholls Warm Sprg	33 36 21N	114 43 49W	city/town	390
Nichols	38 02 29N	121 59 13W	city/town	20
Nicklin	33 56 37N	117 00 48W	city/town	2400
Nicks Cove	38 11 59N	122 55 12W	city/town	10
Nicolaus	38 54 12N	121 34 36W	city/town	34
Nielsburg	38 57 26N	121 01 56W	city/town	1540
Nielson Place	40 00 25N	123 20 36W	city/town	2580
Niland	33 14 24N	115 31 05W	city/town	141
Niles District	37 34 44N	121 58 36W	city/town	80
Niles Junction	37 34 35N	121 58 13W	city/town	60
Nimbus	38 37 45N	121 12 51W	city/town	145
Nimshew	39 50 37N	121 37 05W	city/town	2430
Ninetynine Oaks	34 28 33N	118 36 57W	city/town	1110
Ninth Street Jct.	34 01 13N	118 13 11W	city/town	240
Nipinnawasee	37 24 15N	119 43 55W	city/town	2940
Nipomo	35 02 34N	120 28 30W	city/town	330
Nipton	35 28 00N	115 16 17W	city/town	3042
Nitro	38 00 33N	122 21 49W	city/town	20
Noel Heights	38 29 38N	122 57 40W	city/town	240
Nojoqui Falls	34 31 42N	120 10 15W	falls	
Norco	33 55 52N	117 32 52W	city/town	640
Nord	39 46 47N	121 57 22W	city/town	148

California GPS Companion

Place Name	Latitude	Longitude	Type	Elev
Norden	39 19 05N	120 21 18W	city/town	6960
Normal Heights	32 45 48N	117 07 19W	city/town	402
Norman	39 24 29N	122 11 27W	city/town	92
Norman Clyde Peak	37 04 30N	118 28 19W	summit	13851
Normandy Village	37 52 32N	122 15 52W	city/town	260
North Beach	37 48 21N	122 24 40W	city/town	10
North Beach (1)	34 02 45N	118 56 43W	beach	
North Beach (2)	38 04 38N	122 58 29W	beach	
North Beach Museum	37 47 57N	122 24 28W	museum	
North Belridge	35 32 47N	119 47 23W	city/town	625
North Bloomfield	39 22 06N	120 53 54W	city/town	3300
North Clairemont	32 49 58N	117 11 57W	city/town	343
North Columbia	39 22 22N	120 59 10W	city/town	3018
North Cucamonga	34 05 36N	117 34 51W	city/town	1120
North Dinuba	36 34 03N	119 23 37W	city/town	340
North Edwards	35 01 00N	117 49 55W	city/town	2295
North Elsinore	33 41 24N	117 20 18W	city/town	1275
North Fillmore	34 24 24N	118 55 57W	city/town	450
North Fork	37 13 47N	119 30 31W	city/town	2640
North Fork Mount	41 01 00N	122 06 36W	summit	5342
North Glendale	34 09 38N	118 15 49W	city/town	525
North Guard	36 43 00N	118 29 24W	summit	13327

California GPS Companion

Place Name	Latitude	Longitude	Type	Elev
North Head Lighth.	33 01 49N	118 35 42W	lighthous	189
North Highland Pk.	34 07 28N	118 12 10W	city/town	610
North Highlands	38 41 09N	121 22 16W	city/town	100
North Hollywood	34 10 20N	118 22 41W	city/town	650
North Jamul	32 43 32N	116 52 07W	city/town	1022
North Landing	37 38 07N	118 44 37W	city/town	6825
North Long Beach	33 51 36N	118 11 05W	city/town	45
North Ontario	34 05 39N	117 39 01W	city/town	1215
North Palisade	37 05 38N	118 31 19W	summit	14242
North Palm Springs	33 55 22N	116 32 32W	city/town	860
North Park	32 44 27N	117 07 47W	city/town	340
North Peak	37 58 57N	119 18 46W	summit	12242
North Placerville	38 45 18N	120 49 50W	city/town	1840
North Point Public	37 48 18N	122 24 47W	city/town	20
North Pomona	34 05 24N	117 44 58W	city/town	1040
North Richmond	37 57 32N	122 21 59W	city/town	15
North Ridge C C	38 39 40N	121 16 59W	golf	
North Sacramento	38 36 22N	121 27 23W	city/town	35
North Salmon Creek	38 21 26N	123 04 00W	beach	
North San Juan	39 22 10N	121 06 10W	city/town	2125
North Santa Maria	34 57 25N	120 26 37W	city/town	208
North Shafter	35 30 41N	119 17 01W	city/town	346

California GPS Companion

Place Name	Latitude	Longitude	Type	Elev
North Sherman Way	34 12 02N	118 26 54W	city/town	746
North Shore	34 16 05N	117 11 00W	city/town	5120
North Shore Marina	34 15 47N	117 10 03W	marina	
North Star	39 35 12N	121 04 33W	city/town	4000
North Star Beach	33 37 30N	117 53 33W	beach	
North Star Museum	39 12 29N	121 04 07W	museum	
North Star Ski Ar.	39 15 21N	120 07 18W	ski area	7900
North Wawona	37 32 52N	119 38 37W	city/town	4200
North Windmill	37 46 13N	122 30 30W	building	
Northridge	34 13 42N	118 32 09W	city/town	812
Northspur	39 25 22N	123 33 03W	city/town	320
Northstar-at-Tahoe	39 16 24N	120 06 05W	ski area	6500
Northwood	38 28 32N	123 00 02W	city/town	47
Northwood Heights	38 28 47N	122 59 54W	city/town	80
Northwood Lodge	38 28 38N	122 59 48W	city/town	40
Norton (1)	38 04 51N	121 14 30W	city/town	46
Norton (2)	38 35 10N	121 58 12W	city/town	176
Norton Simon Mus.	34 08 47N	118 09 30W	museum	
Nortonville	37 57 28N	121 52 46W	city/town	800
Norvell	40 29 11N	121 00 16W	city/town	5740
Norwalk	33 54 08N	118 04 51W	city/town	92
Norwalk Golf Crs	33 54 24N	118 03 19W	golf	

California GPS Companion

Place Name	Latitude	Longitude	Type	Elev
Notarb	37 00 40N	120 07 05W	city/town	253
Notchko	41 17 47N	123 52 07W	city/town	160
Notleys Landing	36 23 54N	121 54 09W	city/town	120
Novato	38 06 27N	122 34 07W	city/town	18
Novato -Gnoss Fld	38 08 39N	122 33 28W	airport	2
November Pier	32 41 23N	117 14 15W	pier	
Noverd	38 05 28N	121 41 12W	city/town	10
Noyo	39 25 42N	123 48 08W	city/town	110
Nubieber	41 05 45N	121 10 55W	city/town	4117
Nuestro	39 11 02N	121 39 40W	city/town	61
Nuevo	33 48 05N	117 08 42W	city/town	1480
Nutwood	33 48 25N	117 56 57W	city/town	105
Nyland	34 13 32N	119 08 03W	city/town	72
Nystrom Village	37 55 38N	122 21 20W	city/town	14

◎

Place Name	Latitude	Longitude	Type	Elev
Oak Creek Golf Crs	40 08 50N	122 13 38W	golf	
Oak Creek Hills	38 42 51N	121 04 33W	city/town	590
Oak Glen (1)	34 02 58N	116 56 49W	city/town	4880
Oak Glen (2)	40 16 57N	123 44 24W	city/town	860
Oak Grove (1)	33 23 06N	116 47 18W	city/town	2787
Oak Grove (2)	36 27 02N	118 47 28W	city/town	2680

California GPS Companion

Place Name	Latitude	Longitude	Type	Elev
Oak Grove (3)	38 07 01N	120 53 09W	city/town	290
Oak Grove (4)	39 25 38N	121 36 15W	city/town	125
Oak Grove Stage St	33 23 25N	116 47 38W	park	
Oak Hill	34 03 55N	118 47 03W	city/town	1225
Oak Knoll (1)	34 07 28N	118 08 06W	city/town	740
Oak Knoll (2)	38 21 30N	122 20 02W	city/town	109
Oak Park (1)	38 33 05N	121 28 12W	city/town	25
Oak Park (2)	35 38 52N	120 41 23W	city/town	720
Oak Ridge Golf Clb	37 14 30N	121 48 19W	golf	
Oak Ridge Village	38 40 46N	121 04 31W	city/town	800
Oak Run	40 41 07N	122 01 25W	city/town	1620
Oak Tree Village	38 42 25N	121 04 27W	city/town	660
Oak Valley	39 29 55N	121 02 13W	city/town	3025
Oak View	34 24 00N	119 17 57W	city/town	480
Oak Village	34 23 32N	118 57 45W	city/town	464
Oakbar	41 50 15N	122 56 15W	city/town	1715
Oakdale	37 46 00N	120 50 46W	city/town	155
Oakdale Airport	37 45 22N	120 48 00W	airport	234
Oakhurst	37 19 41N	119 38 54W	city/town	2289
Oakhurst C C	37 56 56N	121 56 15W	golf	
Oakland	37 48 16N	122 16 11W	city/town	42
Oakland -Metropol.	37 43 16N	122 13 14W	airport	6

California GPS Companion

Place Name	Latitude	Longitude	Type	Elev
Oakland Army Term.	37 49 01N	122 18 09W	military	
Oakland City Col 1	37 50 33N	122 16 04W	univ/coll	
Oakland City Col 2	37 47 46N	122 15 24W	univ/coll	
Oakland Civic Aud.	37 47 52N	122 15 38W	building	
Oakland Convention	37 48 08N	122 16 20W	building	
Oakley	37 59 51N	121 42 41W	city/town	18
Oakmont	38 26 27N	122 36 12W	city/town	460
Oakmont Country Cl	34 11 37N	118 13 58W	golf	
Oakmoore Golf Crs	37 59 40N	121 16 11W	golf	
Oaks	35 07 08N	120 35 38W	city/town	90
Oakville	38 26 13N	122 24 04W	city/town	155
Oasis (1)	38 58 58N	123 00 10W	city/town	1920
Oasis (2)	33 27 57N	116 05 53W	city/town	140
Oban	34 46 28N	118 08 50W	city/town	2300
Obelisk	36 54 30N	118 51 15W	pillar	9700
Obie	41 10 11N	121 42 49W	city/town	4220
Obregon	32 51 29N	114 47 18W	city/town	660
O'Brien	40 48 44N	122 19 23W	city/town	1240
Observation Peak	37 01 24N	118 31 52W	summit	12322
Occidental	38 24 27N	122 56 50W	city/town	578
Occidental College	34 07 39N	118 12 36W	univ/coll	
Ocean Beach	32 44 40N	117 15 40W	city/town	30

California GPS Companion

Place Name	Latitude	Longitude	Type	Elev
Ocean Beach	37 45 34N	122 30 35W	beach	
Ocean Beach City B	32 44 24N	117 15 16W	beach	
Ocean Beach Fish.	32 44 55N	117 15 19W	pier	
Ocean Park	34 00 08N	118 28 58W	city/town	23
Ocean Roar	38 12 58N	122 55 26W	city/town	40
Ocean View	33 42 56N	117 59 16W	city/town	26
Ocean West Mobile	40 57 20N	124 06 37W	city/town	90
Oceano	35 05 56N	120 36 41W	city/town	25
Oceano Beach	35 06 20N	120 37 45W	city/town	10
Oceano County Airp	35 06 04N	120 37 19W	airport	14
Oceanside	33 11 45N	117 22 43W	city/town	47
Oceanside City Bch	33 11 43N	117 23 04W	beach	
Oceanside Municip	33 13 04N	117 21 07W	airport	28
Oceanside-Carlsbad	33 11 51N	117 21 52W	golf	
Oceanview	37 42 34N	122 26 15W	city/town	400
Ockenden	37 05 20N	119 19 00W	city/town	5880
Ocotillo	32 44 19N	115 59 36W	city/town	380
Ocotillo Airport	33 09 00N	116 07 58W	airport	160
Ocotillo Badlands	33 07 10N	116 05 55W	locale	
Ocotillo Wells	33 08 40N	116 08 00W	city/town	163
Octol	36 07 26N	119 19 39W	city/town	266
Odd Fellows Park	38 30 08N	122 56 46W	city/town	200

California GPS Companion

Place Name	Latitude	Longitude	Type	Elev
O'Donald Golf Crs	33 49 36N	116 32 53W	golf	
Ogilby	32 49 01N	114 50 17W	city/town	356
Ohlone College	37 31 50N	121 54 41W	univ/coll	
Ohm	37 37 36N	121 16 59W	city/town	105
Oil City	35 25 35N	118 57 34W	city/town	450
Oil Junction	35 25 11N	119 03 22W	city/town	441
Oil Piers Beach	34 21 03N	119 25 27W	beach	
Oildale	35 25 11N	119 01 13W	city/town	455
Ojai	34 26 53N	119 14 31W	city/town	746
Ojai Country Club	34 26 15N	119 15 19W	golf	
Ojala	34 29 04N	119 17 54W	city/town	820
Olacha Peak	36 15 56N	118 06 59W	summit	12123
Olancha	36 16 55N	118 00 20W	city/town	3648
Olancha Dunes	36 17 29N	117 58 27W	locale	
Olancha Peak	36 15 56N	118 06 59W	summit	12123
Olcott	38 16 38N	121 49 23W	city/town	23
Old Adobe	35 44 16N	120 41 56W	city/town	630
Old Bailey Place	39 10 05N	123 28 53W	city/town	952
Old Bretz Mill	37 04 54N	119 17 52W	city/town	5373
Old Castro House	35 39 16N	121 13 12W	building	
Old Coloma Theatre	38 47 43N	120 53 23W	building	
Old Corral	37 21 25N	119 36 22W	city/town	3280

California GPS Companion

Place Name	Latitude	Longitude	Type	Elev
Old Dale	34 07 21N	115 47 40W	city/town	1268
Old Forbestown	39 31 41N	121 16 47W	city/town	2840
Old Fort Jim	38 42 38N	120 43 04W	city/town	2260
Old Fort Tejon	34 52 25N	118 53 36W	city/town	3200
Old Garlock	35 22 33N	117 49 27W	city/town	1979
Old Gilroy	36 59 59N	121 31 31W	city/town	175
Old Hilltown	36 37 53N	121 40 06W	city/town	40
Old Hopland	38 58 33N	123 05 57W	city/town	500
Old Hulbert Place	41 26 18N	121 03 06W	city/town	4620
Old Lighthouse	32 40 18N	117 14 50W	lighthous	
Old Mammoth	37 37 34N	118 58 56W	city/town	8050
Old Mint Building	37 46 58N	122 24 23W	building	30
Old Ornbaun Hot Sp	38 54 45N	123 18 35W	city/town	1200
Old Pino	38 49 05N	120 38 46W	city/town	3160
Old Point Comfort	34 24 55N	117 49 58W	city/town	4160
Old Point Loma Lt.	32 40 18N	117 14 24W	lighthous	
Old Red Rock Place	38 47 35N	123 26 27W	city/town	1760
Old River	35 16 02N	119 06 29W	city/town	340
Old Sacramento St.	38 35 04N	121 30 15W	park	
Old Station	40 40 31N	121 25 47W	city/town	4382
Old Town (1)	34 24 16N	119 31 45W	city/town	30
Old Town (2)	38 05 45N	122 34 04W	city/town	20

California GPS Companion

Place Name	Latitude	Longitude	Type	Elev
Old Town (3)	35 08 34N	118 29 38W	city/town	3824
Old Town San Diego	32 45 15N	117 11 46W	city/town	20
Old Town San Diego	32 45 15N	117 11 46W	park	
Oleander	36 38 04N	119 45 14W	city/town	283
Olema	38 02 27N	122 47 13W	city/town	60
Oleum	38 02 41N	122 14 50W	city/town	260
Olga	34 06 45N	118 09 53W	city/town	660
Olin Hall of Engin	34 01 14N	118 17 19W	building	
Olinda	40 26 38N	122 24 23W	city/town	762
Olivas Adobe	34 14 39N	119 14 27W	locale	41
Olive	33 50 10N	117 50 43W	city/town	226
Olive Hill	39 17 18N	121 28 09W	city/town	190
Olive View	34 19 28N	118 26 34W	city/town	1440
Olivehurst	39 05 44N	121 33 04W	city/town	60
Olivenhain	33 02 46N	117 14 02W	city/town	127
Olympia	37 04 11N	122 03 27W	city/town	380
Olympia Glade	39 13 59N	121 02 04W	city/town	2620
Olympic Golf Club	37 42 34N	122 29 38W	golf	
Olympic Heights	39 20 09N	120 09 24W	city/town	5880
Olympic Yacht Club	37 46 57N	122 15 54W	locale	
Omaha Heights -sub	34 04 53N	118 11 15W	city/town	760
Omega	39 20 00N	120 44 54W	city/town	4280

California GPS Companion

Place Name	Latitude	Longitude	Type	Elev
Omira	39 58 01N	120 04 35W	city/town	4340
Omo Ranch	38 34 53N	120 34 20W	city/town	3480
Omus	38 43 11N	122 55 07W	city/town	220
O'Neals	37 07 42N	119 41 36W	city/town	1313
Onehundred Palms	33 33 43N	116 10 18W	city/town	-70
O'Neil Place	39 41 56N	122 57 33W	city/town	5120
Ono	40 28 31N	122 37 01W	city/town	981
Ontario	34 03 48N	117 39 00W	city/town	988
Ontario Internat.	34 03 21N	117 36 04W	airport	943
Ontario Motor Spdw	34 04 21N	117 33 55W	track	
Onyx	35 41 25N	118 13 11W	city/town	2800
Opal Cliffs	36 57 39N	121 57 47W	city/town	48
Opera Plaza -sub.	37 46 53N	122 25 11W	city/town	85
Ophir	38 53 28N	121 07 21W	city/town	700
Ophir Hill Acres	39 11 35N	121 02 22W	city/town	2890
Ora	36 09 05N	120 19 32W	city/town	640
Orange	33 47 16N	117 51 08W	city/town	187
Orange Avenue Jct.	34 05 33N	117 56 32W	city/town	415
Orange Coast Col.	33 40 10N	117 54 39W	univ/coll	
Orange County Mar.	33 27 42N	117 42 27W	marina	
Orange Cove	36 37 28N	119 18 46W	city/town	425
Orange Park Acres	33 48 07N	117 46 53W	city/town	480

California GPS Companion

Place Name	Latitude	Longitude	Type	Elev
Orangevale	38 40 43N	121 13 29W	city/town	240
Orchams	34 28 32N	119 53 02W	city/town	402
Orchard	38 20 10N	122 46 22W	city/town	220
Orcutt	34 51 55N	120 26 06W	city/town	400
Ord Mountain	34 40 28N	116 48 54W	summit	6309
Ordbend	39 37 47N	122 00 16W	city/town	120
Ordway	34 00 15N	117 10 01W	city/town	1540
Oregon City	39 35 38N	121 31 42W	city/town	1200
Oregon House	39 21 23N	121 16 41W	city/town	1530
Orford	37 58 38N	121 11 18W	city/town	47
Orick	41 17 13N	124 03 31W	city/town	34
Orinda	37 52 38N	122 10 43W	city/town	500
Orinda Country Clb	37 53 32N	122 11 42W	golf	
Orinda Village	37 53 15N	122 11 40W	city/town	540
Orita	32 58 38N	115 24 16W	city/town	-92
Orland	39 44 51N	122 11 43W	city/town	256
Orland -Haigh Fld	39 43 16N	122 08 47W	airport	215
Orleans	41 18 06N	123 32 24W	city/town	400
Orleans Flat	39 25 44N	120 50 02W	city/town	4147
Ormand	34 00 40N	117 25 03W	city/town	900
Ormond Beach	34 08 13N	119 11 00W	beach	
Oro Fino	41 34 50N	122 55 13W	city/town	2841

241

California GPS Companion

Place Name	Latitude	Longitude	Type	Elev
Oro Grande	34 35 56N	117 20 00W	city/town	2631
Oro Loma	36 53 27N	120 41 22W	city/town	171
Oroleve	39 31 36N	121 10 42W	city/town	3330
Orosi	36 32 42N	119 17 11W	city/town	373
Oroville	39 30 50N	121 33 19W	city/town	174
Oroville Dam	39 32 20N	121 29 04W	dam	
Oroville Junction	39 30 35N	121 38 58W	city/town	161
Oroville Municipal	39 29 23N	121 37 10W	airport	192
Oroville Seaplane	39 33 59N	121 28 03W	airport	900
Orris	35 51 14N	119 03 37W	city/town	530
Orrs Springs	39 13 46N	123 21 49W	city/town	920
Ortega (1)	37 54 17N	121 16 16W	city/town	15
Ortega (2)	34 24 59N	119 35 05W	city/town	70
Ortonville	34 19 17N	119 17 26W	city/town	160
Orwood	37 56 24N	121 34 04W	city/town	7
Osborne	40 43 06N	122 01 45W	city/town	1860
Ostrom	39 04 10N	121 30 38W	city/town	65
Oswald	39 04 09N	121 37 30W	city/town	49
Otay	32 35 41N	117 03 49W	city/town	66
Oteys Sierra Villa	37 21 31N	118 27 30W	city/town	4470
Otterbein	33 59 15N	117 53 02W	city/town	508
Ottoway Peak	37 38 32N	119 23 32W	summit	11480

California GPS Companion

Place Name	Latitude	Longitude	Type	Elev
Outingdale	38 37 00N	120 43 44W	city/town	1660
Overlook	32 46 17N	117 11 54W	city/town	100
Ovis Bridge	41 42 11N	121 30 59W	arch	
Owens Point	36 30 04N	118 09 20W	summit	11372
Owens Valley Radio	37 14 00N	118 16 58W	observtry	
Owenyo	36 40 42N	118 02 36W	city/town	3697
Owl	33 55 40N	116 49 00W	city/town	1998
Oxalis	36 54 43N	120 32 56W	city/town	137
Oxford	38 18 26N	121 37 11W	city/town	0
Oxford Mill	39 34 19N	120 49 28W	city/town	3300
Oxnard	34 11 51N	119 10 34W	city/town	52
Oxnard Airport	34 12 02N	119 12 25W	airport	43
Oxnard Beach	34 09 48N	119 13 37W	city/town	10
Oxnard Shores	34 11 27N	119 14 26W	city/town	7
Ozol	38 01 36N	122 09 43W	city/town	20

ℙ

Place Name	Latitude	Longitude	Type	Elev
Pabrico	37 34 58N	122 00 19W	city/town	45
Pacer	34 56 07N	120 29 20W	city/town	170
Pachappa	33 56 48N	117 23 03W	city/town	870
Pacheco (1)	37 59 01N	122 04 27W	city/town	20
Pacheco (2)	40 30 46N	122 19 58W	city/town	448

California GPS Companion

Place Name	Latitude	Longitude	Type	Elev
Pacific	38 45 37N	120 30 22W	city/town	3400
Pacific Asia Mus.	34 08 49N	118 08 24W	museum	
Pacific Beach	32 47 52N	117 14 22W	city/town	120
Pacific Christian	33 46 58N	118 08 08W	univ/coll	
Pacific Coast Bapt	34 05 22N	117 49 48W	univ/coll	
Pacific College	36 43 33N	119 44 02W	univ/coll	
Pacific Grove	36 37 04N	121 54 56W	city/town	125
Pacific Grove Acre	36 37 44N	121 55 44W	city/town	140
Pacific Heights	37 47 06N	122 27 04W	city/town	225
Pacific Heritage M	37 47 38N	122 24 08W	museum	
Pacific Manor	37 39 01N	122 29 19W	city/town	150
Pacific Marina	37 47 02N	122 15 45W	marina	
Pacific Oaks Coll.	34 09 07N	118 09 35W	univ/coll	
Pacific Palisades	34 02 53N	118 31 32W	city/town	300
Pacific Shores	41 51 20N	124 12 01W	city/town	20
Pacific States U.	34 02 40N	118 18 28W	univ/coll	
Pacific Union Coll	38 34 12N	122 26 16W	univ/coll	
Pacifica	37 36 50N	122 29 09W	city/town	76
Packers Bay Marina	40 46 33N	122 20 19W	marina	1150
Pacoima	34 15 45N	118 25 34W	city/town	980
Pacoima Dam	34 20 05N	118 23 44W	dam	2015
Paicines	36 43 43N	121 16 39W	city/town	680

California GPS Companion

Place Name	Latitude	Longitude	Type	Elev
Paige	36 10 55N	119 25 11W	city/town	254
Paige Bar	40 34 53N	122 32 29W	city/town	950
Painted Lady	36 47 33N	118 23 59W	summit	12126
Paintersville	38 19 12N	121 34 30W	city/town	10
Pajaro	36 54 15N	121 44 51W	city/town	42
Pala	33 21 55N	117 04 33W	city/town	400
Pala Mesa	33 19 56N	117 09 46W	city/town	350
Pala Mesa Golf Clb	33 21 22N	117 09 36W	golf	
Palace of Fine Art	37 48 10N	122 26 54W	building	
Palace' Legion' Hon.	37 47 05N	122 29 59W	building	
Palermo	39 26 08N	121 32 13W	city/town	190
Palisade Crest	37 04 40N	118 29 09W	summit	13550
Palisades Beach	34 01 24N	118 30 44W	beach	
Palisades Del Rey	33 56 25N	118 26 13W	city/town	140
Palm Beach	36 52 02N	121 49 01W	beach	
Palm City	32 35 01N	117 05 00W	city/town	44
Palm Desert	33 43 20N	116 22 25W	city/town	243
Palm Grove	32 44 07N	116 12 32W	city/town	1720
Palm Lake Golf Crs	34 02 41N	117 46 00W	golf	
Palm Lakes Golf C.	36 47 24N	119 43 22W	golf	
Palm Springs	33 49 49N	116 32 40W	city/town	466
Palm Springs Reg.	33 49 41N	116 30 22W	airport	462

California GPS Companion

Place Name	Latitude	Longitude	Type	Elev
Palm Springs-Berm.	33 44 54N	116 16 29W	airport	73
Palm Springs-Therm	33 37 40N	116 09 35W	airport	-117
Palm Wells	34 04 40N	116 32 19W	city/town	2720
Palmdale	34 34 46N	118 06 56W	city/town	2659
Palmetto	39 49 26N	121 19 05W	city/town	5160
Palmo	35 33 33N	119 19 49W	city/town	337
Palms	34 01 22N	118 24 17W	city/town	90
Palo Alto	37 26 31N	122 08 31W	city/town	23
Palo Alto Airport	37 27 39N	122 06 53W	airport	5
Palo Alto Hills	37 22 24N	122 10 17W	golf	
Palo Alto Munic.	37 27 24N	122 07 03W	golf	
Palo Cedro	40 33 50N	122 14 16W	city/town	462
Palo Verde	33 25 58N	114 43 53W	city/town	233
Palo Verde College	33 37 06N	114 36 18W	univ/coll	
Paloma	38 15 34N	120 45 44W	city/town	1360
Palomar College	33 08 58N	117 11 02W	univ/coll	
Palomar Mountain	33 19 22N	116 52 40W	city/town	6140
Palomar Mountain	33 21 48N	116 50 07W	summit	6140
Palomar Mountain S	33 20 15N	116 54 34W	park	
Palomar Observator	33 21 16N	116 51 58W	observtry	
Palos Verdes C C	33 47 43N	118 22 20W	golf	
Palos Verdes Est.	33 48 02N	118 23 21W	city/town	217

California GPS Companion

Place Name	Latitude	Longitude	Type	Elev
Palos Verdes Point	33 46 26N	118 25 38W	cape	
Palos Verdes Shore	33 43 32N	118 19 30W	golf	
Pan Pacific Aud.	34 04 29N	118 21 13W	building	
Panama	35 16 01N	119 03 21W	city/town	347
Panamint	36 07 06N	117 05 40W	city/town	6280
Panamint Springs	36 20 23N	117 28 01W	city/town	1940
Panoche	36 35 49N	120 49 57W	city/town	1220
Panoche Junction	36 32 46N	120 29 13W	city/town	513
Panorama City	34 13 29N	118 26 56W	city/town	810
Panorama Hts (1)	33 46 40N	117 47 50W	city/town	400
Panorama Hts (2)	35 48 18N	118 37 42W	city/town	5000
Panorama Hts (3)	34 07 27N	116 13 12W	city/town	2720
Pape Place	40 10 17N	121 48 06W	city/town	1560
Paradise	39 45 35N	121 37 15W	city/town	1708
Paradise Cove Mob.	34 01 13N	118 47 20W	city/town	100
Paradise Cove Pier	34 01 12N	118 47 06W	pier	
Paradise Knolls	33 58 25N	117 29 20W	golf	
Paradise Park	37 00 37N	122 02 33W	city/town	80
Paradise Pines	39 49 49N	121 35 42W	city/town	2600
Paradise Skypark	39 42 34N	121 36 58W	airport	1300
Paradise Springs	34 23 45N	117 48 20W	city/town	4740
Paramount	33 53 22N	118 09 32W	city/town	67

247

California GPS Companion

Place Name	Latitude	Longitude	Type	Elev
Paramount Studios	34 05 08N	118 19 04W	studio	
Pardee	34 24 54N	118 32 23W	city/town	1170
Pardee Home Museum	37 48 18N	122 16 37W	museum	
Paris	34 28 19N	118 10 48W	city/town	2771
Park View Commons	37 45 57N	122 27 07W	city/town	275
Park Village (1)	36 30 40N	116 51 17W	city/town	200
Park Village (2)	38 39 28N	121 04 26W	city/town	700
Parker Dam	34 17 14N	114 08 32W	city/town	400
Parker Junction	34 46 13N	114 35 43W	city/town	740
Parker Peak	37 48 52N	119 11 02W	summit	12861
Parkfield	35 53 59N	120 25 54W	city/town	1535
Parkfield Junction	36 04 55N	120 28 46W	city/town	1192
Parkhill	39 43 21N	121 29 44W	city/town	1965
Parklabrea	34 03 57N	118 21 15W	city/town	180
Parkway	38 29 46N	121 27 28W	city/town	18
Parkway Golf Crs	37 32 41N	121 58 15W	golf	
Parlier	36 36 42N	119 31 34W	city/town	340
Parramore Springs	39 18 49N	122 52 44W	city/town	2140
Parsons Landing	33 28 22N	118 33 03W	beach	
Parsons Peak	37 46 32N	119 18 24W	summit	12147
Pasadena	34 08 52N	118 08 37W	city/town	865
Pasadena City Coll	34 08 41N	118 07 02W	univ/coll	

California GPS Companion

Place Name	Latitude	Longitude	Type	Elev
Pasadena Civic Aud	34 08 37N	118 08 34W	building	
Pasadena College	34 10 20N	118 07 06W	univ/coll	
Pasadena Historic.	34 08 58N	118 09 35W	museum	
Pasatiempo	37 00 16N	122 01 29W	city/town	360
Paskenta	39 53 05N	122 32 41W	city/town	743
Paso Robles	35 37 36N	120 41 24W	city/town	721
Paso Robles Munic.	35 40 22N	120 37 37W	airport	836
Patch	35 15 10N	118 53 42W	city/town	417
Patrick Creek	41 52 31N	123 50 38W	city/town	840
Patricks Point	41 07 25N	124 09 20W	city/town	253
Patricks Point	41 08 10N	124 09 30W	cape	
Patricks Point St.	41 08 10N	124 09 37W	park	
Patterson	37 28 18N	121 07 43W	city/town	97
Patterson, Mount	38 26 12N	119 18 15W	summit	11673
Patton	34 08 09N	117 13 23W	city/town	1280
Patton Beach	39 13 42N	120 04 03W	beach	
Patton Village	40 08 28N	120 09 14W	city/town	4108
Pauley Pavilion	34 04 12N	118 26 45W	building	
Paulsell	37 43 06N	120 41 22W	city/town	200
Paulson Place	39 50 40N	121 08 40W	city/town	5560
Pauma Valley	33 18 12N	116 58 50W	city/town	800
Paumaville C C	33 18 04N	116 59 12W	golf	

California GPS Companion

Place Name	Latitude	Longitude	Type	Elev
Pavilion Dome	37 13 50N	118 48 27W	summit	11846
Pawnee	40 36 45N	122 02 00W	city/town	1160
Paxton	40 02 17N	120 59 38W	city/town	3080
Paymaster Landing	33 14 45N	114 41 20W	city/town	220
Payne	40 14 35N	123 05 30W	city/town	3100
Payne Place	40 14 00N	121 52 35W	city/town	1360
Paynes Creek	40 20 08N	121 54 50W	city/town	1850
Paynesville	38 48 33N	119 46 42W	city/town	5120
Peaceful Pines	38 24 22N	119 47 18W	city/town	6200
Peach Tree Golf	39 08 31N	121 32 25W	golf	
Peachton	39 22 50N	121 39 37W	city/town	100
Peacock Gap Golf	37 59 40N	122 27 49W	golf	
Peak Eight	41 33 02N	123 46 30W	city/town	5193
Peanut	40 28 05N	123 10 03W	city/town	2499
Pearblossom	34 30 23N	117 54 32W	city/town	3049
Pearblossom Arts C	34 30 22N	117 53 55W	building	
Peardale	39 11 28N	120 59 56W	city/town	2716
Pearland	34 33 40N	118 02 22W	city/town	2670
Pearson (1)	38 07 49N	121 14 46W	city/town	60
Pearson (2)	39 03 43N	121 34 35W	city/town	50
Pearsonville	35 48 35N	117 52 20W	city/town	2505
Peavine	39 40 40N	120 00 20W	city/town	5080

California GPS Companion

Place Name	Latitude	Longitude	Type	Elev
Pebble Beach (1)	38 41 48N	123 26 19W	beach	
Pebble Beach (2)	36 34 00N	121 56 47W	beach	
Pebble Beach (3)	41 45 55N	124 13 47W	beach	
Pebble Beach (4)	38 07 43N	122 53 09W	beach	
Pebble Beach (5)	37 14 13N	122 24 55W	beach	
Pebble Beach Golf	36 33 56N	121 56 19W	golf	
Pecwan	41 20 39N	123 51 10W	city/town	100
Pedley	33 58 31N	117 28 30W	city/town	718
Pedro Valley	37 35 36N	122 29 49W	city/town	25
Peethill	38 35 03N	121 31 16W	city/town	15
Pelican State Bch.	41 59 34N	124 12 32W	park	
Peligreen Place	40 12 32N	121 47 14W	city/town	3168
Pellow Place	39 58 36N	122 37 43W	city/town	1520
Peltier	38 11 19N	121 14 35W	city/town	66
Pendleton, Camp	33 12 37N	117 23 31W	locale	50
Pendola Gardens	37 31 05N	120 06 15W	garden	1810
Peninsula Bridge	41 44 12N	121 29 58W	arch	
Peninsula C C	37 32 30N	122 19 18W	golf	
Peninsula Village	40 16 24N	121 07 46W	city/town	4650
Penmar Golf Course	34 00 22N	118 27 35W	golf	
Penney	40 11 54N	123 06 02W	city/town	3200
Penngrove	38 17 59N	122 39 56W	city/town	81

California GPS Companion

Place Name	Latitude	Longitude	Type	Elev
Pennington	39 17 28N	121 47 32W	city/town	84
Penoyar	41 40 03N	122 03 42W	city/town	4819
Penryn	38 51 08N	121 10 06W	city/town	619
Pentland	35 03 36N	119 21 20W	city/town	650
Pentz	39 39 19N	121 34 58W	city/town	435
Penvir	36 32 19N	121 28 59W	city/town	112
Pepper Corner	33 51 06N	117 32 59W	city/town	902
Pepperdine -Malibu	34 02 26N	118 42 30W	univ/coll	
Pepperdine College	33 58 06N	118 17 40W	univ/coll	
Pepperwood	40 26 46N	123 59 30W	city/town	110
Pepperwood Falls	40 27 51N	123 51 17W	falls	
Pepperwood Grove	39 03 29N	122 46 49W	city/town	1340
Peral	36 25 41N	119 17 09W	city/town	325
Peralta Adobe	37 20 13N	121 53 32W	building	
Peralta Hills	33 50 40N	117 49 01W	city/town	400
Perez	41 40 35N	121 15 11W	city/town	4179
Perkins	38 32 47N	121 23 50W	city/town	45
Perkins, Mount	36 55 38N	118 22 58W	summit	12591
Perks Corner	38 42 41N	120 50 17W	city/town	1760
Permanente	36 22 27N	118 00 28W	city/town	3640
Perris	33 46 57N	117 13 40W	city/town	1457
Perris Valley Airp	33 45 39N	117 13 06W	airport	1413

California GPS Companion

Place Name	Latitude	Longitude	Type	Elev
Perry (1)	33 51 56N	118 20 37W	city/town	73
Perry (2)	37 11 01N	121 42 19W	city/town	300
Perrys Corner	32 51 42N	115 22 45W	city/town	-52
Pescadero	37 15 18N	122 22 49W	city/town	31
Pescadero Beach	37 15 44N	122 24 44W	beach	
Pescadero State B.	37 15 50N	122 25 43W	park	
Petaluma	38 13 57N	122 38 08W	city/town	12
Petaluma Adobe St.	38 15 21N	122 35 00W	park	
Petaluma Municipal	38 15 27N	122 36 18W	airport	87
Pete Hoff Place	40 13 02N	122 36 35W	city/town	1080
Peter Peak	37 08 43N	118 44 42W	summit	12543
Peters	37 58 51N	121 02 49W	city/town	97
Peterson Mill	37 15 16N	118 28 39W	city/town	8970
Peterson Place	39 52 42N	122 45 46W	city/town	3160
Petroglyphs Big	36 02 28N	117 39 53W	locale	
Petroglyphs Little	35 59 40N	117 36 30W	locale	5020
Petrolia	40 19 32N	124 17 09W	city/town	120
Pettit Place	35 38 23N	118 37 00W	city/town	4985
Pettyjohn Place	40 10 25N	122 40 29W	city/town	1362
Pfeiffer Beach	36 14 19N	121 48 59W	beach	
Pfeiffer Big Sur S	36 14 56N	121 46 54W	park	
Pfeiffer Falls	36 15 25N	121 46 50W	falls	

California GPS Companion

Place Name	Latitude	Longitude	Type	Elev
Phelan	34 25 34N	117 34 17W	city/town	4112
Phelps Corner	32 43 20N	116 48 35W	city/town	1640
Philbrick Mill	39 04 56N	123 29 39W	city/town	520
Philbrook Lake Boa	40 01 47N	121 28 29W	locale	5546
Phillip Burton Mem	37 42 25N	122 30 05W	beach	
Phillips	38 49 05N	120 04 36W	city/town	6880
Phillipsville	40 12 33N	123 47 05W	city/town	278
Philo	39 03 57N	123 26 38W	city/town	280
Picacho	33 01 23N	114 36 37W	city/town	200
Picacho Mill Ruins	33 01 22N	114 36 01W	locale	
Picacho State Recr	33 02 02N	114 40 19W	park	
Pickering, Mount	36 31 42N	118 17 27W	summit	13485
Picket Guard Peak	36 34 35N	118 28 18W	summit	12302
Pico	34 22 39N	118 36 40W	city/town	1625
Pico Rivera	33 58 59N	118 05 45W	city/town	161
Pico Rivera Sports	34 01 33N	118 02 40W	building	
Picture Puzzle	37 07 41N	118 32 17W	summit	13280
Piedmont	37 49 28N	122 13 50W	city/town	400
Piedra	36 48 37N	119 22 52W	city/town	540
Piedras Blancas L.	35 39 56N	121 17 00W	lighthous	
Pier 39	37 48 35N	122 24 33W	pier	
Pier 41	37 48 36N	122 24 41W	pier	

California GPS Companion

Place Name	Latitude	Longitude	Type	Elev
Pierce (1)	38 07 32N	122 05 58W	city/town	5
Pierce (2)	41 16 07N	122 12 49W	city/town	4478
Pierce College	34 11 07N	118 34 26W	univ/coll	
Pierce Mitchell H.	37 25 17N	122 10 00W	city/town	115
Piercy	39 57 59N	123 47 39W	city/town	800
Pierpont Bay	34 15 35N	119 16 06W	city/town	10
Pieta	38 55 36N	123 03 15W	city/town	480
Pigeon Point Light	37 10 55N	122 23 33W	lighthous	
Pike	39 26 21N	120 59 49W	city/town	3440
Pilgrimage Theater	34 06 49N	118 20 00W	building	
Pilibos Ranch	36 41 01N	120 30 48W	city/town	308
Pillar Point	37 29 56N	122 29 49W	cape	
Pillar Point Harb.	37 30 00N	122 29 00W	harbor	
Pilliken	38 41 11N	120 21 12W	city/town	5600
Pilot Creek House	38 53 43N	120 35 01W	building	4200
Pilot Hill	38 50 06N	121 00 48W	city/town	1185
Pilot Knob	37 16 25N	118 45 23W	summit	12245
Pinchot, Mount	36 56 49N	118 24 23W	summit	13495
Pine Acres	38 23 46N	120 38 33W	city/town	2680
Pine Cove	33 45 38N	116 44 13W	city/town	6165
Pine Cove Boat L.	40 45 37N	122 47 06W	locale	1903
Pine Falls	36 18 03N	121 38 39W	falls	

California GPS Companion

Place Name	Latitude	Longitude	Type	Elev
Pine Flat	35 52 41N	118 39 02W	city/town	3720
Pine Grove (1)	38 24 47N	120 39 28W	city/town	2500
Pine Grove (2)	40 39 54N	122 21 08W	city/town	700
Pine Grove (3)	38 49 42N	122 43 48W	city/town	2520
Pine Grove (4)	32 56 43N	116 42 42W	city/town	2492
Pine Grove (5)	39 20 58N	123 48 47W	city/town	182
Pine Hill	40 45 53N	124 10 24W	city/town	120
Pine Hill State Ec	38 43 10N	120 59 22W	park	
Pine Hills	33 02 54N	116 37 48W	city/town	4400
Pine Island Beach	39 14 00N	121 12 42W	beach	
Pine Land	39 08 12N	120 09 27W	city/town	6270
Pine Meadows Golf	37 59 11N	122 05 57W	golf	
Pine Mountain Club	34 50 47N	119 08 55W	city/town	5800
Pine Mountain Club	34 51 13N	119 10 08W	golf	5400
Pine Town	40 18 15N	120 59 23W	city/town	5085
Pine Valley	32 49 17N	116 31 42W	city/town	3736
Pine Wood	33 48 51N	116 44 12W	city/town	6000
Pinecrest (1)	38 11 19N	119 59 23W	city/town	5680
Pinecrest (2)	39 09 46N	120 58 02W	city/town	2435
Pinecroft	39 04 35N	120 58 37W	city/town	2040
Pinedale	36 50 34N	119 47 20W	city/town	340
Pinehurst	36 41 43N	119 00 56W	city/town	4020

California GPS Companion

Place Name	Latitude	Longitude	Type	Elev
Pineridge	37 03 48N	119 21 36W	city/town	4921
Pinewood Camp	36 34 26N	118 45 54W	city/town	6600
Pinewood Cove	40 50 43N	122 50 43W	city/town	2559
Pinezanita	34 09 52N	116 57 09W	city/town	4880
Pinnacles	36 31 51N	121 08 39W	city/town	1269
Pinnacles National	36 28 00N	121 10 30W	park	
Pinnio	41 04 27N	120 28 06W	city/town	5454
Pino Grande	38 52 13N	120 37 30W	city/town	4027
Pinoche Peak	37 38 05N	119 46 29W	summit	5765
Pinole	38 00 16N	122 17 52W	city/town	21
Pinole Point	38 00 44N	122 21 56W	cape	
Pinon Hills	34 26 00N	117 38 45W	city/town	4160
Pinon Pines Estate	34 49 44N	119 02 31W	city/town	5500
Pinoso House -hist	35 57 52N	120 19 36W	building	
Pinto Wye	34 01 15N	116 01 07W	city/town	3660
Pinyon Crest	33 36 31N	116 26 11W	city/town	4120
Pinyon Pines	33 35 22N	116 27 07W	city/town	4080
Pioneer (1)	41 17 33N	122 18 33W	city/town	3434
Pioneer (2)	38 25 55N	120 34 15W	city/town	2970
Pioneer Memorial M	37 47 08N	122 26 45W	museum	
Pioneer Point	35 47 09N	117 21 45W	city/town	1658
Pioneertown	34 09 24N	116 29 43W	city/town	4033

257

California GPS Companion

Place Name	Latitude	Longitude	Type	Elev
Pippin Corner	35 17 56N	120 24 07W	city/town	137
Piru	34 24 55N	118 47 35W	city/town	692
Pisgah	34 45 35N	116 21 16W	city/town	2171
Pismo Beach	35 08 34N	120 38 25W	city/town	33
Pismo State Beach	35 06 28N	120 37 47W	park	
Pit River Falls	40 59 10N	121 28 15W	falls	
Pitas Point	34 19 10N	119 23 15W	cape	
Pitco	36 21 24N	119 39 46W	city/town	251
Pittsburg	38 01 41N	121 53 01W	city/town	30
Pittsburg Marina	38 02 23N	121 53 06W	marina	
Pittsburg Yacht Cl	38 02 19N	121 53 03W	locale	
Pittville	41 02 55N	121 20 00W	city/town	3270
Pitzer College	34 06 12N	117 42 15W	univ/coll	
Piute	35 24 00N	118 24 00W	city/town	0
Piute Mountain	37 32 17N	118 13 52W	summit	12564
Pixley	35 58 07N	119 17 27W	city/town	271
Pixley Airport	35 57 37N	119 18 29W	airport	256
Pizona	37 58 18N	118 33 26W	city/town	7000
Placentia	33 52 20N	117 52 10W	city/town	250
Placer County Hist	38 53 29N	121 04 18W	museum	
Placerville	38 43 47N	120 47 51W	city/town	1866
Placerville Airprt	38 43 27N	120 45 11W	airport	2583

California GPS Companion

Place Name	Latitude	Longitude	Type	Elev
Plainfield	38 35 27N	121 47 45W	city/town	65
Plainsburg	37 13 59N	120 19 24W	city/town	216
Plainview	36 08 39N	119 07 59W	city/town	352
Planada	37 17 27N	120 19 03W	city/town	225
Plano	36 02 37N	119 00 27W	city/town	462
Plaskett	35 55 00N	121 28 04W	city/town	200
Plasse	38 38 14N	120 07 32W	city/town	7280
Plaster City	32 47 33N	115 51 28W	city/town	100
Playa del Rey	33 56 56N	118 26 41W	city/town	47
Pleasant Grove	38 49 26N	121 28 58W	city/town	48
Pleasant Hill	37 56 53N	122 03 35W	city/town	60
Pleasant Hills	37 20 20N	121 47 56W	golf	
Pleasant Valley	38 40 59N	120 39 43W	city/town	2460
Pleasant View	35 48 20N	118 38 24W	city/town	4480
Pleasanton	37 39 45N	121 52 25W	city/town	352
Pleyto	35 51 37N	120 59 33W	city/town	720
Plum Valley	39 26 55N	120 57 35W	city/town	3960
Plumas	39 45 24N	120 04 56W	city/town	4840
Plumas County Mus.	39 56 08N	120 56 48W	museum	
Plumas Eureka St.	39 45 40N	120 42 20W	park	
Plumas Pines Golf	39 47 32N	120 39 06W	golf	
Plumbago	39 27 08N	120 49 00W	city/town	4280

California GPS Companion

Place Name	Latitude	Longitude	Type	Elev
Plymouth	38 28 55N	120 50 37W	city/town	1086
Poche Beach	33 26 27N	117 38 41W	beach	
Poe	39 44 40N	121 28 13W	city/town	1200
Poffenbergers Land	38 56 20N	121 49 41W	city/town	33
Point Arena	38 54 32N	123 41 31W	city/town	219
Point Arena	38 57 21N	123 44 25W	cape	
Point Arena Lighth	38 57 17N	123 44 22W	lighthous	
Point Arguello	34 34 38N	120 38 59W	cape	
Point Bennett	34 01 48N	120 27 04W	cape	
Point Bonita Light	37 48 56N	122 31 43W	lighthous	
Point Buchon	35 15 19N	120 53 53W	cape	
Point Cabrillo	39 20 58N	123 49 38W	cape	
Point Cabrillo Lt.	39 20 55N	123 49 34W	lighthous	
Point Castillo	34 24 10N	119 41 28W	cape	
Point Conception	34 26 55N	120 28 14W	cape	
Point Conception L	34 26 56N	120 28 11W	lighthous	
Point Delgada	40 01 18N	124 04 05W	cape	
Point Dume Mobile	34 00 53N	118 48 50W	city/town	200
Point Dume State B	34 00 10N	118 48 15W	park	
Point Estero	35 27 47N	121 00 04W	cape	
Point Fermin	33 42 18N	118 17 35W	cape	112
Point Fermin Light	33 42 19N	118 17 34W	lighthous	

California GPS Companion

Place Name	Latitude	Longitude	Type	Elev
Point La Jolla	32 51 04N	117 16 20W	cape	
Point Lobos (1)	36 31 18N	121 57 06W	cape	
Point Lobos (2)	37 46 52N	122 30 47W	cape	
Point Lobos State	36 31 10N	121 56 41W	park	
Point Loma Lighth.	32 39 54N	117 14 30W	lighthous	
Point McCloud	40 55 26N	122 14 33W	city/town	1100
Point Molate Beach	37 56 43N	122 24 47W	beach	
Point Montara Lt.	37 32 11N	122 31 06W	lighthous	
Point Mugu	34 05 08N	119 03 36W	cape	
Point Mugu Beach	34 05 08N	119 03 22W	beach	
Point Pinos Light	36 38 01N	121 55 57W	lighthous	
Point Pleasant	38 19 54N	121 27 46W	city/town	12
Point Reyes	38 00 05N	122 59 45W	cape	
Point Reyes Beach	38 05 00N	122 58 20W	beach	
Point Reyes Lighth	37 59 45N	123 01 20W	lighthous	
Point Reyes Nat'l	38 04 00N	122 53 00W	park	
Point Reyes Stat.	38 04 09N	122 48 21W	city/town	35
Point Richmond	37 54 35N	122 23 22W	cape	
Point Richmond	37 55 27N	122 23 17W	city/town	200
Point Richmond His	37 55 35N	122 23 04W	museum	
Point Sal	34 54 11N	120 40 10W	cape	
Point Sal Beach St	34 54 05N	120 38 49W	park	

California GPS Companion

Place Name	Latitude	Longitude	Type	Elev
Point San Luis	35 09 39N	120 45 26W	cape	
Point San Pedro	37 59 08N	122 26 45W	cape	
Point Sur	36 18 19N	121 53 54W	cape	
Point Sur Lighth.	36 18 23N	121 54 02W	lighthous	
Point Tiburon	37 52 22N	122 27 02W	cape	
Point Vicente Lt.	33 44 31N	118 24 35W	lighthous	
Poker Flat	39 41 36N	120 50 40W	city/town	4760
Polaris	39 20 21N	120 08 05W	city/town	5701
Pole Garden	39 13 11N	122 38 11W	city/town	3450
Polemonium Peak	37 05 37N	118 30 40W	summit	14080
Poleta	37 21 41N	118 19 31W	city/town	4075
Polk	38 31 56N	121 24 28W	city/town	38
Polk Springs	40 07 02N	121 39 51W	city/town	2480
Pollard Flat	40 59 45N	122 25 02W	city/town	1500
Pollock (1)	38 29 22N	121 28 03W	city/town	15
Pollock (2)	40 55 00N	122 23 05W	city/town	1180
Pollock Pines	38 45 41N	120 35 08W	city/town	3960
Polvadero C C	36 07 41N	120 12 05W	golf	578
Pomins	39 04 00N	120 07 33W	city/town	6240
Pomo	39 18 24N	123 05 41W	city/town	940
Pomo Visitors Cent	39 14 06N	123 10 59W	building	
Pomona	34 03 19N	117 45 05W	city/town	850

California GPS Companion

Place Name	Latitude	Longitude	Type	Elev
Pomona College	34 06 42N	117 42 49W	univ/coll	
Pomona Islander M.	34 02 47N	117 48 56W	city/town	693
Pomona Junior Coll	34 03 42N	117 44 15W	univ/coll	
Pomona Raceway	34 05 27N	117 46 19W	track	
Pomponio Beach	37 17 32N	122 24 22W	beach	
Pomponio State Bch	37 17 35N	122 24 23W	park	
Ponca	36 02 31N	119 00 58W	city/town	459
Pond	35 43 04N	119 19 40W	city/town	283
Ponderosa	36 06 20N	118 31 38W	city/town	7200
Ponderosa Fairway	39 19 40N	120 09 45W	city/town	5830
Ponderosa Golf Crs	39 19 28N	120 09 45W	golf	
Ponderosa Palisade	39 18 55N	120 11 30W	city/town	6160
Pondosa	41 11 58N	121 41 16W	city/town	4140
Ponto State Beach	33 04 01N	117 18 20W	park	
Pony Express State	38 41 58N	120 59 41W	park	
Ponytail Falls	41 55 55N	123 07 43W	falls	
Pope (1)	33 21 57N	115 43 19W	city/town	-200
Pope (2)	38 08 30N	121 14 33W	city/town	59
Pope Beach	38 56 14N	120 01 40W	beach	
Pope Valley	38 36 55N	122 25 36W	city/town	706
Poplar	36 03 12N	119 08 32W	city/town	374
Porphyry	33 52 33N	117 32 20W	city/town	650

California GPS Companion

Place Name	Latitude	Longitude	Type	Elev
Port Chicago	38 02 46N	122 01 11W	city/town	10
Port Costa	38 02 47N	122 10 56W	city/town	17
Port Hueneme	34 08 52N	119 11 39W	city/town	12
Port Hueneme Hist.	34 08 54N	119 11 50W	museum	
Port Hueneme Light	34 08 42N	119 12 32W	lighthous	
Port Kenyon	40 35 43N	124 16 43W	city/town	12
Port of Hueneme	34 08 57N	119 12 28W	harbor	
Port of Long Beach	33 45 15N	118 12 56W	harbor	
Port Orford	34 28 13N	120 13 39W	city/town	20
Port San Luis	35 10 30N	120 45 15W	city/town	40
Port Watsonville	36 52 29N	121 49 26W	city/town	10
Portal Inn	40 44 09N	122 19 06W	city/town	1000
Porter	38 23 39N	120 25 27W	city/town	3560
Porter Valley C C	34 16 48N	118 33 14W	golf	
Porterville	36 03 55N	119 00 57W	city/town	459
Porterville Colleg	36 03 02N	119 00 48W	univ/coll	
Porterville Munic.	36 01 46N	119 03 45W	airport	442
Portola	39 48 38N	120 28 05W	city/town	4860
Portola Railroad M	39 48 14N	120 28 31W	museum	
Portola State Park	37 15 04N	122 12 15W	park	
Portola Valley	37 23 03N	122 14 03W	city/town	455
Portugese Beach	38 22 55N	123 04 50W	beach	

California GPS Companion

Place Name	Latitude	Longitude	Type	Elev
Portuguese Bend	33 44 23N	118 22 07W	city/town	200
Posey	35 48 17N	118 40 55W	city/town	3600
Poso Park	35 48 39N	118 38 02W	city/town	4680
Posts	36 13 42N	121 45 48W	city/town	960
Potem Falls	40 50 20N	122 01 38W	falls	
Potrero	32 36 17N	116 36 44W	city/town	2323
Potrero District	37 45 35N	122 23 49W	city/town	250
Potter Valley	39 19 20N	123 06 43W	city/town	945
Potwisha	36 31 03N	118 47 56W	city/town	2160
Poverty Hill	39 37 21N	121 00 21W	city/town	4450
Poway	32 57 46N	117 02 06W	city/town	503
Poway Grove	32 56 24N	117 03 48W	city/town	525
Poway Grove Park	32 56 27N	117 03 52W	city/town	480
Powder Bowl Ski Ar	39 10 54N	120 12 04W	ski area	6500
Powell, Mount	37 08 10N	118 37 42W	summit	13364
Powellton	39 55 44N	121 34 17W	city/town	3635
Pozo	35 18 13N	120 22 32W	city/town	145
Prado Dam	33 52 45N	117 38 57W	locale	
Prairie City	38 38 32N	121 09 17W	city/town	300
Prater, Mount	37 02 15N	118 26 08W	summit	13328
Prather	37 02 15N	119 30 47W	city/town	1642
Pratt Place	39 54 47N	123 43 14W	city/town	1740

California GPS Companion

Place Name	Latitude	Longitude	Type	Elev
Pratton	36 44 48N	119 53 55W	city/town	257
Prattville	40 12 32N	121 09 20W	city/town	4535
Prenda	33 55 17N	117 23 15W	city/town	1000
Prentice Park	33 44 38N	117 50 35W	park	
Presidio Golf Link	37 47 27N	122 27 41W	golf	
Presidio Heights P	37 47 19N	122 26 54W	park	
Presidio Park	32 45 26N	117 11 37W	park	
Presidio Terrace	37 47 18N	122 27 35W	city/town	240
Presswood	39 10 06N	123 12 17W	city/town	620
Preston	38 50 07N	123 00 59W	city/town	330
Preston Falls	37 53 04N	119 52 49W	falls	
Price Laboratory	37 25 47N	122 10 55W	building	
Priest	37 48 51N	120 16 18W	city/town	2457
Princeton (1)	37 30 18N	122 29 09W	city/town	13
Princeton (2)	39 24 12N	122 00 32W	city/town	80
Proberta	40 04 54N	122 10 10W	city/town	254
Professorville	37 26 12N	122 08 45W	city/town	34
Progress	39 03 48N	121 48 00W	city/town	33
Prospero	35 28 16N	119 07 33W	city/town	405
Prosser Lake Hts.	39 21 05N	120 10 50W	city/town	6150
Prosser Lakeview E	39 21 47N	120 10 12W	city/town	6160
Prunedale	36 46 33N	121 40 07W	city/town	90

California GPS Companion

Place Name	Latitude	Longitude	Type	Elev
Pudding Creek Bch.	39 27 20N	123 48 18W	beach	
Puente Junction	34 00 51N	117 57 34W	city/town	320
Puerco Beach	34 01 53N	118 43 04W	beach	
Pulga	39 48 11N	121 26 51W	city/town	1440
Pumpkin Center (1)	35 16 01N	119 01 57W	city/town	346
Pumpkin Center (2)	41 06 36N	121 06 20W	city/town	4138
Punch Bowl, The	34 27 48N	119 03 07W	falls	2200
Punta	34 21 45N	119 26 45W	city/town	40
Punta Gorda Lighth	40 14 58N	124 20 57W	lighthous	
Purdys Gardens	39 06 44N	123 05 34W	garden	
Pushawalla Palms	33 49 27N	116 16 51W	city/town	570
Putah Creek State	38 30 40N	122 05 00W	park	
Pywiack Cascade	37 47 14N	119 29 16W	falls	

Q

Place Name	Latitude	Longitude	Type	Elev
Quail	36 00 35N	119 18 09W	city/town	273
Quail Park Botanic	33 03 12N	117 16 45W	park	
Quail Valley	33 42 25N	117 14 39W	city/town	1560
Quail Valley C C	33 42 15N	117 14 25W	golf	
Quaker Meadow	36 06 37N	118 33 13W	city/town	7120
Quality	35 47 02N	119 07 07W	city/town	505
Quarry Beach	37 51 33N	122 25 12W	beach	

California GPS Companion

Place Name	Latitude	Longitude	Type	Elev
Quartz	37 55 41N	120 25 11W	city/town	1375
Quartz Hill	34 38 43N	118 13 02W	city/town	2450
Queen City	39 39 53N	120 56 21W	city/town	4880
Queen Mary	33 45 10N	118 11 20W	locale	
Quincy	39 56 13N	120 56 46W	city/town	3432
Quincy Junction	39 57 48N	120 53 50W	city/town	3520
Quincy-Gansner Fld	39 56 37N	120 56 48W	airport	3415
Quintette	38 54 54N	120 41 10W	city/town	4040

ℝ

Place Name	Latitude	Longitude	Type	Elev
R Flourney	41 12 40N	120 31 33W	city/town	4400
Racimo	34 03 45N	117 36 38W	city/town	962
Rackerby	39 26 23N	121 20 25W	city/town	1400
Raco	36 48 02N	119 58 41W	city/town	262
Radec	33 27 51N	116 54 47W	city/town	1695
Radisson Plaza	33 53 55N	118 23 14W	golf	
Radnor	35 49 49N	119 15 39W	city/town	295
Radum	37 40 13N	121 51 29W	city/town	359
Rafael Village	38 04 08N	122 32 55W	city/town	80
Raffetto	38 51 49N	120 26 25W	city/town	4800
Ragby	37 36 43N	120 08 03W	city/town	816
Ragtown	34 39 54N	116 09 04W	city/town	2092

California GPS Companion

Place Name	Latitude	Longitude	Type	Elev
Rail Road Flat	38 20 36N	120 30 40W	city/town	2606
Railroad Museum	37 23 58N	118 20 43W	museum	
Rainbow (1)	33 24 37N	117 08 49W	city/town	1050
Rainbow (2)	39 18 37N	120 30 27W	city/town	5800
Rainbow Mountain	36 25 25N	118 32 55W	summit	12043
Rainbow Wells	35 12 17N	115 39 03W	city/town	4457
Raines Houses	37 25 21N	122 09 38W	city/town	67
Raisin City	36 36 09N	119 54 11W	city/town	235
Ralph	37 57 56N	120 16 12W	city/town	2825
Ralph Leggett Plc.	39 51 33N	123 24 04W	city/town	2100
Ramada	39 33 20N	121 42 36W	city/town	134
Ramal	38 13 17N	122 23 37W	city/town	10
Ramirez	39 16 03N	121 32 16W	city/town	91
Ramona (1)	38 32 51N	121 24 28W	city/town	45
Ramona (2)	33 02 30N	116 52 02W	city/town	1442
Ramona Airport	33 02 20N	116 54 49W	airport	1393
Ramona Bowl	33 43 11N	116 56 58W	city/town	
Ramona Park -sub.	34 04 18N	118 07 19W	city/town	400
Rampart	39 09 53N	120 10 38W	city/town	6200
Ramsey (1)	41 16 56N	120 30 26W	city/town	4400
Ramsey (2)	39 58 21N	123 26 46W	city/town	618
Ramsey Crossing	38 59 54N	120 33 12W	city/town	3760

California GPS Companion

Place Name	Latitude	Longitude	Type	Elev
Rana	34 05 22N	117 19 09W	city/town	1060
Ranch House Estate	38 24 23N	120 37 05W	city/town	2550
Rancheria Falls	37 57 18N	119 42 34W	falls	
Ranchita	33 12 36N	116 30 57W	city/town	4065
Rancho Bernardo	33 01 07N	117 03 36W	city/town	500
Rancho Bernardo CC	33 01 54N	117 03 55W	golf	
Rancho Cordova	38 35 21N	121 18 06W	city/town	90
Rancho Cucamonga	34 06 23N	117 35 32W	city/town	1200
Rancho Del Campo	32 36 06N	116 28 06W	city/town	2640
Rancho Dos Palmas	33 29 55N	115 49 49W	city/town	-115
Rancho Duarte Golf	34 08 27N	117 56 35W	golf	
Rancho Llano Seco	39 36 30N	121 57 07W	city/town	110
Rancho Loma Rica	39 18 32N	121 21 11W	city/town	800
Rancho Los Cerrito	33 50 23N	118 11 41W	museum	
Rancho Los Penasq.	32 59 03N	117 05 11W	golf	
Rancho Mirage	33 44 23N	116 24 43W	city/town	320
Rancho Murieta	38 29 19N	121 06 08W	airport	141
Rancho Palos Verde	33 44 40N	118 23 10W	city/town	653
Rancho Park & Golf	34 02 35N	118 24 41W	golf	
Rancho San Joaquin	33 39 49N	117 49 54W	golf	
Rancho Santa Ana B	33 52 54N	117 42 28W	locale	
Rancho Santa Clar.	34 26 24N	118 31 52W	city/town	350

California GPS Companion

Place Name	Latitude	Longitude	Type	Elev
Rancho Santa Fe	33 01 13N	117 12 07W	city/town	245
Rancho Seco	35 16 59N	117 59 20W	city/town	2025
Rancho Sierra Golf	34 44 37N	118 01 31W	golf	
Rancho Vista	34 37 16N	118 13 05W	city/town	2740
Rand	35 25 19N	117 41 30W	city/town	2690
Randall	38 20 42N	121 32 03W	city/town	10
Randolph	39 34 47N	120 22 11W	city/town	4980
Randsburg	35 22 07N	117 39 26W	city/town	3540
Rat Beach	33 48 13N	118 23 38W	beach	
Ratto Landing	38 13 55N	122 17 18W	city/town	9
Ratto Theatre	38 23 36N	120 48 06W	building	
Ratto Winery	38 50 32N	122 59 16W	wine/vin	
Ravendale	40 47 55N	120 21 51W	city/town	5299
Ravendale Airport	40 48 11N	120 21 59W	airport	5299
Ravenna	34 26 19N	118 13 28W	city/town	2468
Ravenswood	37 28 35N	122 08 03W	city/town	10
Ravenswood Point	37 30 27N	122 08 09W	cape	
Rawhide	39 12 01N	120 44 38W	city/town	2180
Rawson	40 07 04N	122 11 36W	city/town	280
Raymer	34 12 53N	118 27 52W	city/town	785
Raymond	37 13 02N	119 54 16W	city/town	938
Raymond Hill	34 07 27N	118 08 50W	city/town	820

California GPS Companion

Place Name	Latitude	Longitude	Type	Elev
Rayo	36 27 00N	119 11 14W	city/town	374
Reading Adobe	40 23 32N	122 11 56W	building	
Recess Peak	37 22 58N	118 51 14W	summit	12836
Recreation Park	33 46 37N	118 07 47W	golf	
Rector	36 18 19N	119 14 31W	city/town	344
Red and White Mt.	37 28 49N	118 51 19W	summit	12850
Red Apple	38 10 44N	120 22 50W	city/town	3228
Red Bank	40 05 58N	122 26 39W	city/town	540
Red Bluff	40 10 43N	122 14 05W	city/town	309
Red Bluff Municip.	40 09 03N	122 15 08W	airport	349
Red Castle	39 15 39N	121 00 53W	building	
Red Dog	39 13 00N	120 53 54W	city/town	2621
Red Fir	36 36 20N	118 45 55W	city/town	7060
Red Hill C C	34 06 36N	117 37 22W	golf	
Red Kaweah	36 32 23N	118 30 17W	summit	13720
Red Mountain	35 21 30N	117 36 57W	city/town	3600
Red Rock Beach	37 53 22N	122 37 54W	beach	
Red Slate Mountain	37 30 27N	118 52 09W	summit	13163
Red, White & Blue	36 58 35N	122 08 27W	beach	
Redbanks	36 25 20N	119 08 36W	city/town	427
Redcrest	40 24 02N	123 56 56W	city/town	380
Redding	40 35 12N	122 23 26W	city/town	557

California GPS Companion

Place Name	Latitude	Longitude	Type	Elev
Redding -Benton	40 34 29N	122 24 29W	airport	719
Redding -Seaplane	40 45 27N	122 19 24W	airport	1065
Redding Convention	40 35 23N	122 22 43W	building	
Redding Municipal	40 30 32N	122 17 36W	airport	502
Redding Museum&Art	40 35 40N	122 23 33W	museum	
Redinger Boat Ramp	37 08 42N	119 26 36W	locale	1414
Redlands	34 03 20N	117 10 54W	city/town	1360
Redlands C C	34 01 27N	117 08 57W	golf	
Redlands Heights	34 02 02N	117 09 28W	city/town	1740
Redlands Municipal	34 05 06N	117 08 46W	airport	1571
Redman	34 45 50N	117 58 08W	city/town	2342
Redondo Beach	33 50 57N	118 23 15W	city/town	59
Redondo Beach	37 26 25N	122 26 33W	beach	
Redondo Beach Pier	33 50 23N	118 23 29W	pier	
Redondo Beach St.	33 49 45N	118 23 22W	park	
Redondo Junction	34 00 57N	118 13 35W	city/town	220
Redway	40 07 13N	123 49 20W	city/town	538
Redwood City	37 29 07N	122 14 07W	city/town	15
Redwood Corral	35 58 57N	118 39 42W	city/town	5960
Redwood Empire C C	40 33 56N	124 06 24W	golf	
Redwood Estates	37 09 23N	121 59 08W	city/town	1600
Redwood Grove	37 09 27N	122 07 59W	city/town	560

California GPS Companion

Place Name	Latitude	Longitude	Type	Elev
Redwood Junction	37 28 38N	122 13 13W	city/town	22
Redwood Lodge (1)	37 06 28N	121 56 37W	city/town	1350
Redwood Lodge (2)	39 26 28N	123 41 22W	city/town	
Redwood Nat'l Pk.	41 45 58N	124 02 48W	park	1800
Redwood Point	37 32 06N	122 11 37W	cape	
Redwood Terrace	37 18 53N	122 17 38W	city/town	280
Redwood Valley	39 15 56N	123 12 12W	city/town	708
Redwoods	40 35 47N	121 56 04W	city/town	2000
Reed	37 54 18N	122 29 58W	city/town	60
Reedley	36 35 47N	119 26 58W	city/town	348
Reedley Municipal	36 39 58N	119 26 59W	airport	383
Reef Station	35 54 06N	120 03 14W	city/town	550
Reeves Place (1)	35 09 54N	120 18 32W	city/town	940
Reeves Place (2)	39 53 21N	123 06 45W	city/town	2640
Refugio Beach	34 27 46N	120 04 09W	beach	
Refugio Beach St.	34 27 38N	120 04 22W	park	50
Regina Heights	39 08 54N	123 10 21W	city/town	900
Reilly Heights	39 06 35N	123 30 53W	city/town	352
Reinstein, Mount	37 04 15N	118 44 15W	summit	12586
Relief	39 21 41N	120 51 35W	city/town	
Remnoy	36 20 23N	119 33 12W	city/town	255
Rendalia	33 53 25N	118 07 59W	city/town	70

California GPS Companion

Place Name	Latitude	Longitude	Type	Elev
Reno Junction	39 47 31N	120 05 56W	city/town	4990
Renoville	35 33 10N	116 11 18W	city/town	675
Renshaw Place	35 10 20N	120 15 42W	city/town	1610
Renwood-Santino W.	38 32 17N	120 48 05W	wine/vin	
Requa	41 32 49N	124 03 55W	city/town	200
Reseda	34 12 04N	118 32 08W	city/town	738
Retzlaff Vineyards	37 40 18N	121 45 08W	wine/vin	
Reward (1)	36 44 51N	118 03 15W	city/town	3936
Reward (2)	35 19 21N	119 40 42W	city/town	1275
Rex	34 56 43N	120 22 34W	city/town	280
Reyes Place	39 50 46N	123 24 24W	city/town	1240
Reynolds	38 08 54N	122 52 55W	city/town	9
Rheem (1)	37 58 33N	122 21 12W	city/town	15
Rheem (2)	37 51 39N	122 07 34W	city/town	600
Rheem Valley	37 51 36N	122 07 22W	city/town	602
Rhinehart Cabin	40 00 52N	120 51 36W	building	5580
Rialto	34 06 23N	117 22 10W	city/town	1240
Rialto Municipal	34 07 45N	117 24 05W	airport	1455
Ribbon Beach	33 26 59N	118 34 43W	beach	
Ribbon Fall	37 44 09N	119 38 50W	falls	
Ribbonwood	33 34 13N	116 29 53W	city/town	4400
Ribier	35 15 10N	118 52 43W	city/town	444

California GPS Companion

Place Name	Latitude	Longitude	Type	Elev
Ricardo	35 22 26N	117 59 18W	city/town	2580
Riccas Corner	38 25 24N	122 47 13W	city/town	94
Rice	34 05 01N	114 50 56W	city/town	935
Rice Air Base -his	34 03 56N	114 48 48W	military	
Rice Fork Summer H	39 23 59N	122 56 58W	city/town	1971
Rices Junction	37 09 10N	122 07 59W	city/town	550
Riceton	39 26 58N	121 43 28W	city/town	95
Rich	34 58 35N	117 43 36W	city/town	2345
Rich Gulch	38 19 49N	120 37 48W	city/town	1914
Richardson Springs	39 50 24N	121 46 33W	city/town	580
Richfield	39 58 30N	122 10 32W	city/town	267
Richfields	33 52 02N	117 49 30W	city/town	250
Richgrove	35 47 48N	119 06 25W	city/town	510
Richland	33 09 15N	117 08 25W	city/town	700
Richmond	37 56 09N	122 20 48W	city/town	50
Richmond -San Rafa	37 56 05N	122 25 57W	bridge	
Richmond Art Cent.	37 56 17N	122 20 36W	building	
Richmond District	37 46 50N	122 28 17W	city/town	150
Richmond Golf Club	37 59 21N	122 20 52W	golf	
Richmond Museum	37 56 12N	122 21 52W	museum	
Richmond Pier	37 54 28N	122 23 05W	pier	
Richvale	39 29 38N	121 44 37W	city/town	106

California GPS Companion

Place Name	Latitude	Longitude	Type	Elev
Rico	32 48 24N	115 23 48W	city/town	-24
Ridge	39 20 12N	123 18 00W	city/town	1900
Ridge Tavern -hist	34 42 43N	118 47 48W	building	
Ridge View	39 13 44N	121 04 36W	city/town	2640
Ridgecrest	35 37 21N	117 40 12W	city/town	2289
Ridgeview Village	38 40 10N	121 05 01W	city/town	1100
Ridgeville	40 51 53N	122 48 07W	city/town	2560
Ridgewood	39 12 57N	120 05 29W	city/town	6460
Ridgewood Park	39 19 51N	123 20 25W	city/town	2160
Ridgewoods Heights	40 44 08N	124 08 50W	city/town	400
Riego	38 45 05N	121 29 01W	city/town	45
Rimforest	34 13 47N	117 13 27W	city/town	5955
Rimlon	33 50 15N	116 26 33W	city/town	344
Rimrock	34 11 53N	116 33 13W	city/town	4540
Rinckel	41 08 00N	122 04 27W	city/town	2500
Rincon (1)	37 00 44N	122 03 05W	city/town	300
Rincon (2)	33 17 17N	116 57 27W	city/town	1018
Rincon Beach	34 20 08N	119 24 22W	beach	
Rinconada	37 13 39N	121 58 00W	city/town	393
Rio Bravo	35 23 53N	119 17 24W	city/town	312
Rio Del Mar	36 58 06N	121 53 57W	city/town	120
Rio Del Mar Beach	36 57 50N	121 53 48W	beach	

California GPS Companion

Place Name	Latitude	Longitude	Type	Elev
Rio Dell (1)	38 29 57N	122 54 22W	city/town	160
Rio Dell (2)	40 29 58N	124 06 19W	city/town	126
Rio Hondo	33 58 30N	118 07 25W	city/town	155
Rio Hondo C C	33 57 13N	118 08 39W	golf	
Rio Hondo Junior C	34 01 10N	118 01 57W	univ/coll	
Rio Linda	38 41 28N	121 26 51W	city/town	50
Rio Linda Airport	38 40 33N	121 26 43W	airport	45
Rio Nido	38 31 16N	122 58 33W	city/town	80
Rio Oso	38 57 40N	121 32 36W	city/town	43
Rio Vista	38 09 21N	121 41 25W	city/town	22
Rio Vista Junction	38 12 22N	121 52 27W	city/town	112
Rio Vista Municip.	38 10 15N	121 41 20W	airport	45
Ripley	33 31 31N	114 39 19W	city/town	248
Ripon	37 44 30N	121 07 24W	city/town	62
Ripperdan	36 51 05N	120 03 18W	city/town	244
Ritter, Mount	37 41 22N	119 11 53W	summit	13140
River Mansion	38 16 10N	121 35 11W	building	
River Oaks	36 53 59N	121 35 36W	city/town	140
River Pines	38 32 47N	120 44 35W	city/town	2040
Riverbank	37 44 10N	120 56 04W	city/town	140
Riverbend	36 45 25N	119 30 37W	city/town	406
Riverbend Golf Crs	38 35 55N	121 31 11W	golf	

California GPS Companion

Place Name	Latitude	Longitude	Type	Elev
Riverdale (1)	39 53 16N	123 44 47W	city/town	760
Riverdale (2)	36 25 52N	119 51 31W	city/town	230
Riverkern	35 47 23N	118 26 46W	city/town	2800
Riverside (1)	40 51 50N	123 58 10W	city/town	110
Riverside (2)	33 57 12N	117 23 43W	city/town	830
Riverside (3)	38 31 09N	121 31 10W	city/town	12
Riverside (4)	37 38 17N	120 56 50W	city/town	101
Riverside -Flabob	33 59 23N	117 24 38W	airport	764
Riverside Grove	37 10 26N	122 08 32W	city/town	720
Riverside Junction	33 59 07N	117 21 37W	city/town	881
Riverside Mun. A.	33 57 06N	117 26 42W	airport	816
Riverside Mun. G.	36 50 45N	119 54 13W	golf	
Riverside Park	40 29 43N	123 59 30W	city/town	256
Riverton	38 46 16N	120 26 54W	city/town	3220
Riverview (1)	38 30 13N	121 33 32W	city/town	20
Riverview (2)	40 55 22N	122 24 06W	city/town	1260
Riverview (3)	32 51 21N	116 55 52W	city/town	390
Riverview C C	40 32 54N	122 22 10W	golf	
Riverview Farms	32 50 42N	116 55 52W	city/town	440
Riviera	34 03 28N	118 30 02W	city/town	500
Riviera Country Cl	34 03 00N	118 30 01W	golf	
Riviera Villas	32 43 38N	117 15 02W	city/town	210

California GPS Companion

Place Name	Latitude	Longitude	Type	Elev
Rixford, Mount	36 47 04N	118 23 54W	summit	12890
Roadrunner Dunes	35 10 01N	116 02 30W	golf	
Roads End	35 55 36N	118 29 54W	city/town	3630
Roaring River Fall	36 46 50N	118 37 12W	falls	
Robbers Creek	40 22 13N	121 00 14W	city/town	5320
Robbins	38 52 13N	121 42 19W	city/town	18
Robert W Matthews	40 22 08N	123 25 54W	dam	2760
Roberts Army Air F	35 48 53N	120 44 37W	military	630
Roberts Place	40 02 28N	121 51 23W	city/town	1760
Robertson Gymnas.	34 24 58N	119 50 53W	building	
Robertsville	37 15 48N	121 52 31W	city/town	173
Robinson Mills	39 29 42N	121 19 11W	city/town	2576
Robinson, Mount	37 07 04N	118 30 59W	summit	12967
Robinsons Corner	39 21 52N	121 36 25W	city/town	101
Robla	38 39 41N	121 26 44W	city/town	45
Roblar	38 19 17N	122 45 28W	city/town	210
Roble	39 39 52N	121 48 18W	city/town	170
Roble Gymnasium	37 25 34N	122 10 25W	building	
Robles Del Rio	36 28 12N	121 43 56W	city/town	480
Rochedale Village	37 51 57N	122 15 30W	city/town	230
Rochester	34 05 30N	117 32 48W	city/town	1120
Rock City	37 50 59N	121 56 04W	city/town	1520

Place Name	Latitude	Longitude	Type	Elev
Rock Creek	39 54 10N	121 21 07W	city/town	1840
Rock Creek Camp	39 55 36N	121 18 54W	city/town	
Rock Creek Dam	39 59 13N	121 16 54W	dam	2212
Rock Crest	39 55 37N	121 18 56W	city/town	1850
Rock Haven	37 07 33N	119 19 06W	city/town	5600
Rock House	33 37 48N	116 31 45W	building	
Rockaway Beach	37 36 31N	122 29 39W	city/town	68
Rockaway Beach	37 36 36N	122 29 47W	beach	
Rocket Fuel Test S	33 51 03N	117 42 08W	military	
Rocking K	37 21 40N	118 28 48W	city/town	4593
Rockland	41 58 52N	123 57 38W	city/town	910
Rocklin	38 47 27N	121 14 05W	city/town	248
Rockport	39 44 20N	123 48 54W	city/town	30
Rocktram	38 15 27N	122 16 46W	city/town	8
Rockville	38 14 39N	122 07 16W	city/town	60
Rockwood	33 02 56N	115 30 43W	city/town	-154
Rocky Hill	36 18 05N	119 07 00W	city/town	408
Rodeo	38 01 59N	122 15 57W	city/town	20
Rodeo Beach	37 49 48N	122 32 09W	beach	
Rodeo Marina	38 02 22N	122 16 15W	marina	
Rodgers Crossing	36 51 43N	119 07 12W	city/town	1040
Rodgers Flat	39 57 35N	121 16 40W	city/town	2100

California GPS Companion

Place Name	Latitude	Longitude	Type	Elev
Rodgers Peak	37 43 29N	119 15 23W	summit	12978
Roe Island	38 04 21N	122 02 01W	island	
Rogerville	39 36 41N	121 13 17W	city/town	3450
Rohnert Park	38 20 23N	122 42 00W	city/town	106
Rohnerville	40 34 02N	124 08 04W	city/town	200
Rolands	38 30 39N	122 58 46W	city/town	60
Rolinda	36 44 07N	119 57 39W	city/town	249
Rolling Greens	38 44 00N	121 11 49W	golf	
Rolling Hills	33 45 25N	118 21 11W	city/town	1000
Rolling Hills C C	33 46 52N	118 19 35W	golf	
Rolling Hills Est.	33 47 16N	118 21 26W	city/town	500
Roma	38 08 35N	121 14 14W	city/town	64
Romaggi Adobe	38 02 28N	120 31 16W	building	
Romoland	33 44 45N	117 10 27W	city/town	1440
Roop Fort -hist.	40 25 07N	120 39 21W	military	
Roosevelt (1)	34 43 10N	118 00 17W	city/town	2383
Roosevelt (2)	33 51 53N	118 18 10W	city/town	50
Roosevelt Municip.	34 07 09N	118 17 26W	golf	
Rosamond	34 51 51N	118 09 45W	city/town	2326
Rosamond Skypark	34 52 14N	118 12 33W	airport	2415
Rose Hill -subdiv.	34 04 55N	118 11 45W	city/town	600
Rose Place	39 09 57N	122 49 00W	city/town	3080

California GPS Companion

Place Name	Latitude	Longitude	Type	Elev
Rose Valley Falls	34 31 34N	119 10 42W	falls	
Rosedale	35 23 01N	119 08 40W	city/town	368
Rosemary	34 56 44N	120 23 37W	city/town	260
Rosemead	34 04 50N	118 04 19W	city/town	281
Rosemont (1)	33 00 03N	116 55 27W	city/town	1480
Rosemont (2)	38 33 07N	121 21 49W	city/town	48
Rosemont Pavilion	34 09 19N	118 09 48W	building	
Roseville (1)	38 45 08N	121 17 13W	city/town	160
Roseville (2)	32 43 41N	117 13 53W	city/town	180
Roseville Teleph.	38 45 02N	121 16 54W	museum	
Rosewood (1)	40 16 11N	122 33 19W	city/town	669
Rosewood (2)	40 46 05N	124 09 52W	city/town	130
Rosicrucian Museum	37 20 04N	121 55 18W	museum	
Ross (1)	37 57 45N	122 33 14W	city/town	23
Ross (2)	38 27 31N	122 53 05W	city/town	170
Ross Auditorium	33 58 05N	118 08 37W	building	
Ross Corner	32 46 53N	114 35 22W	city/town	130
Rossi	36 17 44N	119 49 54W	city/town	212
Rossmoor	33 47 08N	118 05 03W	city/town	13
Rossmoor Walnut Cr	37 51 52N	122 04 07W	golf	
Rotavele	39 41 04N	121 59 57W	city/town	130
Rough and Ready	39 13 49N	121 08 06W	city/town	1880

California GPS Companion

Place Name	Latitude	Longitude	Type	Elev
Round Hill C C	37 51 20N	122 00 24W	golf	
Round Mountain	40 47 39N	121 56 27W	city/town	2080
Round Valley	40 14 23N	121 30 20W	city/town	4795
Round Valley Peak	37 26 56N	118 40 57W	summit	11943
Rovana	37 24 46N	118 36 52W	city/town	5060
Rowen	35 14 27N	118 34 33W	city/town	2412
Rowland	34 00 06N	117 55 44W	city/town	391
Rowland Heights	33 58 34N	117 54 16W	city/town	540
Royal Arch Cascade	37 44 59N	119 34 11W	falls	
Royal Gorge	39 13 41N	120 26 06W	locale	
Royal Presidio Ch.	36 35 44N	121 53 20W	mission	
Royal Vista Golf	33 59 28N	117 51 50W	golf	
Royce Peak	37 19 08N	118 46 11W	summit	13282
Rubicon Properties	39 00 50N	120 07 00W	city/town	6400
Rubidoux	33 59 46N	117 24 17W	city/town	773
Ruby Hill C C	37 38 55N	121 48 45W	golf	
Rucker	37 03 15N	121 35 28W	city/town	235
Rumsey	38 53 18N	122 14 11W	city/town	419
Running Springs	34 12 28N	117 06 30W	city/town	6040
Runnymede Poultry	34 12 50N	118 31 26W	city/town	752
Rupert Boat Ramp	40 28 05N	122 16 40W	locale	
Ruskin, Mount	36 58 42N	118 28 23W	summit	12920

Place Name	Latitude	Longitude	Type	Elev
Russ	34 26 23N	118 18 50W	city/town	2025
Russ Place	40 08 45N	123 16 40W	city/town	3340
Russell	38 14 20N	122 05 41W	city/town	40
Russell City	37 39 10N	122 07 57W	city/town	15
Russell, Mount	36 35 27N	118 17 16W	summit	14086
Russian Gulch St.	39 19 59N	123 46 26W	park	
Russian Peak	41 16 58N	122 57 03W	summit	8196
Russian River Terr	38 30 17N	122 55 32W	city/town	80
Ruth	40 16 11N	123 19 13W	city/town	2720
Ruth Airport	40 12 40N	123 17 51W	airport	2781
Rutherford	38 27 31N	122 25 17W	city/town	170
Ruthven	32 57 09N	115 00 38W	city/town	375
Ryan	36 19 23N	116 40 14W	city/town	3040
Ryde	38 14 19N	121 33 34W	city/town	11
Ryer Island	38 14 26N	121 37 59W	island	

S

Place Name	Latitude	Longitude	Type	Elev
S F B Morse Botan.	36 35 34N	121 56 11W	park	
Sablon	34 10 29N	114 59 37W	city/town	710
Sacanap	37 53 36N	122 04 30W	city/town	210
Sacate	34 28 20N	120 17 33W	city/town	40
Saco	35 26 40N	119 05 29W	city/town	450

California GPS Companion

Place Name	Latitude	Longitude	Type	Elev
Sacramento	38 34 54N	121 29 36W	city/town	20
Sacramento City C.	38 32 27N	121 29 23W	univ/coll	
Sacramento Exec.	38 30 45N	121 29 36W	airport	21
Sacramento Int'l	38 41 43N	121 35 26W	airport	24
Sacramento Landing	38 08 59N	122 54 19W	city/town	0
Sacramento State C	38 33 48N	121 25 29W	univ/coll	
Sacramento Valley	39 09 07N	122 09 34W	museum	
Sacramento-Natomas	38 38 17N	121 30 54W	airport	22
Saddle Junction	33 46 26N	116 40 24W	city/town	8080
Sage	33 34 54N	116 55 53W	city/town	2320
Sage Hen	41 06 39N	120 28 37W	city/town	5540
Sageland	35 28 48N	118 12 42W	city/town	4011
Sahl Court	39 14 03N	121 04 03W	city/town	2620
Saint Andrews Vlg.	38 41 51N	121 04 48W	city/town	740
Saint Bernard	40 15 36N	121 22 15W	city/town	4850
Saint Francis Sq.	37 47 03N	122 25 41W	city/town	150
Saint Francis Wood	37 44 05N	122 28 01W	city/town	350
Saint Francis Yt.C	37 48 25N	122 26 40W	locale	
Saint Helena	38 30 19N	122 28 09W	city/town	257
Saint James Park	34 01 52N	118 16 45W	city/town	202
Saint John Mount	39 26 04N	122 41 31W	summit	6746
Saint Johns	36 23 05N	119 05 51W	city/town	427

California GPS Companion

Place Name	Latitude	Longitude	Type	Elev
Saint Louis	39 41 55N	120 55 26W	city/town	5040
Saint Marys Coll.	37 50 28N	122 06 25W	univ/coll	
Saint Vincent	38 01 47N	122 32 00W	city/town	20
Salesian College	36 59 16N	121 55 34W	univ/coll	
Salida	37 42 21N	121 05 02W	city/town	67
Salinas	36 40 40N	121 39 16W	city/town	53
Salinas Fairways	36 40 09N	121 37 06W	golf	
Salinas Municipal	36 39 47N	121 36 22W	airport	84
Salinas River St.	36 46 59N	121 47 40W	park	
Salminas Resort	38 52 33N	122 43 39W	city/town	2610
Salmon Creek	38 21 02N	123 03 40W	city/town	40
Salmon Creek Falls	35 54 38N	118 26 06W	falls	
Salmon Falls	38 45 33N	121 04 08W	falls	
Salmon Mountain	41 11 00N	123 24 36W	summit	6956
Salt Point	38 33 59N	123 19 54W	cape	
Salt Point State P	38 34 31N	123 18 43W	park	
Saltdale	35 21 33N	117 53 12W	city/town	1927
Salton	33 28 26N	115 53 02W	city/town	-200
Salton Beach	33 28 11N	115 52 59W	beach	
Salton Sea Airport	33 14 29N	115 57 09W	airport	-85
Salton Sea Beach	33 22 30N	116 00 40W	city/town	-220
Salton Sea Nat'l	33 09 00N	115 44 00W	park	

California GPS Companion

Place Name	Latitude	Longitude	Type	Elev
Salton Sea State P	33 25 04N	115 49 51W	park	
Saltus	34 32 16N	115 41 21W	city/town	590
Salvador	38 20 27N	122 19 11W	city/town	75
Salvia	33 52 21N	116 30 03W	city/town	550
Salyer	40 53 25N	123 35 00W	city/town	600
Sam Snead Golf Crs	34 04 18N	117 21 32W	golf	
Samoa	40 49 08N	124 11 07W	city/town	20
San Andreas	38 11 46N	120 40 46W	city/town	1008
San Andreas -Calav	38 08 46N	120 38 53W	airport	1325
San Anselmo	37 58 29N	122 33 38W	city/town	45
San Antonio	38 11 02N	122 35 25W	city/town	15
San Antonio Dam	34 09 27N	117 40 38W	dam	2238
San Antonio Falls	34 16 19N	117 38 01W	falls	
San Antonio Height	34 09 20N	117 39 20W	city/town	2000
San Antonio Miss.	36 00 55N	121 14 56W	mission	
San Antonio Winery	34 03 51N	118 13 23W	wine/vin	
San Ardo	36 01 14N	120 54 15W	city/town	459
San Augustine	34 27 34N	120 21 26W	city/town	86
San Benito	36 30 35N	121 04 51W	city/town	1340
San Benito County	36 46 38N	121 18 31W	golf	
San Bernardino	34 06 30N	117 17 20W	city/town	1200
San Bernardino Int	34 05 43N	117 14 04W	airport	1156

California GPS Companion

Place Name	Latitude	Longitude	Type	Elev
San Bernardino Pk.	34 07 20N	116 55 21W	summit	10649
San Bernardino Vly	34 05 14N	117 18 43W	univ/coll	
San Bruno	37 37 50N	122 24 36W	city/town	16
San Buenaventura S	34 16 03N	119 16 40W	park	
San Carlos	37 30 26N	122 15 34W	city/town	76
San Carlos Airport	37 30 39N	122 14 58W	airport	2
San Carlos Beach	36 36 35N	121 53 40W	beach	
San Carlos Golf	32 48 02N	117 01 57W	golf	
San Clemente	33 25 37N	117 36 40W	city/town	160
San Clemente City	33 25 38N	117 37 39W	beach	
San Clemente Dam	36 26 09N	121 42 27W	dam	525
San Clemente Golf	33 24 29N	117 35 42W	golf	
San Clemente Is.	32 54 00N	118 30 00W	island	
San Clemente Pier	33 25 06N	117 37 16W	pier	
San Clemente State	33 24 11N	117 36 14W	park	
San Diego	32 42 55N	117 09 23W	city/town	40
San Diego -Brown	32 34 20N	116 58 48W	airport	524
San Diego -Gillesp	32 49 34N	116 58 20W	airport	385
San Diego -Montgom	32 48 57N	117 08 25W	airport	423
San Diego C C	32 37 21N	117 03 42W	golf	
San Diego City Col	32 43 04N	117 09 08W	univ/coll	
San Diego Int'l	32 44 00N	117 11 15W	airport	15

California GPS Companion

Place Name	Latitude	Longitude	Type	Elev
San Diego Mesa Col	32 48 16N	117 10 07W	univ/coll	
San Diego Stadium	32 47 00N	117 07 08W	stadium	
San Diego State C.	32 46 36N	117 04 12W	univ/coll	
San Diego Yacht Cl	32 43 06N	117 13 42W	locale	5
San Diego-Coronado	32 41 22N	117 09 15W	bridge	
San Dimas	34 06 24N	117 48 21W	city/town	952
San Dimas Canyon	34 08 15N	117 46 45W	golf	
San Elijo St. Bch.	33 01 29N	117 17 08W	park	
San Emidio	35 05 40N	119 18 13W	city/town	480
San Felipe (1)	36 58 15N	121 25 05W	city/town	182
San Felipe (2)	33 11 57N	116 35 52W	city/town	3477
San Fernando	34 16 55N	118 26 17W	city/town	1061
San Fernando Vly.	34 09 17N	118 35 33W	golf	
San Fernando Vly.	34 14 19N	118 31 49W	univ/coll	
San Francisco	37 46 30N	122 25 06W	city/town	63
San Francisco Fire	37 47 09N	122 26 45W	museum	
San Francisco Golf	37 42 38N	122 28 37W	golf	
San Francisco Ice	37 45 27N	122 30 26W	arena	
San Francisco Int.	37 37 08N	122 22 29W	airport	11
San Francisco Mus.	37 46 46N	122 25 11W	museum	
San Francisco Oper	37 46 43N	122 25 11W	building	
San Francisco St P	37 33 38N	122 25 23W	park	

California GPS Companion

Place Name	Latitude	Longitude	Type	Elev
San Francisco St.	37 43 20N	122 28 34W	univ/coll	
San Francisco Toy	37 48 26N	122 25 04W	museum	
San Francisco Wom.	37 46 47N	122 27 04W	univ/coll	
San Francisco-Oakl	37 48 58N	122 21 07W	bridge	
San Gabriel	34 05 46N	118 06 18W	city/town	400
San Gabriel C C	34 06 39N	118 05 43W	golf	
San Geronimo	38 00 48N	122 39 46W	city/town	299
San Gorgonio Mount	34 06 02N	116 49 40W	summit	11490
San Gregorio	37 19 38N	122 23 08W	city/town	62
San Gregorio Beach	37 19 23N	122 24 08W	beach	
San Gregorio State	37 19 24N	122 24 09W	park	
San Ignacio	33 18 17N	116 31 03W	city/town	4918
San Jacinto	33 47 02N	116 57 28W	city/town	1567
San Jacinto Peak	33 48 52N	116 40 42W	summit	10804
San Joaquin	36 36 24N	120 11 17W	city/town	170
San Joaquin C C	36 51 01N	119 51 06W	golf	
San Joaquin Delta	37 58 34N	121 18 34W	univ/coll	
San Joaquin Mount	37 43 09N	119 06 17W	summit	11600
San Joaquin River	37 40 51N	121 16 19W	city/town	40
San Jose	37 20 22N	121 53 38W	city/town	87
San Jose -Reid-Hlv	37 19 58N	121 49 11W	airport	133
San Jose Bible Col	37 19 51N	121 52 05W	univ/coll	

California GPS Companion

Place Name	Latitude	Longitude	Type	Elev
San Jose C C	37 23 16N	121 49 11W	golf	
San Jose City Coll	37 18 54N	121 55 37W	univ/coll	
San Jose Civic Aud	37 19 51N	121 53 19W	building	
San Jose Convent.	37 19 50N	121 53 15W	building	
San Jose Int'l	37 21 43N	121 55 40W	airport	58
San Jose M. of Art	37 20 02N	121 53 21W	museum	
San Jose Speedway	37 19 46N	121 49 09W	track	
San Jose State Col	37 20 04N	121 52 48W	univ/coll	
San Juan Bautista	36 50 44N	121 32 13W	city/town	220
San Juan Capistran	33 30 06N	117 39 42W	city/town	120
San Juan Hills C C	33 29 45N	117 39 08W	golf	
San Juan Hot Sprgs	33 35 27N	117 30 31W	city/town	720
San Lawrence Terr.	35 44 45N	120 40 57W	city/town	700
San Leandro	37 43 30N	122 09 18W	city/town	50
San Leandro Bay	37 45 03N	122 13 24W	bay	
San Leandro Marina	37 41 52N	122 11 24W	marina	
San Lorenzo	37 40 52N	122 07 24W	city/town	40
San Lorenzo Park	37 11 46N	122 08 40W	city/town	703
San Lucas	36 07 44N	121 01 10W	city/town	406
San Luis Obispo	35 16 58N	120 39 31W	city/town	234
San Luis Obispo CC	35 12 46N	120 37 28W	golf	
San Luis Obispo Co	35 14 13N	120 38 32W	airport	209

California GPS Companion

Place Name	Latitude	Longitude	Type	Elev
San Luis Rey	33 13 55N	117 19 22W	city/town	60
San Luis Rey Hts.	33 19 08N	117 12 30W	city/town	340
San Marcos	33 08 36N	117 09 55W	city/town	590
San Marino	34 07 17N	118 06 20W	city/town	566
San Martin	37 05 06N	121 36 33W	city/town	282
San Martin -S.Cnty	37 04 54N	121 35 48W	airport	281
San Martin Rock	35 53 17N	121 27 54W	island	122
San Mateo	37 33 47N	122 19 28W	city/town	15
San Mateo Bridge	37 36 07N	122 12 13W	bridge	
San Mateo Coast St	37 17 48N	122 24 18W	park	
San Mateo Park	37 34 00N	122 20 39W	city/town	75
San Miguel	35 45 09N	120 41 43W	city/town	640
San Miguel Island	34 02 23N	120 22 28W	island	
San Miguel Mission	35 44 40N	120 41 49W	mission	
San Nicolas Island	33 14 58N	119 29 58W	island	
San Onofre	33 22 52N	117 34 20W	city/town	30
San Onofre Beach	33 22 22N	117 33 53W	beach	
San Pablo	37 57 44N	122 20 40W	city/town	50
San Pablo Bay	38 04 00N	122 23 00W	bay	
San Pasqual	33 05 30N	116 57 11W	city/town	540
San Pasqual Battle	33 05 10N	116 59 21W	park	407
San Pedro	33 44 09N	118 17 29W	city/town	120

California GPS Companion

Place Name	Latitude	Longitude	Type	Elev
San Pedro Bay	33 44 00N	118 12 00W	bay	
San Pedro Beach	37 35 54N	122 30 06W	beach	
San Pedro Hill	33 44 46N	118 20 07W	city/town	1460
San Quentin	37 56 29N	122 29 02W	city/town	32
San Rafael	37 58 25N	122 31 48W	city/town	12
San Ramon	37 46 48N	121 58 37W	city/town	480
San Ramon National	37 44 04N	121 55 41W	golf	
San Ramon Village	37 43 17N	121 55 44W	city/town	350
San Simeon	35 38 38N	121 11 23W	city/town	20
San Simeon Point	35 38 10N	121 11 38W	cape	
San Tomas	37 16 08N	121 58 28W	city/town	235
San Ysidro (1)	32 33 07N	117 02 32W	city/town	80
San Ysidro (2)	33 15 19N	116 33 56W	city/town	4110
Sanborn	35 00 02N	118 06 20W	city/town	2560
Sand Beach	37 16 17N	122 24 34W	beach	
Sand Canyon	35 18 27N	118 25 40W	city/town	2700
Sand City	36 37 02N	121 50 50W	city/town	60
Sand Dollar Beach	35 55 26N	121 28 03W	beach	
Sand Hill	37 58 25N	121 41 40W	city/town	43
Sandberg	34 44 28N	118 42 31W	city/town	4164
Sanders	39 12 10N	121 39 39W	city/town	64
Sandia	32 53 08N	115 24 18W	city/town	-80

California GPS Companion

Place Name	Latitude	Longitude	Type	Elev
Sandia Nat'l Labs	37 40 28N	121 42 20W	locale	
Sandoz	38 20 53N	120 25 46W	city/town	3320
Sands	35 00 55N	115 56 31W	city/town	1232
Sandy Beach (1)	37 44 34N	122 12 59W	beach	
Sandy Beach (2)	33 11 08N	115 49 58W	beach	
Sandy Beach (3)	36 30 25N	121 56 18W	beach	
Sandy Beach (4)	40 41 16N	120 46 16W	beach	
Sandy Gulch	38 22 49N	120 31 54W	city/town	2597
Sandy Korner	33 38 32N	116 10 49W	city/town	96
Sandyland	34 24 17N	119 32 44W	city/town	10
Sandyland Cove	34 23 48N	119 31 49W	city/town	10
Sanger	36 42 29N	119 33 18W	city/town	363
Sanger Peak	41 55 14N	123 39 17W	summit	5862
Sanger Winery	36 41 37N	119 33 07W	wine/vin	
Sanitarium	38 32 42N	122 28 28W	city/town	500
Sankey	38 46 42N	121 29 53W	city/town	40
Santa Ana	33 44 44N	117 52 01W	city/town	110
Santa Ana -Orange	33 40 32N	117 52 05W	airport	54
Santa Ana C C	33 39 52N	117 53 07W	golf	
Santa Ana College	33 45 32N	117 53 13W	univ/coll	
Santa Ana Heights	33 39 09N	117 53 41W	city/town	70
Santa Anita	34 08 44N	118 02 56W	city/town	

California GPS Companion

Place Name	Latitude	Longitude	Type	Elev
Santa Anita Dam	34 11 01N	118 01 07W	dam	1317
Santa Anita Golf	34 08 01N	118 02 00W	golf	
Santa Barbara	34 25 15N	119 41 50W	city/town	50
Santa Barbara C.-1	34 26 20N	119 42 15W	univ/coll	
Santa Barbara C.-2	34 24 23N	119 41 47W	univ/coll	70
Santa Barbara Harb	34 24 26N	119 41 16W	harbor	
Santa Barbara Is.	33 28 32N	119 02 07W	island	
Santa Barbara Lt.	34 23 47N	119 43 17W	lighthous	
Santa Barbara Mis.	34 26 18N	119 42 45W	mission	
Santa Barbara Mun.	34 25 34N	119 50 25W	airport	10
Santa Barbara Zool	34 25 10N	119 39 47W	park	
Santa Catalina Is.	33 23 00N	118 25 00W	island	
Santa Clara	37 21 15N	121 57 15W	city/town	88
Santa Clarita	34 23 30N	118 32 30W	city/town	1200
Santa Cruz	36 58 27N	122 01 47W	city/town	20
Santa Cruz -hist.	36 57 05N	122 01 32W	lighthous	
Santa Cruz Bay	34 34 57N	119 55 13W	bay	
Santa Cruz Beach	36 57 49N	122 01 03W	beach	
Santa Cruz City M.	36 57 52N	122 00 30W	museum	
Santa Cruz Island	34 01 00N	119 43 00W	island	
Santa Cruz M Wharf	36 57 37N	122 01 08W	wharf	
Santa Cruz Surfing	36 57 05N	122 01 32W	museum	

California GPS Companion

Place Name	Latitude	Longitude	Type	Elev
Santa Fe Dam	34 06 57N	117 58 18W	dam	524
Santa Fe Springs	33 56 50N	118 05 04W	city/town	145
Santa Margarita	35 23 24N	120 36 29W	city/town	1000
Santa Maria (1)	34 07 53N	118 34 25W	city/town	1400
Santa Maria (2)	34 57 11N	120 26 05W	city/town	216
Santa Maria Airprt	34 53 56N	120 27 26W	airport	259
Santa Maria C C	34 54 23N	120 26 28W	golf	
Santa Monica	34 01 10N	118 29 25W	city/town	101
Santa Monica City	34 01 00N	118 28 03W	univ/coll	
Santa Monica Civic	34 00 32N	118 29 18W	building	
Santa Monica Muni.	34 00 56N	118 27 04W	airport	175
Santa Monica Mus.	34 00 13N	118 29 01W	museum	
Santa Nella	38 29 50N	122 57 56W	city/town	78
Santa Nella Vlg.	37 05 52N	121 00 57W	city/town	150
Santa Paula	34 21 15N	119 03 30W	city/town	274
Santa Paula Airprt	34 20 49N	119 03 40W	airport	245
Santa Rita	36 43 26N	121 39 18W	city/town	80
Santa Rita Pk (1)	37 02 51N	120 35 39W	city/town	120
Santa Rita Pk (2)	36 20 48N	120 36 02W	city/town	5165
Santa Rosa	38 26 26N	122 42 48W	city/town	160
Santa Rosa -Sonoma	38 30 32N	122 48 46W	airport	125
Santa Rosa Golf	38 27 46N	122 37 44W	golf	

California GPS Companion

Place Name	Latitude	Longitude	Type	Elev
Santa Rosa Island	33 57 00N	120 06 00W	island	
Santa Susana	34 16 18N	118 42 29W	city/town	961
Santa Susana Knoll	34 15 44N	118 40 22W	city/town	1150
Santa Teresa Golf	37 13 14N	121 46 33W	golf	
Santa Venetia	37 59 55N	122 31 27W	city/town	60
Santa Ynez	34 36 52N	120 04 44W	city/town	600
Santa Ynez Airport	34 36 24N	120 04 32W	airport	671
Santa Ysabel	33 06 33N	116 40 20W	city/town	2984
Santa Ysabel Chap.	33 07 51N	116 40 37W	mission	
Santee	32 50 18N	116 58 23W	city/town	345
Santiago Dam	33 47 10N	117 43 28W	dam	789
Santiago Golf Crs	33 46 41N	117 50 12W	golf	
Santiago Peak	33 42 38N	117 32 00W	summit	5687
Santino Winery	38 32 40N	120 47 30W	wine/vin	
Saranap	37 53 06N	122 04 30W	city/town	420
Saratoga	37 15 50N	122 01 19W	city/town	412
Saratoga Springs	39 10 31N	122 58 47W	city/town	1420
Sardine Falls	38 18 31N	119 37 17W	falls	
Sardine Peak	39 32 25N	120 11 15W	summit	8134
Sargent	36 55 10N	121 32 49W	city/town	150
Saticoy	34 16 59N	119 08 56W	city/town	151
Saticoy C C	34 16 21N	119 06 24W	golf	

California GPS Companion

Place Name	Latitude	Longitude	Type	Elev
Sattley	39 36 58N	120 25 34W	city/town	4944
Saugus	34 24 41N	118 32 21W	city/town	1170
Saunders Place	40 03 02N	122 32 47W	city/town	920
Sausalito	37 51 33N	122 29 03W	city/town	14
Sausalito Point	37 51 24N	122 28 41W	cape	
Savage Dam	32 36 36N	116 55 31W	dam	491
Savercool Place	40 11 23N	121 41 31W	city/town	360
Sawmill Flat	36 58 10N	119 00 59W	city/town	6720
Sawpit Dam	34 10 32N	117 59 11W	dam	1359
Sawtelle	34 01 50N	118 27 45W	city/town	168
Sawtooth Peak	36 27 15N	118 33 15W	summit	12343
Sawyers Crossing	36 57 26N	121 31 14W	city/town	147
Saxon	38 28 00N	121 39 19W	city/town	19
Scaath	41 30 53N	123 58 06W	city/town	70
Scales	39 35 54N	120 59 29W	city/town	4320
Scarface	41 24 42N	121 17 38W	city/town	4388
Scheelite	37 22 41N	118 40 33W	city/town	6894
Schellville-Sonoma	38 13 24N	122 26 58W	airport	10
Schelville	38 14 46N	122 26 19W	city/town	12
Schilling	36 24 32N	119 54 46W	city/town	210
Schooner Gulch St.	38 52 05N	123 39 15W	park	
Schramsberg Winery	38 32 59N	122 32 15W	wine/vin	

California GPS Companion

Place Name	Latitude	Longitude	Type	Elev
Sciots Camp	38 47 10N	120 09 09W	city/town	5640
Scissors Crossing	33 05 47N	116 28 28W	city/town	2280
Scotia	40 28 57N	124 05 59W	city/town	164
Scotland	34 14 32N	117 29 50W	city/town	3040
Scott Bar	41 44 31N	123 00 11W	city/town	1740
Scott Creek Beach	37 02 25N	122 13 44W	beach	
Scott Museum	40 59 12N	122 41 47W	museum	
Scott Place	40 12 24N	124 01 56W	city/town	1160
Scotts	39 50 47N	120 05 29W	city/town	4820
Scotts Corner	37 35 20N	121 52 12W	city/town	260
Scotts Flat	39 17 00N	120 54 45W	city/town	3100
Scotts Valley	37 03 04N	122 00 49W	city/town	570
Scottsville	38 20 05N	120 45 17W	city/town	1260
Scotty Place	41 07 27N	120 52 22W	city/town	4530
Scottys Castle	37 01 56N	117 20 21W	locale	
Scovern Hot Spring	35 37 17N	118 28 24W	city/town	2490
Scranton	36 27 07N	116 30 10W	city/town	2231
Scripps College	34 06 11N	117 42 31W	univ/coll	
Scylla	37 04 50N	118 41 25W	summit	12939
Sea Cliff	34 20 40N	119 25 02W	city/town	
Sea Hawk Stadium	33 50 49N	118 22 45W	stadium	
Sea Ranch	38 42 55N	123 27 12W	city/town	119

California GPS Companion

Place Name	Latitude	Longitude	Type	Elev
Sea View Beach	33 12 31N	115 50 35W	beach	
Sea World Aquatic	32 45 58N	117 13 41W	park	
Seabee Museum	34 10 07N	119 11 48W	museum	
Seabright	36 57 58N	122 00 24W	city/town	50
Seabright Beach	36 57 48N	122 00 25W	beach	
Seacliff -subdiv.	37 47 19N	122 29 09W	city/town	80
Seacliff State Bch	36 58 17N	121 54 40W	park	
Seal Beach	33 44 29N	118 06 14W	city/town	15
Seal Beach Pier	33 44 13N	118 06 25W	pier	
Seal Cove	37 31 09N	122 30 42W	city/town	75
Seal Rocks Beach	37 47 10N	122 30 26W	beach	
Seaplane Harbor	37 37 56N	122 22 50W	harbor	
Searles	35 29 02N	117 38 04W	city/town	3243
Sears Point	38 09 04N	122 26 48W	city/town	12
Seaside	36 36 40N	121 51 02W	city/town	60
Seaside Creek Bch.	39 33 33N	123 45 55W	beach	
Seaview	38 32 44N	123 13 37W	city/town	1425
Sebastopol (1)	39 21 46N	121 07 12W	city/town	1875
Sebastopol (2)	38 24 08N	122 49 22W	city/town	78
Secline Beach	39 14 15N	120 01 52W	beach	
Second Falls	37 08 03N	118 27 17W	falls	
Second Garrotte	37 49 30N	120 11 47W	city/town	2875

Place Name	Latitude	Longitude	Type	Elev
Secret Town	39 09 26N	120 52 36W	city/town	3000
Sedco Hills	33 38 30N	117 17 24W	city/town	1275
Seeley	32 47 35N	115 41 25W	city/town	-42
Seguro	35 25 11N	119 01 13W	city/town	470
Seiad Valley	41 50 26N	123 11 29W	city/town	1371
Seigler Springs	38 52 30N	122 41 15W	city/town	2280
Selby	38 03 24N	122 14 34W	city/town	20
Selma	36 34 15N	119 36 40W	city/town	308
Selma Airport	36 34 53N	119 39 30W	airport	305
Selma Speedway	36 33 12N	119 36 23W	track	
Seminary Park -sub	37 46 25N	122 11 12W	city/town	80
Seminole Hot Sprgs	34 06 23N	118 47 23W	city/town	875
Seminole Springs T	34 06 36N	118 47 27W	city/town	925
Semitropic	35 36 07N	119 30 27W	city/town	255
Seneca	40 06 38N	121 05 01W	city/town	3580
Seneger, Mount	37 16 38N	118 51 26W	summit	12271
Sentinel Fall	37 43 30N	119 35 44W	falls	
Sentinel Rock	37 43 44N	119 35 37W	pillar	7038
Sentous	34 01 35N	118 22 16W	city/town	103
Sepulveda (1)	34 09 42N	118 16 55W	city/town	470
Sepulveda (2)	34 13 51N	118 28 02W	city/town	820
Sequoia (1)	37 48 36N	119 53 29W	city/town	5512

California GPS Companion

Place Name	Latitude	Longitude	Type	Elev
Sequoia (2)	36 25 39N	119 06 58W	city/town	449
Sequoia Nat'l For.	36 00 01N	118 30 01W	forest	
Sequoia Nat'l Pk.	36 33 51N	118 46 22W	city/town	6409
Sequoyah C C	37 45 58N	122 07 56W	golf	
Serena	34 24 45N	119 33 19W	city/town	13
Serena Park	34 25 07N	119 34 18W	city/town	50
Serra Mesa	32 48 10N	117 08 15W	city/town	410
Serrano	35 20 06N	120 39 13W	city/town	960
Serrano Place	33 38 49N	117 41 20W	city/town	480
Serrano Village	34 10 44N	117 19 15W	city/town	1470
Sespe	34 24 00N	118 56 58W	city/town	460
Sespe Village	34 23 11N	118 57 17W	city/town	385
Seven Gables	37 18 41N	118 49 58W	summit	13075
Seven Oaks	34 11 11N	116 54 48W	city/town	5340
Seven Pines	36 47 08N	118 17 35W	city/town	6232
Seville	36 29 09N	119 13 20W	city/town	353
Shackleford Place	40 07 37N	122 44 00W	city/town	1600
Shadelands Ranch H	37 55 33N	122 01 10W	museum	
Shadow Hills	34 15 43N	118 21 03W	city/town	1200
Shadow Mountain M.	41 16 32N	122 17 53W	city/town	3300
Shady Dell	32 58 22N	116 54 58W	city/town	1242
Shady Glen	39 07 05N	120 56 55W	city/town	2440

California GPS Companion

Place Name	Latitude	Longitude	Type	Elev
Shafter (1)	35 30 02N	119 16 15W	city/town	345
Shafter (2)	38 00 16N	122 42 27W	city/town	199
Shafter - Minter F	35 30 21N	119 11 29W	airport	422
Shake Cabin	40 14 28N	120 46 36W	building	5160
Shake City	39 25 52N	123 27 58W	city/town	540
Shakespare, Mount	37 02 10N	118 32 22W	summit	12151
Shalow Beach	38 07 25N	122 52 53W	beach	
Shandon (1)	35 39 19N	120 22 28W	city/town	1038
Shannon (2)	37 13 59N	121 57 47W	city/town	370
Shannon Place	40 09 17N	123 21 40W	city/town	1880
Sharktooth Peak	37 28 55N	119 01 33W	summit	11640
Sharon	37 05 53N	120 07 44W	city/town	293
Sharon Valley	39 28 56N	121 14 45W	city/town	2275
Sharp Park	37 38 10N	122 29 13W	city/town	100
Sharp Park Beach	37 37 57N	122 29 37W	beach	
Sharp Park Golf	37 37 28N	122 29 18W	golf	
Sharpe Army Air F.	37 50 11N	121 16 23W	military	18
Shasta	40 35 58N	122 29 27W	city/town	1026
Shasta Dam	40 43 07N	122 25 03W	dam	
Shasta Junior Coll	40 37 38N	122 19 01W	univ/coll	
Shasta Lake	40 40 50N	122 22 11W	city/town	790
Shasta Marina	40 49 05N	122 19 40W	marina	

California GPS Companion

Place Name	Latitude	Longitude	Type	Elev
Shasta Retreat	41 14 08N	122 16 17W	city/town	2620
Shasta Springs	41 14 49N	122 15 36W	city/town	2535
Shasta State Hist.	40 35 47N	122 29 38W	park	
Shasta, Mount	41 24 34N	122 11 38W	summit	14162
Shastina	41 24 33N	122 13 21W	summit	12330
Shaver Lake	37 06 15N	119 19 00W	city/town	5640
Shaver Lake Height	37 06 25N	119 19 10W	city/town	5600
Shaws Flat	38 00 28N	120 24 30W	city/town	2060
Shay Creek Summer	38 41 39N	119 49 58W	city/town	6000
Sheep Mountain (1)	37 31 38N	118 13 00W	summit	12497
Sheep Mountain (2)	41 48 09N	121 53 05W	summit	6210
Sheep Peak	37 58 57N	119 20 23W	summit	11842
Sheep Ranch	38 12 34N	120 27 47W	city/town	2371
Sheepshead	40 51 20N	120 49 24W	city/town	5770
Sheldon	38 25 51N	121 17 57W	city/town	74
Shell	36 19 44N	119 37 20W	city/town	250
Shell Beach	35 09 19N	120 40 17W	city/town	60
Shell Beach (1)	38 25 17N	123 06 43W	beach	
Shell Beach (2)	38 07 03N	122 52 24W	beach	
Shell Mountain (1)	36 41 47N	118 47 43W	summit	9594
Shell Mountain (2)	40 06 44N	123 04 44W	summit	6700
Shellville Colony	38 14 38N	122 24 57W	city/town	22

California GPS Companion

Place Name	Latitude	Longitude	Type	Elev
Shelter Cove (1)	37 35 47N	122 30 42W	city/town	25
Shelter Cove (2)	40 01 50N	124 04 19W	city/town	200
Shelter Cove Airp.	40 01 39N	124 04 24W	airport	69
Shelter Cove B.-1	34 15 56N	117 10 34W	bay	
Shelter Cove B.-2	40 01 28N	124 03 45W	bay	
Shelter House -his	34 37 29N	118 39 34W	building	
Shenandoah Valley	38 32 42N	120 46 30W	museum	
Shenandoah Viney.	38 32 10N	120 47 15W	wine/vin	
Shepards	34 23 56N	119 27 09W	city/town	270
Shepherd Crest	38 00 32N	119 19 01W	summit	11880
Sheridan (1)	38 58 47N	121 22 28W	city/town	115
Sheridan (2)	38 27 56N	123 02 06W	city/town	60
Sherman	40 42 53N	122 14 26W	city/town	920
Sherman Acres	38 26 50N	120 04 15W	city/town	7040
Sherman Island	38 03 34N	121 43 56W	island	
Sherman Oaks	34 09 04N	118 26 54W	city/town	657
Sherman Peak	36 00 36N	118 23 27W	summit	9909
Sherwood Forest -1	39 11 03N	121 04 51W	city/town	2380
Sherwood Forest -2	38 01 45N	120 13 24W	city/town	3600
Shields Grove Arb.	38 31 46N	121 45 41W	arboretum	
Shiloh	38 31 25N	122 47 41W	city/town	110
Shingle Springs	38 39 57N	120 55 30W	city/town	1420

California GPS Companion

Place Name	Latitude	Longitude	Type	Elev
Shingle Springs St	38 39 58N	120 54 27W	park	
Shingletown	40 29 33N	121 53 17W	city/town	3489
Shingletown Airp.	40 31 19N	121 49 03W	airport	3880
Shinn	37 34 00N	121 58 56W	city/town	65
Shinn Mountain	40 41 30N	120 12 48W	summit	7562
Ship Ashore Race T	41 56 10N	124 11 36W	track	
Shippee	39 32 24N	121 41 13W	city/town	131
Shipyard Acres	38 15 36N	122 16 12W	city/town	30
Shirley (1)	36 23 55N	119 39 48W	city/town	255
Shirley (2)	33 49 28N	118 01 23W	city/town	52
Shirley Meadow Ski	35 42 33N	118 33 30W	ski area	7090
Shirley Meadows	35 42 39N	118 33 20W	city/town	6560
Shively	40 25 51N	123 58 07W	city/town	150
Sholun	37 40 20N	122 28 35W	city/town	100
Shorb -subdivision	34 04 45N	118 09 05W	city/town	450
Shore Acres	38 02 09N	121 57 52W	city/town	30
Shorecliffs C C	33 27 10N	117 38 43W	golf	
Short Place	38 46 48N	120 28 23W	city/town	3600
Shoshone	35 58 23N	116 16 13W	city/town	1569
Shoshone Airport	35 58 06N	116 16 10W	airport	1568
Shrine Auditorium	34 01 24N	118 16 48W	building	
Shrub	38 35 33N	120 57 13W	city/town	1020

California GPS Companion

Place Name	Latitude	Longitude	Type	Elev
Shubert Theatre	34 03 32N	118 24 50W	building	
Shuman	34 52 01N	120 31 18W	city/town	398
Shumway	40 41 49N	120 29 24W	city/town	5077
Siberia	34 37 36N	115 59 06W	city/town	1295
Sicard Flat	39 13 52N	121 20 42W	city/town	340
Sids Place	40 25 09N	123 27 20W	city/town	3640
Sierra Cedars	37 04 34N	119 18 26W	city/town	5800
Sierra City	39 33 57N	120 37 58W	city/town	4186
Sierra College	38 47 27N	121 12 41W	univ/coll	
Sierra Glen	36 38 22N	118 59 57W	city/town	3120
Sierra Heights	36 11 14N	119 03 40W	city/town	407
Sierra Knoll Est.	39 04 02N	121 02 00W	city/town	1820
Sierra La Verne	34 08 18N	117 45 57W	golf	
Sierra Madre	34 09 42N	118 03 07W	city/town	800
Sierra Nevada Aq.	37 36 52N	118 49 54W	aquarium	
Sierra Ski Ranch	38 47 49N	120 04 41W	ski area	8120
Sierra Sky Park	36 50 32N	119 51 53W	city/town	325
Sierra Subdivision	39 38 33N	120 12 56W	city/town	5180
Sierra View C C	38 45 45N	121 17 14W	golf	
Sierra Village	38 04 19N	120 10 19W	city/town	4845
Sierra Vista	37 09 05N	120 17 07W	city/town	235
Sierra Vista -sub.	34 05 43N	118 09 27W	city/town	530

California GPS Companion

Place Name	Latitude	Longitude	Type	Elev
Sierra Vista Park	39 13 52N	121 04 36W	city/town	2630
Sierraville	39 35 23N	120 21 59W	city/town	4952
Sierraville Dearw.	39 34 51N	120 21 15W	airport	4984
Signal Butte	41 16 49N	122 11 15W	city/town	4240
Signal Hill	33 48 16N	118 10 01W	city/town	150
Sill, Mount	37 05 40N	118 30 07W	summit	14153
Silt	34 59 59N	117 44 55W	city/town	2330
Silver Apron	37 43 37N	119 32 23W	falls	
Silver Basin Ski A	38 37 57N	120 12 24W	ski area	7400
Silver City	36 27 58N	118 38 42W	city/town	6935
Silver Falls	38 20 38N	119 32 44W	falls	
Silver Lake Height	34 05 58N	118 15 20W	city/town	600
Silver Peak	37 28 13N	119 01 12W	summit	11878
Silver Spray Falls	36 54 52N	118 47 12W	falls	
Silver Strand	34 09 10N	119 13 03W	city/town	10
Silver Strand Bch.	34 09 01N	119 13 05W	beach	
Silver Strand Fall	37 42 16N	119 40 06W	falls	
Silver Strand St.	32 37 46N	117 08 24W	park	
Silverado	33 44 46N	117 38 10W	city/town	1210
Silverado C C	38 20 54N	122 15 29W	golf	
Silvergate Yacht C	32 42 56N	117 13 22W	locale	11
Silverthorn	40 38 52N	122 23 26W	city/town	720

California GPS Companion

Place Name	Latitude	Longitude	Type	Elev
Silverwood Falls	34 04 31N	116 49 01W	falls	
Silverwood Lake St	34 17 28N	117 19 39W	park	
Simerson	39 25 16N	123 21 14W	city/town	1380
Simi	38 38 24N	122 52 24W	city/town	
Simi Civic Center	34 16 42N	118 44 01W	building	
Simi Valley	34 16 10N	118 46 50W	city/town	760
Simmler	35 21 05N	119 59 10W	city/town	2049
Simmons Peak	37 45 38N	119 17 36W	summit	12503
Simms	37 47 53N	121 05 39W	city/town	72
Simons	33 59 15N	118 07 56W	city/town	162
Sims	41 04 19N	122 21 14W	city/town	1675
Singing Hills Golf	32 47 04N	116 53 00W	golf	
Singing Springs	34 19 16N	118 07 40W	city/town	3160
Sintorosa C C	33 08 56N	117 17 13W	golf	
Siskiyou County M.	41 43 26N	122 38 14W	museum	
Sisquoc	34 51 53N	120 17 26W	city/town	440
Sisquoc Falls	34 44 33N	119 43 49W	falls	
Sisson Museum	41 18 32N	122 19 40W	museum	
Sites	39 18 32N	122 20 15W	city/town	300
Sitton Peak	33 35 15N	117 26 43W	summit	3273
Sixmile House -his	37 00 45N	119 57 48W	building	
Ski Beach	32 46 32N	117 13 57W	beach	

California GPS Companion

Place Name	Latitude	Longitude	Type	Elev
Ski Echo Tahoe	38 48 24N	120 02 06W	ski area	7400
Ski Hi	39 37 22N	122 43 12W	ski area	
Ski Run Marina	38 56 59N	119 57 41W	marina	
Skidoo	36 26 08N	117 08 48W	city/town	5620
Skinner Mill Place	40 09 24N	122 42 07W	city/town	1520
Skinner Winery-his	38 42 00N	120 59 46W	wine/vin	
Skinners	38 41 57N	120 59 39W	city/town	1360
Sky Haven	37 08 40N	118 30 15W	summit	12840
Sky Londa	37 23 01N	122 15 42W	city/town	1520
Sky Valley	33 53 24N	116 21 06W	city/town	1047
Skyforest	34 14 07N	117 10 42W	city/town	5800
Skyhigh	38 25 36N	120 05 55W	city/town	7000
Skyland	34 14 00N	117 17 07W	city/town	5080
Skyline Golf Crs	33 49 07N	118 08 13W	golf	
Skyline Junior Col	37 37 47N	122 28 02W	univ/coll	
Skytop	35 42 05N	117 29 53W	city/town	2477
Skywest Golf Crs	37 39 48N	122 07 48W	golf	
Slagger	41 19 33N	121 43 19W	city/town	4564
Slate Castle	39 32 08N	120 48 34W	pillar	5236
Slater	35 32 58N	119 11 47W	city/town	450
Slates Hot Springs	36 07 25N	121 38 10W	city/town	120
Sleepy Hollow	33 56 52N	117 46 40W	city/town	880

California GPS Companion

Place Name	Latitude	Longitude	Type	Elev
Sleepy Valley	34 30 33N	118 21 52W	city/town	2280
Sloat	39 52 00N	120 43 35W	city/town	4140
Sloughhouse	38 29 45N	121 11 34W	city/town	107
Sly Park Dam	38 42 55N	120 33 43W	dam	3471
Smartville	39 12 27N	121 17 51W	city/town	683
Smeltzer	33 43 49N	117 59 37W	city/town	22
Smiley Heights	34 01 53N	117 11 27W	city/town	1555
Smiley Park	34 11 54N	117 07 36W	city/town	5520
Smith	40 36 17N	122 03 11W	city/town	1040
Smith Corner	35 28 42N	119 16 40W	city/town	328
Smith Mill	36 05 25N	118 39 27W	city/town	5920
Smith River	41 55 42N	124 08 45W	city/town	60
Smithe Redwoods St	39 54 00N	123 44 39W	park	
Smithflat	38 44 05N	120 45 15W	city/town	2240
Smithsonian Obser.	34 22 55N	117 40 38W	observtry	
Smoke Tree	34 08 07N	116 05 22W	city/town	2119
Smugglers Cave	35 10 26N	120 42 55W	arch	
Snelling	37 31 09N	120 26 11W	city/town	259
Snoboy	37 30 41N	121 56 43W	city/town	33
Snow Bend	37 16 02N	119 07 31W	city/town	8200
Snow Creek	33 53 24N	116 41 00W	city/town	1252
Snow Creek Falls	37 46 00N	119 32 00W	falls	

312

California GPS Companion

Place Name	Latitude	Longitude	Type	Elev
Snow Summit	34 13 14N	116 53 30W	summit	8182
Snowden	41 47 36N	122 28 33W	city/town	2960
Snyder Date Garden	33 46 53N	116 26 17W	garden	
Soapweed	38 50 31N	120 40 37W	city/town	3577
Soboba Hot Springs	33 47 59N	116 55 42W	city/town	1680
Sobon Estate Vin.	38 32 22N	120 46 15W	wine/vin	
Sobrante	38 00 08N	122 20 54W	city/town	20
Soda Bay	39 00 04N	122 47 17W	city/town	1380
Soda Springs (1)	39 19 24N	120 22 44W	city/town	6768
Soda Springs (2)	39 25 22N	123 25 59W	city/town	780
Soda Springs (3)	36 02 21N	118 45 26W	city/town	1400
Soda Springs (4)	39 01 27N	123 18 53W	city/town	1400
Soda Springs Ski A	39 19 09N	120 22 57W	ski area	7352
Solana Beach	32 59 28N	117 16 13W	city/town	52
Soledad	36 25 29N	121 19 31W	city/town	200
Soledad State Pris	36 28 09N	121 22 56W	locale	
Soledad Sulphur Sp	34 26 00N	118 21 35W	city/town	1770
Solemint	34 24 59N	118 27 05W	city/town	1442
Solomons, Mount	37 06 28N	118 40 28W	summit	13016
Solromar	34 03 00N	118 57 10W	city/town	100
Solvang	34 35 45N	120 08 12W	city/town	496
Solyo	37 36 34N	121 15 48W	city/town	92

California GPS Companion

Place Name	Latitude	Longitude	Type	Elev
Somerset (1)	41 51 09N	121 59 24W	city/town	4241
Somerset (2)	38 38 52N	120 41 05W	city/town	2089
Somersville	37 57 25N	121 51 48W	city/town	900
Somes Bar	41 22 35N	123 28 30W	city/town	720
Somis	34 15 26N	118 59 43W	city/town	300
Sonoma	38 17 31N	122 27 25W	city/town	84
Sonoma Coast State	38 23 12N	123 05 00W	park	
Sonoma Golf & C C	38 18 49N	122 30 02W	golf	
Sonoma Mission	38 17 38N	122 27 18W	mission	
Sonoma Skypark	38 15 27N	122 26 03W	airport	20
Sonoma State Col.	38 20 24N	122 40 30W	univ/coll	
Sonora	37 59 03N	120 22 52W	city/town	1826
Sonora Junction	38 20 55N	119 27 03W	city/town	6920
Sonora Peak	38 21 14N	119 38 03W	summit	11459
Soquel	36 59 17N	121 57 20W	city/town	40
Sorensens	38 46 28N	119 54 07W	city/town	6920
Sorenson	37 38 44N	122 03 53W	city/town	65
Sorrento	32 54 03N	117 13 20W	city/town	30
Sorroca	38 20 32N	121 36 32W	city/town	3
Soto Street Jct.	34 01 08N	118 13 06W	city/town	225
Souas Corner	38 26 47N	122 51 37W	city/town	221
Soudan	38 36 10N	121 16 30W	city/town	105

314

California GPS Companion

Place Name	Latitude	Longitude	Type	Elev
Soulsbyville	37 59 05N	120 15 46W	city/town	2925
South Anaheim	33 48 32N	117 54 01W	city/town	150
South Beach (1)	38 03 00N	122 59 14W	beach	
South Beach (2)	34 02 45N	118 55 48W	beach	
South Berkeley	37 50 56N	122 16 14W	city/town	100
South. Cal. Bible	33 39 38N	117 54 02W	univ/coll	
South Carlsbad St.	33 06 14N	117 19 07W	beach	
South Coast Botan.	33 47 00N	118 20 39W	garden	
South Corcoran	36 05 28N	119 33 11W	city/town	205
South Coyote	37 11 56N	121 43 14W	city/town	282
South Creek Falls	35 58 18N	118 29 31W	falls	
South Dos Palos	36 57 52N	120 39 08W	city/town	115
South El Monte	34 03 07N	118 02 45W	city/town	250
South Fontana	34 03 46N	117 29 17W	city/town	1004
South Fork (1)	37 13 52N	119 29 36W	city/town	2720
South Fork (2)	39 25 34N	123 43 34W	city/town	40
South Gate	33 57 17N	118 12 40W	city/town	111
South Guard	36 41 35N	118 29 00W	summit	13224
South Hills C C	34 03 25N	117 53 15W	golf	
South Laguna	33 30 02N	117 44 32W	city/town	140
South Lake	35 38 13N	118 21 58W	city/town	2760
South Lake Tahoe	38 56 00N	119 59 00W	city/town	6260

California GPS Companion

Place Name	Latitude	Longitude	Type	Elev
South Landing	37 34 55N	118 43 58W	city/town	6822
South Leggett	39 50 55N	123 42 23W	city/town	1120
South Los Angeles	33 55 39N	118 16 38W	city/town	150
South Oceanside	33 10 38N	117 21 20W	city/town	50
South Oceanside B.	33 10 20N	117 21 52W	beach	
South Oroville	39 29 48N	121 33 04W	city/town	235
South Park	32 43 12N	117 07 42W	city/town	240
South Pasadena	34 06 58N	118 08 58W	city/town	660
South Salmon Creek	38 20 22N	123 04 01W	beach	
South San Diego	32 35 01N	117 05 46W	city/town	25
South San Francisc	37 39 17N	122 24 24W	city/town	19
South San Gabriel	34 03 45N	118 05 22W	city/town	272
South Santa Ana	33 42 41N	117 52 02W	city/town	45
South Shore -sub.	37 45 35N	122 15 24W	city/town	10
South Shore Marina	34 15 06N	117 11 13W	marina	
South Shore Port	37 25 36N	122 02 24W	city/town	0
South Sister	38 28 57N	119 17 57W	summit	11339
South Taft	35 08 05N	119 27 19W	city/town	1050
South Trona	35 42 56N	117 23 47W	city/town	1640
South Vallejo	38 05 16N	122 14 32W	city/town	40
South Wawona	37 32 33N	119 38 38W	city/town	4200
South Whittier	33 57 39N	118 02 27W	city/town	170

Place Name	Latitude	Longitude	Type	Elev
South Yuba	39 07 32N	121 35 04W	city/town	65
Southport Landing	40 41 42N	124 14 52W	city/town	10
Southside Highland	39 18 57N	120 16 10W	city/town	6080
Southwest Museum	34 06 02N	118 12 17W	museum	
Southwest Village	33 50 48N	118 18 34W	city/town	50
Southwestern Col.	32 38 26N	116 59 47W	univ/coll	
Southwestern Univ.	34 03 40N	118 17 20W	univ/coll	
Spadra	34 03 08N	117 47 57W	city/town	740
Spalding Corner	41 07 50N	121 34 45W	city/town	3340
Spalding Tract	40 39 11N	120 46 15W	city/town	5120
Spangler	35 32 56N	117 27 02W	city/town	2099
Spanish Bay Resort	36 36 42N	121 56 39W	golf	
Spanish Flat (1)	38 49 24N	120 48 30W	city/town	2340
Spanish Flat (2)	38 32 07N	122 13 26W	city/town	
Spanish Flat Res.	38 31 12N	122 12 31W	city/town	480
Spanish Ranch	39 57 03N	121 03 22W	city/town	3660
Sparkle	37 55 42N	122 03 20W	city/town	85
Sparr Heights -sub	34 11 45N	118 13 30W	city/town	1120
Spartan Stadium	37 19 11N	121 52 02W	stadium	
Spear Creek Summer	35 49 12N	118 35 36W	city/town	6100
Spellacy	35 06 47N	119 28 14W	city/town	1675
Spence	36 36 46N	121 33 56W	city/town	80

California GPS Companion

Place Name	Latitude	Longitude	Type	Elev
Spencer, Mount	37 09 17N	118 40 49W	summit	12431
Sperry	35 44 30N	116 13 17W	city/town	839
Spicer City	35 30 04N	119 36 13W	city/town	245
Spieker Aquatics C	37 52 08N	122 15 40W	building	
Spillway Boat Ramp	39 32 52N	121 29 29W	locale	
Spinks Corner	36 12 43N	119 13 56W	city/town	308
Spinnaker Yacht Cl	37 41 32N	122 11 16W	locale	
Split Mountain	37 01 16N	118 25 20W	summit	14058
Spoonbill	38 03 38N	121 54 10W	city/town	0
Spreckels	36 37 19N	121 38 45W	city/town	60
Spreckels Junction	36 39 30N	121 37 47W	city/town	60
Spreckels Mansion	37 47 33N	122 25 35W	building	
Sprekelsville	38 37 58N	120 58 35W	city/town	970
Spring Creek	38 55 45N	120 03 50W	city/town	6340
Spring Creek Golf	37 44 45N	121 06 20W	golf	
Spring Gap	38 10 07N	120 06 04W	city/town	4900
Spring Garden	39 53 42N	120 47 06W	city/town	3880
Spring Hill	39 13 57N	121 02 35W	city/town	2680
Spring Valley (1)	38 46 46N	120 31 36W	city/town	3800
Spring Valley (2)	32 44 41N	116 59 53W	city/town	400
Spring Valley Golf	37 27 02N	121 51 08W	golf	
Springbrook Golf	34 00 26N	117 21 33W	golf	

California GPS Companion

Place Name	Latitude	Longitude	Type	Elev
Springfield	38 01 15N	120 24 41W	city/town	2056
Springfield Meadow	38 38 50N	121 04 20W	city/town	580
Springtown Golf	37 42 45N	121 44 29W	golf	
Springville (1)·	34 13 14N	119 05 42W	city/town	70
Springville (2)	36 07 49N	118 49 02W	city/town	1033
Spruce Point	40 44 36N	124 11 48W	city/town	30
Spyglass Hill Golf	36 35 07N	121 57 03W	golf	
Spyrock	39 52 36N	123 26 34W	city/town	821
Squab	38 11 50N	122 16 35W	city/town	33
Squabbletown	38 00 53N	120 23 07W	city/town	2040
Squaw Hill	39 54 29N	122 05 31W	city/town	195
Squaw Valley	36 44 25N	119 14 45W	city/town	1630
Squaw Valley Ski A	39 11 29N	120 15 03W	ski area	8885
Squaw Valley State	39 11 32N	120 13 53W	park	
Squires Dam	33 09 03N	117 15 32W	dam	505
Squirrel Mountain	35 37 24N	118 24 32W	city/town	2961
St George Point	41 46 57N	124 15 07W	cape	
Stacy	40 13 48N	120 01 13W	city/town	4015
Stafford	40 27 15N	124 03 09W	city/town	139
Staircase Falls	37 44 07N	119 34 26W	falls	
Stalder	34 01 19N	117 31 25W	city/town	800
Staley	41 53 18N	121 22 47W	city/town	4040

California GPS Companion

Place Name	Latitude	Longitude	Type	Elev
Stallion Oaks	32 52 24N	116 38 08W	city/town	3480
Standard	37 58 00N	120 18 39W	city/town	2300
Standiford	37 41 21N	121 00 09W	city/town	90
Standish	40 21 55N	120 25 16W	city/town	4048
Standish-Hickey St	39 52 46N	123 44 14W	park	
Stanfield Hill	39 20 33N	121 19 55W	city/town	1221
Stanford Golf Crs	37 25 28N	122 11 04W	golf	
Stanford Linear Ac	37 25 00N	122 12 05W	locale	
Stanford Mount (1)	36 42 14N	118 23 41W	summit	13969
Stanford Mount (2)	37 29 21N	118 47 44W	summit	12838
Stanford Museum	37 25 58N	122 10 11W	museum	
Stanford Stadium	37 26 04N	122 09 37W	stadium	
Stanford Univ.	37 25 38N	122 10 09W	univ/coll	
Stanislaus	38 08 18N	120 22 09W	city/town	1120
Stanislaus State C	37 31 30N	120 51 29W	univ/coll	
Stanley	38 14 41N	122 17 34W	city/town	15
Stanton	33 48 09N	117 59 32W	city/town	62
Stanton Peak	38 03 30N	119 21 45W	summit	11666
Starbright Acres	39 11 43N	121 05 12W	city/town	2360
Stardust C C	32 45 41N	117 10 22W	golf	
Starr, Mount	37 25 37N	118 45 54W	summit	12870
State Peak	36 55 55N	118 32 41W	summit	12620

California GPS Companion

Place Name	Latitude	Longitude	Type	Elev
Stateline	38 57 30N	119 56 34W	city/town	6240
Stauffer	34 45 16N	119 03 57W	city/town	5067
Stearns Wharf	34 24 33N	119 41 02W	wharf	
Stedman	34 37 48N	116 10 02W	city/town	2380
Steel Canyon Res.	38 30 29N	122 12 08W	city/town	480
Steele Peak	33 45 20N	117 18 22W	summit	2529
Steelhead (1)	40 10 13N	123 38 39W	city/town	340
Steelhead (2)	41 46 37N	123 02 17W	city/town	1600
Stege	37 55 00N	122 19 34W	city/town	20
Stegeman	39 21 28N	122 01 39W	city/town	74
Steinhardt Aquar.	37 46 10N	122 27 53W	aquarium	
Stent	37 55 04N	120 24 44W	city/town	1401
Steuben Place	39 57 52N	122 44 37W	city/town	6120
Stevens	35 18 51N	119 11 23W	city/town	335
Stevinson	37 19 40N	120 51 02W	city/town	82
Stewart Mansion	39 15 33N	121 01 20W	building	
Stewart, Mount	36 34 10N	118 33 11W	summit	12205
Stewarts Point	38 39 07N	123 23 53W	city/town	109
Stewartville	37 56 47N	121 50 51W	city/town	600
Stinson Beach	37 53 40N	122 38 15W	beach	
Stinson Beach	37 54 02N	122 38 36W	city/town	18
Stinson State Bch.	37 53 39N	122 38 13W	park	

California GPS Companion

Place Name	Latitude	Longitude	Type	Elev
Stirling City	39 54 28N	121 31 37W	city/town	3532
Stirling Junction	39 42 51N	121 48 44W	city/town	200
Stockdale C C	35 20 45N	119 04 43W	golf	
Stockton	37 57 28N	121 17 23W	city/town	15
Stockton -Seaplane	38 00 14N	121 27 23W	airport	0
Stockton C C	37 57 51N	121 21 23W	golf	
Stockton Metropol.	37 53 38N	121 14 17W	airport	30
Stoil	35 55 05N	119 25 28W	city/town	205
Stomar	37 21 43N	121 02 41W	city/town	101
Stone	40 30 44N	124 06 47W	city/town	80
Stone Place	35 54 09N	118 44 00W	city/town	1800
Stonegate Village	38 41 15N	121 04 22W	city/town	740
Stonehurst	34 15 04N	118 22 10W	city/town	960
Stoneman	34 05 19N	118 07 17W	city/town	456
Stoneridge Winery	38 23 30N	120 45 56W	wine/vin	
Stones Landing	40 42 45N	120 43 20W	city/town	5140
Stonestown	37 43 42N	122 28 42W	city/town	150
Stony Creek Vlg.	36 39 51N	118 50 23W	city/town	6460
Stony Point	38 18 39N	122 44 02W	city/town	220
Stony Ridge Winery	37 39 57N	121 43 45W	wine/vin	
Stonyford	39 22 31N	122 32 35W	city/town	1168
Storey	36 58 27N	120 01 05W	city/town	289

California GPS Companion

Place Name	Latitude	Longitude	Type	Elev
Storrie	39 55 03N	121 19 20W	city/town	1800
Story Vineyards	38 32 30N	120 49 00W	wine/vin	
Stout	36 10 58N	119 04 46W	city/town	387
Stover Mountain Sk	40 17 22N	121 17 18W	ski area	
Stratford	36 11 22N	119 49 20W	city/town	200
Strathearn	34 16 52N	118 47 54W	city/town	740
Strathmore	36 08 44N	119 03 35W	city/town	402
Strathmore -Eckert	36 09 44N	119 03 00W	airport	426
Strawberry (1)	38 11 54N	120 00 30W	city/town	5100
Strawberry (2)	38 47 49N	120 08 39W	city/town	5800
Strawberry Park	33 54 03N	118 18 38W	city/town	47
Strawberry Valley	39 33 51N	121 06 21W	city/town	3725
Striped Mountain	36 57 56N	118 24 18W	summit	13175
Stronetta	38 56 50N	123 42 05W	city/town	60
Stronghold	41 54 20N	121 24 31W	city/town	4036
Strybing Arboretum	37 46 06N	122 28 08W	arboretum	
Stuart	33 15 04N	117 25 12W	city/town	70
Studebaker	33 55 11N	118 05 43W	city/town	102
Studio City	34 08 55N	118 23 44W	city/town	610
Studio City Golf	34 08 44N	118 24 22W	golf	
Stump Beach	38 34 55N	123 20 04W	beach	
Sturtevant Falls	34 12 42N	118 01 08W	falls	

California GPS Companion

Place Name	Latitude	Longitude	Type	Elev
Styx	33 52 41N	114 47 40W	city/town	1033
Subaco	38 55 43N	121 44 18W	city/town	20
Subeet	38 13 42N	122 04 48W	city/town	20
Success Dam	36 03 42N	118 55 19W	dam	652
Sucker Flat	39 12 43N	121 17 46W	city/town	600
Sucro	38 28 11N	121 48 13W	city/town	60
Sugar Bowl Ski Ar.	39 18 16N	120 20 05W	ski area	7000
Sugar Pine	37 26 28N	119 38 00W	city/town	4280
Sugar Pine Point L	39 03 41N	120 06 47W	lighthous	
Sugarfield	38 42 50N	121 45 09W	city/town	57
Sugarloaf (1)	34 14 36N	116 49 41W	city/town	7024
Sugarloaf (2)	40 51 30N	122 23 45W	city/town	1140
Sugarloaf Mountain	35 50 20N	118 36 13W	city/town	6000
Sugarloaf Ridge St	38 26 42N	122 30 04W	park	
Sugarloaf Village	35 49 33N	118 38 00W	city/town	5200
Sugarpine	38 03 30N	120 12 02W	city/town	4471
Suisun City	38 14 18N	122 02 21W	city/town	5
Sulfer Springs	34 28 46N	118 36 48W	city/town	1106
Sullivan	39 12 12N	121 38 04W	city/town	66
Sullivans Beach	33 27 42N	118 31 19W	beach	
Sulphur Springs	34 25 37N	119 05 37W	city/town	1000
Sultana	36 32 44N	119 20 21W	city/town	360

California GPS Companion

Place Name	Latitude	Longitude	Type	Elev
Summer Home	37 50 51N	121 11 05W	city/town	41
Summerhome Park	38 29 48N	122 56 18W	city/town	120
Summerland	34 25 17N	119 35 44W	city/town	100
Summertown	40 32 40N	121 33 59W	city/town	5880
Summerville	41 05 56N	123 04 00W	city/town	2900
Summit	35 07 40N	118 24 47W	city/town	4032
Summit City	39 24 32N	120 30 05W	city/town	7320
Summit University	34 06 03N	118 42 15W	univ/coll	
Summit Village	38 43 38N	121 05 42W	city/town	640
Sun City	33 42 33N	117 11 47W	city/town	1440
Sun Valley	34 13 03N	118 22 10W	city/town	810
Suncrest	32 48 15N	116 51 49W	city/town	1580
Sunfair	34 09 50N	116 14 47W	city/town	2412
Sunfair Heights	34 14 25N	116 13 05W	city/town	2580
Sunken Gardens Pk.	37 40 35N	121 44 57W	park	
Sunkist	34 04 38N	117 11 24W	city/town	1320
Sunland (1)	34 16 01N	118 18 05W	city/town	1503
Sunland (2)	36 01 21N	118 58 53W	city/town	546
Sunny Acres Trail.	37 57 43N	122 01 38W	city/town	80
Sunny Brae	40 51 30N	124 03 55W	city/town	40
Sunny Hills	33 54 04N	117 56 08W	city/town	360
Sunny Oak Farm and	38 41 46N	120 56 34W	wine/vin	

California GPS Companion

Place Name	Latitude	Longitude	Type	Elev
Sunny Vista	32 38 41N	117 04 02W	city/town	80
Sunnybrook	38 20 35N	120 52 33W	city/town	800
Sunnyhills Golf	37 27 40N	121 54 53W	golf	
Sunnymead	33 56 24N	117 14 34W	city/town	1630
Sunnyside (1)	32 40 27N	117 00 56W	city/town	140
Sunnyside (2)	39 50 39N	122 51 51W	city/town	5000
Sunnyside (3)	36 44 57N	119 41 54W	city/town	327
Sunnyside (4)	39 08 36N	120 09 09W	city/town	6240
Sunnyside C C	36 43 43N	119 41 34W	golf	
Sunnyslope (1)	39 22 03N	121 25 51W	city/town	550
Sunnyslope (2)	34 00 43N	117 25 57W	city/town	920
Sunnyvale	37 22 08N	122 02 07W	city/town	150
Sunol	37 35 40N	121 53 15W	city/town	280
Sunol Valley Golf	37 34 40N	121 53 16W	golf	
Sunrise	34 40 23N	118 07 51W	city/town	2424
Sunrise Heights	39 13 54N	121 04 15W	city/town	2660
Sunrise Ski Area	34 23 18N	117 41 00W	ski area	
Sunrise Vista	38 52 48N	122 43 59W	city/town	2600
Sunset	39 15 02N	121 39 03W	city/town	74
Sunset Beach	33 42 59N	118 04 05W	city/town	11
Sunset Beach	36 53 17N	121 49 56W	beach	
Sunset Cliffs	32 43 44N	117 15 39W	city/town	60

California GPS Companion

Place Name	Latitude	Longitude	Type	Elev
Sunset District	37 45 13N	122 29 39W	city/town	250
Sunset Mobile Home	38 38 49N	121 03 40W	city/town	580
Sunset Oaks C C	38 48 15N	121 14 35W	golf	
Sunset Peak Look.	34 13 00N	117 41 19W	overlook	5796
Sunset State Beach	36 52 54N	121 49 38W	park	
Sunset View	39 13 46N	121 05 43W	city/town	2500
Sunshine Camp	37 59 16N	120 16 54W	city/town	2850
Sunsweet	34 03 36N	117 41 02W	city/town	960
Surf	34 41 04N	120 36 09W	city/town	42
Surfside	33 43 40N	118 04 53W	city/town	11
Surfside Beach	33 43 32N	118 04 54W	beach	
Surgone	41 20 06N	123 51 12W	city/town	160
Surprise Station	41 34 26N	120 26 07W	city/town	4516
Susanville	40 24 59N	120 39 07W	city/town	4258
Susanville -Spaul.	40 39 01N	120 46 06W	airport	5116
Susanville Municip	40 22 36N	120 34 22W	airport	4144
Suscol	38 14 38N	122 17 02W	city/town	15
Sutro Baths -hist.	37 46 48N	122 30 45W	building	
Sutter	39 09 36N	121 45 06W	city/town	20
Sutter County Mus.	39 08 49N	121 38 08W	museum	
Sutter Creek	38 23 35N	120 48 05W	city/town	1198
Sutter Hill	38 22 42N	120 48 02W	city/town	1556

California GPS Companion

Place Name	Latitude	Longitude	Type	Elev
Sutter Ridge Vin.	38 23 14N	120 46 26W	wine/vin	
Sutters Fort State	38 34 20N	121 28 11W	park	
Sutters Mill	38 48 11N	120 53 27W	locale	
Sutterville	38 32 50N	121 30 28W	city/town	12
Suval	38 14 48N	122 04 36W	city/town	32
Sveadal	37 05 01N	121 47 17W	city/town	1180
Swain Place	40 10 42N	122 34 33W	city/town	1110
Swall	36 14 27N	119 17 10W	city/town	314
Swansea	36 31 29N	117 54 11W	city/town	3625
Swanston	38 36 18N	121 26 09W	city/town	35
Swanton	37 03 51N	122 13 35W	city/town	135
Sweeneys Crossing	38 39 10N	120 37 26W	city/town	2080
Sweetbriar	41 07 48N	122 19 09W	city/town	1900
Sweetland	39 20 35N	121 07 09W	city/town	2075
Swenson Park Golf	38 00 33N	121 20 37W	golf	
Swingle	38 33 30N	121 40 28W	city/town	25
Swiss Bar	41 51 55N	122 42 45W	city/town	1910
Swobe	41 16 37N	121 54 48W	city/town	3750
Sycamore	39 08 02N	121 56 27W	city/town	49
Sycamore Cove	34 04 16N	119 00 50W	city/town	25
Sycamore Flat	36 16 00N	121 23 33W	city/town	500
Sycamore Springs	35 11 11N	120 42 48W	city/town	40

California GPS Companion

Place Name	Latitude	Longitude	Type	Elev
Sykes	36 02 12N	117 57 34W	city/town	3546
Sylmar	34 18 28N	118 26 54W	city/town	1258
Sylvan Lodge	38 05 03N	120 09 22W	city/town	5000
Sylvia Park	34 06 54N	118 34 51W	city/town	1100

𝕋

Place Name	Latitude	Longitude	Type	Elev
Table Bluff	40 39 30N	124 12 55W	city/town	320
Table Bluff Light.	40 41 43N	124 16 28W	lighthous	
Table Bluff Ranch.	40 41 03N	124 14 40W	city/town	239
Table Mountain (1)	36 39 38N	118 28 23W	summit	13630
Table Mountain (2)	37 12 30N	118 35 30W	summit	11696
Table Mountain Mun	39 29 42N	121 37 36W	golf	
Taft	35 08 33N	119 27 20W	city/town	950
Taft - Kern County	35 08 27N	119 26 28W	airport	875
Taft Heights	35 08 05N	119 28 18W	city/town	1150
Taft Junior Col.	35 08 54N	119 27 40W	univ/coll	
Tagus	36 16 17N	119 22 02W	city/town	295
Tahoe City	39 10 20N	120 08 16W	city/town	6280
Tahoe City Golf	39 10 15N	120 08 37W	golf	
Tahoe Donner Ski A	39 21 09N	120 16 14W	ski area	7000
Tahoe Estates	39 14 39N	120 03 20W	city/town	6400
Tahoe Keys -subdiv	38 55 54N	120 00 45W	city/town	6235

California GPS Companion

Place Name	Latitude	Longitude	Type	Elev
Tahoe Keys Marina	38 56 16N	120 00 17W	marina	
Tahoe Marina Est.	39 14 27N	120 03 39W	city/town	6380
Tahoe Paradise	38 51 14N	120 00 36W	golf	
Tahoe Paradise Jct	38 51 22N	120 00 38W	univ/coll	
Tahoe Park	39 08 32N	120 09 25W	city/town	6280
Tahoe Pines	39 06 17N	120 09 33W	city/town	6240
Tahoe Ski Bowl Ar.	39 03 54N	120 09 33W	ski area	6856
Tahoe State Park	39 10 31N	120 08 02W	park	6250
Tahoe Valley	38 54 49N	120 00 12W	city/town	6270
Tahoe Vista	39 14 24N	120 03 00W	city/town	6232
Tahoe Woods	39 08 57N	120 09 02W	city/town	6490
Tahoma	39 04 03N	120 07 38W	city/town	6280
Tahoma Meadows	39 03 55N	120 08 49W	city/town	6320
Tahquitz Falls	33 48 13N	116 33 39W	falls	
Tajiguas	34 28 00N	120 06 27W	city/town	80
Talich	33 12 00N	117 19 00W	city/town	120
Tall Timber Camp	38 04 25N	120 10 17W	city/town	
Tallac Village	38 55 19N	120 01 15W	city/town	6320
Talmage	39 08 00N	123 10 00W	city/town	620
Talmont	39 08 42N	120 09 57W	city/town	6840
Talus	36 05 13N	117 58 19W	city/town	3746
Tamalpais Vly	37 52 47N	122 32 41W	city/town	40

California GPS Companion

Place Name	Latitude	Longitude	Type	Elev
Tamalpais Vly Jct	37 52 55N	122 31 25W	city/town	5
Tamarack	38 26 20N	120 04 30W	city/town	6960
Tamarack Mountain	37 10 51N	119 13 16W	summit	7921
Tamarack Winter Sp	37 10 20N	119 11 49W	ski area	7691
Tamarisk C C	33 46 30N	116 25 39W	golf	
Tambo	39 14 22N	121 34 34W	city/town	79
Tan Oak Park	39 49 40N	123 36 11W	city/town	1340
Tancred	38 45 55N	122 09 45W	city/town	295
Tanforan	37 38 19N	122 24 37W	city/town	30
Tangair	34 45 16N	120 36 36W	city/town	211
Tara Hills	37 59 37N	122 18 55W	city/town	90
Tarke	39 08 43N	121 50 53W	city/town	50
Tarpey	36 47 16N	119 41 59W	city/town	350
Tarpey Village	36 47 35N	119 42 00W	city/town	350
Tarzana	34 10 24N	118 33 11W	city/town	780
Tassajara	37 47 45N	121 51 45W	city/town	713
Tassajara Hot Sprg	36 14 03N	121 32 52W	city/town	1540
Tatu	39 39 30N	123 20 37W	city/town	1005
Taurusa	36 25 04N	119 15 09W	city/town	343
Taylor	33 35 54N	116 25 03W	city/town	3619
Taylor Junction	34 03 47N	118 13 20W	city/town	290
Taylorsville	40 04 32N	120 50 19W	city/town	3545

California GPS Companion

Place Name	Latitude	Longitude	Type	Elev
Teachers Beach	38 06 50N	122 52 08W	beach	
Teakettle Junction	36 45 37N	117 32 30W	city/town	4138
Teal	38 10 24N	122 04 40W	city/town	5
Tecate	32 34 38N	116 37 36W	city/town	1800
Tecopa	35 50 54N	116 13 32W	city/town	1329
Ted Runner Stadium	34 04 03N	117 09 51W	stadium	
Tehachapi	35 07 56N	118 26 53W	city/town	3973
Tehachapi -Mt. Vly	35 06 03N	118 25 23W	airport	4220
Tehachapi Mountain	35 04 07N	118 28 57W	park	
Tehachapi Municip.	35 08 07N	118 26 23W	airport	3996
Tehama	40 01 38N	122 07 20W	city/town	210
Tehama County Mus.	40 01 39N	122 07 19W	museum	
Tehan Falls	37 40 24N	121 56 20W	falls	
Telegraph City	37 56 04N	120 44 20W	city/town	652
Telegraph Hill	37 48 10N	122 24 17W	summit	275
Television City	34 04 58N	118 21 33W	studio	
Temecula	33 29 37N	117 08 51W	city/town	1006
Temescal	33 45 46N	117 29 04W	city/town	1115
Temple City	34 06 26N	118 03 25W	city/town	381
Temple Crag	67 06 35N	118 29 30W	summit	12999
Templeton	35 32 59N	120 42 18W	city/town	800
Ten Mile Beach	39 31 35N	123 46 31W	beach	

Place Name	Latitude	Longitude	Type	Elev
Ten Mile Dunes	39 31 11N	123 46 22W	locale	
Tenmile House -his	39 13 17N	121 26 50W	building	
Tennant	41 35 02N	121 54 44W	city/town	4800
Tenth Avenue Mar.	32 41 57N	117 09 22W	marina	
Terminal Geyser	40 25 15N	121 22 31W	locale	
Terminal Island M.	33 45 56N	118 14 10W	marina	
Terminous	38 06 48N	121 29 40W	city/town	-5
Terminus Dam	36 25 01N	119 00 09W	dam	694
Termo	40 51 57N	120 27 33W	city/town	5300
Terra Bella	35 57 45N	119 02 36W	city/town	487
Terra Cotta	33 42 11N	117 22 26W	city/town	1340
Terra Linda	38 00 15N	122 32 55W	city/town	200
Terra Lindo	38 00 42N	122 32 30W	city/town	175
Teutonia Peak	35 17 59N	115 33 47W	summit	5755
The Badlands	33 57 15N	117 06 45W	locale	
The Cannery Shopng	37 48 27N	122 25 06W	locale	
The Cascades	37 43 37N	119 42 43W	falls	
The Castle	39 08 25N	121 35 15W	building	
The Cedars	39 15 11N	120 21 08W	city/town	5840
The Citadel	37 03 54N	118 37 06W	summit	11744
The Crags C C	34 05 52N	118 43 42W	golf	
The Crossing	40 29 11N	120 28 23W	city/town	4480

California GPS Companion

Place Name	Latitude	Longitude	Type	Elev
The Forks	39 11 28N	123 12 24W	city/town	640
The Grotto	33 35 17N	115 53 50W	locale	
The Grove	37 24 14N	120 35 38W	city/town	197
The Hermit	37 09 44N	118 43 02W	summit	12360
The Homestead	37 56 20N	121 17 05W	city/town	15
The Hunchback	37 10 51N	118 31 26W	summit	12226
The Jumpoff	37 48 48N	118 21 03W	summit	13484
The Meadows C C	33 12 50N	117 06 29W	golf	
The Miter	36 32 02N	118 15 51W	summit	12770
The Oakland Museum	37 47 56N	122 15 45W	museum	
The Oaks (1)	38 54 17N	123 13 30W	city/town	1040
The Oaks (2)	39 13 10N	121 04 48W	city/town	2530
The Oaks (3)	34 30 38N	118 21 16W	city/town	2373
The Pines	37 19 08N	119 33 08W	city/town	3420
The Plaza	34 09 01N	116 03 12W	city/town	1998
The Sphinx	36 46 16N	118 33 00W	pillar	9146
The Springs	40 47 56N	124 02 05W	city/town	1260
The Thumb	37 04 10N	118 27 00W	summit	13388
The Tombstone	37 16 09N	118 54 50W	pillar	10794
The Vineyards	38 31 37N	120 48 54W	wine/vin	
The Willows (1)	37 06 10N	121 55 25W	city/town	1560
The Willows (2)	32 50 05N	116 43 18W	city/town	2220

California GPS Companion

Place Name	Latitude	Longitude	Type	Elev
Thenard	33 47 12N	118 14 30W	city/town	20
Thermal	33 38 25N	116 08 19W	city/town	120
Thermalito	39 30 41N	121 35 09W	city/town	220
Thermalito Forebay	39 30 44N	121 37 08W	locale	
Thoman	38 29 28N	122 27 03W	city/town	220
Thomas Lane	35 29 15N	119 17 02W	city/town	331
Thomas Mountain	33 36 45N	116 37 34W	city/town	6825
Thomas Paine Sq.	37 46 49N	122 25 42W	city/town	105
Thomas Place	35 10 32N	115 27 50W	city/town	4315
Thomas/Wright Bat.	41 46 12N	121 32 09W	site	
Thomasson	38 13 02N	122 06 23W	city/town	15
Thompson	38 14 21N	122 16 50W	city/town	15
Thompson Place	40 09 37N	121 58 22W	city/town	1600
Thompson, Mount	37 08 35N	118 36 45W	summit	13494
Thor Peak	36 34 36N	118 15 54W	summit	12300
Thorn	34 28 33N	117 16 48W	city/town	2960
Thorn Junction	40 03 49N	123 57 45W	city/town	977
Thornton	38 13 34N	121 25 25W	city/town	11
Thornton Beach St.	37 41 48N	122 29 53W	park	
Thousand Oaks	34 10 14N	118 50 12W	city/town	900
Thousand Oaks -sub	37 53 44N	122 16 42W	city/town	250
Thousand Palms	33 49 12N	116 23 22W	city/town	240

California GPS Companion

Place Name	Latitude	Longitude	Type	Elev
Three Arch Bay	33 29 27N	117 43 53W	city/town	220
Three Arches	33 29 20N	117 44 10W	arch	
Three Chimneys	38 15 12N	119 48 01W	summit	9882
Three Crossing	39 19 00N	122 55 13W	city/town	2883
Three Points (1)	34 44 09N	118 35 52W	city/town	3424
Three Points (2)	34 20 36N	117 58 53W	city/town	5911
Three Rivers	36 26 20N	118 54 13W	city/town	825
Three Rivers Golf	36 25 45N	118 54 54W	golf	
Three Rocks	36 30 09N	120 23 26W	city/town	420
Three Sirens, The	37 04 52N	118 41 08W	summit	12640
Thunder Mountain	36 40 10N	118 28 27W	summit	13588
Thunderbird C C	33 45 22N	116 25 27W	golf	233
Thunderbolt Peak	37 05 53N	118 31 00W	summit	14003
Thyle	35 20 28N	120 37 57W	city/town	1300
Tiber	35 10 42N	120 37 03W	city/town	160
Tiburon	37 52 25N	122 27 20W	city/town	100
Tiburon Peninsula	37 53 30N	122 28 30W	cape	
Tierra Buena	39 08 56N	121 39 57W	city/town	55
Tierra Del Sol	32 37 20N	116 19 18W	city/town	3680
Tiger Lily	38 40 52N	120 46 26W	city/town	2080
Tilden Park Golf	37 53 19N	122 14 28W	golf	
Timba	37 20 34N	121 01 48W	city/town	96

California GPS Companion

Place Name	Latitude	Longitude	Type	Elev
Timber Cove Marina	38 56 56N	119 57 58W	marina	
Timber Trails	39 14 55N	121 02 35W	city/town	2760
Timberland	39 07 39N	120 09 53W	city/town	6300
Timbuctoo	39 13 01N	121 19 03W	city/town	420
Tinemaha, Mount	37 02 10N	118 23 47W	summit	12561
Tioga Peak	37 56 58N	119 14 45W	summit	11513
Tionesta	41 38 46N	121 19 37W	city/town	4280
Tipton	36 03 34N	119 18 40W	city/town	272
Tisdale	39 02 26N	121 47 06W	city/town	31
Titus	32 37 57N	116 10 44W	city/town	2750
Toadtown	39 53 17N	121 35 22W	city/town	2800
Tobin	39 56 17N	121 18 27W	city/town	1960
Tocaloma	38 03 01N	122 45 30W	city/town	74
Todd Place	35 16 27N	120 09 45W	city/town	2080
Todd Valley	38 59 53N	120 51 02W	city/town	2680
Tokay	36 33 07N	119 21 29W	city/town	355
Tokopah Falls	36 36 31N	118 41 21W	falls	
Toland Landing	38 05 18N	121 45 01W	city/town	30
Tolenas	38 15 55N	122 00 16W	city/town	42
Tollhouse	37 01 08N	119 23 54W	city/town	1920
Tom, Mount	37 20 19N	118 39 27W	summit	13652
Tomales	38 14 47N	122 54 16W	city/town	79

California GPS Companion

Place Name	Latitude	Longitude	Type	Elev
Tomales Bay State	38 07 28N	122 53 20W	park	
Tomales Beach	38 10 23N	122 55 19W	beach	
Toms Place	37 33 41N	118 40 49W	city/town	7072
Tomspur	38 03 26N	121 16 33W	city/town	34
Toners Place	38 31 51N	123 10 37W	city/town	975
Tony Lema Golf Crs	37 41 38N	122 10 53W	golf	
Tonyville	36 14 55N	119 05 23W	city/town	360
Toolville	36 17 15N	119 07 00W	city/town	390
Toomey	34 55 15N	116 44 40W	city/town	1075
Top of the World	33 32 54N	117 45 12W	city/town	1000
Topanga	34 05 37N	118 36 02W	city/town	800
Topanga Beach	34 02 19N	118 34 50W	beach	
Topanga Beach	34 02 24N	118 34 43W	city/town	29
Topanga Oaks	34 06 04N	118 35 22W	city/town	950
Topanga Park	34 06 27N	118 37 42W	city/town	1021
Topanga State Bch.	34 02 19N	118 34 50W	park	
Topaz PO	38 36 40N	119 31 04W	city/town	5042
Tormey	38 03 02N	122 14 53W	city/town	20
Torrance	33 50 09N	118 20 23W	city/town	84
Torrance County B.	33 48 39N	118 23 27W	beach	
Torrance-Zamperini	33 48 12N	118 20 22W	airport	101
Torrey Pines City	32 52 38N	117 15 01W	beach	

California GPS Companion

Place Name	Latitude	Longitude	Type	Elev
Torrey Pines State	32 56 10N	117 15 38W	beach	
Tortuga	33 10 04N	115 20 31W	city/town	187
Tourmaline Surfing	32 48 18N	117 15 39W	park	
Towle	39 12 15N	120 47 53W	city/town	3640
Town and Country V	38 37 05N	121 23 59W	city/town	60
Town Talk	39 14 36N	121 01 47W	city/town	
Toyon	38 12 18N	120 45 52W	city/town	990
Trabucco Gardens	37 33 36N	120 06 43W	garden	
Trabuco Canyon	33 39 45N	117 35 22W	city/town	1040
Trabuco Peak	33 42 08N	117 28 27W	summit	4604
Tracy	37 44 23N	121 25 27W	city/town	48
Tracy Municipal	37 41 20N	121 26 30W	airport	190
Tracy-NewJerusalem	37 40 44N	121 17 58W	airport	62
Trail Mountain	41 25 43N	123 36 47W	summit	4834
Trail Peak	36 25 40N	118 11 22W	summit	11623
Trancas	34 01 52N	118 50 32W	city/town	25
Trancas Beach	34 01 59N	118 50 55W	beach	
Tranquillity	36 38 56N	120 15 06W	city/town	167
Transamerica Pyram	37 47 41N	122 24 07W	building	
Travel Town Museum	34 09 16N	118 18 25W	museum	
Traver	36 27 19N	119 29 02W	city/town	285
Travis A F B	38 16 09N	121 58 30W	airport	51

California GPS Companion

Place Name	Latitude	Longitude	Type	Elev
Travis Field	38 16 20N	121 55 54W	city/town	60
Treasure Island M.	37 49 02N	122 22 11W	museum	
Trent	37 04 39N	120 52 47W	city/town	115
Trenton	38 29 07N	122 51 03W	city/town	130
Tres Pinos	36 47 24N	121 19 12W	city/town	530
Trestles Beach	33 23 07N	117 35 35W	beach	
Trevarno	37 41 26N	121 44 47W	city/town	534
Triangle Court	37 56 50N	122 21 35W	city/town	26
Trigo	36 54 47N	119 57 34W	city/town	285
Trimmer	36 54 18N	119 17 43W	city/town	1020
Trinidad	41 03 34N	124 08 31W	city/town	170
Trinidad Harbor	41 03 20N	124 08 46W	harbor	
Trinidad Head Lt.	41 03 07N	124 09 01W	lighthous	
Trinidad State Bch	41 03 56N	124 08 57W	beach	
Trinity Alps	40 51 27N	122 53 21W	city/town	2490
Trinity Alps Golf	40 43 08N	122 55 45W	golf	
Trinity Alps Mar.	40 48 46N	122 46 07W	marina	2395
Trinity Business C	37 47 02N	122 23 52W	univ/coll	
Trinity Center	40 58 59N	122 41 39W	airport	2390
Trinity Center	40 59 00N	122 41 55W	city/town	2795
Trinity Center Boa	40 58 20N	122 41 26W	locale	
Trinity Village	40 52 32N	123 31 38W	city/town	700

California GPS Companion

Place Name	Latitude	Longitude	Type	Elev
Triple Falls	36 59 05N	118 33 16W	falls	
Triunfo Corner	34 09 27N	118 49 26W	city/town	933
Trocha	35 47 53N	119 08 46W	city/town	455
Trojan Peak	36 38 35N	118 18 50W	summit	13950
Trolley Museum	33 45 39N	117 13 52W	museum	
Trona	35 45 46N	117 22 19W	city/town	1659
Trona Airport	35 48 44N	117 19 38W	airport	1716
Trousdale Estates	34 06 18N	118 23 40W	city/town	1140
Trowbridge	38 54 39N	121 31 27W	city/town	48
Troy	39 18 42N	120 27 43W	city/town	6360
Truckee	39 19 41N	120 10 56W	city/town	5840
Truckee -Tahoe	39 19 12N	120 08 22W	airport	5900
Truckhaven	33 17 49N	115 58 35W	city/town	-55
Trull	37 56 19N	121 30 02W	city/town	2
Truth Home	38 34 48N	123 08 15W	city/town	920
Tryon Corner	41 52 39N	124 08 43W	city/town	30
Tuber	41 56 13N	121 27 01W	city/town	4037
Tucker Oaks Golf	40 29 03N	122 18 13W	golf	
Tudor	39 00 18N	121 37 21W	city/town	40
Tueeulala Falls	37 57 47N	119 46 32W	falls	
Tufa Falls	36 26 37N	118 35 43W	falls	
Tujunga	34 15 08N	118 17 15W	city/town	1765

California GPS Companion

Place Name	Latitude	Longitude	Type	Elev
Tulare	36 12 28N	119 20 47W	city/town	288
Tulare -Mefford	36 09 22N	119 19 34W	airport	271
Tulare Golf Links	36 12 05N	119 18 00W	golf	
Tulare Peak	36 24 43N	118 33 44W	summit	11588
Tulelake	41 57 22N	121 28 35W	city/town	4035
Tulelake Municipal	41 53 14N	121 21 33W	airport	4044
Tulloch Dam	37 52 35N	120 36 14W	dam	510
Tunemah Peak	36 59 43N	118 41 13W	summit	11894
Tunitas Beach	37 21 28N	122 23 56W	beach	
Tunnabora Peak	36 36 17N	118 16 53W	summit	13565
Tunnel Inn	40 43 35N	122 19 25W	city/town	920
Tuolumne	37 57 39N	120 14 11W	city/town	2577
Tuolumne Falls	37 54 21N	119 25 00W	falls	
Tupman	35 17 53N	119 21 01W	city/town	320
Turk	36 10 16N	120 13 16W	city/town	500
Turlock	37 29 41N	120 50 44W	city/town	101
Turlock Country Cl	37 26 32N	120 49 45W	golf	
Turlock Lake State	37 37 38N	120 34 53W	park	
Turlock Municipal	37 29 14N	120 41 48W	airport	159
Turner (1)	38 20 28N	122 46 35W	city/town	200
Turner (2)	37 51 36N	121 13 02W	city/town	31
Turret Peak	37 15 49N	118 50 28W	summit	12091

California GPS Companion

Place Name	Latitude	Longitude	Type	Elev
Tustin	33 44 45N	117 49 31W	city/town	130
Tuttle	37 17 46N	120 22 40W	city/town	202
Tuttletown	37 59 30N	120 27 31W	city/town	1450
Twain	40 01 13N	121 04 15W	city/town	2862
Twain Harte	38 02 23N	120 13 54W	city/town	3640
Twentieth Century	34 05 49N	118 18 25W	studio	357
Twentynine Palms	34 07 55N	115 56 44W	airport	1905
Twentynine Palms	34 08 08N	116 03 12W	city/town	2001
Twin Bridges	38 48 41N	120 07 23W	city/town	6117
Twin Buttes	36 28 00N	119 12 20W	city/town	651
Twin Cities	38 17 28N	121 18 36W	city/town	51
Twin Creeks	37 09 22N	121 50 35W	city/town	624
Twin Falls	37 36 42N	119 00 33W	falls	
Twin Lakes (1)	36 58 03N	121 59 49W	city/town	40
Twin Lakes (2)	34 16 41N	118 36 02W	city/town	1300
Twin Lakes (3)	34 59 14N	118 30 49W	city/town	5160
Twin Lakes Beach	36 57 48N	122 00 08W	beach	
Twin Lakes Golf	34 04 04N	118 00 15W	golf	
Twin Oaks (1)	33 11 07N	117 09 14W	city/town	720
Twin Oaks (2)	35 18 45N	118 24 32W	city/town	2825
Twin Peaks	34 14 20N	117 13 58W	city/town	5800
Twin Peaks Estates	39 08 37N	120 10 24W	city/town	7000

California GPS Companion

Place Name	Latitude	Longitude	Type	Elev
Twin Pines	39 01 32N	120 58 42W	city/town	2200
Twin Rocks	39 49 22N	123 33 51W	city/town	1430
Two Eagle Peak	37 07 47N	118 31 19W	summit	12966
Two Harbors	33 26 24N	118 29 54W	city/town	175
Two Rivers	39 49 23N	120 40 09W	city/town	4280
Two Rock	38 15 59N	122 47 28W	city/town	80
Tyee City	40 55 21N	124 07 32W	city/town	10
Tylers Corner	38 31 42N	120 41 07W	city/town	2100
Tyndall Landing	38 52 59N	121 49 01W	city/town	35
Tyndall, Mount	36 39 20N	118 20 10W	summit	14019
Tyrone	38 26 57N	122 59 58W	city/town	50

Ⓤ

Place Name	Latitude	Longitude	Type	Elev
U of C Davis	38 32 25N	121 44 53W	univ/coll	50
U of C Irvine	33 38 46N	117 50 31W	univ/coll	
U of C Los Angeles	34 04 17N	118 26 15W	univ/coll	
U of C Riverside	33 58 24N	117 19 48W	univ/coll	
U of C San Diego	32 52 37N	117 14 24W	univ/coll	401
U of C Santa Barb.	34 24 58N	119 50 53W	univ/coll	
U of C Santa Cruz	36 59 51N	122 03 06W	univ/coll	
U of Redlands	34 03 50N	117 09 45W	univ/coll	
U of San Diego	32 46 19N	117 11 27W	univ/coll	

California GPS Companion

Place Name	Latitude	Longitude	Type	Elev
U of San Francisco	37 46 32N	122 26 59W	univ/coll	
U of Santa Clara	37 20 57N	121 56 20W	univ/coll	
U of the Pacific	37 58 47N	121 18 37W	univ/coll	
U S C	34 01 15N	118 17 05W	univ/coll	
U S Navy Golf Crs	36 35 29N	121 51 45W	golf	
Ueland Place	40 18 47N	123 23 44W	city/town	2720
Ukiah	39 09 01N	123 12 24W	city/town	639
Ukiah Mun. Aprt	39 07 33N	123 12 03W	airport	614
Ukiah Mun. Golf	39 09 17N	123 13 20W	golf	
Ukiah Rancheria	39 05 25N	123 09 30W	city/town	640
Ulmar	37 42 11N	121 42 54W	city/town	555
Ultra	35 57 51N	118 59 51W	city/town	512
Una	35 25 28N	119 10 37W	city/town	347
Underwood Park	39 51 36N	123 42 57W	city/town	980
Union (1)	38 19 17N	122 18 32W	city/town	75
Union (2)	35 38 15N	120 33 36W	city/town	1026
Union City	37 35 45N	122 01 05W	city/town	59
Union Hill (1)	39 12 20N	121 02 15W	city/town	2720
Union Hill (2)	39 35 50N	121 00 08W	city/town	4200
Union Landing	39 41 58N	123 48 02W	city/town	80
Union Mills	39 21 14N	120 06 22W	city/town	5830
Union Square	37 56 55N	121 16 24W	park	

California GPS Companion

Place Name	Latitude	Longitude	Type	Elev
Union Square Park	37 47 16N	122 24 23W	park	
Universal City	34 08 20N	118 21 09W	city/town	780
Universal City St.	34 08 27N	118 21 20W	studio	
University Art Mus	37 52 08N	122 15 17W	museum	
University City	32 51 17N	117 12 11W	city/town	360
University Heights	32 45 20N	117 08 19W	city/town	340
University of Cal.	40 49 03N	121 28 05W	observtry	
University Peak	36 44 53N	118 21 38W	summit	13632
University Vlg (1)	34 03 57N	117 09 40W	city/town	1470
University Vlg (2)	37 53 06N	122 18 00W	city/town	23
Upland	34 05 51N	117 38 51W	city/town	1300
Upland -Cable	34 06 41N	117 41 11W	airport	1439
Upland College	34 05 58N	117 39 33W	univ/coll	
Upp	39 25 38N	123 21 21W	city/town	1340
Upper Beach	33 44 30N	118 22 41W	beach	
Upper Falls	41 14 27N	122 00 25W	falls	
Upper Forni	38 49 20N	120 10 18W	city/town	7500
Upper Lake	39 09 53N	122 54 34W	city/town	1343
Upper Lake-Gravel.	39 26 59N	122 57 19W	airport	1900
Upper Town	38 21 16N	119 07 01W	city/town	8040
Upper Yosemite Fls	37 45 23N	119 35 45W	falls	
Upton	41 20 28N	122 20 49W	city/town	3742

California GPS Companion

Place Name	Latitude	Longitude	Type	Elev
Urgon	38 09 29N	121 16 14W	city/town	51
USS San Fran. Mem	37 46 58N	122 30 38W	park	
Uva	36 37 08N	119 29 20W	city/town	352

𝕍

Place Name	Latitude	Longitude	Type	Elev
Vaca Valley Racew.	38 24 27N	121 53 54W	track	
Vacation Beach	38 29 23N	123 00 44W	city/town	60
Vacaville	38 21 24N	121 59 12W	city/town	179
Vacaville Junction	38 17 44N	121 57 51W	city/town	94
Vacaville-Nut Tree	38 22 36N	121 57 44W	airport	114
Val Verde (1)	33 50 54N	117 15 11W	city/town	1506
Val Verde (2)	34 26 42N	118 39 24W	city/town	1200
Valdez	38 19 34N	121 36 44W	city/town	2
Vale	38 19 13N	121 47 04W	city/town	15
Valencia	34 26 37N	118 36 31W	city/town	1010
Valencia -subdiv.	34 08 48N	117 16 18W	city/town	1240
Valencia Gardens	37 46 00N	122 25 20W	city/town	40
Valerie	33 34 08N	116 10 46W	city/town	-88
Valinda	34 02 43N	117 56 34W	city/town	350
Valjean	35 35 08N	116 07 26W	city/town	1029
Valla	33 57 29N	118 03 31W	city/town	150
Valle Vista (1)	37 49 22N	122 08 16W	city/town	520

California GPS Companion

Place Name	Latitude	Longitude	Type	Elev
Valle Vista (2)	33 44 52N	116 53 33W	city/town	1767
Vallecito	38 05 25N	120 28 21W	city/town	1745
Vallecito Stage St	32 58 34N	116 21 13W	park	
Vallecitos Atomic	37 36 33N	121 50 31W	building	
Vallejo	38 06 15N	122 15 20W	city/town	60
Vallejo Beach	37 29 47N	122 27 47W	beach	
Vallejo Home State	38 17 55N	122 27 43W	park	
Vallejo Mill Ruins	37 34 40N	121 58 16W	locale	
Vallejo Municipal	38 07 19N	122 11 44W	golf	
Vallemar	37 36 49N	122 28 47W	city/town	125
Valleton	35 53 22N	120 42 17W	city/town	960
Valley Acres	35 12 22N	119 24 21W	city/town	415
Valley Center	33 13 06N	117 02 00W	city/town	1300
Valley Crossing	38 41 59N	123 24 45W	city/town	120
Valley Ford	38 19 05N	122 55 23W	city/town	42
Valley Gardens	34 04 59N	117 16 45W	city/town	1010
Valley Hi C C	38 24 44N	121 26 19W	golf	
Valley Home	37 49 44N	120 54 40W	city/town	150
Valley Oaks Mobile	39 24 43N	123 18 49W	city/town	1380
Valley of Enchant.	34 14 48N	117 18 14W	city/town	4440
Valley of the Fall	34 05 00N	116 54 42W	falls	
Valley Springs	38 11 30N	120 49 41W	city/town	680

California GPS Companion

Place Name	Latitude	Longitude	Type	Elev
Valley View Park	34 14 06N	117 18 26W	city/town	5200
Valley Vista	33 44 29N	117 04 20W	city/town	1625
Valley Wells	35 49 42N	117 19 51W	city/town	1750
Valley Wells Stat.	35 26 05N	115 42 05W	city/town	3690
Valona	38 03 08N	122 13 24W	city/town	62
Valyermo	34 26 46N	117 51 05W	city/town	3698
Van Allen	37 47 54N	121 03 05W	city/town	90
Van Damme State Pk	39 16 35N	123 46 24W	park	
Van Ness	33 58 57N	118 19 07W	city/town	131
Van Nuys	34 11 12N	118 26 53W	city/town	708
Van Nuys Airport	34 12 35N	118 29 23W	airport	799
Van Nuys Golf Crs	34 11 26N	118 29 17W	golf	
Van Vleck	38 46 41N	120 30 52W	city/town	3880
Vance	36 13 27N	119 06 09W	city/town	363
Vandenberg A F B	34 43 46N	120 34 36W	military	368
Vanderbilt	35 19 50N	115 15 01W	city/town	4231
Vandever Mountain	36 23 55N	118 34 48W	summit	11947
Vanguard	36 15 19N	119 57 29W	city/town	252
Vann	39 15 10N	122 57 16W	city/town	1500
Vasona Junction	37 15 26N	121 57 49W	city/town	280
Vega	34 11 31N	118 21 00W	city/town	675
Vega Mar -historic	34 25 10N	119 39 47W	building	

California GPS Companion

Place Name	Latitude	Longitude	Type	Elev
Venado	38 36 20N	123 00 25W	city/town	1100
Venice	33 59 27N	118 27 33W	city/town	20
Venice Beach (1)	33 58 35N	118 27 57W	beach	
Venice Beach (2)	37 28 47N	122 26 58W	beach	
Venice Fishing Pr.	33 58 39N	118 28 06W	pier	
Venice Pavilion	33 59 11N	118 28 24W	building	
Venida	36 19 58N	119 07 45W	city/town	410
Vennacher Needle	36 59 55N	118 28 28W	summit	12996
Venola	35 18 39N	119 03 12W	city/town	370
Ventucopa	34 49 53N	119 28 08W	city/town	2896
Ventura	34 16 42N	119 17 32W	city/town	100
Ventura College	34 16 38N	119 13 53W	univ/coll	
Ventura County His	34 16 49N	119 17 53W	museum	
Ventura Harbor	34 14 58N	119 15 50W	harbor	
Ventura Junior Col	34 16 42N	119 15 59W	univ/coll	
Ventura Municipal	34 14 25N	119 12 34W	golf	
Ventura Pier	34 16 24N	119 17 28W	pier	
Venus	35 14 54N	116 47 39W	city/town	3540
Verano	38 18 10N	122 28 26W	city/town	124
Verdant	33 07 03N	115 33 29W	city/town	-200
Verde	35 10 18N	120 33 25W	city/town	346
Verdemont	34 11 35N	117 22 00W	city/town	1720

California GPS Companion

Place Name	Latitude	Longitude	Type	Elev
Verdi-Sierra Pines	39 31 28N	120 00 44W	city/town	5120
Verdugo City	34 12 41N	118 14 19W	city/town	1300
Verdugo Hills Golf	34 14 05N	118 16 21W	golf	
Vernal Fall	37 43 39N	119 32 34W	falls	
Vernalis	37 37 51N	121 17 10W	city/town	104
Vernon	34 00 14N	118 13 45W	city/town	200
Verona (1)	38 47 10N	121 37 03W	city/town	20
Verona (2)	37 37 37N	121 52 49W	city/town	303
Versteeg, Mount	36 38 48N	118 19 28W	summit	13448
Vestal	35 50 23N	119 05 02W	city/town	500
Vestil	41 14 12N	120 33 30W	city/town	4900
Veteran Heights	38 34 27N	122 26 06W	city/town	1800
Veterans Memorial	33 49 42N	118 08 08W	stadium	
Via Verde C C	34 05 01N	117 49 52W	golf	
Vichy Springs (1)	38 20 16N	122 15 36W	city/town	90
Vichy Springs (2)	39 10 01N	123 09 25W	city/town	800
Vickers Hot Spring	34 29 52N	119 20 13W	city/town	1230
Victor	38 08 17N	121 12 18W	city/town	75
Victor Valley C C	34 34 23N	117 20 43W	golf	
Victoria	34 04 25N	117 15 06W	city/town	1080
Victoria Beach	33 31 01N	117 45 37W	beach	
Victoria Golf Crs	33 51 12N	118 16 10W	golf	

California GPS Companion

Place Name	Latitude	Longitude	Type	Elev
Victoria Mews -sub	37 45 37N	122 23 55W	city/town	75
Victoria Peak	38 10 04N	119 25 19W	summit	11732
Victorville	34 32 10N	117 17 25W	city/town	2715
Victory Palms	33 42 20N	115 45 04W	city/town	3000
Vidal	34 07 08N	114 30 34W	city/town	626
Vidal Junction	34 11 19N	114 34 24W	city/town	930
View Park	33 59 56N	118 20 30W	city/town	350
Viewland	40 25 49N	120 16 45W	city/town	4520
Vikingsholm	38 57 10N	120 06 22W	locale	
Villa Grande	38 28 23N	123 01 28W	city/town	60
Villa Montalvo	37 14 38N	122 01 47W	building	760
Villa Park	33 48 52N	117 48 44W	city/town	370
Villa Park Dam	33 48 54N	117 45 51W	dam	566
Village Square	37 44 39N	122 26 12W	city/town	525
Villinger	38 08 39N	121 22 21W	city/town	20
Vin	38 38 57N	121 36 04W	city/town	25
Vina	39 55 59N	122 03 10W	city/town	208
Vincent	34 30 02N	118 06 56W	city/town	3260
Vincent Landing	38 13 10N	122 56 27W	city/town	0
Vine Hill	38 00 31N	122 05 42W	city/town	23
Vineburg	38 16 21N	122 26 15W	city/town	51
Vineyard -subdiv.	34 02 50N	118 20 10W	city/town	150

California GPS Companion

Place Name	Latitude	Longitude	Type	Elev
Vineyard Mobile V.	37 40 00N	121 51 05W	city/town	370
V.Mission Soledad	36 19 51N	121 21 54W	wine/vin	
Vinland	35 42 54N	119 14 02W	city/town	320
Vino Noceto Winery	38 31 10N	120 49 15W	wine/vin	
Vinton	39 48 16N	120 10 38W	city/town	4945
Vinvale	33 57 13N	118 09 46W	city/town	109
Viola	40 31 05N	121 40 36W	city/town	4400
Virgilia	40 01 07N	121 06 16W	city/town	2760
Virginia C C	33 50 21N	118 11 35W	golf	
Virginia Colony	34 17 16N	118 51 27W	city/town	580
Virginia Peak	38 03 57N	119 21 24W	summit	12001
Virginiatown	38 54 02N	121 12 49W	city/town	320
Visalia	36 19 49N	119 17 28W	city/town	331
Visalia -Sequoia	36 26 54N	119 19 08W	airport	313
Visalia Golf Club	36 20 05N	119 18 58W	golf	
Visalia Municipal	36 19 07N	119 23 34W	airport	292
Vista	33 12 00N	117 14 30W	city/town	340
Vista del Mar	33 49 08N	118 11 52W	city/town	21
Vista Del Monte	37 44 35N	122 26 08W	city/town	475
Vista Robles	39 25 15N	121 33 05W	city/town	141
Vista Valencia	34 23 08N	118 33 42W	golf	
Vogelsang Peak	37 46 39N	119 20 54W	summit	11516

Place Name	Latitude	Longitude	Type	Elev
Volcano	38 26 35N	120 37 47W	city/town	2053
Volcano Falls	36 21 07N	118 23 33W	falls	
Volcano Jail House	38 26 35N	120 37 50W	building	
Volcanoville	38 58 55N	120 47 17W	city/town	3036
Vollmers	40 56 35N	122 26 20W	city/town	1391
Volta	37 05 51N	120 55 30W	city/town	103
Vorden	38 16 38N	121 32 24W	city/town	5
Voss	38 39 26N	120 23 12W	city/town	5500

W

Place Name	Latitude	Longitude	Type	Elev
Waddell Creek Bch.	37 05 43N	122 16 38W	beach	
Waddington	40 34 02N	124 12 02W	city/town	37
Wade Place	40 17 46N	121 54 51W	city/town	1560
Wadstrom	34 18 58N	119 17 26W	city/town	150
Wages Creek Beach	39 39 05N	123 47 02W	beach	
Wagner (1)	38 21 31N	119 52 37W	city/town	5480
Wagner (2)	37 47 53N	121 04 49W	city/town	75
Wagon Wheel Mobile	39 23 20N	123 20 55W	city/town	1410
Wagoner	40 33 57N	122 01 34W	city/town	760
Wahtoke	36 40 37N	119 27 25W	city/town	358
Wahtoke Winery	36 41 27N	119 27 12W	wine/vin	
Waldo	37 52 16N	122 30 09W	city/town	11

California GPS Companion

Place Name	Latitude	Longitude	Type	Elev
Waldo Junction	39 06 40N	121 18 29W	city/town	250
Waldorf	34 54 40N	120 33 15W	city/town	200
Waldrue Heights	38 21 52N	122 33 36W	city/town	739
Walerga	38 40 30N	121 21 53W	city/town	110
Walker (1)	33 58 49N	118 10 19W	city/town	135
Walker (2)	41 50 03N	122 50 18W	city/town	1845
Walker (3)	38 30 54N	119 28 33W	city/town	5400
Walker Landing	38 12 55N	121 36 15W	city/town	0
Walker Mountain	38 14 10N	119 28 16W	summit	11563
Wallace	38 11 39N	120 58 37W	city/town	206
Wallace Center	35 10 11N	119 27 53W	city/town	860
Wallace, Mount	37 08 46N	118 39 19W	summit	13377
Walltown	38 34 27N	121 06 10W	city/town	340
Walmort	38 22 50N	121 14 35W	city/town	80
Walnut	34 01 13N	117 51 52W	city/town	569
Walnut Creek	37 54 23N	122 03 50W	city/town	200
Walnut Grove	38 14 32N	121 30 38W	city/town	5
Walnut Heights	37 52 36N	122 03 00W	city/town	180
Walnut Hills Mob.	34 02 40N	117 49 03W	city/town	685
Walnut Park	33 58 05N	118 13 27W	city/town	145
Walong	35 11 51N	118 32 13W	city/town	3066
Walsh Landing	38 33 20N	123 17 58W	city/town	120

California GPS Companion

Place Name	Latitude	Longitude	Type	Elev
Walsh Station	38 31 44N	121 20 01W	city/town	62
Walter Springs	38 39 13N	122 21 25W	city/town	1000
Walteria	33 48 18N	118 21 01W	city/town	95
Walthal	37 58 43N	121 08 43W	city/town	62
Waltz	34 21 37N	118 31 14W	city/town	1425
Wanhala	39 28 15N	123 32 38W	city/town	540
Wapama Falls	37 57 59N	119 45 52W	falls	
Wards Cabin	41 03 12N	122 20 29W	building	1120
Warlow, Mount	37 07 40N	118 40 28W	summit	13206
Warm Creek Golf	34 04 10N	117 17 51W	golf	
Warm Springs	34 07 13N	117 14 46W	city/town	1100
Warm Springs Dist.	37 29 14N	121 55 41W	city/town	80
Warner	34 03 39N	117 08 44W	city/town	1560
Warner Brothers St	34 09 01N	118 20 05W	studio	
Warner Springs	33 16 56N	116 37 58W	city/town	3132
Warnerville	37 43 57N	120 35 44W	city/town	225
Warren, Mount	37 59 25N	119 13 23W	summit	12327
Wasco	35 35 39N	119 20 24W	city/town	325
Wasco -Kern County	35 37 10N	119 21 13W	airport	313
Waseck	41 13 01N	123 45 15W	city/town	800
Washington	39 21 34N	120 47 53W	city/town	2640
Washoe	38 18 21N	122 44 05W	city/town	216

California GPS Companion

Place Name	Latitude	Longitude	Type	Elev
Washtub Falls	33 10 21N	116 47 10W	falls	
Waterford	37 38 29N	120 45 34W	city/town	165
Waterford Village	38 43 38N	121 04 40W	city/town	660
Waterloo	38 02 05N	121 11 09W	city/town	57
Watermans Corner	32 46 52N	115 26 49W	city/town	-25
Waterwheel Falls	37 55 37N	119 27 28W	falls	
Watson (1)	33 48 30N	118 14 02W	city/town	19
Watson (2)	40 03 14N	122 41 12W	city/town	3300
Watson Cabin	39 40 00N	121 16 27W	locale	3720
Watson Junction	33 47 58N	118 15 11W	city/town	40
Watsonville	36 54 37N	121 45 21W	city/town	29
Watsonville Golf	36 52 21N	121 45 06W	golf	
Watsonville Jct.	36 53 42N	121 44 41W	city/town	25
Watsonville Munic.	36 56 08N	121 47 22W	airport	160
Watterson Business	34 08 47N	118 07 35W	univ/coll	
Watts	33 56 26N	118 14 31W	city/town	105
Watts Tower	33 56 20N	118 14 26W	locale	
Watts Towers State	33 56 19N	118 14 26W	park	
Waucoba Mountain	37 01 20N	118 00 23W	summit	11123
Waukena	36 08 19N	119 30 31W	city/town	192
Wawona	37 32 13N	119 39 19W	city/town	4012
Wayne	37 23 09N	121 53 52W	city/town	50

California GPS Companion

Place Name	Latitude	Longitude	Type	Elev
Weaverville	40 43 52N	122 56 27W	city/town	2011
Weaverville-L.Pool	40 44 44N	122 55 19W	airport	2350
Webster	38 33 44N	121 39 15W	city/town	20
Weed	41 25 22N	122 23 06W	city/town	3466
Weed Airport	41 28 29N	122 27 11W	airport	2938
Weed Golf Club	41 25 43N	122 23 40W	golf	
Weed Museum	41 25 32N	122 22 55W	museum	
Weed Patch	35 14 17N	118 54 51W	city/town	385
Weeds Point	39 28 39N	121 02 55W	city/town	2900
Weeks Poultry Colo	34 12 30N	118 34 44W	city/town	791
Weeks Tract	39 19 08N	120 17 53W	city/town	5980
Weibel Vineyards	37 30 15N	121 54 40W	wine/vin	
Weimar	39 02 15N	120 58 17W	city/town	2280
Weisel	33 48 36N	117 29 56W	city/town	880
Weitchpec	41 11 18N	123 42 26W	city/town	400
Welby	36 11 19N	121 04 07W	city/town	320
Weldon	35 39 57N	118 17 22W	city/town	2653
Weldons	34 20 42N	119 17 46W	city/town	200
Wellhouse Falls	34 31 42N	119 47 14W	falls	2000
Wellington Heights	34 02 10N	118 11 05W	city/town	300
Wells Place	40 11 53N	121 55 52W	city/town	1540
Wellsona	35 41 50N	120 41 33W	city/town	675

California GPS Companion

Place Name	Latitude	Longitude	Type	Elev
Wendel	40 20 54N	120 13 57W	city/town	4009
Wengler	40 54 51N	121 54 27W	city/town	2699
Wente Brothers Win	37 39 51N	121 43 29W	wine/vin	
Weott	40 19 19N	123 55 14W	city/town	338
Werner	37 56 26N	121 36 29W	city/town	0
West Anaheim	33 49 56N	117 56 30W	city/town	135
West Anaheim Jct.	33 47 46N	117 53 40W	city/town	140
West Arcadia	34 07 34N	118 03 14W	city/town	480
West Beach	34 24 04N	119 41 54W	beach	
West Berkeley -sub	37 52 28N	122 17 51W	city/town	20
West Butte	39 11 14N	121 53 13W	city/town	87
West Coast Bible C	36 50 12N	119 44 42W	univ/coll	
West Coast Univ.	34 03 58N	118 17 19W	univ/coll	
West Colton	34 04 01N	117 21 07W	city/town	1040
West Covina	34 04 07N	117 56 17W	city/town	381
West End -subdiv.	37 46 21N	122 16 48W	city/town	10
West Glendale	34 08 54N	118 16 21W	city/town	461
West Hartley	37 56 26N	121 48 42W	city/town	440
West Highlands	34 08 22N	117 13 50W	city/town	1320
West Hollywood	34 05 24N	118 21 39W	city/town	287
West Los Angeles	34 02 47N	118 26 50W	city/town	241
West Manteca	37 47 50N	121 15 03W	city/town	25

California GPS Companion

Place Name	Latitude	Longitude	Type	Elev
West March	33 54 12N	117 16 37W	city/town	1560
West Oakland	37 48 43N	122 17 38W	city/town	15
West Park	36 42 37N	119 51 01W	city/town	270
West Pittsburg	38 01 37N	121 56 10W	city/town	50
West Point	38 23 57N	120 31 35W	city/town	2790
West Sacramento	38 34 50N	121 31 45W	city/town	15
West San Leandro	37 42 22N	122 10 35W	city/town	25
West Saticoy	34 17 07N	119 09 34W	city/town	220
West Venida	36 20 28N	119 07 44W	city/town	405
West Whittier	33 59 19N	118 03 22W	city/town	200
Westchester	33 57 35N	118 23 59W	city/town	120
Westchester Golf	33 57 26N	118 24 38W	golf	
Westend	35 42 25N	117 23 29W	city/town	1660
Westend Galatin Pl	40 01 28N	122 31 05W	city/town	760
Western Addition	37 47 07N	122 26 45W	city/town	300
Western Avenue	33 55 13N	118 18 42W	golf	
Western University	32 42 50N	117 02 11W	univ/coll	
Westgate	34 03 03N	118 28 42W	city/town	317
Westgate Heights	34 03 59N	118 28 20W	city/town	510
Westhaven (1)	36 13 36N	119 59 38W	city/town	277
Westhaven (2)	41 02 10N	124 06 36W	city/town	295
Westlake	37 41 52N	122 28 46W	city/town	100

California GPS Companion

Place Name	Latitude	Longitude	Type	Elev
Westlake Village	34 08 50N	118 49 25W	city/town	900
Westlake Village	34 09 00N	118 48 47W	golf	
Westley	37 32 58N	121 11 53W	city/town	85
Westlund Place	40 14 02N	124 00 58W	city/town	1700
Westminster	33 45 33N	118 00 21W	city/town	35
Westminster Garden	34 08 17N	117 57 40W	garden	523
Westmont College	34 27 01N	119 39 37W	univ/coll	
Westmorland	33 02 14N	115 37 14W	city/town	159
Weston Beach	36 30 45N	121 56 36W	beach	
Westport	39 38 09N	123 46 55W	city/town	115
Westside	36 24 02N	120 08 17W	city/town	248
Westville	39 10 30N	120 38 49W	city/town	5240
Westward Beach	34 00 30N	118 48 50W	beach	
Westwood (1)	40 18 22N	121 00 17W	city/town	5000
Westwood (2)	34 03 22N	118 25 47W	city/town	280
Westwood Junction	40 25 55N	120 56 44W	city/town	5500
Westwood Village	34 03 34N	118 26 36W	city/town	320
Whalers Cove	36 31 12N	121 56 15W	bay	
Wheatland	39 00 36N	121 25 19W	city/town	87
Wheaton Springs	35 27 44N	115 28 31W	city/town	3965
Wheatons	36 01 57N	118 42 06W	city/town	2900
Wheel Mountain	37 02 48N	118 37 42W	summit	12781

California GPS Companion

Place Name	Latitude	Longitude	Type	Elev
Wheeler	39 53 08N	123 54 36W	city/town	40
Wheeler Peak	38 25 07N	119 17 14W	summit	11664
Wheeler Ridge	35 00 16N	118 56 55W	city/town	964
Wheeler Springs	34 30 29N	119 17 26W	city/town	1460
Wherry Housing	34 55 23N	117 56 04W	city/town	2360
Whiskey Springs	39 21 48N	123 39 56W	city/town	560
Whiskeytown	40 38 20N	122 33 31W	city/town	1280
Whiskeytown-Shasta	40 38 00N	122 36 00W	park	
Whisky Falls	37 17 13N	119 26 18W	city/town	5800
Whisky Falls	37 17 17N	119 26 21W	falls	
Whispering Pines-1	38 48 49N	122 42 41W	city/town	2620
Whispering Pines-2	33 05 10N	116 35 06W	city/town	4150
White Cascade	37 54 31N	119 25 07W	falls	
White Hall	38 46 31N	120 24 15W	city/town	3360
White Heather	34 31 13N	118 18 21W	city/town	2760
White Horse	41 18 40N	121 23 50W	city/town	4410
White Pines	38 15 58N	120 20 23W	city/town	3960
White Point Beach	33 42 53N	118 18 48W	beach	
White Point State	33 43 05N	118 18 47W	park	
White River	35 48 40N	118 50 31W	city/town	1100
White River Summer	35 50 58N	118 37 34W	city/town	4220
White Rock	38 37 38N	121 05 28W	city/town	491

California GPS Companion

Place Name	Latitude	Longitude	Type	Elev
White Spot	39 16 53N	121 00 35W	city/town	3075
White Water	33 55 30N	116 38 15W	city/town	1360
White Wolf	37 52 10N	119 38 57W	city/town	7875
Whitesboro	39 12 53N	123 45 48W	city/town	320
Whitethorn	40 01 26N	123 56 31W	city/town	1024
Whitley Gardens	35 39 33N	120 30 24W	city/town	900
Whitlock Place	39 50 07N	122 41 55W	city/town	3800
Whitlow	40 18 55N	123 47 46W	city/town	200
Whitmore	40 37 46N	121 54 56W	city/town	2233
Whitmore Hot Sprgs	37 37 57N	118 48 41W	city/town	6982
Whitney	38 50 01N	121 18 21W	city/town	133
Whitney Falls	41 27 41N	122 14 20W	falls	
Whitney Portal	36 35 21N	118 13 30W	city/town	8000
Whitney, Mount	36 34 45N	118 17 30W	highest	14491
Whittier	33 58 45N	118 01 55W	city/town	365
Whittier College	33 58 43N	118 01 53W	univ/coll	
Whittier Junction	34 00 18N	118 03 51W	city/town	200
Whittier Narrows D	34 01 12N	118 04 55W	dam	200
Whittier Narrows G	34 02 55N	118 04 33W	golf	
Whittington Place	40 42 32N	121 40 50W	city/town	4980
Whorl Mountain	38 04 25N	119 22 57W	summit	12029
Wible Orchard	35 19 04N	119 01 13W	city/town	375

California GPS Companion

Place Name	Latitude	Longitude	Type	Elev
Wicks Corner	39 34 56N	121 37 11W	city/town	260
Wiest	33 03 31N	115 26 51W	city/town	138
Wigdon Place	40 40 31N	123 27 36W	city/town	2380
Wilbur Springs	39 02 22N	122 25 07W	city/town	1350
Wilcox Oaks Golf	40 13 21N	122 15 28W	golf	
Wild Bill Place	39 13 51N	122 46 50W	city/town	2280
Wild Crossing	34 46 48N	117 16 27W	city/town	2400
Wild Goose C C	39 18 24N	121 52 51W	golf	
Wildasin	33 59 20N	118 17 57W	city/town	137
Wildcat Beach	37 57 48N	122 47 14W	beach	
Wilder Place	39 49 34N	122 37 50W	city/town	1200
Wilderness Falls	41 47 28N	123 37 39W	falls	
Wilderness Gardens	33 20 56N	117 02 12W	park	
Wildflower	36 30 14N	119 40 56W	city/town	267
Wildomar	33 35 56N	117 16 45W	city/town	1273
Wildwood (1)	34 05 01N	118 35 55W	city/town	737
Wildwood (2)	37 09 05N	122 08 06W	city/town	500
Wildwood (3)	40 24 01N	123 03 11W	city/town	3504
Wildwood (4)	34 17 44N	118 14 28W	city/town	1760
Wilfred	38 22 02N	122 42 47W	city/town	94
Wilkinson	40 38 50N	122 04 42W	city/town	740
Will Rogers State	34 03 22N	118 30 41W	park	

California GPS Companion

Place Name	Latitude	Longitude	Type	Elev
Willaura Estates	39 06 11N	121 05 49W	city/town	1600
Williams (1)	39 09 17N	122 08 54W	city/town	801
Williams (2)	41 15 48N	120 31 41W	city/town	4350
Williamson, Mount	36 39 22N	118 18 37W	summit	14370
Willie Hoaglin Plc	40 06 51N	123 20 07W	city/town	2240
Willis Palms	33 49 38N	116 19 43W	city/town	400
Willits	39 24 35N	123 21 16W	city/town	1364
Willits -Ells Fld	39 27 03N	123 22 12W	airport	2054
Willota	38 14 40N	122 06 21W	city/town	49
Willow Brook	33 54 58N	118 13 50W	city/town	80
Willow Creek	40 56 23N	123 37 49W	city/town	640
Willow Creek Peak	36 35 09N	121 13 16W	summit	12437
Willow Glen	37 18 31N	121 53 19W	city/town	115
Willow Park Golf	37 43 34N	122 04 54W	golf	
Willow Point	38 25 32N	121 33 05W	city/town	0
Willow Ranch	41 54 09N	120 21 26W	city/town	4738
Willow Springs (1)	34 52 42N	118 17 45W	city/town	2530
Willow Springs (2)	38 11 19N	119 12 13W	city/town	6744
Willow Springs Rac	34 52 26N	118 15 51W	track	
Willow Valley	39 16 19N	120 58 51W	city/town	2740
Willows	39 31 28N	122 11 33W	city/town	135
Willows -Glenn Co.	39 30 58N	122 13 03W	airport	139

California GPS Companion

Place Name	Latitude	Longitude	Type	Elev
Willowville	33 48 20N	118 11 18W	city/town	22
Wilmar -subdiv.	34 04 15N	118 06 27W	city/town	360
Wilmington	33 46 48N	118 15 42W	city/town	35
Wilseyville	38 22 45N	120 30 49W	city/town	2740
Wilshire C C	34 04 38N	118 19 43W	golf	
Wilsie	32 48 00N	115 36 08W	city/town	-38
Wilson	38 58 42N	121 37 29W	city/town	35
Wilson Corner	35 28 07N	120 22 41W	city/town	1496
Wilson Creek Beach	41 36 08N	124 05 57W	beach	
Wilson Golf Course	34 08 07N	118 16 49W	golf	
Wilson Grove	38 31 00N	122 51 13W	city/town	80
Wilson Place	39 40 24N	122 24 06W	city/town	660
Wilson Point	38 00 42N	122 18 55W	cape	
Wilsona Gardens	34 40 04N	117 49 29W	city/town	2562
Wilsonia	36 44 06N	118 57 20W	city/town	6600
Wilton	38 24 43N	121 16 16W	city/town	79
Wimp	36 30 02N	119 14 35W	city/town	380
Winchell, Mount	37 06 12N	118 31 30W	summit	13768
Winchester	33 42 25N	117 05 01W	city/town	1474
Windansea Beach	32 49 52N	117 16 49W	beach	
Windsor	38 32 50N	122 48 55W	city/town	118
Windsor Hills	33 59 20N	118 21 11W	city/town	375

California GPS Companion

Place Name	Latitude	Longitude	Type	Elev
Wineland	36 32 30N	119 34 58W	city/town	305
Wingfoot	33 59 21N	118 15 06W	city/town	172
Wingo	38 12 33N	122 25 32W	city/town	5
Winnetka	34 12 48N	118 34 16W	city/town	795
Winter Gardens	32 49 52N	116 55 57W	city/town	600
Winter Gardens sub	34 00 59N	118 09 52W	city/town	170
Winter Island	38 02 32N	121 50 51W	island	
Winterhaven	32 44 22N	114 38 02W	city/town	130
Winterhaven Vlg.	38 43 05N	121 04 45W	city/town	660
Winters	38 31 30N	121 58 11W	city/town	135
Wintersburg	33 42 57N	117 59 49W	city/town	20
Winterwarm	33 20 27N	117 13 17W	city/town	620
Winton	37 23 22N	120 36 44W	city/town	175
Wister	33 18 55N	115 36 09W	city/town	196
Wofford Heights	35 42 25N	118 27 19W	city/town	2660
Wolf (1)	36 41 43N	119 38 13W	city/town	331
Wolf (2)	39 03 31N	121 08 14W	city/town	1572
Wolfskill Falls	34 10 33N	117 44 55W	falls	
Wonderland of Rock	34 03 51N	116 09 03W	locale	
Wood Ranch	36 44 58N	120 38 17W	city/town	316
Wood Vista	39 14 33N	120 01 53W	city/town	6280
Wood, Mount	37 48 30N	119 09 44W	summit	12637

California GPS Companion

Place Name	Latitude	Longitude	Type	Elev
Woodacre	38 00 46N	122 38 39W	city/town	351
Woodbridge	38 09 15N	121 18 01W	city/town	46
Woodbridge C C	38 09 45N	121 18 17W	golf	
Woodbury College	34 03 09N	118 15 41W	univ/coll	
Woodcrest	33 52 56N	117 21 23W	city/town	1529
Woodcrest Dam	33 54 11N	117 22 42W	dam	1116
Woodford	35 12 46N	118 33 06W	city/town	2728
Woodfords	38 46 40N	119 49 15W	city/town	5640
Woodhouse Laborat.	34 24 48N	119 50 28W	building	
Woodlake (1)	38 09 08N	121 14 32W	city/town	50
Woodlake (2)	36 24 49N	119 05 52W	city/town	440
Woodlake Airport	36 23 55N	119 06 26W	airport	425
Woodlake Junction	36 24 50N	119 06 57W	city/town	438
Woodland	38 40 43N	121 46 20W	city/town	65
Woodland Hills	34 10 06N	118 36 18W	city/town	895
Woodland Watts-W.	38 40 25N	121 52 19W	airport	125
Woodlands	34 14 42N	116 48 02W	city/town	6820
Woodleaf (1)	38 35 20N	122 36 21W	city/town	396
Woodleaf (2)	39 31 03N	121 11 26W	city/town	3130
Woodley Golf Cours	34 10 54N	118 29 16W	golf	
Woodley Island Mar	40 48 28N	124 09 40W	marina	
Woodman	39 46 16N	123 23 20W	city/town	869

California GPS Companion

Place Name	Latitude	Longitude	Type	Elev
Woodside	37 25 48N	122 15 10W	city/town	380
Woodside Glens	37 26 26N	122 15 20W	city/town	460
Woodside Village	34 01 15N	117 53 55W	city/town	700
Woodson Bridge St.	39 55 03N	122 05 25W	park	
Woodstock -subdiv.	37 46 35N	122 17 05W	city/town	10
Woodville (1)	36 05 37N	119 11 53W	city/town	335
Woodville (2)	37 56 41N	122 42 19W	city/town	180
Woodward	38 18 40N	121 38 35W	city/town	24
Woodworth	38 19 56N	122 45 33W	city/town	150
Woodworth, Mount	37 01 13N	118 36 25W	summit	12219
Woody	35 42 15N	118 50 00W	city/town	1647
Woolsey	38 29 02N	122 49 07W	city/town	91
Woolsey Flat	39 24 41N	120 52 01W	city/town	3820
Workman	33 55 47N	118 10 02W	city/town	94
Worswick	40 36 43N	124 11 26W	city/town	40
Worth	36 03 09N	118 56 10W	city/town	538
Wotans Throne	36 33 59N	118 16 43W	summit	12726
Wreck Beach	36 14 05N	121 47 53W	beach	
Wright Beach	38 24 19N	123 05 52W	beach	
Wright Place	41 16 40N	123 40 38W	city/town	900
Wrightwood	34 21 39N	117 37 57W	city/town	5931
Wunpost	35 55 52N	120 51 44W	city/town	490

California GPS Companion

Place Name	Latitude	Longitude	Type	Elev
Wyandotte	39 27 29N	121 28 00W	city/town	677
Wyatt Pavilion	38 32 18N	121 44 44W	building	
Wyeth	36 31 10N	119 15 57W	city/town	370
Wynne, Mount	36 56 18N	118 24 15W	summit	13179
Wynola	33 05 51N	116 38 41W	city/town	3655
Wyntoon	41 11 30N	122 03 48W	city/town	2800
Wyo	39 46 14N	122 11 25W	city/town	266
Wyvernwood -sub.	34 01 27N	118 12 49W	city/town	230

𝕏

𝕐

Place Name	Latitude	Longitude	Type	Elev
Yager Junction	40 32 54N	123 49 24W	city/town	2694
Yaldora	33 13 58N	117 23 34W	city/town	33
Yankee Hill (1)	39 42 13N	121 31 16W	city/town	1990
Yankee Hill (2)	38 02 23N	120 22 37W	city/town	2237
Yankee Jims	39 01 46N	120 51 38W	city/town	2575
Yellowjacket	40 14 26N	121 41 24W	city/town	3327
Yellowjacket Place	40 10 10N	123 19 21W	city/town	2800
Yerba Buena Beach	34 03 06N	118 57 35W	beach	
Yermo	34 54 18N	116 49 10W	city/town	1926
Yeshiva University	34 03 20N	118 23 13W	univ/coll	

California GPS Companion

Place Name	Latitude	Longitude	Type	Elev
Yettem	36 29 11N	119 15 31W	city/town	343
Yokohl	36 19 32N	119 04 53W	city/town	464
Yolano	38 24 37N	121 42 16W	city/town	25
Yolo	38 43 55N	121 48 24W	city/town	77
Yolo Fliers Club	38 40 48N	121 52 08W	golf	
Yontocket	41 54 28N	124 11 52W	city/town	40
Yorba	33 51 55N	117 48 29W	city/town	265
Yorba Linda	33 53 19N	117 48 44W	city/town	397
Yorkville	38 53 53N	123 12 48W	city/town	940
Yosemite Falls	37 45 30N	119 35 39W	falls	
Yosemite Forks	37 22 02N	119 37 51W	city/town	2857
Yosemite Junction	37 53 27N	120 29 14W	city/town	1200
Yosemite National	37 51 00N	119 34 00W	park	
Yosemite Point	37 45 23N	119 35 31W	cliff	6936
Yosemite Village	37 44 43N	119 35 50W	city/town	4000
Yosemite West	37 38 51N	119 43 03W	city/town	6250
You Bet	39 12 33N	120 53 56W	city/town	2920
Young Falls	41 02 34N	121 18 58W	falls	
Young, Mount	36 34 55N	118 19 36W	summit	13177
Youngs Vineyards	38 29 46N	120 49 36W	wine/vin	
Youngstown	38 10 26N	121 14 31W	city/town	64
Yountville	38 24 06N	122 21 35W	city/town	97

California GPS Companion

Place Name	Latitude	Longitude	Type	Elev
Yreka	41 44 08N	122 38 00W	city/town	2625
Yuba City	39 08 26N	121 36 57W	city/town	59
Yuba City -Sutter	39 07 35N	121 36 32W	airport	58
Yuba Col. -Colusa	39 12 37N	122 00 54W	univ/coll	
Yuba College	38 55 56N	122 36 48W	univ/coll	
Yuba Pass	39 19 23N	120 35 57W	city/town	5640
Yucaipa	34 02 01N	117 02 32W	city/town	2622
Yucca Grove	35 24 09N	115 47 29W	city/town	4100
Yucca Inn	34 24 35N	117 35 19W	city/town	4440
Yucca Valley	34 06 51N	116 25 53W	city/town	3279
Yucca Valley Airp.	34 07 40N	116 24 28W	airport	3224

ℤ

Place Name	Latitude	Longitude	Type	Elev
Zamora	38 47 48N	121 52 51W	city/town	50
Zante	36 06 53N	119 02 41W	city/town	416
Zayante	37 05 31N	122 02 33W	city/town	420
Zediker	36 45 26N	119 31 23W	city/town	399
Zee Estates	38 45 50N	121 02 50W	city/town	680
Zenia	40 12 20N	123 29 27W	city/town	2969
Zentner	35 42 11N	119 10 06W	city/town	446
Zinfandel	38 28 58N	122 26 28W	city/town	195
Zmudowski Beach St	36 50 14N	121 48 05W	park	

California GPS Companion

Place Name	Latitude	Longitude	Type	Elev
Zurich	37 10 58N	118 15 33W	city/town	3928
Zuver	38 58 27N	120 35 56W	city/town	3900

Add your own coordinates here

California GPS Companion

Place Name	Latitude	Longitude	Type	Elev

Add your own coordinates here

California GPS Companion

Place Name	Latitude	Longitude	Type	Elev

Add your own coordinates here

California GPS Companion

Place Name	Latitude	Longitude	Type	Elev

Add your own coordinates here

California GPS Companion

Place Name	Latitude	Longitude	Type	Elev

Add your own coordinates here

Place Name	Latitude	Longitude	Type	Elev

Add your own coordinates here

ABOUT LATITUDE AND LONGITUDE

Latitude and Longitude coordinates are commonly expressed two ways: Degrees, Minutes, and Seconds such as DD-MM-SS or Degrees and Minutes where minutes may be stated to one-tenth minute resolution, such as DD-MM.M. Just as 30 seconds equals one half minute on the clock, 30 seconds of Latitude or Longitude equals one half (0.5) minutes on the coordinate system.

Locations North of the equator often include the letter (N) to indicate North Latitude. These are sometimes given a (+) value. Locations South of the equator would be (S) or (-). Locations West of Greenwich, England often include the letter (W) to indicate West Longitude. These are sometimes given a (+) value. Locations East of Greenwich would be (E) or (-).

379

Most GPS units accept data in either the "tenth minute" format or the "minutes and seconds" format. Quick conversion charts follow for your convenience.

FROM

DD-MM.M	to	DD-MM-SS
DD-MM.1	=	DD-MM-06
DD-MM.2	=	DD-MM-12
DD-MM.3	=	DD-MM-18
DD-MM.4	=	DD-MM-24
DD-MM.5	=	DD-MM-30
DD-MM.6	=	DD-MM-36
DD-MM.7	=	DD-MM-42
DD-MM.8	=	DD-MM-48
DD-MM.9	=	DD-MM-54

FROM

DD-MM-SS		to	DD-MM.M
DD-MM-00 to 03	=		DD-MM.0
DD-MM-04 to 09	=		DD-MM.1
DD-MM-10 to 15	=		DD-MM.2
DD-MM-16 to 21	=		DD-MM.3
DD-MM-22 to 27	=		DD-MM.4
DD-MM-28 to 33	=		DD-MM.5
DD-MM-34 to 39	=		DD-MM.6
DD-MM-40 to 45	=		DD-MM.7
DD-MM-46 to 51	=		DD-MM.8
DD-MM-52 to 57	=		DD-MM.9
DD-MM-58 to 60	=		DD-M+1.0 (next minute)

HOW FAR IS A MINUTE?

When using your GPS you will notice the coordinates indicated for a certain location will vary slightly with time. To get a better understanding of the actual distances represented by these values, you may use the following approximations. The number of statute miles represented by a unit of Latitude is constant wherever you go.

So when traveling North-South:
1 Degree=69 miles, 1 Minute=1.15 miles, 1 Second=101 ft.

The number of statute miles represented by a unit of Longitude varies with location, since the lines of Longitude converge at the North and South poles.

For this reason, in Northern California (Yreka) when traveling East-West:
1 Degree=51.4 miles, 1 Minute=0.86 miles, 1 Second=75 ft.

In Southern California (El Centro) when traveling East-West:
1 Degree=58.0 miles, 1 Minute=0.96 miles, 1 Second=85 ft.

NOTES

Points Around the USA

Place Name	Latitude	Longitude	Type	Elev
Aberdeen SD	45 27 53N	098 29 10W	city/town	1304
Akron OH	41 04 53N	081 31 09W	city/town	1050
Albany NY	42 39 09N	073 45 24W	city/town	
Albuquerque NM	35 05 04N	106 39 02W	city/town	4955
Amarillo TX	35 13 19N	101 49 51W	city/town	
Anchorage AK	61 13 05N	149 54 01W	city/town	101
Ann Arbor MI	42 16 15N	083 43 35W	city/town	
Appomattox Mem VA	37 22 38N	078 47 44W	site	
Ashland WI	46 35 33N	090 53 01W	city/town	671
Atlanta GA	33 44 56N	084 23 17W	city/town	1050
Austin TX	30 16 01N	097 44 34W	city/town	501
Baltimore MD	39 17 25N	076 36 45W	city/town	100
Bangor ME	44 48 04N	068 46 42W	city/town	158
Barrow AK	71 17 26N	156 47 19W	city/town	
Baton Rouge LA	30 27 02N	091 09 16W	city/town	53
Bellingham WA	48 45 35N	122 29 13W	city/town	100
Billings MT	45 47 00N	108 30 00W	city/town	3124
Biloxi MS	30 23 45N	088 53 07W	city/town	25
Birmingham AL	33 31 14N	086 48 09W	city/town	600
Bismarck ND	46 48 30N	100 47 00W	city/town	1700
Boise ID	43 36 49N	116 12 09W	city/town	2730
Boston MA	42 21 30N	071 03 37W	city/town	20

Points Around the USA

Place Name	Latitude	Longitude	Type	Elev
Boundary Peak NV	37 50 46N	118 21 00W	summit	13140
Branson MO	36 38 37N	093 13 06W	city/town	722
Brownsville TX	25 54 05N	097 29 50W	city/town	
Buffalo NY	42 53 11N	078 52 43W	city/town	
Burlington VT	44 28 33N	073 12 45W	city/town	113
Cape Hatteras NC	35 13 28N	075 31 50W	cape	
Carbondale IL	37 43 38N	089 13 00W	city/town	415
Casper WY	42 52 00N	106 18 45W	city/town	
Cedar Rapids IA	42 00 30N	091 38 38W	city/town	
Charleston SC	32 46 35N	079 55 52W	city/town	118
Charleston WV	38 20 59N	081 37 58W	city/town	606
Charlotte NC	35 13 37N	080 50 36W	city/town	850
Cheyenne WY	41 08 24N	104 49 11W	city/town	6067
Chicago IL	41 51 00N	087 39 00W	city/town	596
Cincinnati OH	39 09 43N	084 27 25W	city/town	683
Cleveland OH	41 29 58N	081 41 44W	city/town	690
Columbia SC	34 00 02N	081 02 06W	city/town	314
Concord NH	43 12 29N	071 32 17W	city/town	288
Corpus Christi TX	27 48 01N	097 23 46W	city/town	
Corvallis OR	44 33 53N	123 15 39W	city/town	225
Dallas TX	32 47 00N	096 48 00W	city/town	463
Dayton OH	39 45 32N	084 11 30W	city/town	750

Points Around the USA

Place Name	Latitude	Longitude	Type	Elev
Denver CO	39 44 21N	104 59 03W	city/town	5260
Des Moines IA	41 36 02N	093 36 32W	city/town	
Detroit MI	42 19 53N	083 02 45W	city/town	
Disney World FL	28 24 41N	081 34 58W	park	
Disneyland CA	33 48 37N	117 55 05W	locale	
Duluth MN	46 47 00N	092 06 23W	city/town	
El Paso TX	31 45 31N	106 29 11W	city/town	
Empire State B. NY	40 44 55N	073 59 11W	building	
Evansville IN	37 58 29N	087 33 21W	city/town	388
Fairbanks AK	64 50 16N	147 42 59W	city/town	440
Fargo ND	46 52 38N	096 47 22W	city/town	900
Flagstaff AZ	35 11 53N	111 39 02W	city/town	
Ford Museum MI	42 18 12N	083 14 02W	museum	
Fort Sumter SC	32 45 08N	079 52 29W	park	
Fort Wayne IN	41 07 50N	085 07 44W	city/town	781
Gallup NM	35 31 41N	108 44 31W	city/town	6508
Gannett Peak WY	43 11 04N	109 39 12W	summit	13804
Gateway Arch MO	38 37 28N	090 11 14W	other	
Gettysburg PA	39 49 00N	077 14 00W	memorial	
Graceland TN	35 02 46N	090 01 25W	mansion	
Grand Canyon WY	44 20 09N	104 11 47W	valley	
Grand Junction CO	39 03 50N	108 33 00W	city/town	4597

Points Around the USA

Place Name	Latitude	Longitude	Type	Elev
Grand Teton WY	43 44 28N	110 48 06W	summit	13770
Granite Peak MT	45 09 48N	109 48 26W	summit	12799
Greenville SC	34 51 09N	082 23 39W	city/town	966
Hartford CT	41 45 49N	072 41 08W	city/town	
Helena MT	46 35 34N	112 02 07W	city/town	4090
Hilo HI	19 43 47N	155 05 24W	city/town	38
Hilton Head SC	32 11 37N	080 44 18W	island	
Honolulu HI	21 18 25N	157 51 30W	city/town	18
Hoover Dam NV	36 01 00N	114 44 12W	dam	
Houston TX	29 45 47N	095 21 47W	city/town	
Huntsville AL	34 43 49N	086 35 10W	city/town	641
Indianapolis IN	39 46 06N	086 09 29W	city/town	717
Indianapolis S. IN	39 47 41N	086 14 06W	speedway	
Jackson MS	32 17 55N	090 11 05W	city/town	294
Jacksonville FL	30 19 55N	081 39 21W	city/town	12
Jefferson Mem. DC	38 52 53N	077 02 13W	memorial	
Juneau AK	58 18 07N	134 25 11W	city/town	
Kansas City MO	39 05 59N	094 34 42W	city/town	
Kill Devil Hls NC	36 01 00N	075 40 00W	summit	78
Kings Peak UT	40 46 43N	110 22 28W	summit	13528
Knoxville TN	35 57 38N	083 55 15W	city/town	889
Kodiak AK	57 47 24N	152 24 26W	city/town	

Points Around the USA

Place Name	Latitude			Longitude			Type	Elev
Lansing MI	42	43	57N	084	33	20W	city/town	
Las Vegas NV	36	10	30N	115	08	11W	city/town	2000
Lexington KY	37	59	19N	084	28	40W	city/town	
Little Rock AR	34	44	47N	092	17	22W	city/town	350
Los Angeles CA	34	03	08N	118	14	34W	city/town	330
Louisville KY	38	15	15N	085	45	34W	city/town	462
Lubbock TX	33	34	40N	101	51	17W	city/town	
Lynchburg VA	37	24	49N	079	08	33W	city/town	818
Macon GA	32	50	26N	083	37	57W	city/town	400
Madison WI	43	04	23N	089	24	04W	city/town	863
Manassas Battle VA	38	49	19N	077	31	24W	battlefld	
Marquette MI	46	32	37N	087	23	43W	city/town	628
Mayo Clinic MN	44	01	20N	092	27	56W	hospital	
Medford OR	42	19	36N	122	52	28W	city/town	383
Memphis TN	35	08	58N	090	02	56W	city/town	254
Miami FL	25	46	26N	080	11	38W	city/town	11
Milwaukee WI	43	02	20N	087	54	23W	city/town	634
Minneapolis MN	44	58	48N	093	15	49W	city/town	
Missoula MT	46	52	20N	113	59	35W	city/town	3200
Mobile AL	30	41	39N	088	02	35W	city/town	16
Montgomery AL	32	22	00N	086	18	00W	city/town	250
Montpelier VT	44	15	36N	072	34	33W	city/town	525

Points Around the USA

Place Name	Latitude	Longitude	Type	Elev
Mt Elbert CO	39 07 04N	106 26 41W	summit	14433
Mt Hood OR	45 22 25N	121 41 33W	summit	11239
Mt McKinley AK	63 04 10N	151 00 13W	summit	20320
Mt Rainier WA	46 51 10N	121 45 31W	summit	14410
Mt Rushmore SD	43 52 49N	103 27 30W	summit	5725
Mt St Helens WA	46 11 52N	122 11 28W	summit	9677
Mt Whitney CA	36 34 45N	118 17 30W	summit	14491
Mukilteo Light WA	47 56 56N	122 18 12W	lighthous	28
Mystic Seaport CT	41 21 40N	071 58 01W	city/town	
Air & Space Mus OH	40 33 58N	084 10 33W	museum	
Nags Head NC	35 57 26N	075 37 28W	city/town	10
Nantucket Is. MA	41 17 00N	070 05 00W	island	
Nashville TN	36 09 57N	086 47 04W	city/town	440
New Haven CT	41 18 29N	072 55 43W	city/town	
New Orleans LA	29 57 16N	090 04 30W	city/town	11
New York NY	40 42 51N	074 00 23W	city/town	
Newark NJ	40 44 08N	074 10 22W	city/town	95
Newport News VA	36 58 43N	076 25 42W	city/town	15
Newport RI	41 29 24N	071 18 48W	city/town	96
Niagara Falls NY	43 05 00N	079 04 15W	falls	
Nome AK	64 30 04N	165 24 23W	city/town	
North Platte NE	41 07 26N	100 45 54W	city/town	

Points Around the USA

Place Name	Latitude	Longitude	Type	Elev
Oklahoma City OK	35 28 03N	097 30 58W	city/town	
Old Faithful WY	44 27 38N	110 49 41W	geyser	
Omaha NE	41 15 31N	095 56 15W	city/town	
Orlando FL	28 32 17N	081 22 46W	city/town	106
Oshkosh WI	44 01 29N	088 32 33W	city/town	
Peoria IL	40 41 37N	089 35 20W	city/town	
Philadelphia PA	39 57 08N	075 09 51W	city/town	40
Phoenix AZ	33 26 54N	112 04 24W	city/town	
Pierre SD	44 22 06N	100 21 02W	city/town	1484
Pikes Peak CO	38 50 26N	105 02 38W	summit	14110
Pima Air Mus. AZ	32 07 00N	110 51 29W	museum	
Pittsburgh PA	40 26 26N	079 59 46W	city/town	770
Plymouth Rock MA	41 57 30N	070 39 45W	rock	10
Pocatello ID	42 52 17N	112 26 41W	city/town	4464
Portland ME	43 39 41N	070 15 21W	city/town	
Portland OR	45 31 25N	122 40 30W	city/town	50
Providence RI	41 49 26N	071 24 48W	city/town	
Pueblo CO	38 15 16N	104 36 31W	city/town	4662
Raleigh NC	35 46 19N	078 38 20W	city/town	350
Rapid City SD	44 04 50N	103 13 50W	city/town	3247
Redding CA	40 35 12N	122 23 26W	city/town	557
Reno NV	39 31 47N	119 48 46W	city/town	4498

Points Around the USA

Place Name	Latitude	Longitude	Type	Elev
Richmond Battle VA	37 25 45N	077 22 26W	battlefld	
Richmond VA	37 33 13N	077 27 38W	city/town	190
Sacramento CA	38 34 54N	121 29 36W	city/town	20
Saint George UT	37 06 15N	113 35 00W	city/town	2761
Saint Louis MO	38 37 38N	090 11 52W	city/town	
Salina KS	38 50 25N	097 36 40W	city/town	1225
Salt Lake City UT	40 45 39N	111 53 25W	city/town	4266
San Antonio TX	29 25 26N	098 29 36W	city/town	
San Diego CA	32 42 55N	117 09 23W	city/town	40
San Francisco CA	37 46 30N	122 25 06W	city/town	63
Santa Fe NM	35 41 13N	105 56 14W	city/town	6989
Scranton PA	41 24 32N	075 39 46W	city/town	754
Seattle WA	47 36 23N	122 19 51W	city/town	350
Sheridan WY	44 47 50N	106 57 20W	city/town	3742
Sioux City IA	42 30 00N	096 24 00W	city/town	1117
Sioux Falls SD	43 33 00N	096 42 00W	city/town	1442
Smithsonian I. DC	38 53 19N	077 01 34W	museum	
South Bend IN	41 41 00N	086 15 00W	city/town	725
Spokane WA	47 39 32N	117 25 30W	city/town	2000
Springfield IL	39 48 06N	089 38 37W	city/town	
Springfield MA	42 06 05N	072 35 25W	city/town	70
Syracuse NY	43 02 53N	076 08 52W	city/town	